DESIGNING
WITH
PERENNIALS

*A seat placed among the flowers. Plants include red dahlias, blue monkshood (*Aconitum*), pink phlox, white shasta daisies, creamy* Artemisia lactiflora, *and yellow goldenrod. (England; August)*

DESIGNING
WITH
PERENNIALS

PAMELA J. HARPER

Macmillan Publishing Company   *New York*

Collier Macmillan Canada   *Toronto*

Maxwell Macmillan International

New York   Oxford   Singapore   Sydney

Macmillan Publishing Company
866 Third Avenue, New York, NY 10022

Collier Macmillan Canada, Inc.
1200 Eglinton Avenue East, Suite 200
Don Mills, Ontario M3C 3N1

Library of Congress Cataloging-in-Publication Data

Harper, Pamela.
    Designing with perennials/Pamela J. Harper.
        p.   cm.
    Includes index.
    ISBN 0-02-548180-0
    1. Perennials. 2. Landscape gardening. 3.
Gardens—Design.
I. Title.
SB434.H34 1990
716—dc20   90-42166   CIP

Macmillan books are available at special discounts for bulk
purchases for sales promotions, premiums, fund-raising, or
educational use. For details, contact:

Special Sales Director
Macmillan Publishing Company
866 Third Avenue
New York, NY 10022

Design by Laura Hough

10 9 8 7 6 5 4 3

Printed in the United States of America

To my parents with love and gratitude

Whether genes or environment most shape what we each become is a much-debated topic. Both played a part in my all-absorbing passion for gardening. That all of my family are gardeners springs, I think, from the Willmott genes on my father's side. It was he who introduced me, as a toddler, to such old-fashioned flowers as lady-in-the-bath, love-in-a-mist, mignonette, snapdragons, and sweetpeas, taught me to recognize wildflowers along the country lanes, and grew the raspberries, gooseberries, and black currants for my mother's shelves of homemade preserves.

My nurturing mother's mission was that none of her family or friends should ever be cold, hungry, or deprived of books. Many of the books on my shelves are inscribed with her name. Now ninety, she is still gardening and writing me frequent letters of love and encouragement.

Left: *Gray lamb's ears (*Stachys byzantina*) enhances the scarlet flowers of* Geum *'Mrs. Bradshaw'. (England; September)*

Top: Phlox *'Millstream Jupiter'. (Connecticut; May)*

Right: *Small enough for the tiniest garden, or for the rock garden, the miniature dwarf bearded iris is surrounded with bluets (*Hedyotis caerulea, *better known as* Houstonia caerulea*). (Connecticut; May)*

Contents

Acknowledgments

I have been a privileged guest in so many lovely gardens. During the three years spent toying with the manuscript for this book pictures were being set aside. At the end there were over fifteen hundred. Whittling them down to three hundred was a frustrating process. My thanks go not only to the garden owners listed below, but to others who have made me welcome over the years, and to all who share the companionable, helpful, and generous gardening world fundamental to my life.

Gratitude must also be expressed to those computer-literate friends, especially my husband, Patrick, and neighbor George Greene, who came to my rescue so many times, often by means of a program called PC Tools, recovering sections of manuscript that had seemed to be irretrievably lost.

My thanks, too, to friends Edith Eddleman and Elsa Bakalar, who prepared plans to my specification at short notice, and to my editor, Pam Hoenig, who remained calm and helpful throughout: this book is the better for her editing, a form of praise I don't often bestow!

Listed below are the names of the owners, or designers, of gardens, or plant combinations, shown in the photographs. Unless they wished otherwise, these names also appear in the picture captions. Pictures designated only "Virginia" were taken in my own Tidewater garden.

Tony and Michelle Avent
Elsa and Michael Bakalar
Susan Barsky
Doug Bayley
Norman Beal
Mr. G. Beasley
The Reverend and Mrs. John Beck
Elda and Ray Behm
Morris Berd
Keith Bohn
Dan Borroff
Julia Bristow
John Brookes
Susan and Alden Buckles
Mr. and Mrs. R. Cameron
Mr. and Mrs. J. Carnwath
Beth Chatto

Edward C. Childs
Roy Davidson
Sydney and Martin Eddison
The Lord and Lady Fitzwalter
The late Linc and Timmy Foster
Patricia Fountain
Mr. and Mrs. N. Garland
Harland Hand
Rebecca and Cyrus Harvey
Peter and the Honorable Mrs. Healing
Brent and Becky Heath
Mr. and Mrs. David Hodges
Jerri Hopkins
Elaine Horton
Kathleen Hudson
Catherine and Harry Hull
Gladys and Alain Huyghe
Ron Johnson
Herb and Betsie Kinney
Mrs. N. A. Laurie
Mr. and Mrs. D. Lennette
Mary Ley
Christopher Lloyd
Faith and Frank Mackaness
Mrs. J. R. McCutchan
Fred and Mary Ann McGourty
Mr. and Mrs. M. Metianu
The late Richard Meyer
The O'Banion family
Wolfgang Oehme
Marshall Olbrich

Mel Oliver
Ellen and Gordon Penick
J. Liddon Pennock
John and the late Jane Platt
Susie and T. P. Plimpton
Lolita Powell
Rob Proctor
Mrs. Arnold Rakusen
Mrs. J. H. Robinson
Mark Rumary
Susan Ryley
Susan Sasaki
George Schoellkopf
Michael S. Schultz
Mrs. E. R. Slingo
Mr. and Mrs. J. P. Smith
Pam Snow
Mrs. Starr Bruce
Mrs. Jane Stevens
Mr. and Mrs. Clair Stewart
Sir John Thouron
John Treasure
Mr. and Mrs. Henry L. Valentine, II
Jim van Sweden
Mr. and Mrs. A. Van Vlack
Claire and Andre Viette
Mr. and Mrs. Robin Wainwright
Mr. and Mrs. J. P. Weyerhaeuser, III
Doris Willmott
Cynthia Woodyard

Perennials, the Fashionable Plants

Half my gardening years were spent in England, the rest in the United States. In 1970, soon after my arrival, I worked for a landscape contractor not long here from Germany. When I deplored the limited number of plants he used in landscaping he said: "You'll have to learn that in this country you can sell anything, provided it is evergreen and you can clip it." A few years later a neighbor asked me what shrubs she should use as foundation plantings. "Why do you want foundation plantings?" I asked. She looked puzzled, then said: "I don't know, but everybody has them."

Perennials are now in vogue. A lot of clipped evergreens are being ripped out, gardens are getting more colorful, and the plants in them more varied, but I sometimes wonder if the baby is being thrown out with the bathwater! One of the prettiest gardens I have seen began with the typical lawn, solitary tree, and row of clipped evergreens (in this case Japanese hollies) along the base of the house. Wanting color, the owner, an artist, added a narrow flower border between the hollies and the lawn. The dark background of the hollies sets off the flowers, and gives the garden structure in winter when the flowers have gone, a sensible and successful blending of the old style with the new.

Enthusiasm for perennials has been gaining momentum in the United States since the late seventies. In 1982 Longwood Gardens, near Philadelphia, held a well-attended conference on perennials. The following year the New York Botanical Garden held a symposium called, note this, "The New Perennials." The program was not about the latest introductions, as the word "new" might imply. *All* perennials were new to many American gardeners at that time. Most could identify peonies, irises, and Oriental poppies, but often very little else. So enthusiastic was the response that the New York Botanical Garden symposium has become an annual event. In 1988 the program was repeated in five different cities: New York, Boston, Washington, Chicago, and Hamilton, Ontario, Canada.

Meantime, nurseries and landscapers were getting demands for plants they had never heard of, couldn't find, and didn't know how to use. In July 1983 Ohio State University in Columbus sponsored an herbaceous perennials symposium for the trade. Attendance so greatly exceeded expectations that it

*A small border of annuals and perennials curves out from the path to run in front of foundation plantings of Japanese hollies (*Ilex crenata*). A stepping-stone path in the lawn leads to a side gate. See the photograph on page 220 for the area to the left of the front door. (Garden of Gladys and Alain Huyghe, Virginia; early July)*

was decided to form an association for professionals, the Perennial Plant Association, intended primarily as a forum for growers, retailers, and landscape contractors, but also welcoming writers, educators, and keen home gardeners. This association holds its own symposium each year.

Nowadays at least a dozen large conferences featuring perennials are held each year, often drawing so many participants that late registrants have to be turned away. Some symposiums are broadly based, often including one or more speakers from England, but many take a regional approach. Regional groups, some affiliated with the British Hardy Plant Society, arrange lectures, plant sales, seed exchanges, and visits to members' gardens.

Florists are starting to take an interest in annuals and perennials, as designers and flower arrangers move away—none too

soon—from the assembly line "arrangements" of forced flowers plopped into blocks of Oasis that have afflicted us for far too long. The Association of Specialty Flower Growers was formed in 1988 as a forum for arrangers interested in more natural arrangements and those concerned with growing and marketing the annuals and perennials they seek.

Ten years ago only a handful of diehards, notably White Flower Farm and Wayside Gardens, were selling perennials through the mails. Now there are hundreds, some very large, many run by backyard hobbyists whose specialties include: flowers for cutting; fragrant flowers; old-fashioned plants; small perennials for the rock garden; perennials for shade; prairie and meadow flowers; woodland flowers. Some specialize in plants native to their region, others are growing a broad range of plants to test their adaptability to a given

Coreopsis 'Moon-
beam' with Sta-
chys byzantina.

region. There are peony specialists, lily specialists, primrose specialists, and growers galore of the "big three": irises, hostas, and
daylilies. In 1989 Brooklyn Botanic Garden
published a 176-page *Nursery Source Manual
for Perennials*.

Until recently most of the perennials sold
in the United States had been selected or bred
for British gardens. American gardeners have
looked with envy on the range of plants available in England, and English immigrants like
me have looked with amusement at catalogues
describing as "new" plants I grew in England
twenty years ago. Many fine new plants still
come in from Europe, as often now from Germany as from England, but there is now as
much traffic going the other way across the
Atlantic. Many plants "new" to England made
their debut here several years earlier, *Coreopsis* 'Moonbeam', for example. Blue-leaved

hostas such as 'Halcyon', raised by Eric Smith
in England a good many years ago, remain
among the best, but most of the other new
ones originated in the United States, as do the
majority of new irises, daylilies, and peonies.
Some plants bred or selected here are intended to meet a particular regional need, usually cold hardiness, drought resistance, or (a
need unknown in England) tolerance of extreme heat.

For decades the tall, blue-flowered *Baptisia australis* was the only species in that
genus to get a mention, and in English books
it usually still is, but American gardeners now
have many kinds available. *Baptisia minor* is
a daintier version of *B. australis*, *B. pendula*
and *B. alba* are similar species with spires of
white flowers. *Baptisia viridis* has bright yellow flowers on an upright plant, *B. leucophaea*
flowers of a paler yellow, while the clear yel-

low flowers of *B. lanceolata* are borne among narrow leaves on plants of mounding form. *Baptisia perfoliata* makes a wide-spreading mound of slender stems threaded with leaves in a fashion similar to the juvenile foliage of eucalyptus. All these are very tolerant of extreme heat.

With new plants flooding in, are we getting spoilt for choice? I don't think so. It does make it harder to choose which plants to grow from the abundance available, but that is a happy dilemma. There are still many unmet regional needs. Consider chrysanthemums: northern gardeners need hardy, early-flowering kinds, southern gardeners want them in flower from September through November. Chrysanthemum breeders are working to satisfy both needs.

Countless plants, native and foreign, remain untested in our gardens, and in a country with such varied growing conditions truly one man's weed is another's garden treasure. What, for example, could I use as a ground cover over small early bulbs on the sunny side of a surface-rooting tree? It had to be shallow rooting, to tolerate drought and summer temperatures often exceeding 90°F, and if possible it should look presentable twelve months of the year. A tall order, you'll agree, but *Hieracium pilosella* is perfect for the job, quickly making a mat of small evergreen silvery leaves. This species of hawkweed, an immigrant from Europe and West Asia, is described in *Hortus Third* as being "naturalized as a troublesome weed in eastern North America and Oregon." In my garden it is a valued plant, easily curbed under the conditions described provided the flowers are cut off before they go to seed.

Jogging is out, walking is in. Plants, too, are subject to fashion swings: the houseplant boom is over, and "garden" no longer means just a place where vegetables are grown. No one has written a book promising longevity to those who grow perennials nor, heaven be praised, is Madison Avenue promoting them as sexy, so what brought about the present passion for perennials, and will it last? Horticultural institutions are satisfying the thirst for information but they did not initiate the interest. More and more nurseries are selling perennials, but they are responding to demand, not creating it.

A great many perennials come from North America's meadows, prairies, and woods, but growing them in borders was an English innovation, at a time when a leisured class created gardens with the help of highly skilled but poorly paid professional gardeners. When that era ended, to the benefit of the majority, who now have more money and more leisure, interest in labor-intensive herbaceous borders lapsed, but in the intervening years technology has come to our aid with a host of labor-saving devices. Kipling's garden boy who spent his days "grubbing weeds from gravel paths with broken dinner-knives" in exchange for a pittance in *The Glory of the Garden* no longer exists, but there may be a young neighborhood entrepreneur who'll cut your grass with a rider-mower for an affordable fee. As for the gravel path, it can be kept free of weeds with a couple of applications of weedkiller each year.

Nor have plant breeders been idle. They set themselves new goals, and whilst we may have to forgo leggy plants that have to be staked, there are dozens of self-supporting kinds that were not available in the heyday of the herbaceous border. England's Alan Bloom has played a major role in breeding and selecting compact plants for today's smaller gardens. There are still goals to strive for—daylilies that deadhead themselves, and thick-textured, heatproof, and slug-resistant hostas are just two of the challenges that are being

Amsonias—seldom grown in English gardens and accorded faint praise in English gardening books—are among the best perennials for East Coast gardens. The one in the picture, along with Siberian irises 'Super Ego' and 'Summer Skies', is my favorite of the genus. A mystery plant of unknown origin, grown in American gardens for many years, it is now available from nurseries as Amsonia tabernaemontana montana or A. montana. (Virginia; May)

tackled by American breeders.

The question still remains, why perennials? Plant for plant they still require more work than, for instance, shrubs. I found a clue in the slide sets rented out by my Slide Library. Two are in greater demand than all the others put together: both deal with design. We have passed through an era of plantsmanship, where just having a plant and growing it well (or sometimes not!) was enough. Now the emphasis is on the way a plant is used and how it is combined with other plants. A new profession has come into being: garden designer. Unlike landscape architects, who are mainly concerned with structure, garden designers have a more romantic approach and create their effects with plants. Perennials—so varied in texture and form, so colorful, so moveable, and so inexpensive compared with trees and shrubs—lend themselves to creative compositions better than any other group of plants and therefore appeal to garden designers who, whilst they may not have started the perennials fashion ball rolling, have certainly given it impetus.

There is in this emphasis on design some risk of putting the cart before the horse. Extensive knowledge of plants is the foundation stone for their creative use. Design based on the same few perennials, no matter how good they may be, will ultimately become as stereotyped and boring as the lawn and foundation plantings they replace, but the thousands of gardeners, amateur and professional, attending symposiums across the country suggests that knowledge of plants is growing hand-in-hand with interest in design and eagerness to explore new ways of developing gardens.

Perennials are making gardens prettier and providing scope for creativity. The words "perennials" and "border" still tend to be inseparably linked but this is beginning to change. There are many more ways of growing perennials than grouping them in borders. Each of us should consider soil, site, climate, and personal circumstances before deciding how best to incorporate them in our gardens. In the United States there can never be a single prevailing garden style: what works for Boston won't work in New Orleans. Harken to Miss Jekyll, a fount of common sense:

> . . . good gardening means patience and dogged determination. There must be many failures and losses, but by always pushing on there will also be the reward of success. Those who do not know are apt to think that hardy flower gardening of the best kind is easy. It is not easy at all. It has taken me half a lifetime merely to find out what is best worth doing, and a good slice of another half to puzzle out the ways of doing it.

In many parts of the United States we still have to find out what is best worth doing, or do-able at all. By "pushing on" Miss Jekyll did not mean knocking one's head against a brick wall: goals aren't reached by heading in the wrong direction. The place you head for won't always meet your expectations but if you repeatedly fail to get where you meant to go, perhaps you are on the wrong train. In frost-free parts of the South the very concept of a perennial changes to include a great many tender or half-hardy plants grown as annuals or conservatory plants in colder regions. This may call for a different gardening style, with emphasis on foliage. Knowing the hardiness zone of your garden is only a beginning—Zone 10 Florida and Zone 10 California are two different worlds. Where summer drought is normal, it is wasteful of precious water, not to mention precious time, money, and energy, to attempt a perennials border. That doesn't preclude the growing of perennials but does necessitate selection of plants adapted to local conditions. Florida gardeners, for instance, cannot grow bearded irises but they can grow the equally beautiful Louisiana irises envied by many in the north.

The nature of the site and its surroundings should be considered before deciding what kind of garden to make. Gardening of any kind is an unnatural thing, a battle with nature, so think hard before you make it a fight to the death. Forcing on a piece of land a design or plants totally out of character with the soil, climate, and setting can only be done—if at all—at great cost in effort and money, and the result may well be incongruous.

Don't lean too far in the other direction, though. There is a growing interest in native plants by gardeners largely and laudably concerned with conservation. Some, with missionary zeal, think we should grow in our gardens only native plants, but gardening is essentially an artificial thing, a toy with which we play for our own creative satisfaction. From a practical point of view, many native plants are beautiful, equally many are homely or weedy, and whilst both may grow luxuriantly and unattended in the wild that is because, through years of evolution, they have found their niche. When we build a house, with its driveway, well, septic tank, or other accoutrements of human habitation, we make such drastic

Gardeners in the Deep South cannot grow bearded irises but they can grow the equally beautiful Louisiana irises envied by those in cold regions.

Two very different warm-climate gardens. Top: *Foliage plants predominate in the shady Louisiana garden of landscape architects Wayne Womack and Jon Emerson. Plants include aspidistra,* Saxifraga stolonifera, *ferns, and liriope. (April)* Bottom: *Succulents such as agaves, kalanchoes, and aeoniums are used extensively in this summer-dry California garden. The orange flowers are an* Aloe striata *hybrid. The swordlike yellow-striped leaves are New Zealand flax (*Phormium tenax *'Variegata'). (April)*

changes in the soil, the play of sun and shade, and the flow of water that the colonies of lady's slipper once found on that bit of land may never be persuaded to grow there again.

"If you find yourself in hot water," said one of my friends, "decide to take a bath." Similarly, if you find yourself the owner of a wooded lot, decide to make a woodland garden. It would be a pity to remove the trees, at great expense, in order to have a perennials border. But why limit yourself to native plants adapted to shade when woodland plants from other lands will add variety and look every bit as natural. Contradictory though it may seem, many of them will actually prove easier to grow.

In most parts of the United States, excepting the big cities, house sites can be found of such great natural beauty that this should be preserved, whether wooded, rocky, lakeside, meadow, beach, marsh, or desert. If the surroundings are beautiful, why shut them out with walls and hedges or attempt a garden of contradictory mood?

But most of us live in residential developments where little remains of the natural character of the land. With conditions already artificial, is there at least complete freedom of choice in this circumstance? Not as much as you might think. It is a useful exercise to stroll round such a development, look at each house and mentally plan an appropriate garden. It at

*Native wildflowers share a shady patch with others from Japan. Plants include bloodroot (*Sanguinaria canadensis*), foamflower (*Tiarella wherryi*), Phlox divaricata, a selected purple-leaved form of heuchera, ferns, violets, hostas, and white-striped Disporum sessile 'Variegatum'. (Garden of Morris Berd, Pennsylvania; May)*

once becomes apparent that every site is different, each with limitations but most with some advantages. To begin with, assuming a road runs east to west, houses on one side will have sunny front gardens, those on the other side shady ones. Shade at the front may mean sun at the back, but not if the lot is small and backs onto woodland or tall buildings.

Looking round my own neighborhood, it struck me immediately how much attitudes have changed toward walls and fences, reflecting a greater wish for privacy. Twenty years ago fences were seldom acceptable: "Spite fences, we call them," said the builder of our Connecticut house. Now at least half the gardens I pass on my walks have a fence, wall, or hedge of some kind. Where fences and hedges are prohibited, a measure of privacy can be achieved by mounding earth into a ridge, in landscaping called a "berm." Berms can be grassed over or planted with shrubs. If a hedge or fence is permitted but its height restricted, it can effectively be made higher without transgressing bylaws by planting or erecting it atop a berm. Berms vary in breadth and length to fit available space but miniature mountains are seldom attractive, nor, at the other extreme, are the long, narrow ridges that one of my friends calls "mole-runs." Berms not only help provide privacy, they reduce the level of street noise, discourage trespassing by defining the boundaries, and introduce a change of levels that makes a flat site more interesting.

This book is about some of the many ways of using perennials. It will not go into such basics as soil preparation, pruning, and pest control—topics adequately covered in other literature—nor provide a dictionary of plants. By all means copy what you see in the pictures if you wish; there is no copyright on ideas to infringe and the original creators would probably be flattered. My hope, though, is that you will be inspired to create your own gardening style. Recently I read a book (*The Startling Jungle* by Stephen Lacey) that described some of the plant associations in the author's garden. It sent me rushing out to rub elbows with Christmas shoppers in a search for bulbs of white-flowered tulips to interplant with blue starflower (*Ipheion uniflorum*) behind white candytuft (*Iberis sempervirens*) under a pink-flowered magnolia. This combination wasn't described in the book—something quite different sparked the idea.

Not all our dreamed-up schemes work out in practice. A dog—not yours, of course—may decide to bury a bone where you planted bulbs, or a vole may eat the roots of your expensive new hostas. Colors may not look as good together as they did in the imagination, or flowering times may fail to coincide. Don't write off the idea too hastily, though. It is several years since I planted those starflowers under the magnolia, then only a large bush, and at first it seemed a failure. The soil was an acid sand, little improved, and digging substantial holes for the bulbs brought protesting whiffs of ginger from damaged magnolia roots, so the starflower bulbs were dibbled in with a narrow trowel, a few here, a few there. A dry summer followed, then several winters of record-breaking cold. Contrary to traditional (European) wisdom, all the magnolias I grow (*Magnolia grandiflora, M. virginiana, M. stellata, M. kobus, M. soulangiana*) have proved drought resistant, delighting in sandy soil and blazing sun. Starflower bulbs, while multiplying with prodigious speed in rich soil and light shade, were not happy in the hot sun and I would have moved them somewhere else if I'd got around to it. Meanwhile, the magnolia (*M. stellata* 'Pink Stardust') was growing at least three times as fast as one I had in my English garden; its branches spread low and wide, shading the ground beneath, and its falling leaves, aided by a top dressing of compost each autumn, were creating a cooling mulch over the bulbs. Now the starflowers carpet the ground with green leaves from autumn through winter, becoming a sheet of blue flowers in early spring when the magnolia, still leafless, bears its pink stars in profusion. By the time the starflower foliage dies down in early summer the magnolia has leafed out and hidden the now-bare ground.

White candytuft (*Iberis sempervirens*) was added to soften the front edge of this raised bed, where a rail tie separates it from the driveway. Will the tulips do well? Will the flowering times coincide? Time will tell. If not, I'll think of something else. "But star-flower isn't hardy for me," is a reaction I sometimes get from audiences. Then consider alternatives. How about *Scilla sibirica*, which doesn't do well for me—I haven't yet discovered why—or grape hyacinths (*Muscari*), which do well—sometimes *too* well—for nearly everyone. In gardening none of us gets the whole cake, no matter where we live.

Take a walk round your own neighborhood, mentally replanning the gardens as you pass by, with perennials in mind. The new wave hasn't yet struck the neighborhood where I live and what I see is typical of suburbia. There's usually a drive, a path, and foundation plantings, occasionally a tree or two, the rest mown grass.

One front yard is entirely filled with fruit and vegetables. A year's supply is grown and a surplus shared with friends. It is what the owners like to do and they do it well and derive much pleasure from it. I wouldn't change a thing. If they wanted flowers for the house, a bed of annuals or perennials could easily be fitted in among the cabbages and squash, but just because flowers are "in," no law demands that everybody grow them.

Someone has put in a hedge of *Photinia*

× *fraseri*. This undemanding evergreen has become very popular for hedging in the Southeast, being dense, tolerant of poor soil, free from pests and diseases, fast growing at first but slowing down before it starts to tangle with overhead wires, and—probably the most important quality for popularity—it is easy to propagate, therefore inexpensive to buy. For those wanting to grow perennials it has one disadvantage in the very characteristic that makes it popular: its striking coppery red new leaves in spring and early summer. If a border of flowering plants was placed in front of it, colors would have to be more carefully chosen than with the traditional neutral background of dark green yew. Surinam cherry (*Eugenia uniflora*), popular for hedging in parts of California, has the same limitation—or opportunity?

One garden has an attractive close-boarded fence on its north-facing boundary. I'd want a border against that for perennials happiest in shade, such as liriopes, primroses, hostas, ferns, Solomon's seal (especially the variegated *Polygonatum odoratum* 'Variegatum') and hellebores (of which *Helleborus orientalis* is the best), perhaps first dividing the border into bays with groups of shade-tolerant shrubs. If I lived in the house next door, I'd take advantage of the sunny side of that same fence for plants that enjoy a summer baking, such as bearded irises.

The estate developer separated one section from the road with a "serpentine" wall, inside which one owner has planted red maple trees. Nothing will grow under these without more effort than most of us are willing to expend. I envision in their place a colorful mixed border, with vines on the wall and slightly tender plants set back inside its protective curves.

Another well-trodden front "yard" (an appropriate term in this instance) is usually littered with bicycles, and a basketball net is affixed to the front wall of the house. Several young children live here and their needs have priority. If I wanted to grow flowers I'd plant them in containers on the sunny back terrace, threatening the kids with death, or loss of computer privileges, if caught playing among them. Parents have rights too! A lost cause is the house, burgled a year ago, where two Dobermans race back and forth inside the chain-link fence. I hope the question of what to grow under such conditions never comes up where I'm on the problem-solving panel!

A long, wide driveway curves gracefully back through a large front lawn to garages at the side of the house. It cries out for wide borders on either side of the drive, but the owners both work and would not have time to maintain extensive plantings of perennials. I'd plant mainly shrubs, perhaps with an edging of evergreen liriope (*Liriope muscari*). Borders alongside the short drive of a smaller house would certainly be manageable, but there'd scarcely be room to get out of the car onto this narrower drive without treading on the flowers. Perhaps the drive could be widened with bands of cobbles set in cement, providing space for the perennials to overflow and a change of texture too.

Several houses have semicircular drives going in at one side of the lot, out at the other. With this very common layout the space in front of the driveway forms a natural island bed. I picture it planted with shrubs and perennials to form a screen for the house. The screening would be even more effective if soil was added to form a low mound.

There are forest trees on several lots. On such a site the collecting urge could be satisfied with an assemblage of woodland plants from many lands, or a specialist collection of hostas. A massed display of a single plant, say creeping phlox (*Phlox stolonifera*) would in-

Low-growing dianthus and gaillardias will not get big enough to obstruct the path through a plantsman's small front garden. The bright yellow patch near the house is Lysimachia nummularia 'Aurea'. *The variegated shrub in the foreground is* Cornus alba 'Elegantissima'. *(Garden of Tony and Michelle Avent, North Carolina; June)*

A hosta collection in the display gardens of Powell's Nursery, Princeton, North Carolina. (May)

volve much less work and be visually more striking, but only for two or three weeks each year, and not at all where there are rabbits, for rabbits make short work of phlox.

Behind a post-and-rail fence lies one very attractive garden with a simple design of massed evergreen azaleas in boundary borders and large curving island beds, shaded by tall pines. Were that garden mine there'd be perennials in front of and between the azaleas: woodland phlox (*Phlox divaricata*), trilliums, wild ginger (*Asarum*), lungworts (*Pulmonaria*)—the possibilities are endless, but I have to concede the excellence of the garden just the way it is, colorful in spring, serene in summer, neat in winter, and very easy to maintain.

A corner lot has a semicircle of rounded evergreen Japanese hollies (*Ilex crenata*)

where the two roads meet, perhaps intended to discourage shortcuts across the lawn that sweeps unbroken up to the front door. A half moon of flowers would fit nicely inside the evergreens, adding color and interest without interfering with the uncluttered open look.

A Georgian-style brick house has a path leading straight from the sidewalk to the front door, unusual these days when access is usually from the driveway. Neat and symmetrical, it calls for formality and the boxwoods edging the path suit the mood of the place very well. Just the same, I'd like to see them replaced by borders of peonies. When planted in straight rows, peonies have a formal look, especially when all of one kind. The bright pink emerging shoots are beautiful in spring and the foliage is handsome throughout the growing season. They don't flower for long but for that short time they'd be the showpiece of the neighborhood.

This is just one neighborhood, with no two sites quite alike, and with equally varied owners. Your site and circumstances may not match any of these, but these examples serve to show the potential for adding perennials and other plants to the sort of garden most of us have. We all have so much to learn, about the plants themselves, and about the many ways of using them, but never have there been better opportunities for learning. New gardening books appear by the dozen every year, with a growing number of them written by American gardeners. We can travel and visit other gardens or "tour" many of them on video. And then there are the seminars—not, as I perceive them, teams of "experts" dispensing information, but forums where enthusiasts can meet and discuss successes and innovations, and failures too, for we often learn to do something right by first doing it wrong. If this book helps you at all in planning and planting a garden that brings you the happiness I get from mine, that will please me very much.

The colorful Indian pink (Spigelia marilandica) would enliven a planting of hostas. This is one of the many choice wildflowers that have become available from nurseries in recent years. Native to the Southeast, it is usually found in rich, moist soil and light shade. Here it is combined with Japanese painted fern (Athyrium niponicum 'Pictum') and Ligularia dentata. (Virginia; June)

The arbor provides a throughway in a border running parallel to the house. Campanula lactiflora *gains support from trellis attached to the side of the arbor, obviating the need to stake this four-foot plant. Unless blown in another direction by prevailing winds, perennials usually lean toward the strongest light—generally from the south or west, so this would not work with all orientations, nor if the arbor was deeply shaded by vines. (Garden of Elaine Horton, England; July)*

1 | Choosing the Plants:

Some Considerations

It is easy to get carried away when browsing through garden books and catalogues. Books may mention a plant's bad qualities as well as the good but nurseries are, after all, putting their children up for adoption and thus can be expected to gloss over shortcomings. Anyway, "it all depends," as my father used to say when asked a question to which there was no simple answer. Having just, for the umpteenth time, spent half an hour picking tiny barbs out of my fingers, I've decided to dispense with prickly pear (*Opuntia humifusa*), despite its beauty and willingness to grow in poor, dry soil. Pads drop off and somehow get moved a yard or more away, there to make their presence uncomfortably known to weeding fingers. In a more barren region, with rocks and other cacti for company, and no place for the fallen pad to hide, its merits would far outweigh this defect. It just isn't a plant to combine with tall vegetation, nor where the presence of large deciduous trees necessitates hours spent disengaging fallen leaves impaled on prickly pads.

Those of us who don't suffer from allergies are apt to make light of the misery caused to the afflicted by certain plants: gas plant (*Dictamnus albus*), euphorbias, cow parsnip (*Heracleum*), and rue (*Ruta graveolens*) have all been accused of occasionally causing a rash like that from poison ivy, a problem most likely to arise in hot climates. A very few unfortunates are so allergic to bee stings that bee-attracting flowers must be banned from the garden.

Every garden has its problems and advantages. In my own the loblolly pines (*Pinus taeda*) shed needles for months on end, so I seek "comb-ability" in plants grown under them—grassy leaves from which debris can be combed with a rake without damaging them. *Liriope*, *Ophiopogon*, sedges (*Carex*), *Acorus gramineus* 'Variegatus', and Pacific Coast irises are particularly tolerant of this type of grooming, their leaves being not only slender but of a tough, untearable texture. They look so neat when the job is done that I find it a most satisfying process.

THE RIGHT PLANTS FOR THE RIGHT PLACE

A battered, sick, or dead plant doesn't contribute much to the beauty of the garden so the well-being of the plant is an important practical consideration. Delphiniums need protection from wind, Japanese irises must have moist, acid soil—we have to know the individual needs of plants and the varied conditions that exist in different parts of even quite small gardens. Giving plants what they need of sun, air, water, soil texture, and nutrients is more than half the battle. (Tender loving care can be overdone, though. Too much pampering may weaken resistance to pests and diseases, heat, cold, or drought, as well as forcing uncharacteristically lax growth. One of my best plants is *Chrysanthemum* 'Mei Kyo', a sturdy

eighteen-inch tall late-flowering "mum" that spreads rapidly. I gave a clump to a friend who admired it and, a year later, was amazed to see it grown to a sprawling four feet in her double-dug, manure-enriched border.)

Most gardens have exposed places or frost pockets but also sheltered nooks. Finding the right place can make the difference between life and death for a marginally hardy plant. One friend grows blue plumbago (*Ceratostigma plumbaginoides*) in Zone 4, where it usually is not hardy. It surrounds the thick stone slab that forms the front doorstep and if most of the patch gets killed, enough of the roots have crept under the protective stone for the plant to make a comeback. In my own garden, the showy Eastern coral bean (*Erythrina herbacea*) was twice winter-killed but is now established between the trailing outer

A wind-sheltered site has been created for this magnificent bed of delphiniums. (Garden of Sir John Thouron, Pennsylvania; June)

Coral bean (Ery-thrina herbacea) gains winter protection where it is marginally hardy under the sweeping lower branches of an evergreen stranvaesia. (Virginia; late June)

branches of an evergreen *Stranvaesia*, which safeguard the coral bean roots by preventing the ground from deep freezing.

If one plant needs abundant moisture, another very sharp drainage, their different needs might be met by planting the first in a slight hollow with lots of peat moss or compost dug in, the other on a mound with added gravel or road grit. There may not be a need for such contrivances, as many beds and borders have patches that are naturally moister or drier than the rest.

If summers are dry and the water supply inadequate, which plants might survive? Some plants *like* hot, dry sites, provided the soil is deep and there isn't competition for moisture and nutrients from the roots of nearby trees and shrubs. In rich, moist soil *Lespedeza thunbergii* grows six feet high and sprawls. In hot sun and sand it is an airy, arching three to four feet. There are clues in the plants. Tiny leaves, or fleshy ones, and those made silvery by a coating of silky hairs, indicate adaptation to dry conditions. So do the long root thongs of such plants as butterfly weed (*Asclepias tuberosa*), baptisias, *Callirhoe*, *Gaura lindheimeri*, and balloon flower (*Platycodon*). Large leaves usually indicate a need for shade and moisture.

Knowing the natural habitat of a plant helps one decide under what conditions it is likely to do well, but some are exceptionally adaptable: *Hibiscus coccineus* grows in the swamps of Florida and Georgia but it is also very drought resistant, as might be deduced from its far-reaching thonglike roots. Sometimes, however, there are misleading similarities. Red bee balm (*Monarda didyma*) and pale purple bergamot (*M. fistulosa*) look alike except in color and both do well in moist soil, but bergamot is drought resistant, bee balm is not. Many prairie plants are adapted to dry soil, others to wet places. The catalogues of nurseries specializing in native plants suggest solutions for many a problem spot.

Some plants adapted to sun and to soil low in nutrients will not do well when these conditions are combined with prolonged extreme heat. Sea kale (*Crambe maritima*) is one of the sufferers from heat prostration in my garden. It grows on the beaches of Europe and is accustomed to sandy soil but not to temperatures of 100°F. It needs richer, moister soil than in its native habitat to compensate for the summer heat. So do the European sea hollies (*Eryngium*).

If a plant doesn't thrive in shade, yet wilts in sun even when moist—*Ligularia* 'The Rocket' for example—could it be positioned where a taller adjacent plant casts shade for part of the day, or where trees on the perimeter of the lot filter hot sun from the west?

Try as we may, there'll be failures. Moving a plant to another part of the garden sometimes makes all the difference, but enough is enough: getting a garden together requires a measure of ruthlessness. For me that means three attempts to please a pernickety plant. With the third attempt goes the warning, thought or spoken: "Measure up, or out you go"—it does sometimes seem that plants listen. It is also not unusual for a plant that has resisted all blandishments to grow lustily on the rubbish heap to which it has been consigned.

Consolation for failure with one plant can usually be found in success with another: if you live too far south to please *Ligularia* 'The Rocket', you can probably grow the less hardy leopard plant, *Ligularia tussilaginea* 'Aureo-maculata', or the beautiful *L. t.* 'Argentea' with its shining, white-edged leaves.

THE QUESTION OF SPRAYING AND OTHER PEST MANAGEMENT

Are you willing to spray? If not, eschew most of the border phlox, which will be afflicted with mildew sooner or later unless treated with a fungicide. You might take a chance on early-flowering kinds with shiny leaves, such as the old white-flowered 'Miss Lingard', which is less mildew-prone, with the added advantage of being sterile, so you won't have to weed out self-sown progeny in unattractive colors.

The prevalence of mildew on other perennials varies from one region to another. Bee balm (*Monarda*) is often affected and so is lungwort (*Pulmonaria*) when grown in soil that gets dry. Golden star (*Chrysogonum virginianum*) is frequently affected in my garden but if the leaves are cut off at the base it grows a new crop of healthy ones very speedily. There have been promising results from experiments with solutions of baking soda as a mildew preventive, but too strong a solution damages some plants and further testing needs to be done.

If you use insecticides, try to find out what you are killing. No one would choose to

Ligularia 'The Rocket' is placed among other perennials, where the large leaves will not be too conspicuous if they wilt in afternoon heat. (Garden of Elsa and Michael Bakalar, Massachusetts; July)

Aquilegia cana-
densis *'Corbett'*
goes nicely with
the bronze new
fronds of Dryop-
teris erythrosora.
The fronds then
spread out to con-
ceal the colum-
bine's basal
foliage.

be without butterflies, but at the caterpillar stage they have to eat. The *Field Guide to Butterflies*, sponsored by the National Audubon Society, illustrates butterfly larvae and tells you what they feed on. The food of the painted lady, for example, is "chiefly the Everlastings (*Gnaphalium*, *Antennaria*, and *Anaphalis*)" upon which the little caterpillars "live singly in a compact nest of silk, leaves, plant fragments, etc." They obviously have a penchant for furry leaves because *Eriophyllum lanatum* was disfigured in my garden, as well as *Anaphalis*. These I've ceased to grow, but the handsome black-and-yellow banded caterpillars of the monarchs I find on rue (*Ruta graveolens*) some autumns are seldom numerous enough to defoliate the plants (and if they did the rue would probably come back in spring) and I let them be.

If a plant suffers occasional damage, from pest, disease, or some quirk of the weather, it is probably best to ignore it. If the problem occurs year after year, do you deal with it, or discard the plant? Is one of those revolting suspended mortuaries an acceptable remedy for Japanese beetles? If you agree it doesn't contribute to the aesthetics of the garden, then damage done by the beetles will be less apparent on plants with small or ferny leaves and inflorescences containing lots of tiny flowers (astilbes, for instance) than it is on plants with large leaves and flowers. This applies equally to slugs and snails, with damage particularly apparent (and there for the whole season) on large-leaved foliage plants such as hostas and bergenia.

Columbines (*Aquilegia*) are often damaged by leaf miner. They seem able to live

making a suitable match.

Voles are a serious problem in many regions, especially on sandy soils. Nothing is safe from them but they seem to go first for plants of the lily family, especially lilies and hostas. There is no known way of eradicating voles but you can safeguard bulbs and choice plants by planting them in sunken containers. Surrounding the roots and covering the soil surface around vulnerable plants with a good layer of coarse road grit also helps.

Deer and rabbits are enough to make the afflicted give up gardening and it is the rare gardener whose heart does not harden when their own garden is ravaged. When it got to a stage where everything in my garden was encircled with chicken wire, I became a bit less sentimental about "bunnies," and Fred McGourty wrote that "The Bambi lobby has diminished by two" when the garden he and Mary Ann work so hard to keep beautiful suffered deer depredations. The literature abounds with lists of rabbit- and deer-proof plants, but in truth these are few, if any, when food is scarce. The only certain remedy so far is an expensive deer- or rabbit-proof fence. Spraying on Ropel is supposed to make foliage too bitter for rabbits to eat but in my experience it is but an expensive salad dressing. Cats may provide a solution, provided you don't overfeed or otherwise pamper them, but face the fact that they'll probably kill a dozen birds for every rabbit. Some dogs are good rabbiters, especially Jack Russell terriers, but they usually need to be taught by an older dog and in racing through the plants they may do more damage than the rabbits.

All of this is enough to make you give up gardening, but gardeners are a persistent and experimental lot. Writing in the *Hosta Journal* (there is nothing deer like better than hostas), Joyce Descloux reports on a home-brewed mix she has found effective, as follows:

In front is the evergreen Euonymus *'Emerald Gaiety' interplanted with the herbaceous* Carex siderosticta *'Variegata'. (Virginia; May)*

with the problem—it is we who can't abide the worm-tunneled leaves. Try interspersing the columbines with clumps of ferns high enough to hide the basal foliage without overtopping the stems of dancing flowers. In my garden the pale yellow *Aquilegia canadensis* 'Corbett' is combined with autumn fern (*Dryopteris erythrosora*), but both columbines and ferns come in various heights and it is just a matter of

In a kitchen blender, drop two old unshelled eggs, one large clove garlic, a loose cupful of green onion tops, and 2 cups of water. Process to liquify about two minutes. Pour into a wide-mouthed quart jar; stir in 2 tablespoons chili pepper. Add an old piece of deodorant soap and fill with water.

Joyce first diluted this with two gallons of water and poured it on from a watering can, but found it most effective, through a summer of frequent heavy rain, used weekly at full strength, squeeze-dripped on from a saturated kitchen sponge, while wearing rubber gloves. She adds: "I keep a little of the old mix, unrefrigerated, to add to the new batch. The smell is 'ripe' then, but unnoticeable in the garden. I believe this repellent mix depends on a sulfur compound. Both eggs and onions contain a lot of sulfur. The bite of red pepper is also irritating to the deer. But the point is to keep them from even *wanting* to taste the plants. I think deer, like any animal, can be trained, to a certain extent, and therein lies the secret of success. But it does take determination, effort, and perseverance." Don't those last words put gardening in a nutshell? No guarantees but it is certainly worth a try.

TO STAKE OR NOT TO STAKE

We have to consider how much time we are able, or willing, to spend staking plants that can't support themselves. Could some be placed between bushier things to give them support? Is there a compact version of the tall plant you like? There often is. For example (compact version in parentheses): *Amsonia tabernaemontana* (*A. t. montana*), *Anchusa azurea* (*A. a.* 'Little John'), *Anemone* × *hybrida* (*A.* × *hybrida* 'September Sprite'), *He-*lianthus salicifolius* (the two-foot high *Buphthalum salicifolium* or the one-foot *Inula ensifolia*—such similar plants that taxonomists must surely one day put them in the same genus), *Coreopsis lanceolata* (*C.* 'Sunray' or 'Goldfink'), *Delphinium* hybrids (Dwarf Pacific strain), *Gypsophila paniculata* (*G. p.* 'Compacta Flore Pleno' or, for similar airy effect on a rock garden scale, *Petrorhagia saxifraga*, formerly called *Tunica*), *Helenium autumnale* (*H. a.* 'Pumilum'), peonies (choose those with single or anemone-form flowers rather than the heavy full doubles, or, at the midget end of the scale *Paeonia tenuifolia*), *Platycodon grandiflorus* (*P. g.* 'Mariesii', which may still sprawl in rich soil, or the smaller 'Apoyama'). Scan the catalogues and you'll find many more, including, of course, dozens of small daylilies, hostas, and irises.

You don't, however, have to confine yourself to short plants. Tall plants that seldom need staking include *Artemisia lactiflora*, *Aruncus dioicus*, *Dictamnus albus*, *Filipendula rubra*, *Lythrum salicaria* and its hybrids, *Macleaya*, several astilbes, and a number of tall daylilies. There is a host of plants of intermediate height that need no staking.

DEADHEADING

How much time can you—will you—spend deadheading? It can be an enjoyable way to unwind from the day's occupations, companionably or alone, but evening deadheading won't always do: with daylilies and platycodons it needs to be done in the morning. If you can't, won't, or somehow other just don't get around to it, don't make mass plantings of sumptuous modern daylilies with colossal flowers that become gross in sodden decay; plant only the number of clumps within your capacity to deadhead daily, or select those with more elegant flowers—they tend to be older hybrids—that wither less conspicuously.

Other plants that need frequent deadheading if they are not to look disheveled include thrift (*Armeria*), pinks (*Dianthus*), and a lot of the daisies including the shastas (*Chrysanthemum × superbum*) and *Stokesia*.

Many perennials dispose neatly of their own dead flowers: *Astermoea mongolica*, *Belamcanda*, *Boltonia*, *Callirhoe*, *Coreopsis verticillata*, *Gaura lindheimeri*, cranesbill (*Geranium*), *Hibiscus coccineus* (the giant flowered *Hibiscus* hybrids such as Southern Belle, by contrast, collapse into mush and glue themselves to the leaves of the bush), flaxes (*Linum*), rose campion (*Lychnis coronaria*), purple loosestrife (*Lythrum*), primroses (*Primula*), and most salvias (the blue pool of spent flowers surrounding *Salvia azurea grandiflora* each morning is one of its delights). The flowers of *Tradescantia* literally melt away, a process fascinating to observe. Some go one better, not only shedding dead petals cleanly but going on to make ornamental seedheads, among them *Agapanthus*, pasqueflower (*Anemone pulsatilla*), butterfly weed (*Asclepias tuberosa*), *Alstroemeria pulchella* (which forms little acornlike seedheads), *Baptisia australis* (with pods that rustle in the wind), clematis, gas plant (*Dictamnus albus*) (with seedheads like wee starfish), gaillardia, *Monarda*, and *Opuntia*. I enjoy the deadheads of *Sedum* 'Autumn Joy' all winter long. Some flowers, *Gaura lindheimeri* and *Linum perenne* among them, shed their spent flowers by early afternoon, opening a new lot the next morning. If evening is the only time you can enjoy in your garden, you won't want these.

Many flowers need no daily deadheading, only the cutting out of the complete inflorescence when bloom time is done, though this can be tedious and time-consuming where there are numerous separate flowering stalks—Siberian irises, for instance.

Deadheads must, of course, be left on the plant if you want it to self-sow. Some do this overgenerously. Toad flower (*Tricyrtis hirta*) produces seedlings by the thousand, but most of the seed drops close by the parent plants. Many ornamental onions, on the other hand, scatter their progeny all over the garden if not deadheaded before seed ripens: garlic chives (*Allium tuberosum*) is one of the best perennials—easy to grow, with attractive foliage, and flowers that open late in the season—but deadheading is imperative if it is not to become a nuisance.

ORDER OF BLOOM

Whether our goal is massed bloom for a couple of months or scattered color over a longer period, we need to know when each plant can be expected to bloom. This is tricky for beginners. Books and catalogues are unavoidably misleading in a country of such varied climates. Retailers who grow their own plants usually give the flowering time for their locality, but most buy from wholesale growers and these may be located hundreds of miles away. Plants at flowering peak during July and August in Boston will peak in June and July in Philadelphia, and in May and June in South Carolina. Perennials bought in bloom may flower at a different time next year if they've come from a warmer part of the country or wintered in a greenhouse. A young plant puts its energy first into establishing roots and, if planted in spring, may flower later than it will in subsequent years.

Visiting nearby gardens is the best way of learning what can be expected in your own.

Don't be influenced by the way a plant looks in another region. You might admire snakeroot (*Cimicifuga racemosa*) during an August visit to Maine, but south of the Mason-Dixon line it flowers much earlier in the season, sun fades the flowers fast, and it needs a lot of moisture and some shade if the leaves are not to scorch. Conversely, late-flowering *C. simplex* might tempt the Maine gardener traveling south, but in the coldest zones it flowers too late to beat the frost as often as not.

Flowering time can sometimes be manipulated. Many asters and "mum" chrysanthemums are pinched and sheared to make them compact. This also delays flowering. Some perennials can be sheared in this manner, while others treated this way abandon all attempt to flower that year. If cut back *after* they have flowered, some rebloom, some do not, and sometimes whether they do or not depends on what region they're being grown in. The flowering time for *Chrysanthemum × rubellum* 'Clara Curtis' is usually stated to be late summer. In my garden it flowers in June if I let it. Whether or not I do depends on my travel plans—I don't want plants to flower when I am not around to enjoy them if it can be circumvented. Shearing it back after the buds have formed delays flowering for a month or two (varying from year to year, with the weather). If left to flower and then cut back, it flowers again in early autumn. Yet *C. × rubellum* 'Mary Stoker' never attempts to flower before late summer. What an exquisite color this chrysanthemum is, a yellow bright but not brassy, with a hint of apricot. This one is a bit leggier than 'Clara Curtis'. I haven't yet tried shearing it but it probably could be done successfully where autumns are prolonged and warm. Delaying bloom by shearing might render the flowers vulnerable to frost in the north. The little Korean chrysanthemum 'Mei Kyo' opens later still and wouldn't manage to set buds at all, even in the South, if delayed by shearing.

Platycodons produce new flower buds each time the stems are cut back. *Amsonia tabernaemontana* makes a neater bush if sheared back after flowering but it does not bloom a second time, and the same with *Veronica teucrium*, but if I cut back the long stems of the so-called blue butterfly weed (*Oxypetalum caeruleum*) it makes new stems rapidly and continues to bloom through autumn. So does the prickly poppy (*Argemone grandiflora*), an annual north of Zone 8. Blue flax (*Linum perenne*) and *Delphinium grandiflorum* died from the same treatment. So did lavender cotton (*Santolina chamaecyparissus*) when

*Prickly poppy (*Argemone grandiflora*) flowers all summer in my garden. Later in the season it will trail over and help to conceal the foliage, shabby by then, of* Iris pallida *'Aurea-variegata'. Where summers are cool the iris leaves remain attractive through summer. (Virginia; June)*

sheared after flowering, which meant during the heat of summer, though it takes well to pruning if hard pruning is done in early spring, followed by a light trim if and when it starts to get shaggy. It will then not bloom.

Because the effect of cutting back differs from region to region, we each need to experiment in our own gardens, experiments best conducted initially on plants in a nursery bed or out-of-the-way corner, and not, of course, on your solitary specimen of a choice plant. Gardeners in regions where the growing season is very long have the most to gain from such experiments.

HEIGHT AND OTHER CONSIDERATIONS

You'll also need to know how tall a plant gets. This varies a lot with region. In books based on England or the East Coast, one might almost add routinely: "Double that for Seattle." Nothing beats local experience—and local books if you can get them. If not, comparing the height of a plant you know well with the stated height in the book you are reading will give you some idea of the differences to expect. Even within the same area, soil and site can make a great difference: in neighboring gardens you might see *Sedum* 'Autumn Joy' only nine inches high under a tree with competing roots, a little over a foot in better soil but in need of division, and close to three feet where young but well-established clumps (say two to three years) are growing in rich, moisture-retentive soil.

Spread also varies a great deal. Some dictionaries of perennials (such as *Perennial Garden Plants* by Graham Stuart Thomas and *Perennials for American Gardens* by Ruth Rogers Clausen and Nicolas H. Ekstrom) indi-

cate approximate spread as well as approximate height. Bear in mind, though, that a plant growing in sandy soil in a warm region where rainfall is high will spread twice as fast as the same plant in clay soil and a cool region.

Perhaps you like a plant's other qualities but dislike the color. Plants of lurid color often have a white counterpart. Some liatris are a bit loud, others (*Liatris microcephala*, for one) have more blue in them, and there are several white kinds. Though leavened with gray leaves, rose mullein (*Lychnis coronaria*) is still a color to be used in moderation, but there's a white one, and *L. c.* 'Oculata' is mostly white with a pink splash or eye. How about *Geranium psilostemon*'s unabashed magenta? No? Then seek out *G. p.* 'Bressingham Flare', which is less fiercely colored and more compact as well. Perhaps you do like the color but something else about the plant turns you off. Does *Coreopsis verticillata* spread too fast? *C. v.* 'Zagreb' is a bit more restrained. Plants don't have a bill of equal rights and we need to discriminate (a much abused and misused word), choosing the best plant of its kind for our purpose. In this we are often handicapped by the tendency of nurseries to sell as clones plants grown from seed: *Campanula persicifolia* 'Telham Beauty' appears in catalogues but I have yet to receive the real thing. You only have yourself to blame for disappointments such as this if you make a practice of haggling about price and must have a "bargain." "Clone" is a word more often seen in science fiction books and films than in gardening books, but we can and do clone plants. When a plant's name appears in single quotes (*Monarda* 'Croftway Pink', for example), it is a clone, more often referred to as a cultivar. These two terms do not mean precisely the same thing, but the term "clone" is seldom used in gardening books, "cultivar" taking its place. Seed of such perennials will seldom produce plants identical to the parent. New plants must be raised vegetatively, from cuttings or division, and this costs more than raising plants from seed.

FRAGRANCE

Is fragrance important to you? Most gardeners answer yes, yet it seems to be a desideratum more preached than practiced. Surprisingly few perennials have pronounced fragrance. With some the scent is elusive—now you smell it, now you don't, among them sweet violets (*Viola odorata*) and dame's rocket (*Hesperis matronalis*), which seems to save its scent for the evening. Some phloxes, peonies, and daylilies are undoubtedly more fragrant than others. Paul Aden's 'So Sweet', with its white-edged leaves, is a welcome addition to the green-leaved, faintly fragrant hostas 'Royal Standard' and 'Honeybells', but in none of these is the scent very pervasive. Some breeders of bearded irises have fragrance among their goals and Lloyd Zurbrigg, for one, has achieved it with his repeat-blooming 'Immortality'. Many pinks (*Dianthus plumarius*), and some ginger lilies (especially *Hedychium gardneranum*) do have far-flung fragrance, and so do many lilies, especially *Lilium auratum, L. regale,* and the later-blooming *L. speciosum*.

Many perennials, especially those characterized as herbs, have extremely aromatic foliage, and few more so than the little-known mountain mint, *Pycnanthemum virginianum*, native to the Eastern United States and an excellent garden plant, if just a tad invasive in light soil. This is not grown for its flowers, which are white faintly flushed with pink and not at all exciting, but for its neat mounds (if cut back after flowering) of close-packed slender leaves on interlacing stems. Place aromatic plants where they can be pinched, brushed against, or, with a few of the smaller ones, lightly stepped upon. An added advantage is that chewing pests tend to avoid aromatic plants.

A few perennials waft something less than sweetness upon the garden air. *Crambe cordifolia*'s malodorous miasma makes its presence smelt long before you see it, *Chrysanthemum pacificum* has a rank odor very attractive to flies, and if you detect a faint odor of urine it may be emanating from *Cimicifuga racemosa*. These are all excellent plants in spite of their effluvia.

THE VALUE OF FOLIAGE

Consider, for a moment, a pretty woman skillfully made up and attractively coiffeured but wearing a torn and dirty dress. Shabby foliage can similarly mar a flower bed. The influx of new hostas has brought increased awareness of the beauty of foliage alone, but also of how bad it looks if chewed into holes by slugs. Hostas and other plants grown solely, or primarily, for their foliage are discussed in another section. Here I'm concerned with the foliage of perennials grown for their flowers. Good cultivation makes it less likely that perennials will suffer from chewed, diseased, wilting, dead, or dying foliage but the fact remains, some plants are graced with better foliage than others.

Many perennials have foliage that scarcely calls for comment, positive or negative. These include several of such flower-power that they need no advocacy—many sunflowers, for instance (*Heliopsis* and *Helianthus*), *Rudbeckia* 'Goldsturm' and its pink equivalent, the purple coneflower (*Echinacea purpurea*), the bee balms (*Monarda*), and the border phloxes so invaluable for extended summer color in cool regions. Plants with mediocre foliage *and* mediocre flowers usually remain the province of the collector. *Clematis heracleifolia* is, in my experience, such a plant, the flowers being a pretty blue but too sparse in relation to the coarse and overabundant foliage.

Here, however, I'm concerned with those having foliage that does, for good or bad, affect their garden-worthiness. Judged as long-term adornments of the flower bed, I'd group perennials in the following order of merit:

1. Those with attractive foliage that flower for a reasonable length of time. What is "reasonable" depends on where you live. Foliage is particularly important in hot regions because flowers don't last as long as they do where summers are cool.
2. Those with attractive foliage that flower for only a week or two.
3. Those with showy but ephemeral flowers and coarse, shabby, or (in the case of Oriental poppies) short-lived foliage.

GROUP 3

Let's start with group 3. And here, I'm compelled to say, comes a perennial with more devotees than any other except for daylilies: the bearded iris. No matter what is said about rebloomers, and continuity of bloom that can be achieved by planting different kinds, the fact remains you'll be lucky to get a month of bloom from the lot. Which doesn't matter quite as much when the leaves stay handsome through summer, but so often the leaves brown at the tips, getting progressively worse with every week that passes. Hiding them,

while still allowing sun to reach the rhizomes, is not an easy assignment. Bearded irises are sumptuous, and no flower has a lovelier range of colors, but don't ask more of them than they are able to give.

Much the same can be said about Oriental poppies (*Papaver orientale*). That they are gorgeous nobody can deny. The fragility of the crinkled flowers is part of their charm but it also makes them vulnerable to the weather and as often as not the flowers will be spoilt by rain during their short week or so of bloom. Soon afterward they go dormant, leaving a gap. Unlike bearded irises, which must be exposed to the sun, poppies don't mind shade when they are dormant, which makes them easier to deal with. Poppies are so showy that a group of one is probably enough. The gap it leaves is traditionally filled by an adjacent clump of *Gypsophila paniculata*, which gets off to a later start than the poppy but then expands to cover several feet of ground. Gypsophila does best in alkaline soil and mine is acid, so Oriental poppies have been missing from my garden. So have the magnificent foxtail lilies (*Eremurus*), which also go summer dormant. I think I've found alternative screening plants in *Hibiscus coccineus* and *Lavatera* 'Barnsley', both late starters but then growing six feet tall or more, with a similar width. I say "think" because the plan has not yet been put into action and that's the only way one can be sure.

Poppies and foxtail lilies need a sunny site but we don't want gaps in our sunny summer borders. Gaps are natural, and not objectionable, in woodland gardens, where emphasis is on spring flowers and one expects the ground to be bare once the trees leaf out, except for its carpet of rotting leaves. If you are bothered by that seemingly empty ground where such summer-dormant perennials as Virginia bluebells (*Mertensia virginica*), tooth-

Peony 'Henry Bockstoce', Siberian iris 'Dewful', and Baptisia australis *bloom together in the show garden of nurseryman Andre Viette. None flowers for long but all have good, lasting foliage. Behind are creamy* Clematis recta mandshurica, Dictamnus albus *'Purpureus', and (not in bloom)* Achillea *'Moonshine'. (Virginia mountains; June)*

wort (*Dentaria diphylla*), and the painted arum (*Arum italicum* 'Pictum') have gone to rest, tuck small groups of these between winter-dormant ferns which later expand to fill at least part of the gap. A woodland setting isn't essential for summer-dormant shade plants, which could form a spring carpet under a single tree or large shrub.

GROUP 2

Now to group 2, those that flower quite briefly but have lasting attractive foliage. To grasp their importance, think about some of the ways in which perennials can be arranged in a border. Solid color, unalleviated by the greens and grays of foliage, might be too much of a good thing, and anyway impossible to achieve except for a very short time. We could alternate a plant (or group of the same plant) in bloom with one that blooms at a different season, but this would look a bit spotty and we'd lose the pleasure of orchestrating a group of flowers of different color and form. If we group together several that flower at the same time, it follows that they'll also be out of bloom at the same time. This works fairly well even if the foliage of those out of bloom is merely mediocre, but if it is shabby it detracts from the groups in flower. If, however, the foliage is attractive in its own right, interest continues in this part of the border even though color is lacking.

Three fine perennials in this group are peonies, Siberian irises, and amsonias. They look good together when in bloom, in combinations of pink, white, and blue, and when the flowers have gone, there is contrast between the large, divided leaves of the peonies, the bold, swordlike leaves of the irises, and the fine-leaved mounds of *Amsonia tabernaemontana* which, in autumn, give color again when the leaves turn banana yellow. All three are usually pest-free. If the amsonia sprawls, as it may in rich soil, shear it back to six inches when the flowers are spent, or seek out the compact form sold as *A. t. montana* or *A. montana*.

Whether for foliage or flower, everyone has their own favorites. The following are a few of mine in category 2:

Pasqueflower (*Anemone pulsatilla*) is small enough for the rock garden, big enough for the front of the border, and best of all, perhaps, nearer to eye level in a raised bed. It is at its most enchanting when in bloom, the whole plant gossamer-coated and glistening. Then come glistening seedheads, resembling those of clematis. The finely divided leaves remain attractive until winter puts the garden to rest—if it does: pasqueflower is semievergreen in the milder regions, the surviving leaves lying flat enough for early crocuses to peek out from under their sheltering wing.

Baptisia australis has smooth gray-green foliage good for setting off the color of other flowers, if it doesn't sprawl over and smother them. Cut it back by half when it reaches two feet high if it exhibits this tendency in your garden. The smaller *B. minor*, now making an appearance in mail-order catalogues, is likely to prove popular in this age of smaller gardens. No such problem with gas plant (*Dictamnus albus*), a perennial slow to establish but eventually of shrublike proportions. This is entirely self-supporting. If the stems of spent flowers are removed, it may make a few more quite late in the year but I think the loss is greater than the gain, because then you won't get the appealing star-shaped seedpods. So elegant are the glossy, lemon-scented pinnate leaves that any flower at all seems a bonus.

The two-foot tall *Disporum flavens* (or *D. sessile* 'Flavens'—new to American gardens and lacking a common name) bears lemon yellow pendent bells for two or three weeks in early spring. It is a delicate-looking but rugged plant, rather like Solomon's seal (*Polygonatum*) in the way the stout shoots spear through the ground, liking the same conditions of light shade, and spreading at about the same rate. A clump in my garden proved sufficiently sturdy to remain upright when swathed with the wandering strands of the spurred butterfly pea (*Centrosema virginianum*), a vigorous but lightweight vine over which in summer hover inch-wide blue flowers.

I hovered too, torn between conflicting desires: to enjoy the butterfly pea, or to strip it off to display the egg-shaped shining leaves of its host. Silky beneath, and channeled with longitudinal lines, these have textural value from spring to fall. So do those of the so-called hardy orchid (*Bletilla striata*). The flowers alone get this onto my top-twenty list, for they are unique among hardy plants. The clinching factor is the pleated, sword-shaped leaves that flutter, fanlike, in the slightest breeze. There is one snag with this. It comes into growth rather prematurely, even in the south, and that first inch or two of growth is very vulnerable to frost. If it does get frosted, the leaf tips are scorched off and its appearance damaged for the rest of the season, so this is the first thing I rush to cover with shading cloth when a late frost is predicted.

I'll skip lightly over bergenias—none does well for me so I feel a bit cool toward them, but they are of immense value in other regions, especially those with leaves that, in winter, turn the color of a shoe polish that used to be called oxblood but now seems to be called just "brown."

Perennials such as these seldom shame us with conspicuous shabbiness. They play their flowering part well, then take their place in the background. Peonies have such handsome leaves that they can be very satisfying grown in narrow borders on their own. If you'd prefer a second season of flower, intersperse the peonies with autumn-flowering Japanese anemones (*Anemone × hybrida*). All are white or shades of pink so you can mix them if you're a collector, but all-of-a-kind ('September Charm' is a good one) makes a better display.

GROUP 1

And so to group 1, and a few of the elite. There are enough in this group to overcrowd the winner's podium, but which are the very best depends on where you live. I and others have many times attempted a "ten best" list, but on a national basis this cannot be done; such limited lists must be regional. A list of the ten *most popular* is easier to compile but by no means the same thing.

There is, however, consensus about number one: *Sedum* 'Autumn Joy'. This does well nearly everywhere. None of the other tall sedums is anything like as good, though they are, in their less variable shades of pink, easier to place. *Sedum* 'Autumn Joy' belongs with the pinks when in bloom but on its way to the rusty hue of its deadheads it passes through a salmon or brick red stage that is at odds with most pink flowers. It does not, by the way, bloom for long, but it looks as if it does, which for practical purposes amounts to the same thing. When in bloom it is a fairly pale pink. The deeper pink usually assumed to be peak bloom actually comes from the ripening seed capsules—the bees and butterflies know and abandon it at this stage. Blue asters make good companions for *Sedum* 'Autumn Joy'.

Coreopsis verticillata is also a national

success, and its dainty, fine-cut foliage could lay claim to being the most beautiful of all. It is an American native and the wildling can scarcely be improved upon, but slight variations in the forms 'Zagreb' and 'Golden Shower' make them more desirable under some circumstances. The species spreads very fast. 'Zagreb' is a trifle shorter and spreads a bit less fast. These two are the same bright yellow. 'Golden Shower' is a bit taller (still self-supporting) and the flowers are a more golden yellow, which makes this the best choice for hot color schemes of scarlet, orange, and yellow. Pale lemon yellow *Coreopsis* 'Moonbeam' has, in its short existence, won all hearts, most definitely a winner if it likes you. It is now thought to be a hybrid, not a selection of *C. verticillata* as first supposed. In my experience it needs moister, richer soil to do well, and, in the South, some afternoon shade. *Coreopsis rosea*, in the good pink form now available, is a different kettle of fish entirely—low growing, preferring quite wet soil, spreading faster than any of the others but shallow rooting and easy to control. It is inclined to die out where you put it and pop up on either side. I use this as a ground cover among lilies grown near the front of the border. No plant is easier to propagate: lift a clump and it falls into hundreds of separate little rooted pieces.

Yarrows (*Achillea*) get high marks from most gardeners. *Achillea* 'Coronation Gold' is a good plant everywhere, and an excellent one in cool summer regions, but if the soil is rich and moisture-retentive it will certainly need staking. *Achillea* 'Moonshine' is more compact, and a clearer yellow—not, however, the pale yellow implied by the name; for that we turn to the shorter, less robust, *A. × taygetea*. All have attractive feathery gray leaves. If the old stems are cut out they will bloom for a long time where the summers are cool, but only half as long in hot regions.

Achillea millefolium cultivars seem better able to go on flowering in the heat. The dense clumps of feathery bright green foliage appear early in spring, when none is lovelier. This group tend to be invasive, especially on sandy soil, but they are controllable and I wouldn't hold it against them. I have high hopes for the new range of 'Galaxy' hybrids, which greatly extend the color range, especially the exquisite 'Salmon Beauty', but these have not yet been evaluated sufficiently in our various regions. All the achilleas I've grown respond well to shearing.

The Lenten rose (*Helleborus orientalis*) is another general favorite. I would once have said that it must have shade but I recently saw it, healthy and seemingly happy, in full sun in Tennessee, and in October at that, after summer had done its worst. For me it is fully evergreen but the old leaves look so battered by January that they are best cut off, the better to enjoy the flowers for the next three months. The hellebores in my largish patch are now interplanted with bleeding heart (*Dicentra spectabilis*). I've often read that this does not self-sow. Don't believe it, it just depends where you live. In my garden seedlings crop up by the hundred and some of these were dibbled in while small among the hellebores. They have space to grow and flower where the old hellebore leaves have been cut off. Soon after they've flowered they get shabby and are cut down. Meantime the new hellebore leaves have developed to fill the gaps. This probably wouldn't work in the north, where the bleeding heart forms massive clumps of foliage that remain in good condition well into the summer. We each have to develop our own regional tricks.

If one accepts that "good" foliage can include inconspicuous foliage, then the plant known, for want of a more certain name, as *Astermoea mongolica* earns its place among the stars with three months or more of bloom, with no need for deadheading. This has small white double flowers. If you prefer single flowers, get the plant sometimes listed as *Astermoea integrifolia* but more often as *Calimeris* (or *Kalimeris*) *integrifolia*. *Gaura lindheimeri* shares these virtues where soil and climate suit it. It is the worse for pampering and thrives in soil of low to moderate fertility with all the sun you can give it.

The foliage of most asters falls into the mediocre group, which doesn't detract one whit from the deserved popularity of such showy late-blooming New England asters (*Aster novae-angliae*) as the near-red 'Alma Potschke' and violet-blue 'Hella Lacy' (gardening columnist Allen Lacy introduced this one and it is named for his wife). To those who garden where autumns are long and sunny I commend Nancy Goodwin's (Montrose Nursery) 'Our Latest One' (which *was* her latest when named) and the even later November-blooming 'Fanny's Aster'. But if equal points are awarded for foliage and flower, none can equal 'Climax', with its glossy spear-shaped leaves and graceful five-foot panicles of blue single flowers. You can get this from Canyon Creek Nursery. Three generations of English gardeners have enjoyed this old aster but it is fairly new to American gardens. It flowers a bit earlier than the New England asters. In my garden it has needed staking only in a very wet summer.

Allium senescens montanum certainly comes high on the list. It would get more acclaim than it does if its name was known with certainty. It crops up under several species names, all of them probably wrong because it is sterile and sets no seed (a great advantage to gardeners in this all too fecund genus), and is therefore presumably a hybrid. It has bright green glossy leaves for as many months as the temperature stays above 25°F. Mine have the quirk of crooking the tips of their leaves like beckoning fingers, a not unappealing trait, though indicative, I suppose, of a lack of something or other—lime has been suggested and I'm giving it a try. It flowers for several weeks, even in the South, and much longer where the temperature doesn't exceed 80°F. The flowers are lilac-pink—if only they were white, this ornamental onion would be very near the top of my list.

There are dozens of veronicas, many of them excellent. Gray-leaved *Veronica spicata incana* is one of my favorites, but it flowers for only a couple of weeks and the flowers tend to fall over. Of those I've grown, the cream of the crop is the stocky 'Sunny Border Blue'. It is self-supporting, easy to grow, easy to propagate by division or cuttings, and quick to build up into sturdy clumps of bright green toothed and somewhat crinkled leaves, topped week after week after week with sturdy spikes of bright blue flowers.

Boltonia asteroides 'Snowbank' gains extra points for flowering latish in the season but loses a few because it doesn't keep it up for as long as some of the others. The leaves are slender, glaucous, and, unlike the asters it resembles, never get mildew. *B. a.* 'Pink Beauty' flowers a little earlier and a little longer, on a slightly shorter plant, but it does not seem to be quite as robust. The color is hard to pinpoint, sometimes seeming almost blue, sometimes pink, but mostly a very pale lavender. It flowers at the same time as, and makes a good companion for, *Aster* 'Alma Potschke'.

Some daylilies make the list, many don't. If possible, make your selection from living plants, seen in and out of flower, rather than

Boltonia 'Pink Beauty' with Aster 'Alma Potschke' and Lespedeza thunbergii 'Albiflora' in my garden. The grass in the foreground, Miscanthus sinensis 'Purpurascens', has performed poorly here and in several other gardens south of Washington, D.C., but most miscanthus do exceptionally well in the Southeast. (Virginia; September)

from the gorgeous flower close-ups in catalogues. Joining the Daylily Society will make it easier to locate local gardens and nurseries growing daylilies. So many exhibit post-bloom shabbiness, needing "deadleafing" to tidy them up. At least that's what I did for years, laboriously pulling out one by one the dead or disfigured leaves. Now I know that, in my region, a better way is to shave the whole clump off at ground level. Within a couple of weeks new leaves have emerged, and these stay handsome until the end of the season. The much vaunted 'Stella de Oro' does not, in my garden, have the extended bloom period invariably claimed for it. One I bought as 'Mme. Bellum' beats it into a cocked hat for color (lemon yellow), grace, and extended bloom.

Globe thistles (*Echinops*) have always gotten good marks for the quiet charm of their flowers and their distinctive thistlelike foliage. They'll probably climb still higher on the charts now that the bright blue *Echinops ruthenicus* is available from American nurseries. It flowers at daylily time and combines particularly well with the lemon or creamy yellow kinds, my choice being the pale cream-petalled, lemon-yellow-throated 'Ice Cap'. Globe thistle foliage usually stays attractive through summer if the soil is rich and moisture-retentive, but in the sun-baked South they do best with shade from afternoon sun.

Some that are winners where conditions are right must be hedged about with if's and but's of climate or cultivation. *Lespedeza thunbergii* 'Albiflora', a comparative newcomer, was an instant winner in the Southeast. The jury is still out for the north, where it may bloom too late. It flowers for a month or more, in late summer or early autumn, but it earns its place all season long with neat, graceful foliage. It performs best in soil of no more than moderate fertility, a characteristic of

many plants with pea-type flowers. It is really a shrub but for practical purposes regarded as a perennial and cut down to ground level in early spring.

Hibiscus coccineus has deeply lobed leaves that resemble those of some Japanese maples, and I've yet to see them marred by bugs, disease, or weather. The flowers are red, showy without the blowiness of the better-known hybrids, and come late in the season. It loses marks only for limited hardiness, though it still hasn't been thoroughly tested in all regions.

Hemerocallis 'Mme. Bellum' *with* Achillea × taygetea *and* Veronica spicata incana. *The daylily has not been deadheaded; there are dead flowers present but they are not conspicuous. (Virginia; June.)*

Bugbane, *Cimicifuga racemosa*, is first rate where summers are cool, and fairly undemanding, though preferring moisture-retentive soil and a bit of afternoon shade. Where summers are hot it is much less easy to please. Primroses (*Primula vulgaris*) also score high in cool regions. Based on my own experience, the Barnhaven hybrids got nine out of ten for the Southeast as well for fifteen years, but have since been ravaged by spider mite for two successive years. Grown in an east-facing bed, they flower profusely for two months or more. Most years they are evergreen, but they have occasionally gone to earth in exceptionally dry summers and unusually cold winters (which in my region means 0°F). They must be divided every second or third year but this is easily done without much disturbance.

Yellow fumitory (*Corydalis lutea*) has the repeat-flowering quality we seek, and dainty ferny foliage, but it is a wanderer (by seed), often dying out where you put it and popping up where it will, usually in shade. It is pretty, and nearly always welcome, but not very amenable to grouping in beds and borders.

Until very recently chrysanthemums were a vast and varied group. Many have now been put in other genera with unfamiliar names but here I retain the old ones. One or another would go on the "top ten" list in most regions, but which? *Chrysanthemum* 'Mei Kyo' came with me from England and has proved to be a better plant here, where it gets more sun than England provides, winning the hearts of all in the Southeast who see it flowering in November, its foliage having been quietly attractive for the preceding six months. Its pale-brick-red counterpart, 'Bronze Elegance', shows equal promise. But these flower too late for the north, where none of the "mums" is really a top ranker, though invaluable, as bedding plants, for plugging late-season gaps.

Feverfew (*Chrysanthemum parthenium*) loses marks for its comparatively short life and for its weedlike fecundity, and some dislike its pungent smell. Nevertheless it ranks among the best for its months of flower combined with bright green, ferny foliage, as well as for its willingness to grow under less than ideal conditions. Many shasta daisies (*C.* × *superbum*) have top-ten potential of flower and foliage in cool regions, but only the early 'May Queen' in hot ones.

Wild bleeding heart (*Dicentra eximia*) is native from New York to Georgia, but in the southern part of its range it is found in the mountains, not in the hotter coastal regions. *Dicentra formosa* is native to the West Coast. These habitats bespeak the preference of these and their hybrids for cool conditions. The one called 'Luxuriant' is more heat resistant than most but none can be counted a winner where summers are long and hot. Given what they like, there are few better perennials than the exquisite *D. eximia* 'Alba' (also called 'Snowdrift'), elegant in leaf and flower and in bloom for months.

Geraniums flower for months where summers are cool. Shown here, from back to front, are Geranium pratense 'Mrs. Kendall Clark', G. himalayense, and pink G. endressii 'Wargrave'. (Wakehurst Place, England; July)

In cool regions many cranesbills (*Geranium*) have both good foliage and extended bloom, especially *G. endressii*. In hot ones they drop to the good-foliage/short-bloom list. *Geranium sanguineum* blooms longer than most in hot climates. *Geranium endressii* can be treated in two ways. The flowers are born on long, rather sprawling stems, which can be encouraged to weave their way among adjacent plants and even climb a bit. If you think this too untidy, the plants will bush out if the long stems are cut off at the base after they have flowered.

AFTER THE SEASON IS OVER

Plants with good foliage and long-lasting flowers are the mainstays of the border but in regions where autumn isn't the end of the gardening year, plants get bonus points if they hold their foliage through winter. A quick walk round my own garden (Zone 7/8) on a January day found the following still presentable. If you live in a frost-free region many perennials usually considered herbaceous (top growth dying in winter) will be evergreen, though often shorter-lived as a result if the plant has not evolved to be evergreen.

Ajugas vary a lot in weather resistance: green-and-white *Ajuga reptans* 'Variegata' (or 'Silver Carpet') and the newer gray-leaved 'Kingwood' (also sold as 'Gray Lady' or 'Argentea') looked a bit chewed up, and the cream, green, and beet red 'Burgundy Glow' had died back to little nubs. Purple-leaved kinds hold up best against both cold and heat except for the large-leaved 'Jungle Bronze' (which may be synonymous with 'Catlin's Giant') which does get battered by zero temperatures. *Sedum reflexum* 'Oxbow', green in summer, had turned purple with cold, its interwoven stems turned up at the tips like a stand of little conifers.

Gray leaves show up better than green or purple against brown earth. *Artemisia* 'Powis Castle' makes a big bush in one year from a cutting. The lacy foliage stays in good fettle through summer and winter, something of a surprise when the similar but smaller *A.* 'Silver Mound' has repeatedly rotted in summer heat and humidity. 'Powis Castle' is cut back nearly to the base in late winter and then looks bare for a couple of months; for the other ten it is one of the handsomest plants in my garden. The snaking stems of a single plant of *Euphorbia myrsinites* make a sizable circular patch of blue-gray. What a willful plant this is, self-sowing all over the place, but resisting my efforts to assemble the seedlings together in one place.

There were gray-green and silvery pinks, with *Dianthus* 'Inchmery' the most luminous, and the felted leaves of rose mullein (*Lychnis coronaria*) were as pretty on this January day as at any time during the year. This short-lived perennial has its shabby time after flowering, while getting ready to self-sow with weedlike prodigality. The dianthus needs frequent renewal by cuttings.

I lingered to admire first-year plants of velvety leaved verbascums, then passed quickly by the disheveled remains of those that flowered in summer and might, or might not, live for another year. The many cultivars of *Senecio cineraria*, one of several plants called dusty miller, vary in weather resistance: 'Snowcloud', with broad, uncut leaves, is one of the toughest I have grown. The leaves of lamb's ears (*Stachys byzantina*) looked so strokeable, but more practical attention was needed—there are rotting leaves to be picked off all year long. Ignoring this demand for service, I shifted my gaze to *Veronica incana*, less silvery but much more self-sufficient in hot climates. Of the yellow-flowered yarrows (*Achillea*), those of 'Coronation Gold' hold up best in winter.

Variegated plants also show up well. The gold-spotted leaves of leopard plant (*Ligularia tussilaginea* 'Aureo-maculata') looked a bit limp after a 20°F night but would perk up with the rising mercury. Ophiopogons, plain and fancy, winter well, while the taller, broader leaves of the related liriopes alternate from arching to recumbent as the temperature goes up and down. The leaves of *Sedum lineare* 'Variegatum' have more cream in them than green and look quite tender but it is reliably hardy and more-or-less evergreen where the temperature doesn't drop much below 10°F. Among several lungworts (*Pulmonaria*), the long, narrow leaves of 'Roy Davidson' remain unblemished longest in my garden.

Here and there a patch of gold caught the eye, the gold thyme (acquired as *Thymus* 'Clear Gold') a bit the worse for wear, more from wet than cold, I think. Golden oregano (*Origanum vulgare* 'Aureum') would have been painting a brighter patch of yellow on the ground if I'd gotten around to shearing off the stubble of dead top growth.

Some plants that were dormant through summer displayed unblemished new leaves made in fall, none more lovely than the painted arum, *Arum italicum* 'Pictum'. *Dentaria diphylla*, one of the larger toothworts, is a boon under a large fig tree, the solution to a problem spot. In leaf the fig tree conceals a lot of ground but in winter the bare earth was revealed. I need to tramp around it every day at fig-picking time and most ground covers don't take kindly to that. The dentaria bears foot-high stalks of nodding white flowers in May and goes neatly dormant soon afterward. The rhizomes intertwine so densely that it is hard to establish annuals over it, so the best place for it is under a deciduous tree or shrub.

In early autumn fresh new leaves appear, resembling pachysandra, remaining attractive through winter. It is very hardy, being native to Minnesota as well as to the Southeast, but in cold regions it behaves differently, retaining its leaves through summer, going dormant in autumn and staying that way until spring.

Tradescantia hirsuticaulis also has the good sense to take a summer siesta and reappear in fresh new clothes when the weather cools. King's spear (*Asphodeline lutea*) does the same thing some years in my garden and at first I thought it a casualty of summer heat, but if it does go summer dormant it reemerges when the weather cools and retains the slender glaucous leaves, in whorled clumps, through winter. In a friend's garden only a hundred miles further north it behaves in a more traditional way.

The Louisiana irises don't go dormant in summer—if only they would, for the leaves get increasingly brown and tattered until, by late summer, they can no longer be tolerated and are cut off. New leaf swords grow in autumn and remain unmarred through winter down at least to 15°F.

At this time of year, undistracted by the bright colors of flowers, one becomes aware how many different greens there are, and how varied the shapes and textures: the ferny leaves of anthemis, the lacy ones of *Corydalis*, the mottled arrowheads of one of the wild gingers, *Asarum arifolium* (the most reliably evergreen kind I have grown), the deeply veined and wrinkled paddles of the primroses (*Primula vulgaris*), the fingered leaves of potentillas, grassy mounds of thrift (*Armeria maritima*), and the darkly glossy spears and spatulas, in ground-hugging rosettes, of *Coreopsis lanceolata* and *Chrysanthemum leucanthemum* 'May Queen' which, if true to name, is quite the best of the shasta daisies for the Southeast: it sets comparatively little seed but

Leaves of Geranium × cantabrigiense (G. dalamaticum × G. macrorrhizum hybrid). (Harper garden, Virginia; February)

a self-sowing nuisance often masquerades under its name.

That ubiquitous weed sorrel (*Rumex acetosella*) also, I notice with annoyance touched with admiration for its will to live, has ground-hugging rosettes of glossy green spear-shaped leaves, only the little ears at the base distinguishing them from *Coreopsis* 'Gold-fink', among which it had inveigled itself and gone until now undetected. The stringlike roots can't be pulled from frozen ground, but I discouraged it a bit by picking the leaves to go in a lunchtime salad: "vinegar-leaf" my father used to call it.

The aromatic leaves of *Geranium macrorrhizum* turn bright red about Christmas-time. Its hybrids with *G. dalmaticum*, known as *G. × cantabrigiense*, have smaller leaves, a proportion of them turning red, the rest staying green. *Geranium dalmaticum* itself had

gone to earth for the winter and I couldn't rely on a rebirth in spring, for this is one of the hardest geraniums to keep going through hot summers. Other geraniums were soft gray-green, with 'Claridge Druce' and 'Mavis Simpson' two of the leafiest for the time of year. *Geum* leaves change as they age, upright and feather-shaped in youth, becoming round, scalloped, and lying flat in age.

The evergreen candytuft (*Iberis sempervirens*) called 'Autumn Snow' has foliage of a brighter green than the type, but the brightest green winter foliage is that of feverfew (*Chrysanthemum parthenium*), which self-sows around the garden without really being a nuisance. The leaves of *Filipendula vulgaris* 'Flore Pleno' are equally ferny but a much darker green—the foliage is the main attraction and it makes an excellent border edging where the soil doesn't get too dry.

Foliage got for *Penstemon barbatus* a stay of execution. It is stunning in bloom, but for three years in a row the tall stems of almost-scarlet flowers have collapsed under their own weight when they should have been looking their best. The clumps have been moved to a hot spot with less fertile soil, and we shall see. In winter the mats of highly polished dark green leaves certainly earn their place.

Phlox subulata is a native treasure. This is one of rather few evergreen carpeting perennials for full sun. There are dozens of pretty selections and hybrids, so if local nurseries sell only the lurid pink one used all too often in association with red brick walls and paths, get some of the others from the nurseries that advertise in the bulletins of the American Rock Garden Society—a new world will open up to you. In winter some have neat, bright green foliage, others look a bit scruffy. Those with the best foliage aren't always the ones with the prettiest flowers, so one has to compromise.

Along a shaded path the hellebores were getting ready to bloom. *Helleborus foetidus* is the most weatherproof of those I grow, dark green in summer, purplish in winter. Bushy *H. argutifolius* is the biggest, and it has the handsomest leaves—gray-green with spiny edges—but it isn't as hardy as the others and does get badly damaged in unusually cold winters, even in Zone 8. The Lenten rose (*H. orientalis*) is the most reliable and has naturalized in my garden. By February some battered leaves need to be cut out, but they do remain an adornment to the garden through most of winter. *Helleborus viridis* goes summer dormant in my garden, then, at what seems an unpropitious time, with winter about to begin, up pop little tuffets of new leaves, looking so fragile yet undamaged by frost at 15°F. The leaves of the Christmas rose (*H. niger*) are evergreen but sparse and the plant is a poor doer just about everywhere, especially on very acid soils.

A pink-flowered foamflower acquired as *Tiarella cordifolia collina* is a bit of a bother because it roots so shallowly that clumps are pulled out if the rake is used to remove pine needles and leaves, so these have to be picked out by hand. It is worth the extra work, the leaves being semievergreen and the clumps a froth of pale pink flowers for several weeks in spring. *Campanula poscharskyana* is completely evergreen in the Southeast, the leaves heart-shaped, in dense heaps, from which trail out the flowering stems. In my English garden it was overly exuberant but in Virginia summer heat restrains it and it cannot stand full sun as it can in the north. The peach-leaved bellflower (*C. persicifolia*) is also evergreen in mild winter regions.

The sweet violet (*Viola odorata*) seems to have increased its terrain by 25 percent each time I pay it a visit. Already, in January, the mats of evergreen leaves conceal a fragrant flower or two. America has so many kinds of violet but none is as fragrant as this English wildling. It likes it here and a barrowful has to be pulled out now and then to prevent it crowding out other things. My plants came from a friend on Cape Cod, but except for such climatically favored locations the sweet violet isn't reliably hardy northward of Zone 6.

There's good winter foliage from such shrublets as lavender, rue, and germander (*Teucrium chamaedrys*), from quite a lot of ferns (Christmas fern, *Polystichum acrostichoides*, is the hardiest of the evergreen kinds), from several grasses and sedges, notably the arching silver sedge (*Carex conica* 'Marginata') and its yellow-striped counterpart (*Carex* 'Evergold'), also the more upright cream-striped leathery leaves of sweet flag (*Acorus gramineus* 'Variegatus'). Even some bulbs produce in autumn winter-defying leaves, with the hardy autumn-flowering *Cyclamen hederifolium* the loveliest. And then there are the incomparable yuccas, contributing both color and form through the winter months.

Having lauded, or at least listed, some that stay neat, I feel compelled to mention one at the other extreme. *Agapanthus orientalis* is hardy for me, but not evergreen as it is in frost-free regions. By January it is a revolting patch of mushy leaves that can't be quickly scooped up because they are still green at the base and firmly attached to the plant. Kitchen scissors are the best tool I know for cutting them off—the cheap kind with orange handles sold in supermarkets. I wouldn't want to omit such a good plant, but nor do I now put it in too prominent a position.

MAKING YOUR CHOICES

Creating a beautiful garden means walking a fine line between the neatly monotonous and the horticultural zoo, and always within the context of soil and climate. It is easier to start simple, then elaborate, than the other way around. If you are a novice, don't set yourself up for disappointment by choosing the rare and difficult. Price is often a guide. If it is high it may be because the plant is slow to reach salable size, or it may be because it is rare. Why is it rare? If because it is new, the price will soon come down if the plant proves gardenworthy, but it may be rare because it is hard to grow. In how many gardens have you seen the exquisite blue poppies (*Meconopsis*) so coveted by all who see them? Probably none outside of England and the Pacific Northwest. To the plantsman that is more a challenge than a deterrent—why shouldn't *you* be the first to succeed!—but beginners who court failure with difficult plants are

likely to become gardening dropouts, and those concerned primarily with design had better leave it to the plantsmen to do the experimenting.

Yet when all's said and done, head often gives way to heart and a plant is excused its shortcomings for just one endearing quality. Anchusas are short-lived, coarse-leaved, and the taller ones have to be staked, but what an incomparable blue they bring to the garden! Yellow alyssum (*Aurinia saxatilis*) is seldom long-lived, though its life can be extended by cutting it back hard when the flowers are spent, the foliage rots in humid summers, and if it flowered in summer the color would be thought garish, but what a welcome sight it is in spring in brilliant combination with red and yellow tulips. There are, by the way, subtler colors in the lemon yellow *A. s.* 'Citrina' and apricot-buff 'Dudley Neville', or, better still, 'Dudley Neville Variegated' with its handsome white-variegated leaves.

Iris unguicularis needs protection from slugs, the leaves are often untidy (*I. u.* 'Walter Butt' is one of the neatest), and the exquisite flowers are destroyed by frost or rain as often as not, yet those of us in the temperate zones who have picked the delicate buds and watched them unfurl indoors would not wish to be without them.

Similarly with the so-called Christmas rose (*Helleborus niger*). If, just once in a lifetime, you see a large clump massed with flowers, even if it is by that time February, you'll probably struggle for the rest of your gardening years to match that recollection.

Bearded irises, for their beauty and variety, are excused their brief appearance, summer-scruffy leaves, and proneness to disease; daylilies are forgiven their slovenliness; and delphiniums, so choosy about site and climate and so hard to stake inconspicuously, remain on the wish list for many of us. And why not?

Iris unguicularis 'Walter Butt' in my garden on the hottest February day on record for Virginia. It usually opens a few flowers at a time, between periods of frost, spasmodically from December to March. Usually said to need lime, it has thrived for me at pH5. Poor, dry soil is often recommended but in hot regions richer, more moisture-retentive soil suits it better. With the iris is Crocus chrysanthus 'Goldilocks', growing through a variegated ivy. (Virginia; February)

Just don't make them the mainstays of your garden.

Ask yourself these questions. Will it do well in the conditions I have to offer without excessive maintenance? Does it have long-lasting beauty of flower or foliage? Then cut your gardening teeth with good-sized groupings of rather few kinds within your chosen color scheme. They will be easier to manage and, in the hands of the inexperienced, likely to look better. If you want to add more later, you'll see better where they fit with a few good basic kinds first in place. I know whereof I speak, having done it the other way around for most of my gardening years, assembling a great array of plants and only after thirty years of gardening becoming sufficiently ruthless to discard those that don't repay with beauty what they demand in maintenance.

Aurinia saxatilis *makes a welcome splash of color at tulip time.*

Peak bloom comes in mid-June in this Virginia garden. Plants in flower include achilleas, Chrysanthemum leucanthemum *'May Queen', foxgloves,* Nepeta *'Blue Wonder', Oriental poppies,* Penstemon barbatus, Crambe cordifolia, Geranium *'Johnson's Blue',* Salvia × superba *'East Friesland' and 'Rose Queen', and* Potentilla recta *'Warrenii'. The intensity of the summer sun made the pale gray crushed stone used for the path harshly light reflective and it has been replaced with golden brown gravel. (Garden of Ellen and Gordon Penick, Virginia; June)*

2 | Beds, Borders, and Other Ways

Say "perennials" and "border" comes spontaneously to mind. There are countless other ways of growing them, but an "English border" remains the dream of many gardeners. This dream can become a nightmare of scorched and wilting plants in dry regions where over development results in water rationing, but in many parts of the country natural rainfall is adequate—most years, anyway—and borders, or island beds, are then the easiest and least expensive way of making the transition from lawns and foundation plantings to a more relaxed, flower-filled garden.

But even if rainfall is adequate, there are gardens where borders may not be achievable, or appropriate—rocky sites, for example, or wet ones. That doesn't mean eschewing perennials: rock gardens and water gardens are two of the topics covered in this chapter. Small gardens are dealt with more cursorily than the topic deserves. Borders can be discussed as units complete in themselves, needing only to be fitted into the appropriate place in gardens of adequate size. When the garden is small it becomes important that it be integrated architecturally with the house and setting. I rec-

ommend that you browse through the design books of John Brookes, which are packed with inspiring ideas for combining perennials and other plants with structural elements in an orderly yet relaxed and romantic way.

BEDS AND BORDERS

"I'm going to have an English border if it kills me," said one of my friends, and she *did*, with perseverance and considerable expense, create a pair of beautiful English-style borders in her garden near Richmond, Virginia, but peak bloom is in May and June and by mid-July the best is over. Nor are all the plants those that would be seen in an English garden.

When you look with envy at pictures of English borders, don't assume that all perennials do better there than anywhere else. Successful garden making requires that we find out what does well locally. English gardeners have been separating the sheep from the goats for many generations. In the process they have done much of the groundwork for those parts of America where conditions of soil and climate are somewhat similar, most notably the Pacific Northwest, but many perennials need more sun than England provides, among them *Gaura lindheimeri*, butterfly weed (*Asclepias tuberosa*), and chrysanthemums.

The very term "perennial" must often be redefined on a regional basis, for the same plant may be an annual in some regions, a perennial in others, and a shrub in the mildest ones. Blue marguerite (*Felicia amelloides*) is considered an annual in most regions, but in southern California it is a shrub as much as five feet wide. Madagascar periwinkle (*Catharanthus roseus*) is an annual for most of us, but a shrubby perennial where the temperature always stays above freezing, and there's a shrubby impatiens for such favored regions in *Impatiens oliveri*. "Shrublets" such as this are among the best "perennials" in warm regions, where some herbaceous perennials behave as annuals for lack of winter dormancy. Most asters do best where there is some winter cold, so gardeners in southern California might do better with the evergreen shrubaster, *Felicia fruticosa*, which looks just like an aster with its inch-wide lavender flowers but does well where winters are warm and summers are dry.

With the right choice of plants, and if water is available, it is possible to create perennials borders in most parts of the United States. Whether such a border would be fitting, and worth the struggle and expense it would require in regions where soil and climate are less than ideal we must each decide for ourselves. Few traditional herbaceous perennials do well in southern Florida, but why should Floridians mind when they can have massed displays of such tender plants as *Crinum asiaticum* and Egyptian starflower (*Pentas lanceolata*) and magnificent specimens of shellflower (*Alpinia zerumbet*). Such plants could be grouped into borders, but why? Different regions call for different styles.

Where the growing season lasts nine months or more, wise gardeners grow more shrubs, especially the flowering evergreens that are, with a few exceptions, the prerogative of those who live in the warmer zones. Shrubs give the biggest return for the smallest amount of work.

The langorous summers of the Southeast draw two very different reactions: a wish for cool green shade or a desire for very bright color. Also, often, an impelling urge to be somewhere—anywhere—else! (But who will tend those perennials while you are away?) When the heat and humidity are stifling, the need for color is best satisfied with annuals: the hotter it gets, the happier some of these are, though by no means all of them—annuals, too, must be chosen to suit the climate.

The trump card in the hand of the Southeast is the long and lovely autumns. In the north September marks the end of the gardening year, in the South the gentler sun marks a new beginning. Perhaps, in time, autumn borders will become a regional style, with the shimmering plumes of ornamental grasses and such perennials as asters, *Asclepias curassavica*, chrysanthemums, dahlias, plumbago (the sub-shrubby *Ceratostigma willmottianum*, as well as the hardier *C. plumbaginoides*), *Cimicifuga simplex*, *Helianthus angustifolius*, *Lespedeza thunbergii*, the toad lilies (*Tricyrtis*), *Patrinia scabiosifolia*, *Salvia leucantha*, goldenrods (*Solidago*), *Trilisa paniculata*, the Kafir lily (*Schizostylis*), ironweed (*Veronica noveboracensis*), and, about the latest-blooming of them all, *Ligularia tussilaginea* with its bright yellow daisies on branched stems.

Where winter is short and autumn the nicest time of year, perennials should either stay evergreen or else go quickly and neatly dormant. As a foliage plant, rue (*Ruta graveolens*) is outstanding, as is *Artemisia* 'Powis Castle', though why this comes uncomplainingly

One of America's finest perennials gardens is that of Fred and Mary Ann McGourty, Hillside Gardens, Norfolk, Connecticut. This border, at its peak in July, includes Chrysanthemum parthenium, Astilbe 'Fire', Heliopsis 'Gold Greenheart', regal lilies, Cimicifuga racemosa, Coreopsis verticillata, Phlox 'Sir John Falstaff', and Filipendula rubra. (July)

through summer humidity that rots the similar, smaller *A.* 'Silver Mound' is one of gardening's many enigmas. *Hosta tardiflora* is a desirable fall bloomer but most hostas look a mess in autumn—a southern autumn, that is. They may turn pleasingly gold for a week or two but they do not die neatly, and by their decay they seem to suggest the end of the gardening season when two of the best months lie ahead. Visit a specialist nursery in autumn and pick out those that hold their leaves later than the rest; at this late stage of the year relative slug and snail susceptibility will also be apparent. There's no point in northerners choosing hostas that go dormant late because frost mushes them before the natural onset of dormancy.

Where *are* the conditions ideal for the traditional summer-flowering herbaceous border? Consider first what perennials have to offer. There's a conspiracy, of sorts, between photographers, publishers, and—yes—readers. "Beauty is truth, truth beauty," wrote Keats, but few readers of garden books perceive as beautiful a garden pictured at less than its best, though in truth it is at its best for only a very short time. "I don't think much of that," you'd probably say, then spend your money on a less truthful but prettier book. None of us wants to take, publish, or look at pictures of disheveled plants and bare borders, yet that's the way borders look for more than half the year if they rely on perennials alone. And notwithstanding the protestations of their devotees, perennials borders are labor intensive.

The deep, rich soils of the Midwest are well suited to perennials but, as much for its limitations as for its advantages, the Northeast can make a good case for being the ideal place for extensive perennials borders, and indeed it is there that some of the finest borders can be seen. Winter wet may cause heavy losses if the soil is not well drained but most herbaceous perennials can stand a lot of cold weather—they've evolved as winter-dormant plants for that reason. Summer brings the best weather of the year, warm enough for the gardener's comfort, cool enough to discourage many pests and diseases. Plants stay in bloom longer than they do where summers are hot, and because the growing season is fairly short, with spring making a tardy appearance in May and most flowers gone by the end of September, the season of bloom is condensed and it is easier to achieve a display with everything in flower at the same time. Many are willing, eager even, to devote all their spare time to the garden during these halcyon days, knowing that winter will bring a long rest with ample time for other pursuits. And what does it matter if the border is bare of plants for half the year if it is neatly and protectively blanketed with snow?

Choosing the Site

You've decided you do want a perennials bed or border, and that there's a reasonable expectation it can be achieved where you live. Where should it be placed? The usual advice is to put it where it can best be seen from the house, but surely what is seen from the house windows should be pleasant to look upon in *every* month of the year, so far as that can be managed. Seldom does a perennials border meet that requirement, unless the perennials are interspersed with trees and shrubs of attractive winter appearance.

Give first consideration to the needs of the plants. Depending on orientation and the lay of the land, *under* the window might be the best place, or behind a terrace wall. If you want to collect hostas, a north-facing site would serve them well. If you want a varied flower-filled display, there must be sun for four or five hours a day but which way the border should ideally face (ideals are not, in any case, always attainable) depends on where you live and what you want to grow. Where sunny days are neither very numerous nor very hot, south- or west-facing borders will make the most of what there is, but where summers are long and so hot that a week without rain constitutes a drought, plants in east-facing borders stay in bloom longer and need less watering. Protection from wind may be the most important consideration in some regions. If a border follows a house or property line it probably won't be directly north, south, east, or west anyway, but somewhat slanted, with the amount of sun and where it falls affected by buildings, hedges, trees, or other tall plants, so check on site to see when and for how long sun hits the area you have in mind. Do this in summertime; an area shaded in winter by the long shadow of evergreen shrubs or trees might be sunny in summer when the sun is higher in the sky, and an area sunny in winter when deciduous trees are bare might be shady when they are in leaf.

Next consider how you spend your days: not how you think you should, but how you actually do. Standing at windows admiring the flowers is not what most gardeners do. If the weather is good and there are no other commitments, we are out there among the plants. If indoors, we are cooking, cleaning, at our desks, watching TV, reading a book—seldom standing at the window contemplating what we have wrought. If we do glance out of the window at a nearby flower bed, chances are good we'll spot a plant that needs staking, or deadheading, or one that's being overrun by its neighbor and needs a helping hand. So out we go, probably in bedroom slippers, or leaving something to boil over on the stove. There's a case to be made for placing flower beds well away from the house, then putting a seat among or near the flowers where one can sit and enjoy them during leisure hours, out of earshot of the telephone.

Defining the Planting

What form should the planting take? Shall it be a border, an island bed, or perhaps a peninsula? What shape? How large? Your answers to these questions are primarily a matter of good proportions, manageability, and suitability to the site. A place for a border usually suggests itself: along a sunny boundary, on one or both sides of a path, against a wall of a house or outbuilding, or adjacent to a patio. If you are blessed with one of the old stone walls that ramble through many a New England property, it cries out for a border, on one or both sides.

Island beds are not as distinct from borders as is sometimes supposed. Borders tend to be thought of as formal, island beds informal, but either one can be either thing, the difference being one of straight versus flowing lines and of neatness and symmetry versus the "little sweet disorder" of the romantic mind. It has been said that art requires both discipline and abandon. The more discipline there is in a garden, from structure, or from plants trained and restrained, the more formal the garden will be—at the extreme most unwelcoming. The romantic tosses in plants with abandon and lets them have their way—or seems to, for carry this too far and what you have is an unmanageable shambles. Monet or Versailles? The most admired gardens draw from both. In the United States formality has held sway in the lawns and clipped foundation plantings but there is now a noticeable swing toward the more romantic.

Free-flowing curves are informal, straight lines and symmetry are formal. Geometric curves (circles, ovals) give a softened formality. A free-form bed symmetrically placed at each corner of a square lawn would make a contradictory statement that could be disturbing. The flowing curves in a large garden become too sinuous if scaled down; in small gardens the curve should have fewer undulations—there are too many if a mower cannot be easily steered along the edge.

Perennials are meadow flowers. Short of confining them within matching squares, triangles, or circles evenly spaced over a lawn—a style not now in favor even for bedding annuals—it would be difficult to force them into formality, but traditional borders are often semiformal—straight-edged, hedge- or wall-backed, lawn-fronted, perhaps symmetrically paired, with plants graded down from back to front and discouraged from sprawling. Formality demands neatness and few can manage such borders today, preferring something more relaxed, a garden to be

Most gardens are rectangular in shape. When the outline is softened with curved borders along the boundaries the garden wraps itself around you and becomes more welcoming. In this artist's garden the border on the left *curves out to conceal a secret garden,* bottom. *Perennials in the hideaway include catmint, phlox, betony (*Stachys officinalis)*, Achillea 'Salmon Beauty', osteospermum, Sedum 'Autumn Joy', and santolina. Yellow-leaved plants near the seat are* Lonicera nitida 'Baggesen's Gold' *and* Arundinaria viridistriata. *(Garden of Kathleen Hudson, England; late July)*

These twin borders look much less formal than they would if the path was straight. (Glasnevin Botanic Gardens, Dublin, Ireland; June)

The diamond-shaped island bed with its uniform edging of bergenia has a much more formal look than the curving borders in the last picture. (Hestercombe, England. A restored Gertrude Jekyll garden; August)

Annuals and perennials are combined in this city "cottage garden." Plants include sunflowers, cosmos, and Artemisia 'Silver King'. (Garden of Rob Proctor, Denver Colorado; August)

in, to wrap itself around you. A house of formal style does not necessarily demand a formal garden layout; it will look more welcoming if the plants are not strictly regimented, which is not to say that a formal garden cannot be both appropriate and pleasing, only that you have a choice.

Borders Versus Island Beds

The relative merits of borders and island beds have been debated in many books, but invariably in the context of British estate gardens, comparing the traditional hedge- or wall-backed border facing south, southeast, or southwest with an island bed set well out in the lawn. A wall gives privacy and warmth, but reflected heat from walls is a disadvantage where summers are hot. In windy regions walls protect some plants but create eddies damaging to others. Plants against a south wall or hedge start into growth earlier than those against a north one, which might just

make the difference in enabling late bloomers to flower before hard frost. Conversely, if a garden suffers from late spring frosts a cooler location might prevent early risers getting their noses nipped.

Hedges absorb heat and filter instead of deflecting wind, and nothing sets off flowers better than a dark green hedge (traditionally yew) behind them and a well-kept lawn in front, but there is less air circulation against hedges and walls and this makes plants more prone to fungal problems. They will also tend to lean out toward the light. Hedges have to be cut—more often in warm, wet parts of North America than in England—and unless separated by a path at least two feet wide, needed also for access to the back of the border and to prevent the lower part of the hedge from dying out for lack of light and air, hedge roots encroach on the border, aggravating dryness at the back.

In many parts of North America there is another important consideration in whether or not to grow a hedge. Winter, or summer, or both, being more severe than in England, there is the likelihood that part of a hedge will be killed or damaged by unusually heavy snow, exceptional cold, or the many root and branch diseases prevalent where there is humid heat. A gap-toothed hedge is not a thing of beauty, and seldom can a replacement plant of appropriate size be found. This makes any planting dependent for its effect on uniformity risky in many regions. Losses are less apparent, and gaps easier to fill, if the hedge consists of unclipped shrubs, and where space permits this less formal approach is often the better way, but unclipped shrubs do take up more space and do not provide the same neat, neutral background for the perennials. Some gardeners prefer one, some the other; we must each decide for ourselves.

If you do opt for a hedge, this is not the

time to experiment. Choose something known to succeed in your area, and try to inspect a hedge of the kind you are considering at different times of year. Asking the owners whether they'd plant the same kind of hedge again is the most certain way of discovering undesirable characteristics such as the burr-like fragments of dead foliage, painful to the touch, that litter the ground alongside my own juniper hedge. There are excellent assessments of numerous hedging plants in Sunset's *Western Garden Book* and in *Wyman's Gardening Encyclopedia*, two basic texts I would not want to be without.

Because they are seen from only one direction, one-sided borders are easier to design than island beds. The length and width of the border should be in scale with the height of the wall or hedge. A hedge six feet high needs a border at least six feet wide and eighteen feet long. Ten feet wide and thirty feet long would be better. A paved path alongside the border permits plants to flow over the edge and provides a dry place to walk, but when the total width of the hedge, access path behind, border, and front path are added together, the total width is likely to be out of proportion in gardens much smaller than an acre.

If the access path at the back of a border was widened to six feet or more you would have an island bed. Island beds usually do look best if they follow boundary contours and are placed nearer to the edge than in the middle of the lot. Even so, they may obtrude too far into the open space of the lawn in small gardens.

In sunny island beds air circulates freely, reducing the likelihood of mildew. Rain can reach all the plants, and there is no competition for moisture and nutrients from hedge roots. Plants exposed to full sun grow stockier, less likely to need staking. The flowers won't last as long, however, as they would if a hedge cast shade on them for part of the day.

Island beds allow the flowers to be viewed from all directions (translucent poppy petals lit from behind are a magical sight) but this isn't always the advantage it might seem. A border can be compared with a class or group picture, everyone arranged in rows in graduated heights, all facing one way. Now mentally compose that picture with some individuals facing front, some facing back, with the added complication that many have their own ideas about which way they want to face. Plants have less distinct fronts and backs than people but many of them do turn their flowers toward the light. There are more creative possibilities with island beds than with borders, but it requires an extensive knowledge of plants, and a lot of tinkering, to make the vision reality.

If an island bed is to be manageable without walking on it, the width should not be much more than eight feet. The proportions will be most pleasing if the bed is at least twice as long as it is wide. Composition will also be easier. Make the bed round, or square, and it will be much more difficult to arrange the plants in a pleasing way when viewed from all angles. For purposes of composition, though, an eight-foot width, whether in an island bed or border, is a bit skimpy. That's one big advantage, in larger gardens, of having borders on either side of a low stone wall. Each one can be an accessible eight feet wide, yet visually they form a single, wider unit. Lacking a wall, the same effect can be achieved by planting shrubs down the center of a wide island bed, a topic further discussed in the section on shrubs.

Realistically, though, it often isn't practicable to make a bed or border of appropriate size and shape for a particular spot that is narrow enough to manage without stepping among the flowers. All true gardeners know

In this small garden of perennial enthusiasts, the lawn has been reduced to a grass path. (Garden of the Reverend and Mrs. John Beck, England; August)

how one deals with this, balancing on one foot and jumping to the nearest open space, or inserting a foot between the plants and carefully, foot by foot, squiggling one's way through. If frequent access is needed, stepping stones can be placed here and there.

The question of border versus island bed is of only academic interest to many homeowners. If a wall or hedge exists, it is probably much lower than the traditional yew hedge. Because open fences—post-and-rail or picket, for example—don't exclude light and air, borders alongside these have some of the advantages of island beds. What lies beyond the fence will, however, be visible behind the border, and probably won't enhance it, in which case a more solid fence would make a better background. Louvred or alternating board fences provide privacy and a neutral backdrop

while still permitting passage of air. If local bylaws restrict the height of a boundary fence, sometimes this can be got around by adding a strip of trellis to the top subsequent to construction, or even wires attached to occasional posts, on which vines can be trained.

A useful rule of thumb when planning a border or island bed is that the height of the tallest plants should not exceed half the width of the border. One advantage of free-form beds and curving borders is that, being wider in some places than in others, they can accommodate plants of more varied height while still keeping them in scale with the width of the border.

On a flat site, island beds provide the opportunity to create a change of level by mounding the soil. This helps recapture central height lost when avoiding tall plants, because they would be out of scale, or because one wants to avoid the chore of staking and the difficulty of accomplishing this without the stakes looking unsightly. Water drains away faster from mounds or raised beds, so mounding is advantageous in gardens where the soil tends to stay wet. Conversely, mounded beds dry out faster, which could be a disadvantage in dry regions.

Frequently island beds are less a studied choice than a natural evolvement in the gardens of plant enthusiasts. A typical scenario goes like this: Imagine yourself standing in a garden with your back to the house. First come boundary plantings along the two sides, perhaps perennials but more often mixed plantings in order to gain privacy from the height and permanence of shrubs. The front edge of the boundary borders might be straight or curved. When more growing space is wanted, a linking border is made, perhaps along the bottom boundary or, if the lot is long enough, partway down with space behind for vegetables, nursery beds, garden shed, frames, and compost heaps. At this stage, to facilitate mowing, corners will probably be rounded off.

The insatiable plantsman soon again discovers that there are more plants than places to put them, and now there's no choice but to make an island bed. If this process continues, the garden eventually becomes islands of plants with grass paths between them, the paths wide at first but tending to get whittled away each year as the plants spread, until such time as it scarcely seems worthwhile getting out the mower, when the grass might be replaced by mulch or paving.

For most homeowners, however, enthusiasm is tempered by restrictions of time, energy, or other interests. Suppose you want just one or two smaller patches of perennials. Where should they go? Too often a small group of plants is isolated in the lawn, aesthetically the worst possible place. They should go near something else, so first look to see what structural features or existing plantings are on the property. Structural elements such as buildings, walls, fences, and paths have the big advantage that they don't have roots to compete with your plants for moisture.

When, as a child, I drew a house, it always had smoke coming from the chimney, and it always had a path running straight to the front door in the middle of the house. Such paths are still made, but frequently unused because in this era of the automobile, access is more often from the driveway. Often a path goes off at an angle from driveway to front door, creating a corner bed crying out to be filled with plants. Many old houses have an unused path from the road to the front door. If yours has one, don't dispense with it too hastily. It might be the perfect place for borders of flowers, especially if the old stoop is still there as a platform from which to admire them.

What plants are already on the lot? Did you buy a living Christmas tree one year, then plant it in the garden? Not really a good idea; there are better ornamental trees, and it very likely went in the middle of the lawn, which isn't the best place, but there it is and it has sentimental value. You could group your flowers on one side of it, a sunny side (south- or west-facing) for the majority of flowering plants, and not too close because the conifer will continue to spread (its roots are already further out than its branches and you may have to sever some smaller ones when preparing the bed for your flowers). Two feet out would be about right, as most perennials will be ready for division by the time the conifer's branches begin to encroach on them. Don't use those that are slow to get established and

The path to this restored cottage originally ran straight from the street to the front door. A new entrance has been made and shrubs planted to screen the garden from the street. From the stoop, one now looks out over a bed of annuals and perennials and along the imaginative "dry stream," bottom, planted with perennials, that replaced the original path. The gate at the end does open but is primarily ornamental. (Design by Michael S. Schultz for Mr. G. Beasley, Oregon; early August)

don't like to be moved (*Dictamnus albus*, for instance).

Perennials can also be grouped under deciduous ornamental trees but not, usually, under large shade trees—it depends on the degree of shade and whether the tree roots go deep (most oaks) or stay near the surface and prevent other plants from getting water or nutrients (maples, willows, beeches). Avoid walnuts and hickories if there is any alternative site. They are said to secrete a substance in their roots and leaves that kills other plants or inhibits their growth. One of the prettiest island beds I've seen encircles a walnut tree (fallen leaves are removed) but there are probably more failures than successes in such situations.

Do twin arborvitaes, or some other kind of shrub stand sentinel at the entrance to your drive? Could you curve off the corners (easier when mowing than cutting straight across) and

*Those with less vision would have cut down this decrepit old cherry tree but the garden owners saw its potential as a picturesque feature. The gaunt, lichened branches provide just the right amount of shade for a patch of wildflowers and woodlanders that includes trilliums, gingers (*Asarum*), Phlox divaricata, *and primroses. The old apple trees often found on land that was once orchard have similar potential. (Connecticut; May)*

plant perennials at their base? Evergreens would make a good background for them, while a flowering shrub might be the basis of your color scheme: frothy white *Spiraea* × *vanhouttei*, for instance, with a bright pink peony, paler pink gas plant (*Dictamnus albus*), and some blue Siberian irises, a combination harmonious in color and also having attractive, varied, and long-lasting foliage. The spiraea can be pruned as needed to prevent it from encroaching on the flowers.

Is there a post with a name sign or lantern around which flowers could be grouped? Or a mailbox, provided it is inside your property line (the roadside verge is too much of a free-for-all and a post there is too inviting to dogs—and do replace the standard postal service box with something more attractive.) Do you have, or could you acquire a large boulder? *Very* large—it mustn't look as though you might trip over it. This would set off flowers particularly well. Do you have a concrete wellhead that you've tried to disguise with ivy? Instead, try using it as a plinth for an ornament or container and surrounding it with flowers.

If your lawn runs into your neighbor's and a fence or hedge is prohibited, two sections of post-and-rail or other open, ornamental fence at right angles to each other where

Posts, rope, and a clump of drought-tolerant, evergreen Dietes vegeta *make a spot planting of long-lasting good looks at the entrance to a coastal garden. An excellent choice for frost-free gardens, dietes is sometimes called "fortnight lily" because the flowers come in regular bursts for much of the year. (California; August)*

the lots meet often is permissible, and this would mark off a corner where perennials could be planted. Large-mesh chicken wire on the fence is scarcely visible and helps protect the plants from wandering animals.

Foundation Plantings, Paths, and Edgings

Why "plant material"? I used to wonder, surely "plants" is enough. I've now come to regard the term as a descriptive distinction between plants used for ornament, or just for the pleasure of growing them, and plants used for structure. Clipped hedges are as much a part of the garden's structure as a wall or fence. Foundation plantings of clipped evergreens are also part of the garden's structure: don't, merely to be fashionable, rush in and rip them out.

When scorn is heaped on foundation plantings, as it often is, and deservedly, it is usually for one of three reasons. First, the job has been botched: structure requires uniformity, which is not achieved with one of this and one of that, especially when love of a bargain motivates choosing the most to be had for the money, thereby assuring that the infant large shrubs or trees raised fastest, therefore cheapest, to salable size will soon obscure the windows. Second, pruning is often neglected or badly done: plants used structurally must be kept neat. Third, foundation plantings are often all there is except for lawn, which is also a structural element: structure alone, being static, is unsatisfying to creative gardeners.

The original purpose of foundation plantings was to hide the naked concrete below the wood sidings of a house. Modern houses seldom have exposed foundations, but clipped evergreens along the base of a house still have a purpose. When a house sits naked beyond its lawn, clearly visible to passersby, the dark line of evergreens, contrasting with the lighter green of the lawn, frames the house and anchors it to its site. They serve no purpose from inside looking out but, provided the foundation shrubs are not out of scale with the height of the house (as they often are), they do give the property a finished look.

Nowadays a greater need for privacy is made manifest by the growing number of boundary fences and hedges. Foundation plantings often then have no role, but they could be given a new one. A neat row of foundation shrubs makes an excellent background for a border. Such a border, to be in proportion, would not be very wide, in most cases not more than three feet, and the perennials would have to be the shorter, compact kinds, but isn't that about the size, and the kind of plants, manageable by the average homeowner? If a path did not already exist against the house, it would be sensible to make one to facilitate maintenance of both house and plants. If the foundation plantings are hard up against the house with a path in front, then the other side of the path would be a good place for a fairly narrow border.

Where there is no foundation planting or the bushes are overgrown and need to be removed, a bed of perennials could take its place with structure, if called for by the style of the house and the setting, provided by a low hedge in front of the perennials. Boxwood is the most popular plant for low hedges. Hedging box (*Buxus sempervirens* 'Suffruticosa') is of limited hardiness but there are other kinds hardy as far north as Maine. The soft new growth of boxwood that follows spring clip-

Below: Rock garden plants are the main interest of these homeowners (there is a large rock garden not shown in this picture) so they have just a narrow border alongside the path for a few favorite perennials: peonies, irises, and daylilies. Right: The colors in iris 'Gay Geisha' harmonize with the rosy brick of the path and the pink azaleas mixed with conifers in the foundation planting.
(Garden of Herb and Betsie Kinney, Long Island, New York; May)

Above: *Box-edged beds at Goodnestone Park, England. Seen from the front the border seems to be too wide for easy maintenance. In fact, a paved path runs down the middle, under the rose arch. Penstemons predominate in this pink-and-blue color scheme. Other perennials include scabious, phlox, Potentilla 'Miss Willmott', and the frost tender, gentian-blue Salvia patens. (Garden of Lord and Lady Fitzwalter, Goodnestone Park, Kent, England; early July)*

Left: *Clipped privet separates the flower beds from the sidewalk outside a city antique shop. Privet needs frequent clipping and its roots compete with nearby plants for nutrients and moisture but it tolerates city pollution and abuse from pedestrians and dogs better than most plants. Flowers include rudbeckias, artemisias, purple coneflower, feverfew, and scarlet bedding geraniums (Pelargonium). (Garden of Jerri Hopkins, Virginia; late June)*

ping is vulnerable to sun scorch. This is less likely to happen with the small-leaved hollies *Ilex vomitoria* 'Nana' and *I. crenata* 'Helleri', which might be a better choice in the South. The leaves are a darker green but otherwise quite similar to and often mistaken for boxwood, as also is the bright green small-leaved *Euonymus japonicus* 'Microphyllus'. Low hedges could equally well be used in front of borders in other parts of the garden where a touch of formality is wanted.

If house and garden are country-casual, a less formal edging would be more appropriate: one of the dwarf lavenders, perhaps, or germander (*Teucrium*), or gray- or green-leaved lavender cotton (*Santolina*), but don't make a hedge of anything until you've checked out its year-round appearance where you live.

Borders too wide to reach across without stepping on the flowers, or if there is a hedge at the back to be clipped, need an access path behind. This may not be necessary with narrow borders against a wall or fence; it depends what's on the other side of the fence. If it is something invasive, the attack will be easier to repel if there is a path, preferably solid, but wood mulch over newspaper works quite well if supplemented with occasional applications of a weedkiller such as Roundup. Creeping lawn grasses, ivy, bamboo, periwinkle, blackberry bushes, and goutweed (*Aegopodium*) are among the worst offenders, but many perennials spread rapidly where conditions suit them. If your neighbors have a border which includes plume poppy (*Macleaya*), gooseneck loosestrife (*Lysimachia clethroides*), bee balm (*Monarda*), or *Artemisia* 'Silver King', to name just a few, you'll soon be growing them too unless you take defensive action. And vice versa, of course.

If the border is bounded by a lawn of invasive grasses such as Bermuda or centi-

pede, a path separating border from lawn will make it a lot easier to keep the grass under control. Rectangular paving slabs are hard to improve on for this purpose, but don't rule out concrete—it is the least expensive way of making a solid path, and with surface texturing, dividing strips, or an inlay of brick or stone, concrete can be both attractive and more imaginative than paving stone. If bricks are used, they should be cemented into place to prevent the grass from infiltrating them. Paving bricks are more weather resistent than bricks intended for house construction, which may crumble when exposed to frost and rain.

If a solid path is inappropriate, or too expensive, flat stones, or bricks laid ends-out, cemented into place, are time-tested ways of keeping grass in check and permitting plants at the front of the border to flow out a bit without being decapitated by the mower. The edging should be flat, and laid slightly below the level of the lawn.

Birds and wild animals scatter soil from beds and borders when scratching for worms, burying acorns, or digging out your bulbs. A coping alongside paved paths cuts down on the sweeping. If the path is made of gravel, crushed stone, bark chips, or some other unsweepable surface, an edging is needed to prevent soil from spilling out. Bendable edgings of metal or plastic could be used, or bender-board wood strips, or, if the edge is straight, the four-by-six-inch strips with curved edges called landscaping timbers. Wood products are short-lived in hot and humid regions unless pressure treated against rot and termites.

Where there is no lawn, or the grass is not an invasive kind, the type of path is limited only by the imagination. Function should come before form if the path is the main route to the house, or from one part of the garden to another, but in the home garden a secondary path could be primarily an ornamental feature.

Brick inlay adds interest to a simple concrete path. Alongside the path grow lavender, rue, golden oregano, and Coreopsis 'Sunray'. (Garden of Cynthia Woodyard, Oregon; July)

A brick coping prevents soil spilling onto the gravel path. The bed contains red and white bedding geraniums edged with variegated liriope. (Tennessee; July)

In this garden the grass strips framing the borders help keep soil off the paths. The effect would be ruined if the grass was not immaculate and in home gardens, where edging is usually done with hand clippers, maintaining edging bands like this would be very time-consuming. (Old Westbury Gardens, Long Island, New York; May)

In gardens where hardpan impedes drainage, raised beds are often the solution. These may need more substantial edgings, and so will borders alongside driveways if the plants are to be safe from car wheels. Visit local lumber yards, builders' merchants, and garden centers to see what is available and affordable. In my own garden old rail ties have proved unsatisfactory—they are uneven in shape, often ooze creosote damaging to plants, and when they rot they become nesting places for hornets. Treated lumber is much better but also more expensive. Sometimes, when old cobbled roads have been taken up, gray granite sets can be bought: attractive and strong, but usually rather costly.

If you have to make do with something more functional than ornamental, disguise is in order. A functional edging becomes beautiful when draped with swags of moss pink (*Phlox subulata*) or evergreen candytuft (*Iberis sempervirens*). My own solution to wandering wheels that repeatedly crushed parts of a brick edging was to space substantial lumps of broken concrete (stone blocks would, of course, look better) several feet apart along the edge of the gravel drive and disguise these with ivy planted in the gravel. Drivers know when their wheels start to stray and the ivy is tough enough to survive occasional mishaps. This proved to be a good place for some of the ivy collection I'd been growing in pots: ivy is an unruly plant but grown this way each kind is kept separate in mounds kept in check with a couple of clippings each year.

Borders look less formal if the edge is softened with plants of trailing or loosely mounding habit. Suitable plants include *Alchemilla mollis*, artemisias such as 'Silver Mound', *Aurinia saxatilis*, wine-cups (*Callirhoe involucrata*), blue plumbago (*Ceratostigma plumbaginoides*), many kinds of pinks (*Dianthus*), *Coreopis* 'Moonbeam', hardy geraniums, catmints (*Nepeta*), phloxes too numerous to list, including such choice selections of sun-loving *Phlox amoena* as 'Pinstripe' and 'Snowdrift'. Long-lasting gray foliage is provided by lamb's ears (*Stachys byzantina*), the less silvery but less inclined to rot *Veronica incana*, or the silvery, seemingly frost-rimmed *Marrubium cylleneum*. There are trailing sedums to suit your color scheme in yellow-flowered *Sedum kamtschaticum*, *S. lineare* 'Variegatum', and *S.* 'Weihenstephaner Gold', or pink-flowered 'Ruby Glow' and 'Vera Jameson'.

Paths alongside borders nearly always seem fitting but paths round island beds do pose a problem. The rule—not unbreakable but a sound guideline most of the time—requires that a path have, or appear to have, a destination. Depending on the shape of the bed, and from where it is viewed, even uniform edgings of the same plant may lead the eye restlessly round and round. If the bed approaches circular in shape, a path or wide paved edging can all too easily look like an exercise ring.

Island beds are usually set in lawn, so a path is not essential and you may prefer to omit an edging and avoid frontline plants that sprawl over the grass, causing it to rot and impeding the mower. Use instead such compact and upright plants as thrift (*Armeria maritima*), *Astilbe chinensis* 'Pumila', dwarf shasta daisies such as 'Miss Muffet', *Coreopsis* 'Goldfink', *Geranium dalmaticum*, many dwarf hostas and irises including *Iris sibirica* 'Little White', most kinds of coralbells (*Heuchera*), and *Liriope muscari*. If invasive lawn grass needs to be controlled, a metal or plastic edging strip would be inconspicuous.

The more kinds of plants one grows in a border, the more it is likely to benefit from something that unifies them and carries the eye along. This can take the form of punctua-

tion or flow. Punctuation is provided by groups of the same plant, or of different plants of matching color, spaced along the border. Formal punctuation can be achieved with evergreen shrubs of firm outline—natural or clipped, small enough just to punctuate, or large enough to obscure what lies beyond when walking along the border—a useful device for separating color groupings that might otherwise conflict. Flow is achieved by the smoother progression of a continuous line, whether from a hedge, wall, or path, or from a ribbon of the same plant binding the border together. If the effect is to be more than fleeting, such plants will depend on foliage, not flower, for their effect. Plants with silvery leaves are particularly good for both punctua-

tion and flow. An edging of a plant with neat, dark green foliage gives an effect similar to a low hedge—where it is hardy, *Liriope muscari* is outstanding for this purpose. Letting edging plants spread into drifts at the back gives a softer look without disrupting flow, but acquisitive gardeners like me must constantly resist the temptation to nibble away at the front edge to make way for some new treasure. Here, where it can be kept under the eye, is a perfect place for it, but breaking the front line disrupts the flow.

Border Plans

The most beautiful gardens tend to be those created by artistic plantsmen for themselves.

Blue plumbago (Ceratostigma plumbaginoides), a red helianthemum, Geranium sanguineum 'Album', and G. s. 'Striatum' flow over and soften this low edging wall. (Stone House Cottage Nursery, England; June)

BORDER BASICS

These notes are presented as guidelines, not as "rules." Gardens, at their best, are an act of creation. It is the nature of creativity to court failure and nothing original was ever achieved without taking that risk. There must, nonetheless, be a starting place, so here are some fundamental guidelines that may make it easier for the inexperienced to get started.

1. Decide where the border is to go. Along a boundary is often the best place. Mark out the border, using string stretched between stakes for straight lines, a flexible garden hose for curves. If an island bed is being made in a lawn, the shape could be permanently marked, pending digging, by spraying Roundup in a band inside the hose. Autumn is a good time for marking out a border. Plants can then be selected and ordered during the winter, ready for planting in spring.

2. Using quad paper, obtainable from office supply stores, draw a plan of the bed or border. Quad paper is divided into quarter-inch squares and each square can represent one foot. Tracing paper can be laid over the plan to try out different plant combinations but it is easier to make several Xerox copies on which to work.

3. Decide on a color scheme. Include all colors if you wish but it is easier to work within a limited theme. Popular color themes are: (1) gray, white, blue, pinks and (2) gray, white, blue, yellows. Less popular, but especially good for daylily enthusiasts, is a hot color border of scarlets, oranges, and golden yellows.

4. Using an illustrated dictionary of perennials, make a list of the plants you like. *Perennials: How to Select, Grow and Enjoy* by myself and Frederick McGourty, includes most of the basic perennials but not so many that you can't see the wood for the trees. Include only plants hardy in your region and adapted to other existing conditions, such as extreme summer heat or periods of drought. Assuming the border is sunny, omit plants needing shade. If your aim is mass color for a limited season, omit plants that flower earlier or later. Don't forget the importance of good, lasting foliage. Delete any-

thing described as difficult. Later you may want to be adventurous but don't court disappointment with your first attempt.

5. Now send for and peruse nursery catalogues, locating sources for the plants you'd like to include. It is unlikely that you'll be able to find them all at local garden centers in spring. If you can't locate a source, delete the plant from your list.

6. Punctuation, or flow, or both, bring continuity and a basic structure to large borders. Punctuation (repeating the same plant, or the same color, at regular intervals along a border) divides the space into smaller units, which are easier to plan than the unbroken expanse of a newly prepared border. Neither punctuation nor flow (accomplished by means of a uniform edging) may be desirable in small borders, where they tend to emphasize the smallness, as well as limiting the number of different plants that can be fitted in. If the border is to have punctuation, position these plants first.

7. You may want to "anchor" the ends of a border with a plant, or group of plants, of structural quality. If evergreen plants are used (yuccas, for instance), they give the border continuing structure in winter, when herbaceous perennials are dormant. The anchoring plants could form part of the punctuation. Small borders usually look best if anchoring plants are low and mounded rather than upright.

8. Next position any other "permanent" plants. These are the ones that can stay in place for many years, do not need regular division, and may resent disturbance. Permanent plants include peonies, gas plant (*Dictamnus albus*), baptisias, goatsbeard (*Aruncus dioicus*), bugbane (*Cimicifuga*), globe thistles (*Echinops*), sea hollies (*Eryngium*), and butterfly weed (*Asclepias tuberosa*). Most borders aren't big enough to accommodate groupings of such bulky perennials as peonies, gas plant, goatsbeard, or *Baptisia australis*, each of which will ultimately exceed three feet in diameter, but they could be spaced along the border for continuity. Peonies are particularly good because, assuming selec-

tions of similar overall size are chosen, they could have different flowers but still provide continuity of form.

9. Assuming you are planning for extended bloom, divide the remaining plants on your list into four groups: early, midseason, late, and those which either bloom or have attractive foliage all season.

10. Now it is a matter of fitting the less permanent plants among those already in place, grading them more or less by height from front to back. Experiment with drifts (not blocks) of varying size. Groups of three, five, or seven (the larger numbers for the smaller plants) will be about right for borders of average size. Plants are easier to arrange attractively in odd numbers. If you use even numbers, four, for example, don't arrange them in a square; rather make a triangle with three plants, then add the fourth on either side of the single plant. Instead of a row, make a semicircle. In small borders, one of a kind will often be enough. If you intend to include spring bulbs in your border, leave sufficient gaps between the groupings to accommodate these. You may also want to leave gaps for annuals.

Strive for pleasing combinations of color and contrasts of shape and texture. Choose some plants from each seasonal group. If flowers of different seasons are alternated, there'll be little opportunity for creative combinations of color, so it usually works best to group two or more that flower together, interspersed with groups from another season, with foliage plants, or with those that stay in flower for a very long time.

11. Finally, realize that it is unlikely you'll get a border to your satisfaction the first time around, and even if you did, the effect would not be constant. Plants continue to grow in size, so the proportions will change each year. Some may not like the site (*why* they don't is not always apparent). For such reasons, borders need retuning year by year. That's the fun of it.

Top: *A ribbon of gray* Orostachys furusei *flows along one edge of this island bed, interplanted here and there with such small perennials as* Hosta 'Golden Prayers', right, *set sufficiently far back that the clean line of the front edge is not disrupted. (Garden of the late Richard Meyer, Ohio; July)*

Such designers often find working for others extremely frustrating: there are too many limitations. A professional designer must, as a rule, work within the limits of the client's budget and preferences. In the composition of borders, "Don't use any orange," is, for example, one common stipulation. All designers rejoice when an understanding client encourages their artistry, accepting the risk inherent in any work of art that it probably won't be immediately perfect. More often, they must rein their imaginations and work with the predictable, using the limited number of plants

known to be consistently reliable in the region, and planting them sufficiently close for the border to be full in its first, or at most its second year.

Despite the limitations, such borders need not be stereotyped: using no more than a dozen kinds of plants, there are countless permutations, but even supposing they fit the dimensions and orientation of a particular garden, border plans can seldom be used in their entirety, if at all, in a region other than the one for which they were created. They can, however, be very helpful in studying how a border comes together, especially if accompanied by the designer's rationale. With that in mind I asked two friends, both well-known designers, to draw up borders of similar orientation and dimensions. Elsa Bakalar lives and works in Massachusetts, Edith Eddleman in North Carolina.

These hypothetical borders were to face south, against a boundary fence. The front edge could be straight or curved. The width was to be 150 feet and the depth no more than 15 feet. The borders were to be devoted primarily to perennials but bulbs and grasses, and a shrub or two, could be included at the designer's option. The plants used were to be those known to do well in the designers' respective regions.

An extended season of bloom was to be the aim, and one great difference between the two regions is immediately apparent: for Elsa Bakalar this means bloom for about four months, for Edith Eddleman more than twice that time. Limited color schemes were imposed, with both borders incorporating gray, white, and blue, Elsa's then incorporating pink, Edith's yellow.

When the plans came in, it was interesting to note that each designer had used the full fifteen-foot width. Elsa chose a straight front edge, Edith a curved one. A quick count showed something over two hundred plants in each border, of approximately sixty different kinds. Assuming the purchase of perennials in gallon cans, there'd be little change from $1,000 for plants alone. Add the designer's fee, and the cost of the soil amendments usually needed, and such a border is not an inexpensive undertaking. Assuming willingness to wait an extra year for the border to become full, the cost of plants could be more than halved, either by using smaller ones, or by using fewer in a grouping when the plant is one that spreads fairly fast. Where, for instance, a plan indicates three *Cimicifuga simplex*, three should be used, because this increases rather slowly, but where three *Anemone vitifolia* 'Robustissima' is indicated, a single plant could be expected to fill that space within two growing seasons at most.

The artist's renderings are intended to show the different color themes and the intermingling of colors within each border. In reality, there will always be a bigger proportion of green, its place in the borders changing from month to month. Only by choosing plants which all peak at the same time could such overall color be achieved, and for no more than a month. The borders shown spread the flowering times over a much longer period, but seasonal progressions cannot be captured within a single plan.

ELSA BAKALAR'S RATIONALE
"The color will peak in July and August, but there are some pretty things both before and after. Thalictrum, digitalis, verbascum, and *Geranium* 'Johnson's Blue' are early. I have placed them near something else that will take over as they fade. Aconitum, *Anemone vitifolia*, *Cimicifuga simplex*, and *Aster* 'Harrington's Pink' are all late, but have sufficiently good-looking foliage to pay their way during the early part of summer.

Border Plan for the Northeast
(Designer, Elsa Bakalar)

Latin name—number of plants in plan—color, if not indicated by name—type of plant, if not a perennial

1. *Cornus alba* 'Elegantissima'; 1; white-edged leaves; shrub.
2. *Aconitum carmichaelii*; 3; blue.
3. *Thalictrum rochebrunianum*; 3; lavender.
4. *Anemone vitifolia* 'Robustissima'; 3; pink.
5. *Monarda didyma* 'Croftway Pink'; 3.
6. *Digitalis purpurea* 'Alba'; 5; biennial.
7. *Echinops* 'Taplow Blue'; 1.
8. *Digitalis purpurea* 'Alba'; biennial.
9. *Cimicifuga simplex*; 3; white.
10. *Verbascum chaixii* 'Album'; 5.
11. *Anemone vitifolia* 'Robustissima'; 3; pink.
12. *Aster novae-angliae* 'Harrington's Pink'; 3.
13. *Aruncus dioicus*; 3; cream.
14. *Phlox paniculata* 'World Peace'; 3; white.
15. *Astilbe taquetii* 'Superba'; 5; magenta.
16. *Cosmos* 'Sensation White'; annual, seeded in place.
17. *Papaver orientale* 'Helen Elizabeth'; 1; pink.
18. *Cleome*; pink; annual, seeded in place.
19. *Artemisia lactiflora*; 3; cream.
20. *Cleome*; pink; annual, seeded in place.
21. *Helictotrichon sempervirens*; 1; blue-gray grass.
22. *Liatris pycnostachya*; 3; strong pinkish purple.
23. *Cosmos* 'Radiance White'; annual, seeded in place.
24. *Campanula lactiflora*; 3; soft blue.
25. *Iris sibirica* 'White Swirl'; 7.
26. *Paeonia* 'Elsa Sass'; 1; white double.
27. *Phlox paniculata* 'Bright Eyes'; 3; pink.
28. *Aster* × *frikartii* 'Wonder of Staffa'; 3; blue.
29. *Aster novae-angliae* 'Alma Potschke'; 3; bright pink.
30. *Dictamnus albus* 'Purpureus'; 1; soft purplish pink; biennial.
31. *Phlox* 'Miss Lingard'; 3; white.
32. *Delphinium* 'Bellamosum'; 3; blue.

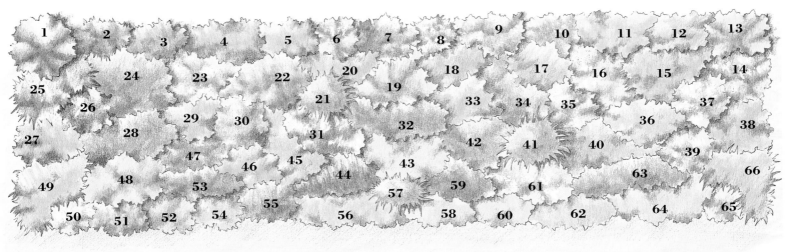

33. *Aster novae-angliae* 'Alma Potschke'; 3; bright pink.

34. *Echinacea purpurea* 'Bravado'; pink.

35. *Gypsophila paniculata* 'Perfecta'; 1; white.

36. *Platycodon grandiflorus* 'Shell Pink'; 3.

37. *Paeonia* 'Elsa Sass'; 1; white double.

38. *Phlox paniculata* 'Bright Eyes'; 3; pink.

39. *Allium tuberosum*; 3; white.

40. *Antirrhinum*, Frontier hybrid; 24; pink; annual.

41. *Helictotrichon sempervirens*; 1; blue-gray grass.

42. *Aster × frikartii* 'Wonder of Staffa'; 3; blue.

43. *Coreopsis* 'Moonbeam'; 5; pale yellow.

44. *Salvia × superba* 'East Friesland'; 5; dark purple.

45. *Antirrhinum*, Frontier hybrid; 24; pink; annual.

46. *Heuchera sanguinea*; 5; pink.

47. *Geranium* 'Johnson's Blue'; 3.

48. *Achillea* 'Moonshine'; 5; yellow.

49. *Hemerocallis* 'Theresa Hall'; 5; gold-dusted pink.

50. *Iberis sempervirens* 'Purity'; 1; white.

51. *Sedum* 'Vera Jameson'; 3; dusty pink flowers, purplish foliage.

52. *Alchemilla glaucescens* (*A. pubescens* of nurseries); 1; lime green flowers, gray-green leaves.

53. *Heliotropium* 'Marine'; 18; dark blue; annual.

54. *Dianthus gratianopolitanus*; 5; pink.

55. *Nepeta* 'Six Hills Giant'; 1; blue.

56. *Geranium sanguineum* 'Striatum'; 5; pale pink.

57. *Festuca ovina glauca*; 3; blue-gray grass.

58. *Gypsophila repens* 'Rosea'; 1; pink.

59. *Heliotropium* 'Marine'; 18; dark blue; annual.

60. *Alchemilla glaucescens* (*A. pubescens* of nurseries); 1; lime green flowers, gray-green leaves.

61. *Aquilegia* hybrid 'Snow Queen'; 7; white.

62. *Stachys byzantina*; 3; pale pink flowers, gray foliage.

63. *Delphinium grandiflorum* 'Blue Butterflies'; 9; bright blue; short-lived perennial usually grown as annual.

64. *Geranium sanguineum* 'Striatum'; 5; pale pink.

65. *Iberis sempervirens* 'Purity'; 1; white.

66. *Hemerocallis* 'Peach Fairy; 5.

"There's some symmetry but very little that's mechanical—just enough to hold the thing together: for instance, the central echinops, flanked by digitalis in early summer and by the annual cleome later in the season, and the hemerocallis and iberis in both front corners.

"There's more subtle symmetry in the placing of *Cornus alba* in one rear corner and *Aruncus dioicus* in the other. I think I've achieved continuity along the front of the border by using gray-foliaged plants with a very soft pink as the only color.

"Mindful of the limited-color requirement, I have used no golden yellow flowers, and only two clear yellows: *Achillea* 'Moonshine' and the very pale *Coreopsis* 'Moonbeam', because they are so good at cutting the saccharine quality of the blues and pinks.

"There are no bulbs, either spring or summer. There's nothing I hate more than spearing bulbs when I'm working around perennials. Just a couple of nods in the direction of ornamental grasses, and I thought they should be tidy ones for this border.

"As for annuals, I find cleome makes a wonderful tall background, as does the tall 'Sensation' cosmos. The pink snapdragons are Parks' Frontier hybrids. The heliotrope is 'Marine', available from most seed houses. I wish it were more available in flats in nurseries: I have to start my own. You might question the quantity of annuals used. I do belong to the school of Cram and Stuff but plants don't get as big as they would where the growing season is much longer. For the same reason *Anemone vitifolia* 'Robustissima' is only mildly invasive here: Other places, other problems, is what I say.

"Much as I love delphiniums, I've stuck only to *Delphinium* 'Bellamosum' here. It's disease-free, has a lovely shape, and is sturdy enough to stand up without staking. The white phlox next to the delphinium must be *Phlox* 'Miss Lingard', as its first wave of bloom coincides with the delphinium. *Phlox* 'World Peace' is a much later one. You might question the use of *Cimicifuga simplex* rather than *C. racemosa*. In my experience *C. simplex* manages to flower before frost most years, and I'd hesitate to put *C. racemosa* in someone's border because I think it has a nasty smell.

"*Hemerocallis* 'Theresa Hall' is a lovely gold-dusted pink. I used to sneer at the hemerocallis fanciers' prose, but there's no way to describe this plant except 'gold-dusted.' It's one of the very few daylilies that I let into the border. 'Mme. Bellum' is another, the hit of my late yellow garden." (Author's note: When this piece arrived, on May 30, my 'Mme. Bellum' was in full bloom. It was an exceptionally early season but June would be usual where I live.)

EDITH EDDLEMAN'S RATIONALE

"This border offers color in flower and foliage from late March/early April to frost, with winter interest provided by the skeletons of the ornamental grasses, the seedheads of the Siberian iris, the gray-blue spiky forms of *Yucca glauca*, the blue-foliaged mounds of *Ruta graveolens*, the silver filigree foliage of *Artemisia* 'Powis Castle', and the gray-green foliage and lavender flowers of *Erysimum* 'Bowles' Mauve'.

"I imagine the fence as tall, providing a suitable background for a spring show of yellow *Lonicera*, white and blue clematis, and pale yellow *Rosa banksiae* 'Lutea'. The annual hyacinth bean (*Dolichos lablab*) blooms from summer to fall, with violet flowers and burgundy seedpods. I assumed an open-ended border, permitting low-growing plants at the sides.

"Early blooms include violet-flowered *Verbena canadensis* (which blooms from

March to frost in a sunny location), *Verbena tenuisecta* 'Alba' (also with a long season of bloom), ice blue *Amsonia tabernaemontana* and its shorter form *A. t. montana*, pale yellow *Aquilegia canadensis* 'Corbett', and the large deep blue flowers of *Aquilegia vulgaris*. White daisies (*Chrysanthemum leucanthemum* 'May Queen') open early in April. Flowering continues with the Siberian iris, pale blue 'Sky Wings', and deep purple 'Ruffled Velvet'. *Centaurea montana*'s dark blue cornflower blossoms contrast with the silver foliage of *Artemisia* 'Valerie Finnis' and the bright yellow flowers of *Chrysogonum virginianum*. The pale green and creamy yellow mottled foliage of *Sedum alboroseum* 'Medio-Variegatus' is good all season long. Its pale pink flowers are negligible.

"Summer is ushered in by the white flowers of *Phlox* 'Miss Lingard' and *Astermoea mongolica*. The see-through green stalks of *Verbena bonariensis* with caps of lavender flowers punctuate the border, flowering from May to frost. Clumps of soft yellow *Anthemis tinctoria* bloom all summer long. *Achillea* 'Coronation Gold' also raises its flat golden clusters of bloom in summer. Deep blue flowers of *Platycodon* and spikes of *Veronica* 'Sunny Border Blue' contrast with the softer blue of *Aster* × *frikartii* 'Monch' and *Nepeta* × *faassenii*. *Aster* × *frikartii* is not very reliable (neither 'Monch' nor 'Wonder of Staffa') here but worthy of replacement as required. A thread of pale yellow *Coreopsis* 'Moonbeam' winds its way through the border, joined by the small graceful yellow flowers of *Hemerocallis* 'Bitsy'. This daylily repeats throughout summer in southeastern gardens. *Calamintha nepeta*, once it begins to bloom, is covered in blue-tinted white blossoms till frost.

"Biennial verbascums lift their candelabras of yellow bloom above silver rosettes of foliage. Allow them to set seed to assure a good crop of flowers the following year. *Salvia argentea*, whose leaves resemble great woolly clouds resting on the earth, also behaves somewhat as a biennial. I usually remove the flower stalks before seed is set. It might be wise to allow one plant to set seed to assure additional plants for the following year.

"Tall (five to six feet) plants of *Salvia guaranitica* bloom from late May to frost. Their flowers are particularly attractive to hummingbirds. Creamy yellow *Canna* 'Creamy Swoon' blooms throughout summer, and its broad green leaves offer a pleasant contrast to the finer-textured plants which surround it.

"Annuals used include white-flowered *Cleome* 'Helen Campbell', deep blue *Salvia farinacea* 'Victoria' (which may persist in southern gardens), soft blue *Ageratum houstonianum*, and the yellow-eyed white *Catharanthus roseus* 'Little Blanche'. Tall *Salvia* 'Indigo Spires' is a tender perennial which often fails to winter over, even in southern gardens, but cuttings root quickly and grow fast if one plant can be brought through winter in a greenhouse or other frost-free place.

"Fall belongs to the tasseled blooms of the ornamental grasses—*Miscanthus sinensis* 'Variegatus' and *M. s.* 'Morning Light' (each with green-and-white leaves and coppery plumes), the white silken puffs of *Pennisetum villosum* (which blooms from late spring through fall and is usually winter hardy in the Raleigh area), and the reddish haze of *Panicum virgatum* 'Heavy Metal' inflorescences rising above their narrow blue-green foliage. Soft blue flowers of *Aster* 'Our Latest One' continue for over a month. *Patrinia scabiosifolia* adds clouds of yellow flowers resembling Queen Anne's lace, and blue blossoms adorn the gray foliage of shrubby *Caryopteris*. *Solidago sempervirens* (a clump-forming goldenrod) carries golden wands up to six feet tall.

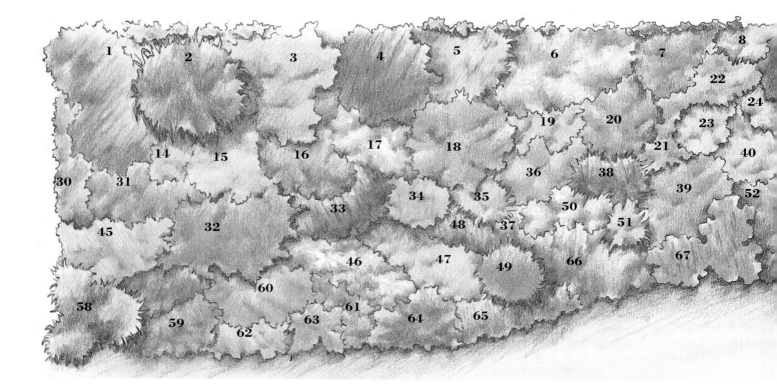

All-Season Border Plan for the Southeast *(Designer, Edith Eddleman)*

Vines on the fence at the back, left to right:

Lonicera sempervirens 'Sulphurea' (yellow) with *Clematis* 'Duchess of Edinburgh' (white).

Rosa banksiae 'Lutea' (yellow) with *Clematis* 'Ramona' (blue).

Dolichos lablab (hyacinth bean); violet; annual.

Lonicera sempervirens 'Sulphurea' (yellow) with *Clematis* 'The President' (blue).

Latin name—number of plants in plan—color, if not indicated by name—type of plant, if not perennial

1. *Salvia* 'Indigo Spires'; 2; blue.
2. *Miscanthus sinensis* 'Variegatus'; 1; white-striped grass.
3. *Thalictrum speciosissimum*; 3; pale lemon-yellow flowers, glaucous foliage.
4. *Salvia guaranitica*; 1; dark blue.
5. *Canna* 'Creamy Swoon'; 2; creamy yellow.
6. *Cleome* 'Helen Campbell'; 3; white; annual.
7. *Perovskia*; 1; lavender-blue.
8. *Patrinia scabiosifolia*; 1; strong yellow.
9. *Salvia guaranitica*; 1; dark blue.
10. *Aster novae-angliae* 'Our Latest One'; 1; blue.
11. *Baptisia pendula*; 1; white.
12. *Miscanthus sinensis* 'Morning Light'; 1; finely striped grass.
13. *Astermoea mongolica*; 3; white.
14. *Solidago sempervirens*; 1; yellow.
15. *Anthemis tinctoria*; 3; pale yellow.
16. *Aster* × *frikartii* 'Monch'; 3; blue.
17. *Phlox* 'Miss Lingard'; 3; white.
18. *Caryopteris* × *clandonensis*; 1; blue; die-back shrub.
19. *Solidago sempervirens*; 1; yellow.
20. *Aster novae-angliae* 'Our Latest One'; 1; blue.
21. *Verbena bonariensis*; 3; pale purple.
22. *Verbascum bombyciferum* 'Silver Spires'; yellow flowers, silver foliage; biennial.
23. *Patrinia scabiosifolia*; 1; yellow.
24. *Lilium formosanum*; 3; white; bulb.

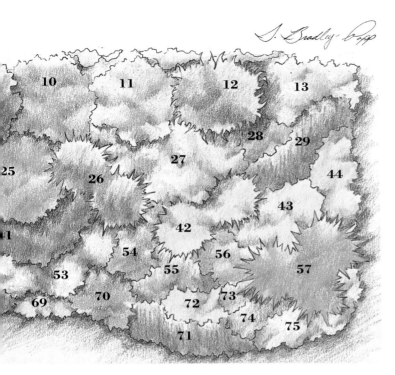

25. *Artemisia* 'Powis Castle'; 1; gray.

26. *Iris sibirica* 'Sky Wings'; 2; pale blue.

27. *Cleome* 'Helen Campbell'; 3; white; annual.

28. *Aquilegia vulgaris*; 1; blue.

29. *Salvia farinacea* 'Victoria'; 15; blue; tender perennial.

30. *Coreopsis* 'Moonbeam'; 5; pale yellow.

31. *Astermoea mongolica*; 3; white.

32. *Echinops ritro*; 3; blue, and *Platycodon grandiflorus* 'Mariesii'; 3; blue, and *Centaurea montana*; 3; blue.

33. *Veronica* 'Sunny Border Blue'; 3.

34. *Achillea* 'Coronation Gold'; 3; yellow.

35. *Hemerocallis* 'Bitsy'; 1; yellow.

36. *Verbena bonariensis*; 2; pale purple.

37. *Verbascum bombyciferum* 'Silver Spires'; 1; yellow flowers, silver foliage; biennial.

38. *Iris sibirica* 'Ruffled Velvet'; 2; purple.

39. *Erysimum* 'Bowles' Mauve'; 1; pale purple.

40. *Anthemis tinctoria*; 3; pale yellow form.

41. *Platycodon grandiflorus* 'Mariesii'; 5; blue.

42. *Kniphofia* 'Primrose Beauty'; 2; pale yellow.

43. *Coreopsis* 'Moonbeam'; 3; pale yellow.

44. *Sedum alboroseum* 'Medio-variegatus'; 5; grown for cream-variegated foliage, though bears pale pink flowers.

45. *Ruta graveolens*; 3; glaucous foliage, yellow flowers.

46. *Catharanthus roseus* 'Little Blanche'; 15; white; annual.

47. *Coreopsis* 'Moonbeam'; 11; pale yellow.

48. *Salvia farinacea* 'Victoria'; 9; blue; tender perennial.

49. *Panicum virgatum* 'Heavy Metal'; 1; gray foliage.

50. *Chrysanthemum leucanthemum* 'May Queen'; 3; white.

51. *Hemerocallis* 'Bitsy'; 1; yellow.

52. *Aster* × *frikartii* 'Monch'; 3; blue, and *Allium christophii*; silvery lilac; bulb.

53. *Chrysanthemum leucanthemum* 'May Queen'; 3; white.

54. *Aquilegia vulgaris*; 1; blue.

55. *Linum perenne*; 3; blue.

56. *Amsonia tabernaemontana*; 1; pale blue.

57. *Yucca glauca*; 3; these anchor the corner and are underplanted with *Verbena tenuisecta* 'Alba' (no.75 on key); tender perennial.

58. *Pennisetum villosum*; 3; grass; anchors corner.

59. *Salvia farinacea* 'Victoria'; 9; blue; tender perennial.

60. *Artemisia* 'Valerie Finnis'; 3; gray.

61. *Ageratum houstonianum*; 11; blue; annual.

62. *Centaurea montana*; 1; blue. Faced down with *Chrysogonum virginianum*; 6; yellow.

63. *Eryngium alpinum*; 3; blue.

64. *Ceratostigma plumbaginoides*; 5; blue.

65. *Calamintha nepeta*; 3; milky blue.

66. *Verbena canadensis*; 5; purple form.

67. *Salvia argentea*; 3; silver-gray.

68. *Salvia* × *superba* 'May Night'; 3; dark violet-blue.

69. *Coreopsis verticillata*; 3; yellow.

70. *Clematis integrifolia*; 1; blue.

71. *Nepeta* × *faassenii*; 5; blue.

72. *Aquilegia canadensis* 'Corbett'; 3; pale yellow.

73. *Centaurea montana*; 1; blue.

74. *Amsonia tabernaemontana* var. *montana*; 2; pale blue.

75. *Verbena tenuisecta* 'Alba'; 7; tender perennial.

"Bulbs—just two. I couldn't resist *Allium christophii*, with its starry flowered silver-lilac orbs in spring and long-lasting seed-heads, or the white trumpets of *Lilium formosanum*, rising on stalks up to six feet tall, against the dark green foliage and blue flowers of *Salvia guaranitica*."

The Evolution of an Unplanned Border

My own borders, beds, and odd patches of flowers are never planned on paper. They are worked out on the ground, evolving gradually, and often impermanently. My garden is also my trials ground and photographic studio. Some combinations please me so much that they are left for years. Others come to maturity, are photographed, and then give way to others. Watching the annual shunting around of long-suffering plants, my husband suggested that it would be easier to grow them in containers, on palettes, and rearrange them with a forklift truck. Actually, that wouldn't work. Plants have a way of growing into their place and something newly planted, or recently moved, takes a while to rearrange its stems and flowers to fit the site, especially if there's been a change of orientation.

Mine is an experimental garden. Many plants are grown in nursery beds at first, to establish their general merit and their adaptability to the climate. The time comes for those that both please and do well (usually, but not always the same thing) to be coordinated with others. I find it easier to do this if I leave gaps in new beds, or those being rearranged, until I find just the right plant to fill them. Moves noted but left until the proper planting season are more likely to be carried out if there is a gap ready and waiting, but often I do not wait: even in a hot climate it is possible, with care, to move large clumps of many perennials

Hot Color Border

On fence at back, left to right:

Lonicera sempervirens; 1; red-flowered vine.

Lonicera 'Dropmore Scarlet'; 1; scarlet-flowered vine.

Lonicera sempervirens 'Superba'; 1; scarlet-flowered vine.

Lonicera sempervirens 'John Clayton'; 1; yellow-flowered vine.

Clematis maximowicziana; 1; white-flowered vine.

Gelsemium sempervirens; 1; yellow-flowered vine.

Latin name—number of plants—color, if not indicated by name—type of plant, if not perennial

1. *Lychnis chalcedonica*; 1; scarlet.
2. *Aquilegia canadensis*; drift; red and yellow.
3. *Asclepias tuberosa*; 1; yellow-flowered form.
4. *Hemerocallis*; 3; tall, orange flowered.
5. *Ipomopsis rubra*; drift; scarlet-flowered biennial.
6. *Nandina domestica*; 3; shrub.
7. *Kerria japonica*; 1; yellow-flowered shrub.
8. *Cornus florida*; 1; tree, about 35 years old.
9. *Coreopsis lanceolata*; drift; yellow.
10. *Achillea* 'Coronation Gold'; 3; yellow.
11. *Heliopsis* 'Gold Feather'; 1; yellow.
12. *Dahlia* 'Bishop of Llandaff'; 3; red flowers, purple foliage.
13. *Iris*, tall bearded 'Buckskin'; 5; light golden yellow.
14. *Curtonus paniculatus*; large clump; scarlet.
15. *Helianthus salicifolius*; 1; yellow but mostly grown for fine foliage.
16. *Coreopsis* 'Early Sunrise'; 5; yellow; grown as an annual.
17. *Dahlia*; 1; orange flowers, purple foliage.
18. *Chrysanthemum*, Korean; 3; orange; grown as an annual.
19. *Hemerocallis*; 3; orange-and-yellow seedlings.
20. *Crocosmia masonorum*; large clump; scarlet.
21. *Coreopsis pulchra*; medium-sized clump; yellow.
22. *Chamaecyparis pisifera* 'Filifera Aurea'; 1; large yellow-leaved evergreen conifer.

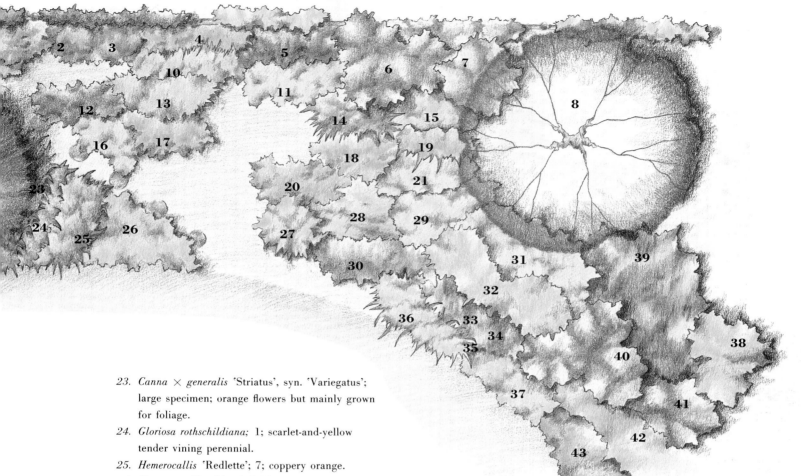

23. *Canna × generalis* 'Striatus', syn. 'Variegatus'; large specimen; orange flowers but mainly grown for foliage.

24. *Gloriosa rothschildiana*; 1; scarlet-and-yellow tender vining perennial.

25. *Hemerocallis* 'Redlette'; 7; coppery orange.

26. *Euonymus* 'Sparkle n' Gold'; about 30 rooted cuttings; yellow foliage turning orange in winter; evergreen shrub.

27. *Spiraea* 'Golden Princess'; 3, to be reduced to 1; golden foliage, pink flowers; shrub.

28. *Coreopsis integrifolia*; large clump; deep golden yellow.

29. *Coreopsis verticillata* 'Golden Shower'; large clump; golden yellow.

30. *Chrysanthemum* 'Bronze Elegance'; large clump; brick red.

31. *Oenothera fruticosa* 'Youngii'; drift; bright yellow.

32. *Spiraea japonica* 'Gold Flame'; 2; golden foliage, purplish pink flowers; shrub.

33. *Tulipa* 'Queen of Sheba'; 25; coppery orange and yellow; bulb.

34. *Lilium* 'Enchantment'; 7; orange; bulb.

35. *Aquilegia canadensis*; drift, from seed; red and yellow.

36. *Hemerocallis dumortieri*; 3; golden yellow.

37. *Sedum aizoon* 'Aurantiacum'; 5; golden yellow.

38. *Abelia* 'Francis Mason'; 3; golden-leaved evergreen shrub.

39. *Ipomopsis rubra*; drift; scarlet-flowered biennial.

40. *Nandina* 'San Gabriel'; 3; dwarf evergreen shrub.

41. *Azalea*, Exbury type; 1; orange-flowered shrub.

42. *Chrysanthemum*, Korean; 7; copper and orange; grown as an annual.

43. *Portulaca oleracea*; 12 rooted cuttings; orange; annual.

Hatched areas along the front of the border show the continuity of color achieved with shrubs having long-lasting golden foliage.

when they are in full bloom, without causing them much of a setback. The plant must, of course, have a fairly compact root system and be well watered in. This is invariably what I do with daylilies, where a nuance of difference in color may make the difference between delight and ho-hum-good-enough combinations. Evening is the best time to move a plant; if it wilts a bit, it usually recovers by morning. If I move plants during hot weather I provide temporary shading by pushing in a spare garden fork and leaning a large board against it to block the sun from the south or west, as the situation dictates. If the plant comes from a container, planting during hot weather poses no problems provided it is well watered in and kept watered during dry spells.

There are reasons other than mine for taking one's time about assembling a border, or changing it: cost; time; obtainability of a desired plant; finding the right balance in color or form; or (a common reason), the desire to grow more plants and the resultant widening of the border.

The plants themselves may dictate changes. If you haven't grown *that* plant in *that* place before, snags may crop up that weren't apparent on paper. A plant that ought, in theory, to do well, languishes for no apparent reason, or, having done well for years, suddenly ceases to flourish. Dividing it and replenishing the soil may or may not help. Or perhaps it prospers too well and becomes unacceptably invasive. A tornado, ice storm, or gypsy moth infestation may kill a tree, creating sun where there was shade, while in the mixed garden the opposite happens: trees and shrubs continue to grow in size, creating shade where there was sun. And then, one may simply tire of a particular plant or combination.

I do try to rearrange one bed or border at a time, so that there are other combinations, more or less complete, to be enjoyed elsewhere in the garden.

My plan demonstrates this piecemeal approach in my hot color border. The approximate position of the plants at present in place is indicated. A year earlier this border was complete, and moderately satisfying. Reworking was prompted by voles destroying so many plants. Most of the surviving perennials were moved to a temporary bed while large quantities of road grit were dug into the border. This isn't the complete answer to voles but it does reduce the losses. Since it had to be done, reworking the border gave me the opportunity to improve it and to try out some new plants. It was widened, for a start, to bring it into better proportion with the large conifer on the left and the dogwood on the right. These have been in the garden for many years and are mature specimens.

This border is now of dimensions similar to the other two garden plans, being fifteen feet deep in the middle but wider at the ends. This is by no means too much when allowing for shrubs at the back. It also has the same orientation, facing south against a post-and-rail fence covered with chicken wire to support vines. I do not have a path at the back of the border because I can get at the vines from the other side of the fence and the shrubs require very little attention. It measures 150 feet from the boundary path behind the gold-thread cypress on the left to the driveway on the right, though, in fact, it does not follow that route but curves as indicated to continue parallel to the driveway, the section not shown being planted primarily with shrubs and small trees. It is a mixed border, with perennials predominating.

There are four kinds of the long-blooming trumpet honeysuckle, *Lonicera sempervirens*, on the fence, put here originally for purposes of comparison. The wild form on the left was grown from a cutting taken from a road-side plant. Next to it is coral-flowered 'Drop-more Scarlet', said to be a hybrid between *L. sempervirens* and *L. hirsuta*. Then comes the best of the three, *L. sempervirens* 'Magnifica', also called *L. s.* 'Superba'. This has larger flowers than the others, so densely borne that they form a solid sheet of scarlet in spring, a wonderful backdrop for a drift of red-and-yellow columbines, *Aquilegia canadensis*, that has almost engulfed a single plant of a yellow-flowered butterfly weed (*Asclepias tuberosa*) that was near the front of this border before it was widened and remains to be moved when time permits and the weather is propitious. The honeysuckle continues to flower, less profusely, until hard frost. A yellow form, *Lonicera sempervirens* 'Sulphurea', proved disappointing, branching very little and flowering only once. It has just been replaced with a new yellow form discovered in a local woods and named *L. s.* 'John Clayton'. Then comes white-flowered sweet autumn clematis (*Clematis maximowicziana*, more often, but, incorrectly, called *C. paniculata*), a bit of an anomaly among the hot colors but it was there first and it is too beautiful, fragrant, and easygoing to discard. To the right of this, behind the dogwood, is the yellow-flowered evergreen Carolina jessamine, *Gelsemium sempervirens*.

At the foot of the vines is a strip of dwarf mondo grass (*Ophiopogon japonicus*), planted years ago along the outside of the fence to deter roadside weeds on the narrow bank between the garden and the ditch, and serving that purpose very well. The ditch itself is stuffed so tightly with blue, yellow, and tawny red water-loving irises (*Iris versicolor, I. pseudacorus, I. fulva*, and hybrid Louisiana irises) that weeds that might otherwise self-sow into the garden have difficulty getting a toehold.

At the back of the border, to the right, is a group of three nandinas (*Nandina domestica*) which bear great bunches of red berries among leaves of red, yellow, and mahogany through winter. On their right is a large bush of the single-flowered *Kerria japonica*, with bright yellow flowers in spring and green canelike stems through winter. This doesn't grow as tall as the more common double-flowered form. It would really prefer a bit of shade in this hot climate but does well enough in its present position. I mean to add a bush of golden privet (*Ligustrum ovalifolium* 'Aureum') center back, between the two honeysuckles, keeping it cut back to the height of the fence. For the present that space is occupied by the feathery spired, scarlet-flowered biennial *Ipomopsis rubra*.

Two of my favorite combinations, as shown on pages 98 and 272, are in this border: a canna against the gold-thread cypress (*Chamaecyparis pisifera* 'Filifera Aurea'), on the left, and 'Queen of Sheba' tulips against a pair of 'Gold Flame' spiraeas on the right. These were left in place but given a thick top-dressing of grit lightly covered with mulch. The canna is flanked on the left by the red-and-yellow *Hemerocallis* 'Screech Owl', which is stunning against the yellow of the cypress. Another daylily will go on the right of the canna when I find just the right one. For the present there is a large, glossy-leaved bright red salvia, *Salvia miniata*, which is either an annual or a tender perennial, kept going by cuttings wintered under lights indoors.

In front of these is a drift of a dainty coppery red daylily called 'Redlette', received as a bonus from a nursery years ago and still among my favorites. Tucked into a gap behind them is a temporary resident, the flamboyant gloriosa lily (*Gloriosa rothschildiana*). This isn't winter hardy but the strange white tubers, almost rootless and curved into strange shapes, are so easily stored, and increase so fast in a single season, that I've usually got several pots to give away or dot into the garden. Come hard frost (which is not, usually, until December) they are tipped out of their pots and stored in the laundry room in buckets of slightly dampened peat moss, along with dahlia tubers.

In front of these, two years ago, went three plants of a new (or new to me) euonymus, *Euonymus fortunei* 'Sparkle 'n Gold', a low-growing evergreen with green-and-yellow foliage through spring and summer, turning glowing orange in winter. I liked this so much that I rooted lots of cuttings, which is very easy to do, without having any particular purpose for them in mind. (There are always fund-raising plant sales!) These corner groupings run sideways from the front of the border, which looks odd on a plan but works particularly well in relationship to the pyramidal conifer when approached from the right. This conifer is one of the most beautiful things in my garden, the year round. Admiring it, early in spring, and noticing how well the yellow of the euonymus matched that of the cypress, it occurred to me that a "reflection" of the conifer's pyramidal shape could be made by planting the euonymus cuttings to make a triangle at the apex of this corner grouping. Though not yet filled in, it looks very promising, but lengthening the diagonal line across the border does now call for a stepping-stone path to make the line more purposeful.

The stepping-stone path will give access to a self-sowing drift of *Coreopsis lanceolata* in the corner. There's a boundary path to the left of the border and I managed quite well before but the stepping stones will make it easier. The coreopsis bears its yellow daisies above glossy, healthy foliage, off and on, all season. The only maintenance it needs is a haircut in midsummer, when it sprawls, and the removal of surplus seedlings. This corner is lightly shaded by the conifer so I've cleared a small patch of the coreopsis to make way for a single plant of scarlet-flowered *Lychnis chalcedonica*. All my previous attempts to please this have failed: it doesn't like 90°F sun for weeks on end but it liked shade even less. I'm hoping that the present spot will be an acceptable compromise.

To the right of the stepping-stone path are some clumps of *Coreopsis* 'Early Sunrise'. This is its first year in my garden. If it lives up to its credentials, I'll never want to part with it, but we shall see. Still within the shadow of the conifer from early afternoon there are two dahlias. To one I have been faithful all my gardening years: purple-foliaged 'Bishop of Llandaff', which bears its clear red flowers on tall stems in summer and then, after being cut back, bears a second crop on shorter stems in autumn. I know no name for the other dahlia, a short one with purple foliage and tawny orange semidouble flowers; it was an impulse purchase that turned out well. With the help of a layer of mulch, these live out of doors through an average Zone 8 winter but I take a tuber or two indoors to be on the safe side.

The grouping to the right of the border consists of two bushes, side by side, of 'Gold Flame' spiraea. In front of them is the tulip 'Queen of Sheba', in sunken laundry baskets, interplanted with orange 'Enchantment' lilies. *Aquilegia canadensis* was recently sown among and around them. It may prove too tall, in which case it will be replaced with a dwarf form I was given as *A. c.* 'Nana'. The tulips flower at the same time as the columbines, against the new bronze-and-yellow foliage of the spiraea. Then come the orange lilies, against the massed circular flowers of a sundrops acquired as *Oenothera fruticosa* 'Youngii'. Though warmed by red buds, the clear bright yellow of the flowers is a trifle cool for this setting but it is such a good-natured plant that I am loath to change it. It forms a wandering patch of evergreen (in mild climates) foliage drifting back under the dogwood and forward around the spiraeas. It flowers for only a couple of weeks and is well away from the golden yellow flowers of *Coreopsis lanceolata* at the other end of the border. If I do decide to try something of warmer coloring, *Rudbeckia triloba* is my candidate. This is an annual but it self-sows so profusely and reliably that it is in effect perennial. It flowers in late summer, so I'd lose the yellow backdrop for the orange lilies.

In front of the tulip and lily bulbs is a narrow strip of the low-growing *Sedum aizoon* 'Aurantiacum'. In my hot garden sedums aren't the grow-anywhere workhorses they are in cooler regions. *Sedum aizoon*, a rather acid yellow, has done well for years in a summer-shaded spot. The flowers of *S. a.* 'Aurantiacum' are a more golden yellow. It doesn't seem to be as robust but perhaps I just haven't found the right place for it. This is its last chance.

In previous years I tried out golden oregano (*Origanum vulgare* 'Aureum') as a possible edging to bind the border together but its lime green color wasn't quite right; it needed a bit more gold in it. Interestingly, the golden oregano, or golden marjoram, grown in English gardens *is* a more golden yellow, and I found the same plant being grown in Vancouver gardens. I grew the two side by side to satisfy myself that it wasn't a matter of soil or climate. Unfortunately, the golden form isn't nearly as reliable or robust in my present garden as the lime green one.

There was already partial punctuation from the matching yellow foliage of the golden conifer, the 'Gold Flame' spiraeas, and a group of three 'Francis Mason' abelias to the right. It was completed by adding three

bushes of *Spiraea* 'Golden Princess'. This is one of the fairly new compact yellow-leaved forms. It is not proving to be as small as I had expected and in autumn the three will be reduced to one. Like 'Gold Flame', it bears pink flowers, but they are a softer pink, quite attractive against the yellowish leaves.

Choice and placement of other perennials so far in place was sometimes based on previous experience, sometimes experimental. *Achillea* 'Coronation Gold' was further forward in the border last year. A combination of soil made rich with sewage compost, a wet season, and my disinclination to stake caused it to topple over surrounding plants: that plants grow taller in wet years than in dry ones is a design factor that usually goes unmentioned. Even if one is able and willing to water copiously, such watering does not stimulate lush growth in the same way as rain. Don't ask me why.

Extra quantities of grit were added to make the soil less rich, and the achilleas were put near the back of the border instead of in the middle third. If we get a dry year there's now the possibility that the height may be insufficient for the back of the border. In that event these are my options: move the plants forward again and shear them in wet seasons, or stake them. I chose 'Coronation Gold' rather than the taller 'Gold Plate' because I knew that the latter would have to be staked. If staking, which I do only as a last resort, is forced upon me, I'll probably substitute 'Gold Plate'. Because of their uncommon platelike form, I do consider one or the other indispensable. Their flowers are a warm, mustardy yellow better suited to hot color borders than the bright canary yellow of the somewhat shorter 'Moonshine', which I grow elsewhere and think the prettiest of the yellow-flowered yarrows.

My garden is strong on coreopsis, for

nearly all do exceptionally well. *Coreopsis ver-ticillata*, in all its forms, is the best of them all and there was a large patch of one I bought as *C. v.* 'Golden Shower' in the middle of the border. It turned out to be the mounding, bright yellow species. This has how been re-placed with the true 'Golden Shower', which is a bit taller and more upright and, more important, a slightly warmer golden yellow, making it the best choice for this bed. Such small changes make all the difference when fine-tuning a color scheme. I moved the clump of 'Golden Shower' from a nursery bed in April, when the weather was already hot, so I left the clump intact. It spreads steadily out and will fill its space soon enough but it would have done so faster, perhaps in one season, had I divided it into three, as I would have, had the weather been cooler.

I used to grow *C. auriculata* and its dwarf form *C. a.* 'Nana'. Often I suddenly realize that a plant I once grew is no longer in the garden, without any clear recollection of hav-ing evicted it, or why. The orange-yellow of one or both of these would be perfect for this hot-color border and I must get them again.

I do know why I finally gave away the delightful little *C.* 'Goldfink': to do its best it needed dividing every year, a job very easily done but I just didn't always get around to it. Instead there are two new kinds of coreopsis in this border. Both have been on trial in a nursery bed and are now getting the chance to show what they can do in the border. They came from Woodlanders Nursery, an invalu-able source of southeastern native plants. *Co-reopsis pulchra* has foliage even more finely cut and feathery than *C. verticillata*. The flowers are similar but with a very dark eye. So far, spread has been very slow, which could be an advantage in some situations, but it also seems to be rather thin on the ground which, being conducive to weed infestation, could be

a mark against it—it is a bit soon to say. The reverse is the case with *C. integrifolia*. I can-not better the description that came with it: "A real winner from Florida, in full bloom now (October), bright egg-yolk yellow with black center." And then the ominous word: "Stoloniferous." So far, though, it has proved a compact spreader, increasing its girth quite rapidly but making dense clumps, less than one foot high. Over the glossy spear-shaped leaves rise flowers that are indeed a rich egg-yolk yellow, if you can remember what egg yolks used to look like before the days of battery hens. In size and shape they resemble the flowers of *C. lanceolata*. This probably flowers too late for the north, and I don't know how hardy it is, but it does show great promise for the South.

In the nursery bed *C. integrifolia* grew side by side with *Chrysanthemum* 'Bronze Ele-gance', which has flowers of light brick red. Their bloom times coincided and I liked the combination so much that I put them together in the revamped border, with the coreopsis behind the chrysanthemum. Their positions may have to be reversed: when in bloom they are of similar height but before they bloom the chrysanthemum is taller.

One could hardly pass up daylilies in a hot-color border. I had a large patch of 'Stella de Oro' but didn't care for it particularly. I like my hot colors hot and Stella is lukewarm. Nor did it rebloom. It is a best-seller and a nurseryman friend was happy to take it off my hands. I retained one small clump to see if it will repeat flower in shade. *Hemerocallis dumortieri* did well here and wherever else I put it. The flowers are golden yellow with a brown reverse, of a size in good proportion with the two-foot height, and they are fra-grant. This flowers very early—April or early May in my garden. At the back of the border there's a "reserved" sign in the shape of an orange daylily soon to be replaced by the six-to-seven-foot *H. altissima*, which bears flowers in abundance for several weeks in late summer and autumn on wiry, self-supporting stems. The flowers are a pale, warm yellow with coppery streaks at the throat, refined and somewhat spidery in form and neater than most in death. Other daylilies will be added when in bloom. So will lilies. Last year I bought a mixed collection, individually beautiful but together a hideous conglomeration of white, pink, yellow, and orange. In autumn they were potted up individually and the pots plunged near this border, the better to pick out suitable colors and move them into place.

Where summers are cool heliopsis can be counted on for a summer-long show of cheerful yellow daisies. Where I live they flower for about six weeks. From the many available kinds I chose 'Gold Feather' because the leaves were feathered with gold, probably an aberration caused by some deficiency in the soil but no less attractive for that. It is easy to overdo the yellow daisies but *Helianthus salicifolius* is grown mainly for its dainty foliage, and separated from the heliopsis by a clump of the bold sword-shaped leaves and scarlet flowers of *Curtonus paniculatus*, an English cottage-garden favorite once called *Antholyza* and familiarly known as Aunt Eliza.

Orange-flowered *Crocosmia masonorum* repeats the shape of *Curtonus paniculatus* on a somewhat smaller scale. Eventually this will (touch wood) be replaced by the scarlet-flowered form called 'Dixter Flame', but it will be several years before the fragment that survived vole depradations has been nursed back to sufficient size.

Among the perennials waiting to be slotted into place is *Buphthalmum salicifolium* 'Dora', which has narrow leaves similar to *Helianthus salicifolius* on a smaller plant. 'Dora' is said to be a particularly compact

form but I've had it only one year and need another season to find out just how tall it gets. Only then can I decide whereabouts to put it. As an infant plant in the nursery bed its show of yellow daisies began in May and continued into autumn, but never in abundance. Also standing by is my latest goldenrod candidate (a good many have been tried and found wanting, usually because they were invasive), *Solidago sphacelata* 'Golden Fleece', a selection found by Dick Lighty in North Carolina, where he admired its ground-covering habit and heart-shaped foliage. It grows less than knee high and flowers in early autumn.

That's as far as it has got. It isn't the textbook way of getting a border together but the scenario will, I'm sure, strike a note familiar to many.

BOG AND WATER GARDENS

If there's a pond or swampy area on your property, count your blessings and take advantage of it by growing the dramatic foliage

When this house was built, a wet hollow lay just in front. Instead of filling it in to make a lawn, as developers would have done, the owners deepened it to make a pond for water lilies. Plants that like moist soil, including massed hostas, grow on the banks, and the pond is encircled by a path of shredded bark. (Garden of the late Richard Meyer, Ohio; August)

Growing in the water are such irises as Iris laevigata *and* I. pseudacorus, *and calla lilies (*Zantedeschia aethiopeca). *Candelabra primroses and* Darmera peltata *grow in the mud near the edge, and hostas, daylilies, and* Euphorbia griffithii *grow higher up on the banks. (Longstock Park, England; July)*

plants that are at their most luxuriant growing in mud, or even shallow water. If these do not exist, plastic pond liners have made small ponds or bog gardens fairly easy and inexpensive to construct—easy meaning uncomplicated, not effortless. Bog plants need a minimum soil depth of six inches, two feet for such giants as *Gunnera*. Making your own pond or bog has the advantage that it can be of the size and in the place you choose.

If a pool is planned (perhaps for growing water lilies) there are two ways of providing for bog-type plants around the edge. In the first, a shallow trough is shaped at the rim of the pool, the liner molded into this, then brought up over the pool edge and anchored with rocks or paving stones. The trough is then filled with earth. This confines the plants and makes for a neat, rather formal look. The shallowness of the trough precludes large bog

plants, which would look out of scale anyway in this limited space, but marsh marigolds (*Caltha palustris*) will grow in three inches of mud covered by shallow water, and so will *Acorus gramineus* 'Variegatus', a Japanese sweet flag with dainty fans of slender cream-striped leaves. Six inches of soil suffices for numerous plants, including many water irises. The catalogue of Lilypons Water Gardens (6800 Lilypons Road, P. O. Box 10, Lilypons, MD 21717) shows how to make this kind of pool and marginal shelf in step-by-step pictures.

Alternatively, put the edges of the liner just below the level of the surounding soil so that water can seep out. This provides varying degrees of moisture for a broad range of plants, and permits them to spread informally. It should be said that with the first method there'll be few weeds, with the second proba-

This pool was constructed in a weekend, using a plastic liner laid over sand, the edges covered with soil or anchored with stone slabs. (Garden of Elaine Horton, England; early July)

bly quite a lot until the plants are dense enough to crowd them out, a job water irises are particularly good at.

If you just want a bog, not a pool, a liner can still be used, but puncture it here and there to let excess water escape. Alternatively, line the excavation with a thick layer of overlapping newspaper. If the soil is clay you may not need a lining at all. There's much to be gained and nothing except time and energy to be lost by digging the excavation as deep as you can manage—aim at a minimum of one foot. If your soil is light, add peat moss to make it more moisture retentive. Lined, sunken areas retain moisture much longer than the surrounding soil. If summer rain is insufficient to keep the bog moist, flood it periodically from a hose. This won't usually be needed unless a month or more has gone by without rain. Don't attempt a bog in regions

where prolonged summer drought is normal—it would be out of character, and using water for the garden might be banned just when it is needed most.

Water irises are among the best plants for bogs. *Iris pseudacorus* (yellow) and *I. versicolor* (blue) are among the toughest and both are quick and easy to grow from seed. Louisiana irises come in a great range of exquisite colors. These all thrive without attention in my roadside ditch, where the water level varies, without seasonal pattern, from zero to well over a foot. Other popular hardy perennials for bogs or very moist soil include *Ligularia dentata*, candelabra primroses (*Primula japonica* is the most readily available but there are many other kinds), rodgersias, umbrella plant (*Darmera peltata*, formerly *Peltiphyllum peltatum*), skunk cabbage (*Symplocarpus* and *Lysichiton*), false hellebore (*Veratrum*

These two streams look so similar but really are very different. The first, left, in the English garden of John Treasure, Burford House, near Tenbury Wells, is a mud-bottomed stream for plants needing abundant moisture. Plants shown include Rodgersia aesculifolia, Primula pulverulenta, Peltiphyllum peltatum *(*Darmera peltata*),* Iris laevigata, *and, on the bank,* Smilacina racemosa. *The second,* right, *at Ladew Topiary Gardens, Maryland, is not a water garden. The water is contained within a concrete channel and most of the perennials grown along the edges are kinds that need sharp drainage, with bearded irises predominating. (June)*

viride), several joe-pye weeds (*Eupatorium*) meadowsweet (*Filipendula ulmaria*—yellow-leaved *F. u.* 'Aurea' is the showiest), *Polygonum bistorta* 'Superbum', American burnet (*Sanguisorba canadensis*), and the loosestrifes (*Lysimachia*). The similarly named but unrelated purple loosestrife (*Lythrum salicaria*) does so well in wet soil that it has crowded native species out of many swamps and this, along with its hybrids, is banned in some states. Then there are such grasses, sedges, and ferns as *Carex stricta* 'Bowles' Golden', sensitive fern (*Onoclea sensibilis*), and ostrich

fern (*Matteuccia struthiopteris*). Popular bog plants for the warmer zones include umbrella palm (*Cyperus alternifolius*), dwarf papyrus (*Cyperus haspans*), water cannas, hardy calla (*Zantedeschia aethiopeca*), and swamp mallows or hibiscus such as *Hibiscus moscheutos* and *H. coccineus*. Daylilies, hostas, and astilbes won't grow in standing water or sodden soil but do exceptionally well in the moist soil at the edge of a pond or bog.

As far as exposure, irises and hibiscus can take the heat anywhere. All the others benefit from light afternoon shade and need it where summers sizzle, especially those such as skunk cabbage and *Veratrum viride* that grow naturally in damp woods.

Streams are more problematical than ponds and bogs. How many have envied the trickling stream of an English garden, with irises and maybe calla lilies wading knee deep, primulas and globeflowers (*Trollius*) dabbling their toes, and daylilies, hostas, and astilbes farther up the bank? England, believe it or not, is drier than much of the United States, with prolonged but gentle rain. The torrential downpours so common here turn trickling streams into raging torrents, while summer heat and drought may leave them dry just when plants need the water most. Under such circumstances an artificial stream, with pumped, controllable water, may be preferable to the real thing, but it may radically change the approach to what is grown. Unless the soil is impermeable clay, such an artificial stream may not retain sufficent water unless it is lined with concrete. The banks above the channel will then be quite dry, so you still have an attractive moving-water feature but

An imaginary stream of Echeveria elegans *rosettes in the California garden of designer Harland Hand.* Aloe striata *hybrids grow along the banks. (April)*

the plants grown alongside will be those liking sharp drainage—bearded irises, for instance.

Small, dry gardens can still grow a few plants that need moist soil (Japanese irises will probably be first choice for many) by making minibogs in holes or containers (sunken or otherwise) lined with punctured plastic or newspapers. One friend grows a collection of pitcher plants (*Sarracenia*) in a plastic-lined half whiskey barrel.

ROCK GARDENS

There are thousands of perennials less than one foot high. If they are chunky and robust enough for the front ranks of the border, we call them perennials. If they are low growing but wide spreading, we call them ground-cover plants. If they are neither, we classify them as "alpines" or "rock garden plants." In the United States the latter category includes, quite properly, a lot of woodland plants. Some of the country's finest rock gardens—gardens that can hold their own with any in Europe—have been made in woodland clearings, a distinctive American style that has evolved naturally in regions of rocky woods rich in wildflowers.

In no gardening genre is there greater variety than in rock gardening as practiced in the United States. There is a single uniting theme—plants. Rock gardens are the province of the plants(wo)man. Rock gardeners (whose plant interests often embrace all kinds of plant) never pretend that their hobby is work-free; rather, it is for those who want the plants for their own sake and who know no more blissful way to relax than taking care of them. Rock gardening is labor intensive but it is not, apart from initial construction, strenuous work, which makes rock gardening particularly well suited to those who love the plants

Top: *Massed phloxes in the garden of the late H. Lincoln and Laura Louise (Linc and Timmy) Foster. Many named forms of carpeting phlox, or moss pinks, originated in this garden, including 'Millstream Laura' (a delicate pink), 'Millstream Daphne' (bright pink), and 'Millstream Jupiter' (the best blue). The photograph* below *shows cowslips growing among boulders in another part of this beautiful garden in a woods. (Connecticut; May)*

but lack the strength for heavy labor. Weeding, the most time-consuming task, is kept to a minimum by disturbing the surface of the soil as little as possible.

If your garden is small and you want to get a quart into a pint pot, rock gardening is for you. If your garden is large you might still want to consider a rock garden for little plants that would be out of scale in beds and borders—rock garden devotees have shown great ingenuity in providing settings that bring the plants into scale with larger properties, standing many of the rules on their heads in the process. If your interests lie in this direction you owe it to yourself to share in the camaraderie of the American Rock Garden Society.

Because of its different and very varied climates and natural settings American rock gardening has developed independently of European tradition, which holds that a rock garden should be out in the open, in full sun, away from the house, and "away from the drip of trees." Full sun at 70°F for a week is a very different matter from full sun at 90°F for three months, and it is constant drizzle that causes trees to drip, not occasional downpours. In America light shade is often preferable to full sun but not if it comes from trees with dense surface roots, particularly maples. The sticky drip from aphids can sometimes be a nuisance, but the main disadvantage of trees in or near a rock garden is autumn's falling leaves, so ideally the shade would come from tall trees well to the south of the rock garden. Under these (or this—a single large tree could cast sufficient shade) would go such woodland plants as trilliums, hepaticas, primroses, the little crested iris (*Iris cristata*) and foamflowers (*Tiarella*). In the lighter, dappled shade further out would go those that want sun but need

An enthusiast's small fenced garden containing hundreds of plants tucked among rocks and incorporating a small pool on the left. (Garden of Mr. and Mrs. Robin Wainwright, England; August)

This long wall of massive boulders brings the small plants grown in the bed above into scale with their surroundings, as well as providing the sharp drainage they require. The plants shown growing between two boulders, below, are Androsace sarmentosa *and a compact form of* Chrysogonum virginianum. *(Garden of Catherine and Harry Hull, Massachusetts; May)*

a little shade during the hottest hours of early afternoon (what these are will vary from region to region, few where summers are cool, the majority where they are extremely hot), and at the extremity go those that like, or at least tolerate, full sun—the moss pinks (*Phlox* species) for example.

Which plants are or aren't in character with a rock garden makes for some lively discussions among purists. It isn't only a question of size, provided the plants are in scale with their surroundings. What it usually boils down to is that the plants should look natural, not flashy. If hybridizers had a hand in their making, this shouldn't be apparent: border daylilies with sumptuous flowers have not gained admittance but the door is opening to some of the dwarf miniatures (in daylily terms "dwarf" and "miniature" are not the same thing—one refers to the size of the plant, the other to the size of the flowers). Some double

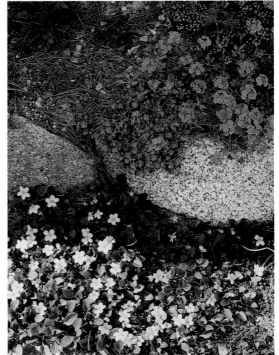

Infrequently used steps house a collection of small plants, including helianthemums, sedums, sempervivums, Geranium dalmaticum, *dwarf irises, campanulas, dwarf veronicas, and* Rhodohypoxis baurii. *(Garden of Sir John Thouron, Pennsylvania; July)*

flowers found in the wild are highly esteemed—anemonellas, bloodroot, and trilliums, for instance, but gaudy manmade doubles will not do, nor will flowers of extravagant size, with occasional exceptions of soft color and simple form.

If you like the idea of a rock garden but aren't sure what form it should take or how to go about it, there's plenty of help at hand. The American Rock Garden Society has chapters in most regions and its members are generous givers of plants as well as advice. Visiting other gardens helps in deciding what style one's own should take and what plants are most likely to do well. The best book on the subject for American gardeners is *Rock Gardening* by H. Lincoln Foster.

To the grower of alpine plants, color and form aren't a major consideration. Most alpines are modest in demeanor and the rocks make peace between those of combative bright color. Unlike the border, where there shouldn't be bare earth, rock garden plants are better presented, jewellike, with some space between. Grown cheek by jowl, such larger, sturdy plants as aubrietia, yellow alyssum (*Aurinia saxatilis*), and the more virulently colored selections of moss pink (*Phlox subulata*) do have the makings of a fine color clash. Dispersed among rocks, gravel chippings, and subtler plants, they become welcome splashes of color.

Spring surfeit, summer dearth is the dominant flowering pattern among rock garden plants. Foliage form and texture, and some color, continues with such plants as dwarf conifers, sempervivums in their multitudinous forms, and the bright reddish leaves of *Sedum* 'Ruby Mantle', but keeping flowers going through summer and autumn is a challenge. Possibilities include asters (*Aster linariifolius* is exceptionally dainty), such small astilbes as *Astilbe × crispa*, dwarf meadowsweet (*Filipendula palmata* 'Nana'), *Patrinia triloba*, dwarf goldenrods such as *Solidago japonica* 'Minutissima' and *S. spathulata* 'Nana', and the latest-blooming of the campions—*Silene schafta*. If you can offer acid soil and a cool climate there is the beautiful late gentian, *Gentiana sino-ornata*, and if you can't please this you probably can grow the less demanding *G. septemfida*. The gray foliage of *Sedum sieboldii* is ornamental all season and this flowers very late—too late for some northern gardens, in which case there's the similar, slightly earlier *S. cauticola*. Then there are the fluffy seedheads of such spring-blooming anemones as *Anemone pulsatilla*, and the ruby red spiny burrs of *Acaena novaezelandiae*, and such small late-blooming bulbs as the dainty autumn snowflake, *Leucojum autumnale*, and the perky little purple-flowered *Allium thunbergii* 'Ozawa's Variety'.

All rock garden plants don't come from the mountains—thrift (*Armeria maritima*), for instance, is found cliff-hanging on the coast. The main requirement is not so much rocks as sharp drainage. Raised beds, walls, and containers are other ways of ensuring that the soil does not get sodden. Plants at the base of small rock gardens, where every inch must be made to count, are sometimes at risk of being trodden on when tending or admiring plants growing higher up. Raised beds have the double advantage of lifting the plants away from the feet and closer to the eye. Dogs and small children, the one undeterred, the other attracted, by the gentle slope of a rock garden, are less likely to jump or climb into a raised bed with vertical sides. Because plants can flow over the edge without getting trodden on, raised beds increase the amount of planting space in small gardens, and if you've reached

Conifers give year-round form to this rock garden. In the center are two fine mature specimens of Juniperus communis *'Compressa'. Among the plants displayed like jewels against the rocks are* Aethionema *'Warley Rose',* Arenaria montana, dianthus, Verbascum dumulosum, *and* Hypericum olympicum. *The golden grass center right is* Deschampsia flexuosa *'Aurea'. (Garden of Jane Platt, Oregon; May)*

*The large rock garden at Longwood Gardens in Pennsylvania once housed an extensive collection of small plants but the planting has been simplified. Butterfly weed (*Asclepias tuberosa*) has naturalized, mingling with lavender and such easy-care perennials as* Alchemilla mollis, Lysimachia vulgaris, Coreopsis verticillata, *and sedums. (June)*

an age where the ground seems a long way down, raised beds help avoid backaches. Raised beds forming part of the structure and making no pretense of being natural may be more appropriate than rocks in a small city garden, but raised beds can also be informal and freestanding if constructed with rocks or stone. One innovative rock gardener made raised beds of stacked newspapers which, weathered to warm brown, resembled the flaking trunks of fallen trees.

Rock garden plants don't always demand rocks and the reverse also is true—rocks don't demand the collector's approach with little plants. Many American homeowners are blessed with large natural outcroppings, often covered with a scant skim of soil. The rock garden enthusiast will strive to develop at least part of this as a home for little plants but another approach, involving much less work, is to drape the rocks with more vigorous plants, none better than that all-American genus, phlox. The many selections of moss pink (*Phlox subulata*, *P. nivalis*, *P. bifida*, *P. douglasii*) and their sundry selections and hybrids do quite well in England (the newer cul-

tivars are among the plants most sought by my English friends), but to see them in America, the more vigorous kinds a tide of color spreading even into lawns, was to me a revelation. A perennials border alongside a rock garden would be incongruous but a cliff clothed in such large patches of color would make a fine backdrop for a border, with interest passing from cliff to border as the season progressed. Overlarge and overfancy flowers are out of character among little rock garden treasures or, for that matter, little rocks, but where the scale is large, whether natural or manmade, larger perennials could certainly be grown, preferably those of "unimproved" form. Letting such wildflowers as butterfly weed, columbines, and asters naturalize might be the solution to a large rock garden which, as the years go by, becomes burdensome to maintain.

For the collector, small garden equals small plants, but it isn't an inevitable equation; rather, it depends on what you want from your garden. If it is to be primarily a place to entertain, sunbathe, read a book, or sip a gin and tonic, a few large architectural plants might best fill the bill, especially in the

Above: *Planter boxes edging the deck make raised beds for such easy-to-grow rock garden plants as* Dianthus *'Tiny Rubies', yellow-flowered dwarf wall-flowers* (Erysimum), *and white-flowered yarrow* (Achillea). *Blue fescue softens the angle between planter and path. (Design by Susan Sasaki, El Cerrito, California, for the O'Banion family; April)*

The Theater Garden at Longwood Gardens demonstrates how arresting simplicity can be in a planting very suitable for small gardens. The perennials used are all of long-lasting good appearance and the garden remains attractive most of the year. Top: Sedum 'Autumn Joy' is massed, along with blue fescue, lamb's ears (Stachys byzantina), *and* Yucca glauca. *The yucca, shown here in autumn, middle,* and *encapsulated in ice, bottom, remains attractive all year long. (Pennsylvania; July, September, and January)*

warmer regions, where such handsome evergreens as *Fatsia japonica* require a little attention and retain their good looks the year around. If flowering perennials are wanted, make large groupings of a few that stay attractive right through the growing season. The theater garden at Longwood Gardens in Pennsylvania is a good example of this approach. *Sedum* 'Autumn Joy', attractive at least six months of the year, is used in quantity, combined with such foliage plants as yuccas, lamb's ears (*Stachys byzantina*) and blue fescue (*Festuca glauca*). The photographs that appear on pages 85 to 91 show a few of the many different approaches to the use of small plants and small spaces.

This retaining wall is also a rock garden, housing such plants as campanulas and hardy geraniums, with ferns in the shade at the foot of the wall. (Garden of Mr. and Mrs. N. Garland, England; June)

Raised beds are an alternative to a rock garden in an enthusiast's small garden. Plants in flower include Alchemilla mollis, *red* Rosa 'Marlena', *foamy pink* Ceanothus 'Marie Simon', *a blue-flowered* penstemon, *pink-flowered* Geranium dalmaticum, Salvia officinalis 'Tricolor', Hypericum × moseranum 'Tricolor', *and, at the back,* Clematis 'Mme. Edouard Andre', Cornus alba 'Elegantissima', *and* Chamaecyparis 'Boulevard'. *(Garden of Patricia Fountain, England; June)*

3 | Placing the Plants:

Size, Shape, Texture

New gardeners fret about spacing, while old hands know that it's a matter of compromise. Plant close for quick results, then divide, restrain or remove some plants in a year or two, or give them ample room and tolerate some bare earth at first or fill the gaps with annuals. A rough guide is one and a half to two feet apart for the majority of plants, half as much for small frontline plants, and at least four feet for those that grow very large and cannot be moved without risking killing the plant or damaging your back. *Aruncus dioicus* is one example of plants in the latter category.

Peonies shouldn't be crowded, they are hungry plants and mustn't be made to contend with other plants for moisture and nutrients. They transplant quite well but tend to put their energy into making roots rather than flowers for a couple of years after being disturbed. Oddly enough, the smallest of them, *Paeonia tenuifolia*, is apt to be intractable about being moved, which may explain its scarcity. Others that prefer not to be shifted around include *Aurinia saxatilis*, *Asclepias tuberosa*, poppy mallow (*Callirhoe*), *Gypsophila*, gas plant (*Dictamnus alba*), *Helleborus niger*, blue flax (*Linum perenne* and *L. nar-*

bonense), sea lavender (*Limonium*), and sundrops (*Oenothera missouriensis*). If these absolutely, positively must be moved, it can be done if you put your back into it and dig a soil ball deep and wide enough not to damage the roots. Do the job on a cloudy day when the weather is likely to stay mild for a week or two. Of course you will first have prepared the new hole!

Romantics like their borders full to overflowing, with no bare earth showing, while those of an engineering frame of mind prefer a less voluptuous approach. What do the *plants* prefer? Some one thing, some the other, and the same plant may enjoy the close company of its fellows where the climate isn't muggy, while the embracing arms of close companions may lead to rotting foliage where air movement is sluggish and the climate humid. Hairy foliage rots more readily than smooth and glossy leaves.

Worry less about spacing and give more thought to form. Combining plants is one of the most satisfying aspects of garden making, also the most challenging. Few of us manage a winning combination more than occasionally, and then by accident more often than

93

most are willing to admit. There's so much to juggle with: shape and color of flower; flowering time; size and shape of plant; quality of foliage and whether it is matte and light-absorbing or shiny and light-reflecting.

There's also the personality of the plant to think about. Tall bearded irises can be grown in any part of the garden that gets sufficient sun but they are at their best in a structured setting—they don't look like meadow flowers, and paving complements them better than grass. A Tennessee gardener gave me a fern known in his area simply as "sun fern" (later identified as *Thelypteris kunthii*) because it tolerates full southern sun although, in the wild, it is a woodland fern. I thought this would be a valuable addition to one of my sunny beds, but because I associate such large ferns with shade it bothers me to see it in sun even though it thrives. Little *Cheilanthes lanosa*, however, grows in sun in the wild and looks right in sun in the garden.

Hostas are also associated with shade, and, gray-leaved plants being associated with sun, I found it upsetting to see hostas side by side with lamb's ears (*Stachys byzantina*). These are gut reactions, not reasoned ones, for in some parts of North America (San Francisco in particular) plants that elsewhere need shade grow happily in sun, and in my own Virginia garden lamb's ears is happier in light shade. Reason should not triumph—if you don't like some combination in your garden, for whatever reason, change it. Equally, if you *do* like it, keep it—doing things differently makes for imaginative and interesting, if sometimes shocking, gardens. If we all looked alike, dressed alike, talked alike, and had the same opinions, how boring, if peaceful, life would be.

Fortunately most perennials reach maturity in a year or two, so our envisioned schemes can soon be assessed, and changed if

Because we associate hostas with shade, they create a feeling of unease among the lamb's ears, lavender, and catmint in the Dutch Garden at Hestercombe, England, and their lime green leaves look chlorotic in association with silver-gray. Hestercombe, in the process of restoration, was designed by Sir Edwin Lutyens and Gertrude Jekyll between 1904 and 1909. (Late August)

they do not please. One friend with a beautiful garden said it resulted not from a well-conceived plan but from "constant tinkering."

THE IMPORTANCE OF CONTRAST

What companions shall we give a plant to show it at its best? The willowy, fair-haired heroine of many a book chooses as best friend either a plain Jane (with a beautiful character, of course) or someone equally attractive but a different type: short, vivacious, with brown eyes and dark curly hair. Whether friends are actually chosen for such reasons is open to debate, but the idea is sound: it is contrast we seek.

There is maximum contrast of analogous colors and of form, left, *between the scarlet pokers of* Kniphofia *'Prince Igor' and the rudbeckia's sheet of bright yellow daisies. The other pair,* right, *are more closely related in color and the scarlet of* Lychnis chalcedonica *is less dense, so the contrast is primarily of form, with colors tending to merge.*

Contrast can come from shape, color, or texture. Color contrasts might be between two different colors (red and yellow, for example), or different tints or shades of the same color (pale blue and dark blue, for example). The more vivid the colors, the greater the contrast. Maximum contrast occurs between plants of different strong colors and different well-defined shapes. Plants of similar color but different shape, or markedly different texture, also contrast. Lesser, but sometimes sufficient contrast, could come from two plants of similar shape and color but different flower form.

The shape and color of a plant influences the mood it evokes. Photographers and artists learn that verticals portray strength, horizontals passivity. Remember those old photographs of grandfather standing behind the chair, grandmother sitting down? Now imagine three standing men to one sitting woman. Overwhelming, isn't it? The same with plants: those of strongest form are best used sparingly, singly or in small groups depending on their individual bulk and the size of the whole composition.

We want contrast in form, but not too much of it. Blobs of form are as restless as blobs of color, so we can't just alternate different forms: chunky, spiky, plumy, cloudy, floppy (they begin to sound like the seven dwarfs) and so on. Plants of strong form stand out better if surrounded by drifts of those less visually assertive in size and shape, though not necessarily in color.

Plants are not static things and character may change with age, or be changed by the gardener. Young plants of snakeroot (*Cimicifuga racemosa*) are spiky, but in long-established clumps, or several clumps tightly grouped, the spikes are so numerous and so close together that they merge into a softer but massive form. Rue (*Ruta graveolens*) and the santolinas can be clipped into architectural domes (they won't then flower) or be allowed to assume their more casual natural habit.

The character of a species may have been so changed by hybridizing that it calls for different treatment than the wildling. Primroses (*Primula vulgaris*), for instance, are woodland plants best suited to informal surroundings, as are the subtly colored Barnhaven hybrids. On the other hand, the brilliantly colored hybrids sold in pots at garden centers toward the end of winter are so chunky in shape and weak of constitution that they have become bedding plants for use in more

formal surroundings. A color change alone, without an accompanying change in form can so alter the character of a plant that it calls for a different setting. This becomes apparent if one compares the prominence of a plant in bloom with its inconspicuousness at other times.

Similar form, different color: Yellow verbascum and white clary sage (a selected form of Salvia sclarea*). If these were the same color they would lose individuality and merge into a single color shape. (Pennsylvania; late June)*

Similar color, different form: Oenothera missouriensis *leans over* Coreopsis 'Moonbeam'. *Contrast in shape and texture is particularly important in monochromatic color schemes. (Virginia; July)*

Combining plants is rather like assembling a well-balanced list of guests. Too many dominating individuals and they'll upstage each other, so we need mostly less forceful types, with just enough lively personalities to make the party go with a swing. Let's take a look at some plant personalities.

SPIKES, SPIRES, AND SPECIMENS

Setting tall plants back behind shorter ones is the logical thing to do but not always the right one. The back of the border usually is the best place for plants with tall spires of flower and undistinguished or short-lived foliage, the foxtail lilies *Eremurus elwesii* and *E. robustus*, for example. *Ligularia* 'The Rocket' might also benefit from being placed behind lower-growing plants: the handsome foliage earns for it frontline placement but it wilts so dejectedly when the sun hits it that kindly concealment by other plants may serve it (and you) best. Those verbascums with coarse green leaves could go at the back (but not the gray-felted ones), and probably *Thermopsis villosa*, because it flowers too briefly to earn a more prominent place. Tall plants that need to be staked are also usually best at the back of the border, where the supports are easier to hide.

Some perennials are of such massive size or imposing character that they are at their most impressive as single specimens, and when a tall plant has attractive, long-lasting foliage it would be a pity to conceal it behind other plants. A bench set near one edge of a lawn, perhaps on its own little apron of paving, flanked by such substantial perennials as goatsbeard (*Aruncus dioicus*), the giant rhubarb (*Rheum palmatum*), or *Rodgersia aesculifolia* would show these plants to advan-

*In this combination of sweet Williams (*Dianthus barbatus*), lupines, and a delphinium, the spires are strongest in form but color dominates. Notice that although they are further back than the blue delphinium, and shorter than the deep pink lupines, the strongest note is struck by the pale yellow lupines, followed by the white of the sweet Williams.*

Shape is accentuated by the presence of the gray santolina among the green and it also draws attention to a planting that might otherwise go unnoticed. Frequent light clippings are needed to maintain the clean outline essential to this architectural grouping. (Virginia)

Euphorbia characias wulfenii makes a fine evergreen specimen in mild winter zones. (England; June)

Gold-thread cypress (Chamaecyparis pisifera 'Filifera Aurea') makes a perfect backdrop for the green-striped butter yellow leaves of Canna × generalis 'Striatus'. The canna leaves are especially handsome from spring to midsummer, then the orange flowers rise up on pinkish purple stems in a splendid, unabashed gaudiness best isolated from other flowers. (Virginia; early September)

tage, as it also would the tall weeping astilbes 'Ostrich Plume' (pink) and 'Professor van der Wielen' (white). These are, of course, herbaceous plants, out of sight through winter. In the milder zone you might prefer the year-round structure of evergreen shrubs alongside your seat.

The plume poppies (*Macleaya*) grace any scene with their seven-foot spires of airy fairy flowers of white (*M. cordata*) or buff (*M. microcarpa*). Soft in form and subtle in color, they are among the cloudlike plants that mix so well with other colors but are exceptional in that they have large, lovely leaves, rounded and deeply lobed, soft green with white veins to match the silky white underside revealed when a breeze flutters the leaf. The leaves are spaced along the slender self-supporting

stems from the ground up, those near the base as much as eight inches wide. For all these reasons, this is one perennial that should go where the whole plant can be seen. The ell of a house or the corner of a courtyard would display them well and also corral their roaming roots. They are winter dormant, and a large bare patch of earth in such a conspicuous spot might not always be acceptable, but plume poppy roots are tough enough to compete with a ground-cover plant such as ajuga or periwinkle.

Acanthus leaves were the inspiration for the sculpted leaves on Corinthian capitals. The mauve and white flowers, in stately spires, are a bit like foxgloves. *Acanthus mollis* and *A. spinosus* usually flower freely in midsummer. *Acanthus mollis latifolius* flowers sparingly and often not at all. Beautiful foliage is not the only reason to put acanthus somewhere more conspicuous than at the back of a border: the hooded flowers, rewarding at close inspection, are a recessive pale mauve color easily overlooked when put behind brighter colors. The plants also spread so rapidly that it is advisable to give them a place to themselves.

If large perennials with good foliage are to be fitted into a border, perhaps they could go at one end, toward the front. The narrow end of an island or peninsula bed might be better still because there, surrounded on three sides by lawn or paving, they would achieve the status of specimens. This is also a good place for such show-offs as the hibiscus hybrids with flowers of dinner-plate size. If these must have companions, they get along well with large but graceful plants such as the various selections of *Miscanthus sinensis*. The wild *Hibiscus moscheutos* (available from wildflower nurseries) is more refined and a better mixer. The corner junction of two borders is another good spot for specimen plants, and so is the narrow inward curve of a free-form border, where the whole plant is visible as one passes by, yet still set back in the overall composition as befits its height.

Nowhere are tall spires of pale colored flowers better displayed than against the dark background of a close-clipped hedge. The hedge should be a little higher than the tallest spire, otherwise its top edge forms a horizontal line that seems to slice off the vertical reach of the plant. Lacking a hedge, perhaps a single dark-leaved evergreen could be so placed that pale spikes would be silhouetted against it, at least from some angles: a big advantage of the traditional hedge-backed border is that by controlling the angle of view, it makes the placing of plants less problematical.

Symmetry, and the anchoring tubbed evergreens, give Crambe cordifolia *an architectural quality. The seat is set back in the center of an expansive border, but it forms a unit complete in itself that could be copied in much smaller gardens. Be aware, though, that crambe has a pungent odor you might not appreciate alongside a seat. (Anglesey Abbey, England; June)*

'Skyrocket' junipers flank the seat, their strong upward thrust contributing stability and form among the amorphous perennials. (Designer Doug Bayley, Seattle; August)

Rodgersia aesculifolia *holds pride of place at one end of an island bed, where its bold foliage contrasts with the ferny leaves of* Selinum tenuifolium, *which contrasts in turn with the large leaves of a hosta on its other side. (Garden of Mrs. N. A. Laurie, England; July)*

Acanthus mollis, *isolated between driveway and house path, makes a hedgelike summer screen. (Garden of Susan and Alden Buckles, Washington; August)*

Tall pale spikes include some foxgloves and hollyhocks, foxtail lilies such as *Eremurus robustus*, *Cimicifuga racemosa*, such white or pale yellow verbascums as *Verbascum chaixii*, and *Thermopsis villosa* (also sold as *T. caroliniana*), which blots its copybook only with brevity of bloom. Then there are delphiniums—the name brings blue to our inner eye but there are exquisite white ones such as 'Galahad'. If you can't grow delphiniums, try the white fireweed (so called because the pink-flowered species tends to spring up in burnt-over areas), *Epilobium angustifolium* 'Album', which has slightly looser spikes than delphiniums. This is easy to grow—you might think *too* easy if the beautiful self-sowing pink wildling grows in your region. Like a good many other native plants, it is more restrained where it isn't quite so much at home, but in any case the white form is less invasive than the pink type.

Not all spires have dominant personalities. Those of *Veronicastrum virginicum* (synonymous with *Veronica virginica*), in its commonest soft white form, are rendered subtler by their slenderness and narrow leaves. When extreme slenderness is combined with gray

lance-shaped leaves in *Lysimachia ephemerum*, the effect is ethereal. Presumably the specific name *ephemerum* refers to its ghostlike appearance, for the flowers are not fleeting as it suggests. Don't by the way, think that you have the wrong thing if you grow this lysimachia from seed or buy young one-year plants: the basal leaves are greener and rounder than those along the flower stalk of mature plants. Graced with narrow gray-green leaves and little snapdragon flowers, the slender three-foot spires of *Linaria purpurea* dance lightly through the landscape where, quite likely, they have sown themselves—'Canon Went' is a pretty pale pink form, readily available.

Nor are all spiky plants statuesque. The short and stocky *Liatris* 'Kobold' has rods of flowers as stiff as pokers. The stiffness and

Epilobium angustifolium *'Album' is mildly invasive but much less so than the pink one. Here its white spires contrast with a cloud of* Crambe cordifolia. *(England; July)*

hard color benefit from the company of fluffily white *Achillea ptarmica* 'The Pearl' or, as an edging plant, the shorter *A. p.* 'Ballerina' or 'Snowball'. If you can't cope with the invasiveness of these, try one of the dwarf gypsophilas. Other liatris vary a lot in height and stiffness. The tallest ones will need supports so put these well back in the border where their props will be less apparent.

The spikes of the two-foot tall knotweed *Polygonum milettii* are so long and slender that, despite their strong crimson color, the plant suggests grace more than strength, and the stubby pale lilac ones of *P. bistorta* 'Superbum' have only moderate upward thrust. The multiple creamy spikes of *Sanguisorba canadensis* merge into a soft and bushy form which, for subtle late-flowering contrast pairs admirably with the platelike inflorescences of *Sedum* 'Autumn Joy'.

Reversing the order of things, with the spike in subordinate role, the violet-blue flowers of *Salvia × superba* 'May Night' contrast strikingly with the yellow plates of *Achillea* 'Gold Plate' or 'Coronation Gold', but color contrast from another plant isn't always wanted: the blending colors from a medley of Russell lupines is sufficient unto itself.

The torch lilies, or red-hot-pokers, (*Kniphofia*) are a mixed bunch and need to be considered individually: the dainty palest primrose wands of 'Little Maid' (as frail, alas, in constitution as in appearance) would be overwhelmed by any but the gentlest of companions—*Coreopsis* 'Moonbeam' would do nicely (similar color, contrasting form), whilst the many glowing red and orange kinds can more than hold their own when combined with the bright yellow daisies of *Rudbeckia fulgida* for a brilliant patch of contrasting color and form. The very tall ones have an overabundance of grassy, floppy foliage, best kept out of sight well back in the bed.

There are also spikes for the front edge of the border. Most astilbes have plumed flowers but in the little *Astilbe chinensis* 'Pumila', the flowers are packed into stiff, fairly narrow inflorescences; small this may be but of assertive character nonetheless. It is a useful edging plant and sturdy enough to discourage encroachment of most lawn grasses—not, however, Bermuda grass. Dwarf knotweeds such as *Polygonum affine* and *P. vacciniifolium* also make good edging plants. Veronicas, with their softer spikes, can be placed as required by their varying heights except that those forms of *Veronica spicata* with mats of gray basal foliage, *V. spicata incana* being the most silvery, should go at the front, where they make good edging plants if one can forgive the tendency of the flower spikes to tumble.

A few plants have amusing curly spikes. These add a touch of whimsy that appeals to the child in us. Burnet (*Sanguisorba obtusa*) and the swan-necked loosestrife (*Lysimachia clethroides*) are two such plants, the latter quite invasive, so best not mixed with other perennials.

I can think of only one hardy perennial with spires of red flowers, the cardinal flower, *Lobelia cardinalis*. It is not an adaptable plant, needing abundant moisture and preferring a little shade. It also seems to need frequent changes of soil, which limits its use in mixed plantings. It is not long-lived but under ideal conditions it will self-sow. Hybrids such as 'Queen Victoria', with purple leaves, are even more stunning, but much less hardy. Cardinal flower is at its best in surroundings otherwise color-quiet: with lots of green, with water, or against a gray stone wall.

What one has to decide before electing to put a plant at the back of the border is whether the flowers are the best thing it has to offer or whether it is the foliage. If it is the foliage, then it is foliage height that must be considered when placing the plant. When, in summer, yuccas hold aloft their plumes of waxy white flowers it calls for a "garden open today" sign so that all may come and admire, but gorgeous though the flowers are, they are temporal, while the leaves are a year-round feature. The hardy yuccas that sit on the ground (those that make trunks are less hardy) should be placed where the architectural V-shaped clumps of evergreen swordlike leaves can be enjoyed when you make your solitary peregrinations during the winter months. *Yucca glauca* and *Y. filamentosa* are the names most frequently encountered. *Yucca glauca* has narrow gray leaf rapiers with a barely perceptible threadlike white margin that doesn't peel into curly filaments like *Y. filamentosa*. The flower spikes—less often borne than in some other kinds—rise about waist high. Watching the flower stalk of true *Y. filamentosa* develop is a Jack-and-the-beanstalk experience as up, up, up it goes to a height of ten feet or more. A backward tilt of the head is needed to admire it, so nothing is lost by putting the plant in the foreground, greatly to the advantage of the stiff leaf swords edged with curling white filaments. Yuccas such as 'Golden Sword', which has softer leaves striped with yellow, are usually sold under the *Y. filamentosa* name but apparently belong to a different species. The flower spikes attain about five feet in height. All are plants for prominent foreground positions. I recommend that you wear some kind of protective glasses when weeding around yuccas with stiff, needle-pointed leaves (*Y. glauca*, *Y. filamentosa*)—skin heals but they could damage an eye.

Rudbeckia maxima—evergray to about 25°F—starts its year as a handsome clump about fifteen inches high of large egg-shaped blue-green leaves very like some of the large blue-leaved hostas but with a smoother, satiny surface. In summer smaller upward pointing leaves mount rigid glaucous stems that hoist aloft solitary yellow-rayed black-coned shuttlecock flowers to a height of as much as ten feet, the whole plant conveying a feeling of upward motion. If anything is to go in front of this it should be a carpeting plant, a purple-leaved ajuga perhaps, or the yellow creeping Charlie (*Lysimachia nummularia* 'Aurea'), both of which thrive in the same kind of moisture-retentive soil preferred by the rudbeckia.

For the foreground of beds with sharply drained soil there are some good gray-leaved biennials or short-lived perennials in *Salvia argentea* and *Verbascum bombyciferum*. Nor is the common mullein (*Verbascum thapsus*) to be despised. All have spires or plumes of pretty flowers that are, however, secondary to the

The silvery felted rosettes of Verbascum bombyciferum *are far too handsome to be tucked back out of sight. Here they combine with* Lonicera nitida *'Baggesen's Gold'. (Denmans, West Sussex, England; September)*

Give the handsome glaucous foliage of Helictotrichon sempervirens *(situated to the right) a place at the front of the border. Plants growing behind will not be concealed by its fountain spray of flowering plumes. (Garden of Kathleen Hudson, England; July)*

beauty of the leaves. *Salvia argentea* covers a circle of ground eighteen inches across with salvers of scalloped leaves surfaced in silvery plush. The verbascums make great rosettes of flannel-textured pale gray leaves that glisten when the sun's rays reflect from moisture held by the silky surface hairs.

One of the nicest spiky plants is king's spear, *Asphodeline lutea*. Flowers in spikes usually open in progression, up or down the spike, and they look a bit tawdry when half the spike is dead. The flowers of king's spear open randomly, one here, one there, all along the spike, and a shiny round seedpod develops where each faded flower has been. But that isn't all, there is a basal swirl of glaucous

linear leaves that it would be a shame to hide. How it behaves varies with where you live, winter dormant in cold regions, winter green in warmer ones where, however, it may go briefly dormant during hot, dry summers.

"SEE-THROUGH" PLANTS

Another kind of plant that can go at the front of the border, even though tall, is what I think of as a see-through plant—one with a veillike inflorescence through which one can glimpse the plants behind. Ornamental grasses are a rich source of these, with *Stipa gigantea* one of the best. *Verbena bonariensis* is the best

Peach-colored alstroemerias can be glimpsed through the dotted veiling of Verbena bonariensis, with Verbascum chaixii behind. (Garden of Christopher Lloyd, Great Dixter, England; July)

haze of the six-foot *Patrinia scabiosifolia*. The trilisa is a plant of the southeastern coastal plain, related to liatris but with flowers in more graceful branched pyramids held over a plinth of basal foliage.

Several of the taller salvias have flowers sufficiently small and scattered that plants behind are not concealed. *Salvia guaranitica* is one of the best for the warmer parts of the country, blooming abundantly and continually through summer and autumn. Blackberry lily (*Belamcanda chinensis*) has such handsome fans of leaves, as much as three feet high in rich, moist soil, that it would be a pity to hide them. The orange flowers are vivid, but small, and so daintily distributed over branched sprays rising well above the leaves that you can see through them to the plants behind. This one, though, is better displayed against something of solid color—a conifer, perhaps, golden for a warm color scheme, blue-gray for a cooler one.

The common name for *Thalictrum rochebrunianum* is lavender mist, but for a real misty effect the meadow rue to get is *T. delavayi* (also known as *T. dipterocarpum*), with myriads of close-set small flowers merging into a haze. The flowers of *T. rochebrunianum* are large for a thalictrum, and sufficiently spaced to be countable. The lavender-violet of thalictrum flowers is a color easily overlooked if the plant is put at the back of a bed, and although *T. rochebrunianum* is six feet tall it is light and lacy enough for the front. A problem, though, is that it may need staking, and stakes are very conspicuous at the front of a bed. One of the burnets, *Sanguisorba tenuifolia purpurea*, is equally tall when in bloom but doesn't need staking. From a clump of attractive bright green pinnate leaves rise slender six-foot stems loosely branched at the top and tipped with cylindrical maroon flowers. Any color can go behind; I like to use the

known see-through plant with colorful flowers. This is a short-lived, rather tender perennial that often returns each year from self-sown seed when the parent plant has died from cold or senility. It is tall, to five feet, but insubstantial, with the leaves at ground level and wiry stems with scattered clusters of lavender flowers. Yellow flowers, both bright and pale, look particularly good seen through the verbena's dotted lavender veiling. Late in the season I enjoy a similar color scheme in reverse, with the two-foot *Trilisa paniculata* glimpsed through the brilliant greenish yellow

The small, sparse flower heads of Dianthus carthusianorum would be lost further back in the border. Here several plants were put close together as a "see-through" group in front of the shrub rose 'Bonica'. (Virginia; early June)

annual purple perilla, of matching but denser color. The sanguisorba prefers moist soil but makes do with any that does not get dry.

Wryly, I read in a catalogue that *Dianthus carthusianorum* is best "planted behind a lower mass of foliage to mask the leggy stems." It's all in the point of view, but I perceive it as a see-through plant. It does, of course, depend also on what is behind, with plants presenting a fairly solid patch of color usually most effective. The dianthus has numerous wiry two- to three-foot stalks topped with small heads of bright pink flowers rising from tufts of narrow leaves. Too sparse a patch isn't effective, so space young plants about six inches apart in groups of five or more.

Painted daisies (*Chrysanthemum coccineum*) do strike me as leggy, which makes them excellent for cutting. Although it hides the basal clumps of bright green ferny leaves, something low and billowy in front is usually an improvement, as it also is when a plant's leaves appear very early in the year and start to die by flowering time. This is a characteristic of some ornamental onions and is natural to the plant, not the result of faulty cultivation. *Allium giganteum* behaves this way—such a handsome plant, though not reliably permanent, with its knobs of purple flowers the size of tennis balls rearing up on four-foot stalks. Put a group of these behind a mound of *Coreopsis verticillata* and the flowers can be admired unbesmirched by its dying leaves.

CLOUDS

At the other extreme from spikes come the cloudlike plants and soft, billowy mounds of romantic mood, the inflorescences, or the combination of inflorescence and foliage, as fluffily soft as bubble-bath suds or the clouds one looks down on from an airplane, ethereal yet dense enough to conceal what lies behind it. These tie together plants of brighter color or stronger form in much the same way as baby's breath (*Gypsophila*) in a flower arrangement.

The impression of softness or solidity is influenced by the shape of the plant, the color and size of the flowers, and how closely packed they are. When the flowers are numerous but small, the form billowy, and the color soft white or leavened with green, the plant looks buoyant and insubstantial. The largest of these is the mistily massive *Crambe cordifolia*. Japanese fleeceflower, *Polygonum cuspidatum*, is another large airy-looking plant, but unfortunately too invasive to be safe in mixed company. The five-foot clump-forming, long-flowering *P. paniculatum* doesn't seem to have crossed the Atlantic yet—keep an eye open for it, its creamy flowers have a similarly frothy look to *Artemisia lactiflora. Lespedeza thunbergii* 'Albiflora' is less ethereal than *Crambe cordifolia* but one of the very best plants for softening a planting. A good mixer, it is billowy in shape with refined foliage and soft white flowers. It keeps its place and is never quarrelsome, varying in height from three to six feet, depending on soil, climate, and how hard you cut it back in spring. It needs a companion with flowers of a brighter color and my candidate is *Aster* 'Alma

Potschke', which flowers at the same time.

Best known of the middle-height diaphanous plants is *Gypsophila paniculata*. Many recently invented "common" names are purposeless, evoking no image and no more familiar than the botanical name, nor easier to pronounce, but the old folk names are often poetically descriptive. Gypsophila is "baby's breath," but this name is also applied to *Galium aristatum* (often confused, according

Lespedeza thunbergii 'Albiflora' *with* Aster 'Alma Potschke' *and* Elymus glaucus. *(Virginia; early October)*

Galium aristatum
is a more diapha-
nous plant than
gypsophila. An
"over the fence"
plant, passed on
from one gardener
to another, it is
seldom sold by
nurseries. (Massa-
chusetts; July)

to *Hortus Third*, with *G. mollugo*, the first being upright, the second sprawling). *Galium aristatum* is an even more ethereal plant than gypsophila, as nebulous as breath on a frosty morning. Only in some of the flowering grasses (*Panicum virgatum*, for instance) is a hazier look to be found. The name *gypsophila* is sometimes used for *Euphorbia corollata*, recognizing a similar airy-fairyness. Soil pH might influence your decision if choosing between them—gypsophila for alkaline soils, euphorbia for acid ones. A single plant of gypsophila will bush out and hide bare earth where Oriental poppies or foxtail lilies

(*Eremurus*) have gone summer dormant. Ethereal though it looks, gypsophila is a heavyweight that needs firm corseting with canes and laces. It takes three plants of the euphorbia, about six inches apart, to fill a similar space; they'll then be mutually self-supporting and they don't mind being crowded. Widely spaced between clumps of bearded irises they'll cast a kindly veil over the summer-shabby iris leaves while still letting sufficient light and air reach the rhizomes.

Chalky white angel's-breath, *Achillea ptarmica*, is not as wraithlike as the name suggests but, in the double form usually grown, is a good fluffy-looking plant for the foreground if you can contend with its wandering ways. For a really cloudy look at the front of the border there are few better plants than *Calamintha nepeta* (*C. nepetoides* of catalogue). What the milky blue flowers lack in size they make up for in profusion, keeping up the display for a very long time on a plant about fifteen inches high and rather more across. The small leaves are mintily aromatic.

Some flowers are of such a bright, sparkling white, and so closely packed, that they dominate a planting even when soft in form. *Iberis sempervirens* is such a plant, if grown in sun, and *Arabis procurrens* another. If grown in light shade they flower less profusely and become less assertive. Such plants are excellent where definition is needed—edging a border, for instance, or for brilliant contrast with other bright, clear colors—but when something light and airy is wanted, or an understated plant to meld together showier ones, select from those—the majority—of a less pure white, or with flowers less densely packed. Strawberry geranium (*Saxifraga stolonifera*) gives a white haze at ground level, and London pride (*Saxifraga × urbium*) a pale pink haze. *Tiarella cordifolia* has a fluffier look well described by its common name, foamflower: creamy white foam as a rule, pale buff or soft pink in *T. cordifolia collina* or *T. wherryi*.

One of the daintiest midheight plants (two to three feet) is *Gillenia trifoliata*, called bowman's root by some, while others use the prettier, more descriptive "fawn's breath." The myriad starry white flowers are loosely spaced and the color modified by pink calyces. The taller *Gaura lindheimeri* is equally good, with delicate white flowers fading to pale pink on willowy stems that branch into besoms of thread-fine red stems as the season progresses. This needs full sun. For light shade

there is the less ethereal *Francoa ramosa*, with wands of pink or creamy white flowers, spikelike in young plants, merging into soft bushiness when mature enough to produce multiple stems.

Astermoea mongolica makes mounds or drifts of twiggy stems clad in small leaves and liberally strewn with petite double daisies of a softer white than the similar but larger flowers of feverfew (*Chrysanthemum parthenium*). Its delicate appearance is belied by a sturdy constitution. If it likes the spot allocated to it, spread is rapid. Each small white star in the flower constellations of garlic chives (*Allium tuberosum*) has a green center, resulting in a cooler, more restful appearance than would have come from unrelieved white. Feverfew's flowers, whether single or double, are bright white, but it remains a good mixer because they are softened by ferny foliage. Similarly, the white form of rose mullein (*Lychnis coronaria* 'Alba') has abundant gray leaves to offset the snowy white flowers. Whether *Boltonia* 'Snowbank' is perceived as soft or showy depends on its neighbors. The white flowers are borne in such abundance that they obliterate the glaucous foliage and make a billowy mound of white. Placed next to soft gray foliage—*Artemisia* 'Powis Castle', for example—it merges in quietly, but put it next to bright pink *Aster* 'Alma Potschke' and the white becomes strong by contrast. This is an example of a plant with white flowers being more dominant than its colored counterpart: *Boltonia* 'Pink Beauty' has flowers of a subtle pale lilac that contrasts with the bright pink of the aster without vying with it for attention as 'Snowbank' does.

Some forms of *Astrantia major* have greenish white flowers that look positively grubby, which sounds disparaging but isn't meant to be; astrantias are endearing plants of great charm. One selection is called 'Shaggy', and that name describes them all. Each flower is composed of a dome of tightly packed florets within a ruff of bracts. Some forms of this variable species are an almost solid muted pink but most are basically white stained with green or pink. Such off-whites make much better mixers and blenders than the sparkling whites that could be flowery ads for a winning brand of detergent. The white form of red valerian (*Centranthus ruber* 'Alba') is a similar "other brand" white, and so is true valerian (*Valeriana officinalis*). The tiny but tightly packed white daisies of *Aster lateriflorus* 'Horizontalis' have deep pink eyes, giving an overall off-white or buff effect that fits in almost anywhere. For late season bloom *Eupatorium rugosum* is another soft, somewhat fluffy looking off-white.

Plants of soft form and subdued color are the harmonizers and unifiers. As demonstrated with the boltonias, they need not be white; pastels can tranquilize as well and sometimes better. Pale lavenders and lilacs are particularly good, including the ubiquitous wild joe-pye weed (*Eupatorium fistulosum*) with its fuzzy domed heads of dusty pink. This is a big plant, and it spreads rapidly. A similar soft smoky pink is found in the low, sprawling *Phuopsis stylosa* (synonym *Crucianella stylosa*), seen at its best frothing over gray paving.

The common name for the sub-shrubby *Caryopteris* is blue mist, and this is apt, the featheriness of the flowers rendered still more hazy by the soft gray foliage, true also of another sub-shrub, *Perovskia*, or Russian sage. One form of sea lavender (*Limonium latifolium*) is called 'Blue Cloud' and this too is descriptive of the diaphanous sprays of violet-blue flowers. This is a recessive color, so put the plant near the front, where the large, shining leaves will also show to advantage. Blue stars (*Amsonia tabernaemontana*) is one

of the best neutralizers as is *Baptisia australis* where there is room for its considerable size.

Thalictrums are all of gentle demeanor, cloudlike in the white or pale lavender *Thalictrum dipterocarpum*, fluffily soft in the white or pale lilac *T. aquilegifolium*, and pale lemon *T. speciosissimum*. *Thalictrum minus* (synonym *T. adiantifolium*) is a misty chartreuse to look down upon; fennel (*Foeniculum vulgare*) contributes a similar gauzy greenish yellow at eye level.

Perennials such as these, gentle in form and color, are the basics in serene compositions. Don't, however, put two of similar color (especially off-white) and form together as they will cancel each other out. Intersperse them with old-fashioned roses, lavender, and lots of gray foliage for the romantic kind of garden that many prefer and none dislike. With the basics in place, such tranquil combinations can then absorb and be enlivened by such flamboyant bright pinks and magentas as *Sedum spectabile* 'Brilliant', *Geranium psilostemon*, and *Lychnis coronaria*.

Plants soft in form are often also soft in color. Just as mist softens a landscape, so these misty plants give a softer look to a planting, at the same time enhancing by their subtlety neighboring plants of stronger form or color. But some plants combine softness of form with brilliance of color. From *Alchemilla mollis* comes a foam of bright chartreuse, but although this greenish yellow is a strong color it is such a good mixer that alchemilla is one of the most used plants for color scheming.

If you seek a cloud of really strong acidic yellow, look to *Patrinia scabiosifolia*, airy in form, brilliant in color, or to the more substantial woad (*Isatis tinctoria*), which is perfectly capable of shouting down its neighbors with its brilliant color. Down nearer ground level equally brilliant color is allied with soft form in *Aurinia saxatilis*. It is less versatile than

The white cloud to the right consists of three plants, six inches apart, of Euphorbia corollata. *Behind it is* Lespedeza thunbergii *'Albiflora', not yet in flower. Other plants include* Arundo donax *'Variegata', top left,* Abelia × grandiflora, *white physostegia wandering among three of the shrub-sized, ruby red* Lagerstroemia *'Victor', gray* Artemisia *'Huntington', and* Spiraea *'Gold Flame', bottom left. Plants not in flower include blue* Aster *'Climax' (in front of the* Arundo*), pale pink shrubby* Ceanothus *'Marie Simon',* agapanthus, Allium tuberosum, *and the late-flowering* Chrysanthemum nipponicum, *bottom right. There is a large dogwood in the background. (Virginia; August)*

off-whites and pastels and at its best in sparkling combination with other bright colors.

SPRAWLERS

Sprawling is sometimes brought about by soil, site, or climate. If one writer says that a plant needs staking, another that it does not, both may be reporting truthfully what they have observed. Not all plants benefit from moist, rich soil. Platycodons fall over in a lightly shaded part of my garden where the soil has been "improved" but remain upright in full sun and sandy, less fertile soil. *Gaura lindheimeri* sprawls in cool, wet climates but remains upright in hot, dry ones unless bowed down by overhead watering. Plants in more shade than they like will lean toward the light.

Some plants will always have to be staked—tall delphiniums for one, others only if exposed to wind, which can be particularly troublesome when funneled along a wall or solid fence. Many perennials, especially the taller daisies, can be kept compact by pinching or shearing: asters, chrysanthemums, helianthus, and heleniums are neater for this treatment. A plant may tend to sprawl when young or widely spaced, becoming self-supporting, or mutually supportive, when bigger or planted closer to its neighbors. With others it is the reverse: the outer stems of *Sedum* 'Autumn Joy' splay out if clumps get overcrowded. If you plant close to begin with and want to postpone division as long as possible, perennials such as this, with compact root systems, can be sliced round with a sharp spade, lifted just enough to detach their roots from the ground, then set back where they came from. Do this at the time of year recommended for planting in your region, usually autumn where summers are hot, spring where winters are very cold.

Alchemilla mollis foams over a path and low hedge. *The soft form and bright but blendable color of alchemilla make it a favorite plant of artistic gardeners in cool summer regions, where it is used in countless ways. It is not as versatile where summers are hot. (England; July)*

Campanula poscharskyana makes long, trailing flowering stems. Here they have been encouraged to climb a topiary yew. (Great Dixter, England; June)

Many plants are by nature trailers or sprawlers. Attempting to make these stand upright will be a losing battle, so the trailing characteristic is best turned to advantage. The smaller ones can flow over and soften a path edge, ledge, or boulder. Some will even climb a bit by weaving their way in and out of the stems of taller neighbors: *Campanula poscharskyana* and the less robust form 'Elizabeth Frost' are good at this. So are *Lithospermum diffusum* (also known as *Lithodora diffusa*), several of the hardy geraniums, especially *Geranium wallichianum* 'Buxton's Blue', *Viola cornuta* (the species especially, in blue or white) and Kenilworth ivy (*Cymbalaria muralis*). I've watched the tiny-leaved *Linaria aequitriloba*, usually considered a carpeter, climb eight inches up a pine tree by insinuating its threadlike stems under the platelets of bark.

With sprawlers the trick is to find some way of displaying them that doesn't force them into postures they resist. They are well suited to containers and raised beds, and after admiring *Clematis recta mandshurica* cascading down a bank in the display garden of nurseryman Andre Viette, I put what I thought was the same plant in a whiskey barrel, where instead of flowing down it grew determinedly up. Mine was the species, *C. recta*, which grows upright, as the name indicates—only the variety *C. r. mandshurica* has decumbent stems.

Many of the catmints (*Nepeta*) flow out as the season progresses, to mingle with and sometimes climb into their neighbors. A single clump of the one called 'Six Hills Giant' spreads each year into a great gray-green mound four feet in diameter, remaining attractive all season. It will smother lowly neighbors but if there is a low-branched tree behind, or a shrub with leafless lower branches, it will wend its way harmlessly up and into it. A good many roses benefit from this concealment of

Clematis recta mandshurica cascades down a bank in a foam of creamy white in the display garden of nurseryman Andre Viette. (Virginia; June)

their gawky framework, and catmint's soft blue flowers harmonize with all colors. In early spring the bare patch of earth later to be occupied by the catmint's all-encompassing skirts can be occupied by early-flowering, summer dormant bulbs.

If lolling plants are not to be staked they'll usually need some other kind of crutch. Gertrude Jekyll taught how well one plant can support another by letting *Aster divaricatus* spread its fleet of tiny white stars over the solid green clumps of *Bergenia cordifolia*. A reinterpretation of this idea I found even more appealing had the aster's dark wiry stems and sprays of little daisies emerging from among the mottled leaves of *Pulmonaria saccharata*, a very subtle combination. If you'd like something brighter, try one of the half-hardy trail-ing verbenas over a compact white-flowered gypsophila such as 'Compacta Plena' or 'Viette's Dwarf'.

Low, bushy deciduous shrubs that flower in spring gain a second spell of vicarious glory when they lend their support, in a mutual give and take, to perennials that need a bit of bol-stering. Useful shrubs for this purpose include dwarf barberries such as *Berberis thunbergii* 'Kobold' and 'Crimson Pygmy', *Deutzia graci-lis* 'Nikko', and such dwarf cultivars of *Spiraea japonica* as 'Little Princess' and 'Lime Mound'. The last makes a good host for blue-flowered *Clematis integrifolia*, which has long trailing stems and is hard to stake inconspicu-ously. Be careful about using evergreen shrubs, which may be scarred for years if so swathed with another plant that their leaves

Aster divaricatus *trails over* Pulmonaria 'Mrs. Moon'. *(England; September)*

Clematis inte-grifolia *is not a vine but it does make long, trail-ing stems. In Jane Platt's Oregon garden it has been skillfully staked to display its blue flowers against a golden conifer but it would be easier to handle if al-lowed to trail over the edge of a raised bed or to sprawl over a mounding shrub such as* Spiraea 'Golden Princess' *or* 'Lime Mound'. *(August)*

are smothered. Evergreen candytuft (*Iberis sempervirens*) is a sub-shrub or woody-based perennial that adapts itself to the climate, remaining evergreen under mild conditions, making vigorous new growth in spring if winterkilled, so it can play a supportive role without long-lasting damage. In the herb garden at the National Arboretum, blue-flowered *Salvia azurea grandiflora* (also known as *S. pitcheri*), a beautiful plant but notorious for its tendency to sprawl, is allowed to tumble over the candytuft.

Some geums and many potentillas (*Potentilla atrosanguinea*, *P. nepalensis*) have neat clumps of leaves but lax sprays of flowers that need some kind of prop. My favorite support plant for these is one of the mountain mints, *Pycnanthemum virginianum*, an aromatic plant that should be placed where it can be squeezed when passing by. Its little white flowers do their job of attracting bees but have no pretensions to beauty; it is the soft mounds of interlaced wiry stems and slender leaves that give the plant its appeal. If sheared after it flowers it makes a bright green cushion against which the red or orange flowers of geums and potentillas can be displayed as tellingly as jewels against black velvet.

FLOWER FORM

The character of a plant is influenced by both color and shape. In the extremes just discussed—the very large, the verticals, the ethereal and subtle, and the low and sprawling, the overall form of the plant has been the main consideration. When a plant is of nondescript shape and middling height, it is the size, form, and color of the flowers that we consider when deciding how best to display the plant or combine it with others.

Form and color are not, however, the only qualities influencing our perception of a scene; a plant may stand out because it is noticeably different from those around it. The familiar is the safe, and the eye, vigilant for signs of danger, is alerted by the different. In a row of seven-foot men, the eye will settle on a single five-foot man among them. Reverse this, with one tall man among a group of short ones and the tall man gets the attention. This is what the fashion game is about. Among a group of women in ankle-length skirts it is the one in the miniskirt that gets the attention. When miniskirts become the norm the woman wanting to be noticed lowers her hemlines again.

Putting this into gardening terms, nearly everyone has seen bedding schemes where a single plant of a different color has been inadvertently included. Attention is riveted on that "odd man out." Mistakes like this are annoying because they negate the designer's intent, but done deliberately it is an effective ploy for highlighting a particular plant and prevailing over the constraints of color. For example, bright pink is much more vivid than pale pink, but put a small patch of the subtler color among an expanse of the bright and attention will center on the pale pink.

Usually, though, bright, solid color is the most assertive element in a garden, so whilst it might be supposed that large flowers such as daylilies, irises, peonies, and Oriental poppies (is it coincidence that the best known perennials are those with the largest flowers?) will be the most visible, this is not always so; we must consider not only the size of a flower but the brightness and density of the color. The flowers of *Aster* 'Alma Potschke' are relatively small, but because they are sufficiently numerous, dense, and brightly colored to create a solid patch of intense color, this is one of the showiest perennials.

Partner a plant, or group of plants, with

another that is clearly different but similar in color and shape and neither shows to advantage. Visualize the yellow spire of a verbascum with the yellow spike of false lupine (*Thermopsis villosa*). They won't clash, they just don't do anything for each other, lacking contrast in either form or color yet not a matching pair. Similarity of form does unify large groupings of such perennials as daylilies, irises, or chrysanthemums where many colors are intermingled. If each flower was also of a different form, the result might be spotty and unsettling, but united by common form such a medley is pleasingly provocative if the colors are bright (most daylilies) or mellifluous if they are soft (irises).

With a few exceptions, such as lupines (provided the near-orange ones are omitted), the effect is apt to be spotty or inharmonious when a small number of plants in assorted colors are mixed together, but two or more of the same kind of plant in different tints and shades of the *same* color can be very appealing—delphiniums in varied tones of blue, for example.

Irrespective of form, flowers of vivid color will usually dominate the scene. Often, though, a particular color scheme is desired, and frequently this means eschewing the showy oranges and bright yellows in favor of pale pinks and blues. Sometimes the theme is even more limiting: white gardens, blue and yellow gardens, and so on. It is in such gardens, with less distraction from color, that flower form is most appreciated and the need for contrasting form the greatest. Perennials are too varied to be neatly classified, but some can be grouped by similarity of flower form.

Large flower size is one attribute that gives a plant impact. Perennials in this group include agapanthus, daylilies, true lilies, many irises, peonies, Oriental poppies, hibiscus, some dahlias, and the large, shaggy double flowers to be found among the sunflowers (*Helianthus* and *Heliopsis*).

Large-flowered daisies comprise another distinctive group, eye-catching in their well-defined flower form, among them the doronicums, gazanias, gaillardias, gerberas, the painted daisy (*Chrysanthemum coccineum*), purple coneflower (*Echinacea purpurea*), rudbeckias, single sunflowers, and shasta daisies (*Chrysanthemum* × *superbum*). Because the petals (ray flowers, actually) of heleniums are gappy and reflexed, they are not as strong in form as the other daisies mentioned. When daisies are very small and numerous, the plant gains in grace but diminishes in impact unless brilliantly colored, becoming cloudlike if white or pastel.

Globular inflorescences are distinctive. There are not a great many perennials with this flower shape; onions are the main contributors, their effect varying with the size, color, and density of the flower heads. The huge pale violet spheres of *Allium christophii* present a softer visual image than the smaller but more solid purple cannonballs of the arresting *A. giganteum*. The globe thistles (*Echinops*) are unique, their flower balls firm in outline but of a tranquil blue or grayish tint. In color they never fail to harmonize but because their flowers are dispersed and subtly colored, they benefit from companions of fairly dense color, such as border phlox, achilleas, bee balm, or sunflowers.

A spherical impression is given by the flowers of two uncommon but very lovely perennials. Both are an unusual and very subtle creamy yellow color. The giant scabious (*Cephalaria gigantea*) bears a great many smallish domed and frilly flowers on slender much-branched six-foot stems, the effect graceful and airy, particularly lovely seen against the blue of the sky but also well set off against a dark green background. The flowers of a very pretty knapweed, *Centaurea ruthenica*, are larger, rounder, fluffier and fewer, on a graceful plant about four feet high. It flowers in summer, a little later than the cephalaria. This too is beautiful against blue sky, an effect that might be achieved in a mounded or raised bed. The ferny foliage is in an unobstructive basal clump, so, the flowers being widely spaced, it could be placed as a see-through plant with massed blue flowers behind.

Some sea hollies (*Eryngium tripartitum* and the similar, shorter *E. bourgatii* among them) have branched stems bearing round, bluish flower balls somewhat like those of the globe thistles but smaller and ringed with spines. These are striking yet adaptable plants, the unusual flower form attracting attention, the subtle color easy to fit into any scheme. Some sea hollies have such large, incised, spine-tipped bracts that these are the dominant feature. The biennial *E. giganteum* is an extremely showy plant, the collar of incised bracts very large and of a gleaming silver-gray. In *E. alpinum*, a general favorite, the bracts are slender and feathery, giving the plant a softer but still striking appearance.

Double flowers often present a somewhat globular appearance, of fairly firm outline in the thrifts (*Armeria*), double marsh marigold (*Caltha palustris* 'Flore Pleno'), and double buttercups (*Ranunculus*), and of blurred outline in *Coreopsis*, *Helianthus*, and *Heliopsis*.

Perennials with platelike inflorescences are conspicuous even when softly colored, and extremely showy when the color is bright. This popular group includes most of the yarrows (*Achillea*), the larger sedums such as *Sedum spectabile* and 'Autumn Joy', *Crassula falcata*, and butterfly weed (*Asclepias tuberosa*). The smaller domed heads of Jerusalem cross (*Lychnis chalcedonica*) fall midway between plates and spheres.

Centaurea ruthenica at Denver Botanic Garden in June.

Plants at the extremes of form, the strong spires and the ethereal clouds were discussed earlier. Plumes come somewhere in between, their character influenced by color, bulk, the stiffness or looseness of the plume, and to some extent by the nature of their companions. Astilbes offer the broadest range of plumes. A few are weeping in habit, and *Astilbe taquetii* is rather dominating in its stiffness and strong color. Most are of feathery appearance but while the pastels seem soft and fluffy the bright red ones may seem to have a firmer, more pyramidal outline. The plumes of false Solomon's seal (*Smilacina racemosa*) are quite pyramidal in shape but softened by their creamy color and slightly arching habit. Queen-of-the-prairie (*Filipendula rubra*) approaches cloudlike in its cotton-candy softness, *Rodgersia* plumes are com-

Artemisia lacti-flora *with a pink phlox. The plumes are not yet fully developed. (England; August)*

Artemisia lacti-flora *combined with* Miscanthus sinensis 'Variega-tus'. *With the flowers fully open, the plumes approach cloudlike. (Longwood Gardens, Pennsylvania; August)*

manding yet elegant, and those of *Artemisia lactiflora* so soft in color and outline that they too approach the cloudlike. Some of the best plumes are found among the despised golden-rods (*Solidago*), and it must have been said often enough by now to get the message across: goldenrods do not cause hay fever. You do, however, need to choose carefully, because many are invasive.

Many perennials change their character when they change their color: bright yellow *Coreopsis verticillata* is sturdy and dynamic despite the ferny foliage, pale lemon yellow 'Moonbeam' very delicate. Bee balm might be vibrant in red ('Cambridge Scarlet'), romantic in pink ('Croftway Pink'), sultry in purple, insipid in white if alone but a good friend to all other colors. Border phloxes encompass such a range of colors that in theory they

ought to mix and match, unified by their common form, but in practice this looks monotonous, perhaps because there is too big a proportion of flower to foliage. In general geraniums are tranquil in form and color, but there are some stunners among them, including the very popular *Geranium sanguineum*, which somehow escapes the widespread disapproval of magenta flowers and is found in a good many gardens where distaste for that color is averred.

Clarity of form plays a part in determining whether a plant is dominant or unobtrusive. Whilst it might be supposed that double flowers would be more noticeable than single ones, the reverse is often the case because doubling makes the shape less clean cut, giving the flower a blurred and softened appearance. This softening of form is apparent in double pinks (*Dianthus*), the fringed knap-weeds (*Centaurea*), and the frilly *Scabiosa caucasica*). Assuming that all were the same color, these would stand out less than flowers of well-defined shape such as single daisies and Japanese anemones. When the flowers face upward, as in the sundrops (*Oenothera*) they are even more noticeable, assuming, of course, that they are below eye level.

Plants of modest height, intermediate form, and subdued color may still have some quality meriting prominent placement, the quaint configuration of toad lily flowers (*Tricyrtis hirta*) for example. The foliage is undistinguished and the flower color a recessive pale purple. Set back among showier plants they serve only as a filler, but put them alongside a path and few will pass by without pausing for a closer look.

Other flowers that need placing where the intriguing flowers will not be overlooked include the dainty, dancing columbines, the hardy (relatively!) begonia (*Begonia grandis*), *Disporum flavens* (also known as *D. sessile* 'Flavens'), and the bleeding hearts (*Dicentra*). Japanese bleeding heart (*D. spectabilis*) presents a challenge in warmer regions because it needs placing where easily seen while in flower but inconspicuous when, soon afterward, it gets shabby. Alternating this with blue-flowered *Brunnera macrophylla* which develops its large basal leaves after the flowers are over, is one popular combination. The low stature of epimediums usually assures them a place where the fascinating little flowers are not ignored. Balloon flowers (*Platycodon*) have beguiling buds and exquisite flowers, and there are selections short enough for the front ranks. If they are near at hand it is easier to nip off daily the spent flowers, which have no more allure than the used handkerchiefs they resemble.

The character of a plant gains emphasis when its neighbors are of contrasting form, so it is usually best to avoid juxtaposition of plate with plate, globe with globe, spike with spike, and so on, but repeated switching from one well-defined form to another is unsettling. This is where plants of nondescript form and soft color play their part, giving the eye a chance to relax and drift after attention has been concentrated on a plant of distinctive form.

Color and form play on the emotions and plants, alone or in combinations, can be stimulating, relaxing, intriguing, endearing, occasionally repulsing. Garden makers usually bring about these varied emotions by accident or instinct, but by thoughtful choice and considered combination we can choose whether we set the heart to dreaming or to dancing. Reflect on your own reactions as you look at the pictures in this and other books.

With so many permutations of form, color, and flower shape, millions of combinations are possible. Not as many, however, as it might at first seem because they don't all flower at the same time. One of the first decisions to be made is whether to concentrate bloom by limiting the season, or to aim at the longest possible period of flower. Climate will influence this decision, favoring the concentration of color where the growing season is short. Bear in mind that many early bloomers flower briefly, and only once, so if maximum flower power is your aim don't give too much space to such spring or early summer beauties as doronicums, Japanese bleeding heart (*Dicentra spectabilis*), irises, peonies, and poppies.

If bloom for six months or more is the aim, will flowers of the different seasons be scattered throughout the planting, or will those in flower at the same time be grouped together? Grouping them provides more scope for artistic combinations (inartistic ones, too,

of course!) but leaves large areas devoid of bloom. A few plants of neutral color and long-lasting good looks distributed through the bed or border provide a constant structural element around which other plants come and go as the season progresses. Many ornamental grasses are excellent for this purpose. So are peonies, and the fact that they don't bloom for long becomes an advantage when their handsome foliage is used to provide a stable element. Red, pink, or white peonies with blue or white Siberian irises make a classic combination, with long-lasting foliage of contrasting texture.

Single clumps of peonies spaced evenly along the middle of a border, with groups of irises in front, form the nucleus of a pink, blue, and white spring theme, to which could be added other early-blooming perennials with pink, blue, or white flowers and attractive long-lasting foliage. Amsonia, *Baptisia australis*, dictamnus, and *Geranium* 'Johnson's Blue' are among the possibilities. Moss pinks (*Phlox subulata*) and *Iberis sempervirens* are among the best edging plants. All these flowers would be gone by early to midsummer. Yellow could, if desired, be the base color for

In this series of photos Pennisetum alopecuroides *is the hub around which other plants revolve. In July,* top left, Sedum *'Autumn Joy' is still at its green stage.* Euphorbia myrsinites *flowered earlier but the glaucous foliage remains attractive.* Imperata cylindrica *'Rubra' adds a splash of red. The main flush of bloom on* Allium senescens, *on the right, is over but it will continue to flower spasmodically. In late August,* opposite page, *the sedum has turned pink and an early blue aster is in bloom. By October,* top right, *the sedum heads have turned to rust and a white Korean chrysanthemum is in full bloom, along with a very late blue aster (*Aster grandiflorus*). (Virginia)*

the rest of the season. Because these, too, have attractive long-lasting foliage, two of the best yellow-flowered, summer-blooming perennials are threadleaf coreopsis (*Coreopsis verticillata*) and yarrows (*Achillea*) such as 'Moonshine' and 'Coronation Gold'. Such a seasonal change from pink to yellow resolves the dilemma of those who like both pink and yellow, but not together.

Though less spectacular, borders with flowers grouped by season, interspersed with those that have gone or are yet to come, often add up to more enjoyment than one grand fling of concentrated color. Because fewer plants are in flower at the same time, such borders are also easier to coordinate.

Right: *A "hot color" arrangement by Jane Platt, cooled by pale yellow, and the border in her Oregon garden from which the flowers were picked. In the arrangement are scarlet and orange crocosmias,* Hypericum *'Hidcote' (a shrub that can be cut back like a perennial),* Coreopsis verticillata, Lysimachia vulgaris, *and* Kniphofia *'Little Maid'. Other plants in the border,* below, *include lavender, lilies,* Anthemis *'Wargrave',* Coreopsis *'Moonbeam', and* Verbascum chaixii. *Sharp eyes might spot an unintended touch of pink from a phlox that usually flowers at a different time. (Early August)*

4 | Color in the Garden

A mnenomic taught me as a child, "*R*obert *O*f *Y*ork *G*ained *B*attles in *V*ain," has been helpful in remembering the order of colors of the spectrum, as we see them in a rainbow: red, orange, yellow, green, blue, and violet. In color technology these hues are formed into a circle in which red meets up with violet, and this color wheel is used in explaining why some color combinations are perceived as harmonious, while others clash. There is little disagreement when discussing these basic hues, but flowers come in such an infinite range of tints (a hue lightened with white, often called pastels), shades (a hue darkened with black), mixtures, and combinations that there is probably some place in the range where any two colors can be felicitously combined. Blue and purple, loved by some, hadn't been a combination of my choice until I found myself won over by violet-blue columbines mixed with a dark purple selection of *Iris tenax*, spiked by a few purple-flowered *Allium giganteum* in front of light violet-purple *Syringa* 'Palibin'. So it is with all color scheming, a tiny change in color, form, or proportion can make the difference between a satisfying combination and one that doesn't quite come off.

The four fans comprising the Royal Horticultural Society's color charts contain over eight hundred color patches, and still sometimes a precise match with a flower color cannot be made. Attempts to count the exact number of reds, pinks, yellows, etc., fail because one color merges imperceptibly into another. Add a little yellow to red and we get scarlet, add more yellow and we get orange. Red and scarlet are enhanced by silver-gray, orange-peel orange is not, but the exact place where scarlet becomes orange would be very hard to define, therefore we cannot say categorically that orange and gray are, or are not, mutually enhancing; it depends what you mean by "orange." And just where does violet become purple? Take two quite similar salvias, 'East Friesland' and 'May Night'. The first is purplish blue, the second dark violet-blue. The difference is very small but, to my eye, a harsh combination became a pleasing one when 'May Night' replaced 'East Friesland' in front of orange 'Enchantment' lilies. Two colors unpalatable in equal measures may be enjoyable in different proportions or with another color added. I don't care for green with silver-gray but was charmed by

123

An arrangement of cooler colors, left, *by designer Susan Barsky and the border,* right, *where the flowers were grown. Flowers include* Filipendula rubra, *echinops,* **Campanula** latifolia, *columbines, liatris,* Campanula persicifolia, *physostegia, stokesia, purple loosestrife,* Lysimachia clethroides, *and pink* Achillea millefolium. *(Massachusetts; July)*

lamb's ears with the green-yellow-and-scarlet jelly-bean leaves of *Sedum rubrotinctum*.

The R.H.S. color fans (out of print for several years but now available again) are invaluable to anyone interested in studying the nuances of color. Recognizing the impossibility of finding meaningful names for over eight hundred colors, each was ascribed only a number. Few own the fans, so the numbers have limited application, but the tables that accompany them are cross-referenced with three earlier charts that do give names, making it easy to see, for example, where chartreuse becomes primrose and primrose in turn becomes sulfur.

The R.H.S. charts define color in terms of three attributes: hue, saturation, and brightness or lightness. *Hue* decides what kind of color it is—whether it is, for example, a red, or a green, or a blue. *Brightness* distin-

guishes the amount of light in or reflected by the color, whether it is a light color or a dark one. Alternative terms for brightness are *tone*, *luminosity*, and *value*. *Saturation* refers to the purity of a color. Spectral colors are fully saturated. The addition of any other color, including white, lessens the saturation.

Pure red, orange, and the glowing golden yellows are considered "hot" colors, but when sufficient white is added they are cooled into delicate, romantic pastels. They also cease to be hot colors when darkened into somberness with the addition of black. Blue and violet are "cool colors" and remain that way when darkened or lightened. Lemon yellows are showy yet refreshing. Green (also considered a cool color) is the great neutralizer—so neutral, in fact, that its presence, its importance, and its variability, is often overlooked.

Space can be visually manipulated by

skillful use of color. Red, bright yellow, orange, luminous white, or silver-gray are advancing colors, seeming closer than they are. Used on a boundary, these colors pull it visually in. Cool, retreating colors push the boundary out or merge it with distant scenery. In this way a garden can be made to seem smaller or larger than it is, but the apparent shape is also changed, so it should be remembered that an oblong is usually more pleasing to the eye than a square.

When we turn to actual flowers, we find that whites, yellows, pinks, and purples are strongly represented among perennials, while orange and clear blue are less common and pure red is rare. With red and orange, a little is often better than a lot—artists long ago discovered that a touch of red brings a picture to life. Could we choose, most of us would wish for a bit more blue and perhaps a bit less bright yellow. Pinks, blues, whites, and grays are probably the easiest group of colors to coordinate and this does seem to be the most popular color scheme, perhaps in part because old-fashioned roses are included in many borders and most of them are pink.

Colors on paper are distinct and, if viewed in the same light, unchanging. In the garden it is much more complex. There are few, if any, flowers of unvaried color. Most have yellow stamens for a start, and even when the rest of the flower is a solid color, it will usually be deeper when newly opened than it is when it starts to fade, or sometimes the reverse. Colors seem more intense on cloudy days than in bright sun, and this has shaped the preference for soft colors evinced in English gardens where sunless days predominate. Where the sun is intense, pale colors may look washed out, while bright ones glow without seeming garish. Color perception is also affected by the changing light at different times of day and in different seasons, by

This thyme lawn at Sissinghurst Castle, England, is oblong in shape but the way the colors are placed makes one corner appear to curve. (June)

the direction from which a flower is lit, and by its association with other colors.

If you find color theory bewildering, take heart. The following quotation comes from a fascinating article by Margaret S. Livingstone in *Scientific American*, January 1988, titled "Art Illusion and the Visual System," in which she discusses the way in which the visual system processes information on color, movement, and form.

Although the neurobiological explanations for many of the phenomena I have described have only recently been clarified, many artists and designers seem to be empirically aware of the underlying principles.

Color precepts attempt to formalize, in order that it can be taught, what was first done instinctively. Human beings are naturally drawn toward activities for which they have innate ability. Those intrigued by color subconsciously observe and analyze everything they see, whether it be a painting, the clothes of passersby, the changing colors of traffic lights against blue sky, or flowers in a garden. Most of us have enough innate color sense to avoid the worst indiscretions, practice develops the eye, and we learn from our mistakes. Our problems most often result from lack of restraint or prior planning when choosing the plants.

Responses to color are remarkably uniform. When I asked audiences in different parts of the country to indicate their reaction to various color combinations, about 90 percent responded similarly. The other 10 percent certainly included some with sufficient color flair to pull off combinations most of us wouldn't risk. The least popular color is orange. Magenta, skillfully used, is not as unpopular as is often suggested but one combination disliked by nearly everyone is purple, magenta, or bright pink with orange. This bears out the color tenet that reds containing blue are best kept at a distance from reds containing yellow. Strong pinks and purples and yellow and orange are, nonetheless, mixed with elan by the artistic, but it must be done with bravado and a sure hand. Most of

Approximately half those asked liked the combination of yellow rudbeckias with purple coneflower, left; *the others did not. Everyone liked the combination of pastels from pink and yellow primroses,* right.

us are too timid to attempt it, and such strong color is not, in any case, well suited to small gardens.

Only with pink and yellow did I find ambivalence. This combination is acceptable to nearly everyone as pastel tints, but some 50 percent would not include stronger pinks and yellows in the same border unless they flowered at different times. Among the other half, opinion varied with the particular combination but reaction to creamy yellows was generally favorable with whatever it was combined. About a quarter of the audience voted against bright yellow rudbeckias with purple coneflower (*Echinacea purpurea*), a percentage that would doubtless have been higher had there not been similarity of form to reconcile the colors. A combination quite repulsive to me is the pink flowers over the greenish yellow leaves of *Lamium maculatum* 'Aureum'—nature doesn't always get it right! With this plant, though, she had a second try and I'm indebted to my friend Henry Ross for sending me *L. m.* 'Beedham's White', which has yellow leaves and white flowers. He reports it to be a bit less robust than the one with pink

Most of the colors in this border are pastels, enlivened by the brighter yellow of verbascums and a touch of magenta from Geranium psilostemon. *Other plants include* Campanula latifolia *'Alba',* penstemons, *pale yellow* Nepeta govaniana, Astrantia major, *and* Eryngium alpinum. *(Garden of Faith and Frank Mackaness, Oregon; July)*

flowers. You can buy it from Glasshouse Works.

One cannot be dogmatic about the conjunction of any two colors, for so many factors are in play: light, texture, proportion, setting, not to mention personal preference. Though often averse to to combinations of bright yellow and bright pink, I greatly enjoyed a combination predominantly white and yellow, with *Hesperis matronalis* 'Alba', *Lonicera* 'Baggesen's Gold', and doronicums, but with touches of pale pink from *Geranium endressii*

and columbines and highlighted with a bright pink peony. The pink touches also brought the yellows into unity with pink rhododendrons in the distant background.

Different colors evoke different emotions and colors are often described accordingly. We might speak of a sunny (cheerful) mood, or a sunny color (yellow), while the somber dark maroon of *Geranium phaeum* got it the name "mourning widow geranium." Dynamic colors can excite, startle, or stun, and soft, passive colors can calm or bore. There is little

A Jekyll-style border in the English garden of Mr. and the Hon. Mrs. Peter Healing, starting with cool colors, moving through hot ones, then back again to cooler colors. The pink on the left is Lavatera cachemiriana *but most of the pink and purple flowers in this garden are grown in another border. (August)*

disagreement about the emotional response, only about its desirability. Few would suggest that orange and magenta are harmonious, but some enjoy the excitement of an occasional raucous note. Others, while agreeing that pastels are compatible, find schemes limited to these pale tints insipid. Some colors whisper, others shout, each may appeal, at different times and in different settings, to our own changing moods, but there usually is an overriding individual preference that determines what we grow in our own gardens.

Combining plants is an art form, and art is not static. Color theory provides guidelines based primarily on our common reactions but also, in gardening, on what has proved successful in the past. Attempting something new is a challenge, but the result is less certain. An experienced chef can take what is available and out of it create a great dish, but the inexperienced cook may prefer to follow a tested recipe. Such a recipe was worked out and refined by Gertrude Jekyll in her English border. Although few now have the space or time

This border in the Healing garden accommodates most of the pinks and purples, together with blue, white, and gray foliage. Perennials include dahlias, bee balm, asters, echinops, gray artemisia, cream-flowered Artemisia lactiflora, Verbena rigida, *and* Eryngium agavifolium. *There are also buddleias and clematis. (August)*

for a border of such dimensions, the color principles demonstrated remain sound and can be applied to much smaller gardens.

The Jekyll border, planned primarily for midsummer and autumn bloom, was two hundred feet long and fourteen feet wide, backed by a wall lined with shrubs, with a wide path between the shrubs and the border. The border was anchored at the ends with yuccas (*Yucca filamentosa, Y. recurvifolia*). The colors progressed from soft yellow, white, blue, mauve, through bright sunny yellows, red, scarlet, and orange, back to cooler yellow, white, blue, and silver. Among the perennials used, grouped in approximate color sequence with the groupings listed roughly from back to front were:

YELLOW, WHITE, BLUE, BLUE-GRAY (WITH SLIGHT TOUCHES OF PINK)
Verbascum olympicum, yellow thalictrum, *Rudbeckia* 'Golden Glow', blue delphiniums, *Miscanthus sinensis* 'Zebrinus', *Aruncus dioicus*, yellow (*Digitalis grandiflora*) and white

(*D. purpurea* 'Alba') foxgloves, *Campanula lactiflora*, white lilies, blue lyme grass (*Elymus glaucus*), meadowsweet (*Filipendula ulmaria* 'Flore Pleno'), blue irises, a pale pink astilbe, sage (*Salvia officinalis*), *Clematis heracleifolia*, and rue (*Ruta graveolens*). Along the front edge of this section were long drifts of *Crambe maritima*, *Iberis sempervirens*, and *Bergenia cordifolia*. Annuals used included snapdragons and primrose yellow marigolds.

HOT COLORS

Helianthus × *multiflorus*, dark red hollyhocks, torch lilies (*Kniphofia*), red and orange dahlias, red canna lilies, *Lychnis chalcedonica*, *Achillea filipendulina*, helenium, sea hollies (*Eryngium* × *oliveranum*, *E. giganteum*), bee balm (*Monarda didyma*), *Coreopsis lanceolata*, tiger lilies. Frontal drifts included a dwarf helenium, *Rudbeckia fulgida* 'Newmanii', and *Salvia* × *superba*. Annuals included marigolds (*Tagetes*), nasturtiums, and celosia.

YELLOW, WHITE, CREAM, BLUE, SILVER

Gypsophila paniculata, blue delphiniums, yellow and white foxgloves, *Echinops ritro*, yellow hollyhocks, *Campanula lactiflora*, *Geranium ibericum*, *Clematis recta*, *Saponaria officinalis*, *Dictamnus*, blue, cream, and light mauve asters, white dahlias. Along the front were three silvery plants of different textures: dusty miller (*Senecio cineraria*), lavender cotton (*Santolina chamaecyparissus*), and lamb's ears (*Stachys byzantina*). Shrubs and vines mixed with the perennials included golden privet (*Ligustrum ovalifolium* 'Aureum'), *Clematis* × *jackmanii*, and white everlasting pea (*Lathyrus latifolius* 'Alba').

Note that the blue-gray glaucous foliage of rue and blue lyme grass at one end of the border is well away from the silvery gray of dusty miller, santolina, and lamb's ears at the other—the silver-grays and the blue-grays are not always good mixers; they can go in the same planting but are usually better for a bit of space between them.

The Jekyll border must be considered in the context of its surroundings. As she herself wrote: "It is important in such a border of rather large size that can be seen from a good space of lawn, to keep the flowers in rather large masses of colour." Plants also need to be of larger size when meant to be viewed from a distance—this is not the place to tuck the little treasures.

Unlike borders seen across a lawn, flower arrangements are seen close at hand, and it used to be thought that distributing similar colors evenly throughout produced the most pleasing effect. Current thought is more along Jekyll lines, which makes the point that "rules" are in part merely fashion. In any case, both approaches can be pleasing or otherwise.

If there is space, or time, for only one fairly small border, it is likely to include the maker's favorite plants, no matter if some are bright pink and others yellow. To designers that is putting the cart before the horse, but to many of us the plants *are* the horse. Borders of mixed colors are frequently more joyous than color schemes more artfully contrived, and two colors that don't please used one-on-one may do so, even side by side, as part of a broader color mix. Still, it usually is best to use the most intense colors sparingly.

If one plant does seem at odds with another, removing it may not be the only solution. It may be the proportions, not the colors, that are wrong. When, in my own garden, a solitary creamy yucca spike seemed at odds with a drift of bright white *Phlox* 'Miss Lingard', adding more cream, in the form of *Arundo donax* 'Variegata', with leaves striped creamy yellow, made for better color balance.

In choosing a color scheme there may be considerations other than the plants, the color of the house, for instance, or a wall, or path. Some bricks are a very unsympathetic red but painting the wall turns a labor-free surface into one requiring maintenance. Could it be clothed with ivy, Boston ivy (*Parthenocissus tricuspidata*), climbing hydrangea (*Hydrangea anomola petiolaris* or *Schizophragma hydrangeoides*), or some other self-clinging vine to overcome the color limitations it otherwise imposes? A purple-leaved plant such as some bugleweeds (*Ajuga*) or black mondo grass (*Ophiopogon planiscapus* 'Nigrescens') would be well displayed against gray paving but visually lost against a brown bark mulch path. This can be turned to advantage if a path is visually too narrow. It will look wider if edged with plants that match it in color.

All too often an element overlooked impairs a color scheme. Plant flowers under a high-branched flowering tree and the distance between them may be enough to avoid a color clash, but what about when the petals fall? Few would enjoy the combination of orange marigolds sprinkled with the watermelon pink petals of a crepe myrtle, and the opportunity has been

In my garden the solitary creamy yucca spike rising up from behind purple barberries was at odds with the sparkling white of Phlox *'Miss Lingard' until more cream was added. (Virginia; May)*

The poppies and foxgloves are harmonious with the pink walls of the house, and orange 'Kwanso' daylilies with the terra-cotta-colored wall. There'd be color clashes if these two plantings were reversed. (Garden of Mrs. E. R. Slingo, England; June, top, and Goodnestone Park, Kent, England; July, bottom)

lost to achieve, with a more sympathetic underplanting, one of those ephemeral touches all the more enchanting for being so fleeting.

Asters and chrysanthemums are two major components of autumn borders. Asters come in a great range of whites, blues, pinks, and purples, and there are also a great many pink and white chrysanthemums, so this color theme seems an obvious one to pursue, but in regions where autumn is ablaze with the reds, yellows, and oranges of leaf and berry, chrysanthemums in these colors are more in tune.

A crepe myrtle has strewn its fallen petals over the Carex glauca and Arabis sturii that edge the bed below. The effect would not be pleasing if orange or yellow flowers grew under the crepe myrtle. (Virginia; August)

BLUE

Miss Jekyll's famous border did not embrace the whole range of colors. There were tentative touches of pink in the outer sections but brighter pinks were omitted. In the cool color sections blue and yellow were the basis of the theme, together with white and gray. This has become a classic combination. Replace the yellow with pink and we have another time-honored combination.

A classic combination of white, yellow, and blue with gypsophila (appearing gray as it starts to open), Chrysanthemum nipponicum, *verbascum,* Adenophora, *and* Achillea 'Moonshine'. *(Garden of Sir John Thouron, Pennsylvania; June)*

Blue, pink, and white is another classic combination. The plants are Iberis sempervirens, Salvia 'East Friesland', Baptisia australis, and a pink peony. (Garden of Ellen and Gordon Penick, Virginia; May)

Blue is a giver and taker, enhancing most colors and being in turn enhanced by them. Blue alone does not have the impact of the hotter colors. A single clump of butterfly weed stands out in a green meadow, but a much bigger quantity of blue is needed to be noticed—sheets of wild blue lupines, for example. Blue never exactly clashes with another color but there is insufficient contrast with green to set it off, and clear blue or greenish blue is not seen at its best one-on-one with violet-blue or purple. That there is a trace of pink in the blue of a flower may not be apparent until we see, for example, the azure-blue of flax (*Linum perenne*) side by side with the less pure blue of a balloon flower (*Platycodon*), or periwinkle with the brilliant blue of *Omphalodes verna*. Pictures of blue flowers are often misleading—not from ill intent but be-

cause blue is extremely difficult to capture on film. Film renders some blues pink, or pinkish—stokesias, for instance, and such geraniums as 'Johnson's Blue'. The European cornflower, *Centaurea montana*, is, at its best, a good deep blue with a red eye, but it may not look that way in pictures. Attempts to compensate for this in the printing process often result in exaggerated color. If what you get is not what you thought you paid for, and you find yourself with conflicting blues, take a tip from an allied art: faced with a blue carpet, a couch of a different blue, and an owner unwilling to part with either, an interior decorator might add scatter cushions in more tones of blue, drawing the disparate blues together by lessening the eye's ability to compare any two.

The borage family, which includes *Anchusa*, *Brunnera*, *Lithospermum*, *Mertensia*, *Myosotis* (forget-me-nots), *Omphalodes*, *Pulmonaria*, and *Symphytum* (comfrey) is particularly rich in clear bright blues and most of these plants are cold hardy. Intense blues are also found among the sages, but the brightest of these are the least hardy. *Salvia guaranitica*, which survives most Zone 8 winters, is a dark but brilliant blue, and *S. patens*, which can take very little frost, a blue of exceptional purity. Sky blue *S. azurea* is hardy in Zone 6, and in much colder zones with snow cover. These brilliant blues combine well with pink but better still with yellow. The somewhat grayed or steely blues of *Echinops ritro*, *Amsonia*, and *Rhazya orientalis* are at ease in any company.

One of my favorite plants, but one I found quite difficult to place, is a rather tender perennial, *Oxypetalum caeruleum*, sometimes called blue butterfly weed. The color, verging on greenish blue, was too dominant among the pinks and violet-blues, and wrong somehow with golden yellow. When I finally got them together, pale lemon yellow 'Moonbeam' coreopsis proved the perfect partner for this unusual and very beautiful color.

My own island bed of blues, yellows, whites, and grays is triangular in shape, each side about thirty feet long, surrounded by paths. Three small trees (*Juniperus rigida*, *Ilex vomitoria* 'Pendula', and white-flowered *Chionanthus retusus serrulatus*) are placed in from the corners and the center is filled with several of the small shrubby *Deutzia gracilis*, with white flowers in spring, and the gray-green foliage mass of blue-flowered baptisia. This means that the three sides are not all seen together, making it possible to keep some colors apart, in particular blue rue and silver lamb's ears.

One side is edged with white-flowered *Phlox subulata*, one with blue-flowered *Veronica teucrium*. The third, most protected side, has various low-growing plants along the front, including *Sedum middendorffianum diffusum* and *S. lineare* 'Variegatum', both with yellow flowers, blue-flowered *Veronica prostrata*, yellow thyme, white variegated *Aurinia saxatilis* 'Dudley Neville Variegated', some dwarf blue irises, and, at present, lamb's ears, but I'm about to get rid of that because it always rots in summer. Just behind these are such early bulbs as *Iris histrioides* 'Major', which flowers in February, and various crocuses.

The taller herbaceous plants, more or less in flowering sequence, include yellow *Asphodeline lutea*, brilliant blue *Delphinium grandiflorum* (not long-lived but quick and easy from seed), *Geranium* 'Johnson's Blue' and *G. pratense*, white vervain (*Valeriana officinalis*), the yellow-striped leaves of *Iris pal-*

In this triangular bed in my garden, the color scheme was limited to blue, white, yellow, and gray until a place had to be found for the peachy-colored daylily. The yellow mounds in the foreground are Ilex crenata 'Helleri Yellow', *with mounds of rue (*Ruta graveolens*) behind. Other plants include prickly poppy (*Argemone grandiflora*),* Iris pallida 'Aurea-variegata', Coreopsis verticillata, *and* Lilium 'Sterling Star'.

lida 'Variegata' interplanted with dainty white-flowered *Euphorbia corollata*, which starts its year late but grows up to conceal the leaves of the iris when they get shabby in midsummer. *Coreopsis verticillata* is underplanted with early yellow tulips and neighbored by white-flowered *Lilium* 'Sterling Star'. Then there's *Coreopsis* 'Moonbeam', blue *Echinops ruthenicus* (a brighter blue than other globe thistles), white-flowered, grayleaved prickly poppy (*Argemone grandiflora*), *Veronica* 'Sunny Border Blue', and yellowstriped liriope. A blue-flowered clematis rambles through the deutzias. Blue rue is kept clipped into mounds, which means that it doesn't flower. Last year, because it was new and I wanted to try it, the yellow drumsticks of *Craspedia* joined the throng and turned out to match exactly the greenish yellow foliage of the mounded Japanese hollies (a yellow-leaved form of *Ilex crenata* 'Helleri') that occupy one corner of this bed. The craspedia, supposedly perennial, did not survive a quite mild winter.

Most of the blue is over by midsummer but *Veronica* 'Sunny Border Blue' keeps going, joined later by *Aster* × *frikartii* and an airy pale blue form of *A. cordifolius*. Two somewhat invasive plants, *Astermoea mongolica* and *Rudbeckia* 'Goldsturm', have been fighting it out on equal terms (postscript—the rudbeckia finally won) but now, having flowed between a group of three gray yuccas (*Yucca glauca*) they are about to overrun a large rosette of silvery *Salvia argentea* at one point of the triangle. White rain lilies (*Zephyranthes candida*) flower off and on, and the season draws to a close with yellow and white chrysanthemums—"mums" and the ferny-leaved *Chrysanthemum indicum* with flowers resembling those of *Anthemis tinctoria*. It roots quickly from cuttings and I treat it as an annual. There used to be a large clump of creamedged *Hosta ventricosa* 'Variegata' in the

shade of one of the trees but the voles got that—just one of the crosses gardeners have to bear.

In this bed I was faithful to my color scheme until faced with the need to find a place for a particularly fine peach-colored daylily that didn't look good with the pinks or oranges in other parts of the garden. It came to rest here, and now I think the change of color pace has wrought an improvement.

Across the path the color narration continues with *Veronica teucrium* 'Trehane', complete unto itself with yellow leaves and bright blue flowers, blue amsonias, and a bright blue native sage not yet as well known as it surely will become: *Salvia urticifolia*. Blue camassias surround the easy, early, yellow-flowered *Rosa hugonis*. There's an early lemon yellow daylily called 'Gracilis', which opens its fragrant small flowers in the evening, a taller, later one of similar color and graceful form bought as 'Mme. Bellum', and the great glaucous hostalike leaf clumps of yellow-flowered *Rudbeckia maxima*. A shrub not yet lauded as much as it deserves, *Amorpha canescens* or leadplant, isn't quite where I want it but it doesn't move well so I'll probably rearrange the other plants around it. If you like Russian sage (*Perovskia*), you'll like leadplant too; there are many similarities, and where one does well probably so will the other. Leadplant is a shrub that can be cut back to ground level each year, if you wish, to keep the height under three feet. The foliage is gray-green and ferny, the flower plumes light violet-blue. It is drought resistant, easy to please, and it is at last available from mail-order nurseries. The violet-blue is matched by the myriad little steeple-shaped flowers of a native verbena, *Verbena hastata*, which flowers for a long time and repeats later if cut back. And it *should* be cut back, removing spent flowers, to prevent it self-sowing too abundantly. These two flower along with the

Doronicums and ajuga enjoy the same conditions of light shade and a moist, humus-rich soil. (Virginia; April)

achilleas and daylilies.

Whether as a twosome, or with gray and white for company, here are some other successful blue-and-yellow partnerships I've noted. For spring flower in light shade yellow doronicums and blue ajuga make a pretty pair, and so do yellow primroses (*Primula vulgaris*) with the blue crested iris (*Iris cristata*). Doronicums with blue and white *Campanula carpatica* make a clean, fresh combination that seems the quintessence of spring, and golden star (*Chrysogonum virginianum*) intermingled with *Campanula poscharskyana* makes a pretty edging for a lightly shaded path. In my garden a little blue violet sowed itself among the golden star and this I found very pleasing, but those who spend a lot of time weeding out violets won't want to hear about that.

In late spring or early summer *Veronica incana* brings gray leaves and blue spikes to accompany pale yellow 'Moonbeam' coreopsis, or the brighter yellow of *Coreopsis* 'Goldfink'. Sandwich the taller *Veronica* 'Blue

Charm' between an early yellow lily such as 'Sunray' and the bushy yellow-starred mounds of *Coreopsis verticillata* for ascending tiers of color. Yarrows (*Achillea*) are the basis for innumerable summer combinations: *Achillea* 'Moonshine' with *Salvia haematodes* or with lavender; creamy yellow *Achillea × taygetea* with deep violet *Salvia* 'May Night'; or *Achillea* 'Coronation Gold' with globe thistle (*Echinops ritro*) and white phlox. Globe thistle (*Echinops*), *Heliopsis* 'Gold Greenheart', and white feverfew (*Chrysanthemum parthenium*) make a long-lasting trio.

Don't forget foliage colors. Hostas alone provide the makings of many happy associations of yellow and blue-green leaves.

If at times there seem to be a surfeit of possibilities, there are also times when we press our noses in vain against the candy shop window. I commend to those in the Pacific Northwest a combination I admired in England: *Perovskia* 'Blue Spire' with the cream-and-lemon-yellow inflorescences (flowers open yellow and fade to cream) of × *Solidaster hy-*

Blue veronica and yellow Sedum kamtschaticum make a simple but striking combination in a rock garden. (Garden of Sir John Thouron, Pennsylvania; July)

Yellow-leaved Hosta fortunei 'Aurea' and blue-leaved Hosta 'Halcyon' are combined with Geranium × magnificum and yellow-leaved Cornus alba 'Aurea' in a narrow border. (Garden of Patricia Fountain, England; June)

Iris tectorum *sowed itself among* Tiarella cordifolia collina *in my garden. (Virginia; May)*

bridus. If, that is, you can get your hands on 'Blue Spire': perovskias sold in the United States (usually as *P. atriplicifolia*) are all, so far, *P. abrotanoides* or a very similar hybrid—quite nice but not as good for this purpose as 'Blue Spire'. In my southeastern garden the flowering times of the two plants did not coincide. I probably could have managed this, with judicious cutting back, but the solidaster flowers bleach out and fade too fast in southern heat to make it worth the effort.

Blue, pink, and white may be the most popular of all combinations, and the easiest to compose, for together with cream and gray, this theme can absorb many of the disparate lavenders, lilacs, and violet-blues without offending anyone's sensibilities. The human eye notices slight differences among pinks much less readily than differences among yellows.

Green is present automatically in any combination, and usually left to take care of itself, but whilst foliage of light greenish yellow blends in with blues and yellows, it may be noticeably out of place among blues and

pinks. And if you can't abide pink with yellow don't overlook the fact that a lot of plants grown for their gray or blue-gray leaves bear yellow flowers, if you let them.

Among the brightest and earliest of the spring blues is *Brunnera macrophylla*, which pairs prettily with Japanese bleeding heart in pink, or white, or both. They will live in harmony for many years provided you remove brunnera's flower stalks before it goes to seed. Omit this attention and it will soon crowd out the bleeding heart and anything else that gets in its way. There are primroses (Barnhaven hybrids of *Primula vulgaris*) in many tints of pink, and Virginia bluebells (*Mertensia virginica*) flowers at the same time. Soon after we are spoilt for choice with the great range of blues and whites from Siberian irises, to mix with peonies, baptisia, candytuft (*Iberis sempervirens*), amsonia, columbines, the early white daisy 'May Queen' and campanulas such as the easy, sturdy *Campanula persicifolia*, which comes in both blue and white. The Japanese roof iris, *Iris tectorum*, will grow

Pink and blue are usually considered soft colors but they can be strong. The equally intense colors of Chrysanthemum coccineum *'Brenda' and Belladonna delphinium 'Wendy' make for a vibrant combination. With them, to the right, is* Nepeta *'Blue Beauty'. (Wisley Gardens, England; June)*

This small garden (only part of which is shown) houses an extensive collection of irises but there are also many other small perennials to extend the flowering season. In this corner pinks and blues predominate. Perennials in flower include bearded irises, white Iris sibirica, *pink snapdragons (perennial in this garden),* Saponaria ocymoides, Felicia amelloides, Dianthus deltoides, *and* Lithodora diffusa. *(Design by Harland Hand for Mr. and Mrs. D. Lennette, Bay Area of California; May)*

in sun or light shade. It comes in blue or white and either or both are lovely with white or pink foamflower (*Tiarella cordifolia, T. wherryi*). Starting about now there's pink, blue, and white galore from hardy geraniums, with *Geranium macrorrhizum, G. sylvaticum, G. maculatum*, and *G.* 'Johnson's Blue' among the first.

In early summer those able to grow them can rejoice in a diversity of delphiniums in harmonizing blues, and pinks, and whites. There are varied pink hues from the painted daisies (*Chrysanthemum coccineum*) to combine with catmints, or *Delphinium grandiflorum*, or *Salvia × superba*. Midsummer brings globe thistle (*Echinops*), to go with white or pink phlox, with purple coneflower (*Echinacea purpurea*), with daylilies, in fact, with anything in flower at the same time—you can't go wrong with globe thistles.

Autumn brings a plethora of blue, pink, and white asters. *Aster × frikartii* has had such good press (deservedly) that it isn't likely to be overlooked (I don't recall anyone pointing out, though, the determined way in which it turns all its flowers toward the sun) but if you haven't tried *Aster* 'Climax', get that too. It is an oldy but a goody, raised in England prior to 1908. I can't do better (correction, I can't do as well!) than quote Graham Thomas in *Perennial Garden Plants* (my bible on the subject): ". . . never surpassed for vigour and elegance. Good broad foliage and huge pyramidal shaped panicles of Spode blue, evenly shaped, single flowers . . . no others equal its quality. The tall willowy stems (to 6′) need staking only in very tidy gardens." To which I would add that the foliage is glossy, seems (so far) to be mildew resistant, and its performance in my Virginia garden, where it flowers along with white physostegia, has been equally praiseworthy. In my sandy soil it tops out at about four feet. Graham Thomas puts it under *Aster novi-belgii*, the New York aster, but A. R. Buckley in *Garden Perennials* attributes it to *A. laevis*, the smooth aster, which given its glossy leaves and earlier flowering time, does seem possible. While all this has been going on mealycup sage (*Salvia farinacea*) will have outbloomed the lot. No blue-flowered plant I know better earns its place, whether grown as a perennial (Zone 7/8 is the borderline) or as an annual. The blue leans toward violet and it is an excellent mixer with the yellows or the pinks.

YELLOW AND GREEN

Green is a taken-for-granted color, so prevalent that we scarcely recognize its presence and variability. An all-green garden is a cool and restful place, saved from monotony by the great range of different greens and the changing patterns of dark and light as the sun moves across the heavens. The dark green of yews, or ground-covering ivy, seem almost black by comparison with the lighter green of a lawn, while other greens verge on yellow or blue.

Green encompasses as many different shades and tints as any other color. In this overall shot what one notices is the contrast between the pool of light green grass and the darker green of the shrubs surrounding it. When one is in the garden the green becomes a taken-for-granted neutral background and attention focuses on the extensive collection of perennials and other plants growing in front of and between the shrubs. (Garden of John Treasure, Burford House, near Tenbury Wells, England; June)

Yellow is the color best perceived by the human eye, a fact made unpleasantly apparent to me when the electric company fitted a bright yellow plastic sheath over a wire pole-stay in my garden—an eyesore soon removed; I'll risk being sued if someone walks into it! The equally showy scintillating whites combine well with yellow.

The eye is quick to notice subtle differences between one yellow and another, so a random mix of yellows is hard to orchestrate unless they are separated by white, gray, or blue. A gradual transition is best: from greenish yellow through lemon yellow, pure yellow, and finally the warm golden yellows. Slight differences in color are hard to visualize and

In the foreground is creamy yellow Chrysanthemum × rubellum 'Mary Stoker', then "mum" chrysanthemum 'Target' separated by blue rue from the acid yellow flowers of Patrinia scabiosifolia. In the background is the hardy orange (Poncirus trifoliata) with its small orange fruits. (Virginia; October)

A garden painting composed entirely of green except for the gray of the rock and reflecting bowl. Plants include baby-tears (Soleirolia soleirolii) in the paving, piggyback plant—so called because infant plantlets develop on top of mature leaves—(Tolmiea menziesii), and aspidistra. (Garden of Mrs. Starr Bruce, northern California; May)

still harder to describe but fanning out the color strips on the R.H.S. color charts makes the progression of color easy to follow.

Yellow is a color we associate with the sun, and in early spring daffodils and forsythia—not to mention dandelions—herald its return, but most yellow-flowered early perennials prefer some shade where summers are hot, including doronicums, columbines, primroses, marsh marigolds (Caltha palustris), the creeping double buttercup (Ranunculus repens 'Flore Pleno'), the exquisite lemon yellow Disporum flavens (synonym D. sessile 'Flavens'), the celandine poppies (Stylophorum), and the Welsh poppy (Meconopsis cambrica). Welsh poppies don't much care for hot climates but in cool summer regions self-sow so prolifically that they are better placed among shrubs than mixed with other perennials: try them scattered among yellow and orange Exbury azaleas. Two early flowerers that do want sun are the dynamic basket-of-gold (Aurinia saxatilis) and the greeny yellow Euphorbia myrsinites. There is a plethora of sun-loving yellow-flowered perennials for summer and autumn.

Yellow is never a shy color—even the pastels do not go unnoticed as can so easily happen with the very pale lavenders and lilacs—but at one end of its range yellow is a warm color, at the other end cool and refreshing. Warm yellows are advancing colors, cool ones more or less neutral but influenced by their neighbors—a greenish or lemon yellow might seem to advance relative to blue, but to recede relative to orange. Lacking color charts and accurate descriptions, there are a few clues in the names of plants. The sun is perceived as warm, the moon as cool, gold as warm, silver as cool. So *Achillea* 'Moonshine' is a cooler color than *Achillea* 'Coronation Gold', *Anthemis* 'Moonlight' is one of the paler colors in the range, and *Coreopsis* 'Moonbeam' is a cool, pale color while *Coreopsis* 'Sunray' is a warm and glowing yellow. "Primrose" means oenotheras, or sundrops, to many Americans, but when used to describe color it means the pale yellow of the English woodland primrose, *Primula vulgaris*. Citrus fruits include oranges but "citron" means lemon yellow: *Aurinia saxatilis* is a brilliant, sunny yellow, *A. s.* 'Citrina' a cooler lemon yellow.

The most versatile yellows, and the best beloved by artistic gardeners, are the pastels, whether light lemons, pale sulfur, or creamy tints of golden yellow. They are at ease in all company, neither overwhelming nor overwhelmed by their companions. There are quite a lot of them but never too many; these are some that come to mind: *Achillea × taygetea*; *Aconitum orientale* and *A. vulparia* (the original wolfsbane); *Anthemis* 'Moonlight' (pale lemon yellow) and 'Wargrave' (creamy yellow); some columbines, especially the new *Aquilegia canadensis* 'Corbett'; *Camassia leichtlinii* 'Plena' (a beauty, don't overlook it); *Centaurea ruthenica*; *Cephalaria gigantea*; *Coreopsis* 'Moonbeam'; *Crocosmia* 'Solfatare'; *Delphinium zalil* (not easy to grow well); several foxgloves but with only *Digitalis grandiflora* at all well known; *Disporum flavens* (*D. sessile* 'Flavens'); *Gladiolus tristis* (for the favored few where winters are warm); *Helichrysum* 'Sulphur Light', *Kirengeshoma palmata*; torch lilies (*Kniphofia*) such as 'Little Maid', 'Maid of Orleans', and 'Vanilla'; *Lysimachia ciliata* and *L. vulgaris*; *Nepeta govaniana*; *Onosma echioides*; some peonies; a

yellow form of *Penstemon barbatus*; *Phlomis russeliana*; *Phygelius* 'Yellow Trumpet'; *Potentilla recta sulphurea*; several primroses including *Primula vulgaris* and the exquisite "moonlight primrose" *P. alpicola*; *Scabiosa ochroleuca*; *Sisyrinchium striatum*; *Thalictrum speciosissimum*; a few globeflowers (*Trollius*), with 'Moonglow' among the best; and the merrybells (*Uvularia*).

Creamy and lemony yellows are also to be had from foliage, especially the young spring growth. The creamy yellow leaves and blue flowers of the variegated periwinkle (*Vinca minor* 'Argenteo-variegata') combine exquisitely with the soft yellow of the wild English primrose (*Primula vulgaris*) or the blue of Virginia bluebells (*Mertensia virginica*). Keep the periwinkle under control by occasionally gathering up a bunch of the trailing stems and cutting them off near the base. The buttery yellow new leaves of an ivy called 'Lemon Swirl', or *Euonymus* 'Emerald Gaiety' (cream in spring becoming white in summer, touched with pink in winter) could echo the

Golden yellow flowers don't harmonize with pink roses but pastel and lemon yellows do. Phlomis russeliana, with whorls of butter yellow flowers, is very hardy (Zone 4) and in the warmer zones it retains its leaves through winter. (England; June)

Primula vulgaris with the cream-edged foliage of Vinca minor 'Argenteo-variegata'. The periwinkle can be used as ground cover, or kept more compact by periodically gathering up and shearing off a handful of its trailing tresses before they've had time to put down roots. (Virginia; May)

pale yellow of *Disporum flavens* (*D. sessile* 'Flavens') or *Aquilegia canadensis* 'Corbett' or contrast with the bright blue flowers of brunnera, *Pulmonaria angustifolia*, or *P. longifolia*, and the variegated Solomon's seal (at its creamiest when newly unfolded) could rise over a carpet of blue ajuga.

In many parts of the United States, yellow foliage has been perceived as chlorotic, therefore undesirable. Hostas have broken through this prejudice. One of the oldest yellow-leaved cultivars, *Hosta fortunei* 'Aurea', has long been popular in England but it fares less well in the United States, where heat often wilts or scorches the thin-textured leaves, which in any case turn green as the season progresses. Among the top twenty hostas in the Hosta Society popularity poll are four more robust yellow-leaved kinds: 'Gold

Standard', 'Sum and Substance' (this has particularly thick, weather- and slug-resistant leaves), 'Piedmont Gold', and 'August Moon'. And nature was kind in making the white and pale purple flowers of hostas so compatible with their yellow leaves.

Yellow foliage can simulate sunshine in a shady place but in dense shade it may turn green, while in hot sun it may scorch, so it often is a matter of trial and error to find the right place for a plant (collectors), or the right plant for a place (designers). Where that right place is varies a lot from one region to another but plants wanting shade can usually take morning sun or shifting sun under high-branched trees. Among my own successes with plants so sited are the ivies 'Lemon Swirl' and 'Buttercup', chartreuse-bracted *Euphorbia* × *martinii*, and the coin-dotted leopard plant

Filipendula ulmaria 'Aurea' shines lantern bright in the slanting rays of the sun. In cool regions it can be grown in full sun provided it gets abundant moisture. Where the growing season is long, cut it back when the foliage gets shabby and it will make new leaves that stay attractive through autumn. (England; early July)

Hosta 'August Moon' with Euphorbia × martinii, growing in dappled shade. (Virginia; May)

(*Ligularia tussilaginea* 'Aureo-maculata') beloved of flower arrangers. The last has bright yellow daisylike flowers nicely matched to the dappled leaves: they are among the last flowers of the year and are borne only where summers are long and hot. Yellow-leaved meadowsweet, *Filipendula ulmaria* 'Aurea', needs more moisture than I could provide but can be splendid in spring (it turns greener in summer) where that need can be met.

"Yellow" foliage and "green" flowers are often greenish yellow or chartreuse, a color seldom seriously amiss and particularly compatible with the blue-greens or blue-grays of rue and many hostas. Chartreuse is not at its best with golden yellow, and silver-gray can make it look jaundiced. Pale pink can make it look sickly too but with red, crimson, magenta, or orange chartreuse is dramatic.

One partnership I admired was *Alchemilla mollis* with a crimson-red dianthus called 'Brympton Red'. In my garden the scarlet fire pink (*Silene virginica*) leaning over golden oregano (*Origanum vulgare* 'Aureum') delighted me for a couple of years, until the fire pink unaccountably took itself off, as plants are wont to do. ("Never mind," wrote a friend, after a particularly harsh winter killed a lot of her plants, "it makes room for something else.")

The blendability of green flowers makes them very popular, though there aren't many of them. Euphorbias and alchemilla head the list. Others that come to mind include pineapple lily (*Eucomis*), several hellebores (*Helleborus*), false hellebore (*Veratrum viride*), fringecups (*Tellima grandiflora*), the calla lily (*Zantedeschia*) called 'Green Goddess', the quaint little green-rose plantain (*Plantago major* 'Rosularis'), the annual bells-of-Ireland (*Molucella laevis*), a green-flowered annual zinnia, the name of which I do not know, and the tender *Bupleurum fruticosum*, which is a shrub in frost-free regions but often used as a perennial in Zone 8. Two somewhat similar greeny yellow plants that look like euphorbias but actually belong to the Umbelliferae, or carrot, family are *Smyrnium perfoliatum* (a biennial) and *Bupleurum rotundifolium* (an annual), both available from seed houses.

ORANGE

In her own border Miss Jekyll worked out color combinations that have been, and will continue to be, widely emulated, but her use of color was far from stereotyped and many different combinations were tried in the gardens she designed for clients. Many other artistic gardeners have contributed to the fund of color knowledge, and continue to do so, but many possibilities remain to be explored by those Karel Čapek so well described as the "creatively discontent." The potential of the "hot" colors, in particular, has been neglected. This is because they need abundant sun to give their best and most color observations in the past have been based on cloudy England.

Orange is often shunned as strident and certainly it is capable of striking a jarring note. Some add a touch of orange to bring zest to a planting of purples and pinks. It does make an exclamation point that concentrates attention but the exclamation is usually "ouch." A few may genuinely like it but I suspect a throwing down of the gauntlet, a perverse satisfaction in hearing one visitor say to another (seldom to the perpetrator) "I don't like *that*." If you are among the majority, watch out for the hybrid border phloxes (*Phlox paniculata*); there are one or two with flowers so nearly orange that they do not mix well with the predominant whites, pinks, and pur-

Two very different effects employing Alchemilla mollis—*brilliant in combination with* Dianthus 'Brympton Red', *left, a subtle echo with* Hosta fortunei 'Obscuramarginata', *right. (England; July)*

In this garden the hot colors have a corner of their own, seen in the background, but a clump of orange torch lilies was put among the pinks and blues in a spirit of experiment. (Garden of Mrs. J. R. McCutchan, Bates Green Farm, Arlington, Sussex, England; July)

Purplish pink foxgloves add zest to a well-composed border of sparkling reds and yellows from achilleas, poppies, and coralbells (Heuchera) of reddish pink, softened by blue delphiniums and erigerons, pale apricot alstroemerias, and pale pink lupines touched with red. (England; June)

*Hot colors at the far end of my garden, with butterfly weed (*Asclepias tuberosa*), prickly pear (*Opuntia humifusa*), red-and-yellow gaillardias, and the yellow-striped leaves of* Yucca *'Golden Sword'. (Virginia; May)*

ples. Similarity of form sometimes unites discordant colors, but not with pink and orange phloxes. *Rosa moyesii* bears orange hips in autumn, bottle-shaped and beautiful, but you may not care for the association with pink and purplish asters.

Scarlet, orange, and golden yellow makes an exhilarating nonclashing scheme best placed away from house windows and main walkways, so that it does not fatigue the eye with its unremitting presence but comes as a surprise. For maximum brilliance use flowers with dense color such as bee balm (*Monarda* 'Cambridge Scarlet'), butterfly weed

(*Asclepias tuberosa*), coreopsis, *Crocosmia* (or *Montbretia*), *Curtonus* (or *Antholyza*), gaillardias, gazanias, lilies, sundrops (*Oenothera fruticosa*), torch lilies (*Kniphofia*), yarrows (*Achillea*), and sunflowers (*Helianthus*, *Heliopsis*).

Daylilies come in such a great array of colors that they are invaluable when a precise tint or shade is sought. For contrast in texture and shape one might add the tall, feathery scarlet-flowered spires of *Ipomopsis rubra*, a biennial, and southern gardeners should certainly try *Clinopodium coccineum* (synonym *Satureja coccinea*), a bushy, drought-tolerant shrublet with wiry stems bearing a succession of tubular scarlet flowers from late summer through autumn. It somewhat resembles California fuchsia (*Zauschneria*), which could also be used where it does well. One of the best selections of this California native arose in Ireland and is called *Zauschneria* 'Glasnevin'.

If a less dazzling but still sunny look is wanted, mix in some plants with less dense inflorescences, such as blackberry lily (*Belamcanda chinensis*), such creamy yellow flowers as *Anthemis* 'Wargrave', *Lysimachia vulgaris*, and torch lilies (*Kniphofia*) such as 'Vanilla' or 'Little Maid'. Pale or dull blues could be added but blue and orange are much more effective together where there is a lot of blue and just a little orange. White and silver-gray are merely inoffensive with orange, neither enhancing nor subduing it but the blue-gray of many hostas does flatter orange. Orange-flowered *Geum* 'Borisii' does well in light shade and hostas such as 'Halcyon' and 'Love Pat' are a very good foil for it. I'm fond of a small-flowered orange daylily called 'Baby Pumpkin' but moved it from pillar to post without finding quite the right place until it finally came to rest in front of *Fothergilla* 'Blue Mist' which has blue-gray leaves.

Orange and scarlet look superb in an

Geum 'Borisii'
with a blue-green
hosta, growing in
light shade and
moist soil. (June)

Attention focuses
on the single
small spot of or-
ange from 'En-
chantment' lilies
among the yellow
of Coreopsis lan-
ceolata and blue
Salvia farinacea.
(Garden of Gladys
and Alain
Huyghe, Virginia;
June)

The combination of vibrant orange poppies with Spiraea 'Gold Flame', top, was photographed in England in late June. The flowers of Oriental poppies stay in bloom for only a week or two and their foliage usually goes summer dormant. The combination was reinterpreted, bottom, in my garden with a paler poppy not certainly identified, grown from seed as Papaver pilosum. This retains its foliage all season, also through mild winters. It blooms profusely in spring, then continues to produce a sprinkling of flowers through summer if dead ones are removed. The effect is less dramatic but longer lasting, with the disadvantage that the apricot poppies and purplish pink spiraea flowers coincide for a week or two.

otherwise green setting: to my mind's eye comes a conflagration of poppies on a California hillside, butterfly weed (*Asclepias tuberosa*) in a New England meadow, an embankment sheeted with dancing columbines on the Yorktown battlefield, and a mountain slope in the Sierras painted scarlet with Indian paintbrush (*Castilleja*). Because orange seems to advance toward you, it has great garden value for spotlighting areas that otherwise might go unnoticed, either because they are distant or because the colors used are cool receding blues and greens. For a single spot of attention-getting orange I know no better plant than the very sturdy lily called 'Enchantment', a splash of vivid color undiluted by green leaves. Orange makes a scintillating but by no means garish combination with the lime green of such perennials as euphorbias, alchemilla, and the chartreuse-leaved feverfew (*Chrysanthemum parthenium* 'Aureum').

Orange Oriental poppies are among the most vibrant of flowers for a week or two each spring or early summer, then they go dormant, leaving a gap. The most imaginative combination my camera has recorded involving poppies was a large clump of a double-flowered bright orange kind planted close enough to *Spiraea japonica* 'Gold Flame' that the flower stalks leaned over and gained support from this bushy shrub. The surrounding plants were green at that early stage of the flowering season. The poppy flowers picked up the bronze tints in the yellow leaves of the spiraea, a combination gay but not gaudy. This small shrub responds well to pruning and if cut back hard in late winter expands during spring and early summer to fill the gap left when the poppy goes dormant in summer. It is unfortunate that it bears bright pink flowers at odds with its yellow leaves, but these do not come until after poppy time.

Vibrant color schemes lift the spirits but

orange can also add sparkle without flamboyance if the individual flowers are of a less dramatic kind thinly sprinkled among green and yellow or white and blue. In one Colonial-style Virginia garden a dainty yet scintillating picture had been composed with small orange poppies sprinkled among early oxeye daisies (*Chrysanthemum leucanthemum* 'May Queen'), with a touch of blue here and there from *Veronica spicata* all contained within low hedges of rounded boxwoods. Orange-flowered trumpet honeysuckle (*Lonicera* 'Dropmore Scarlet') was trained on a nearby fence. These poppies were Iceland poppies (*Papaver nudicaule*), a short-lived perennial often used as an annual. The perennial *P. lateritium* (*P. pilosum* is similar), which is easily raised from seed, also has orange flowers of comparatively modest size and would be an appropriate, longer-lived substitute. A charming early summer combination in moist soil consisted primarily of green foliage, highlighted with touches of orange and yellow from geums, doronicums, and the yellow leaf edge of *Hosta* 'Frances Williams'.

A shade of orange often found in chrysanthemums and sometimes in daylilies but otherwise uncommon is the brick red of *Euphorbia griffithii* 'Fireglow'. This, more than most, is influenced by the color of its companions: bright by comparison with pale blue camassias, sultry with purple-leaved smoke bush (*Cotinus coggygria* cultivars), and at its most brilliant with yellow. You might even find it acceptable with purplish pink. Which of the two pictures on page 153 do you prefer?

Orange is often disdained by the color conscious, though not, in the form of the ubiquitous marigold, by the general public. The few who do favor orange usually let it do what it does best—sing out. Theoretically, it can be toned down by merging it into progressively lighter tints and darker shades, but until re-

A bed, top and bottom, *edged with boxwoods contains geums, poppies, 'May Queen' shasta daisies, and blue Veronica spicata. (Garden of Mr. and Mrs. Henry L. Valentine II, Virginia; May)*

A combination by no means gaudy in moist soil and light shade, with orange Geum *'Borisii', yellow doronicums and geums, and* Hosta *'Frances Williams'. The large incised leaves* top right *are the ornamental rhubarb,* Rheum palmatum. *(Garden of Mrs. Arnold Rakusen, England; June)*

The purplish ornamental onion gives fillip to yellow and orange. Some like it, others don't, but it seldom goes unnoticed. Compare these two similar pictures. Left: Euphorbia griffithii *'Fire Glow' with the yellow foliage of* Cornus alba *'Spaethii'.* Right: Euphorbia griffithii *'Fire Glow' with* Euphorbia palustris *and* Allium aflatunense. *(both England; late June)*

Oriental poppies make a traffic-stopping splash of color in an English village in late June. From the owners' side of the wall the gap will be hidden by other plants when the poppy display is over for the year.

cently the paucity of perennials in tones of orange precluded this approach. Daylilies have amply filled that gap and abundant potential exists for artistic combinations employing orange, possibilities best exploited in America, where the daylily performs best and the widest range is available. Perhaps in due course the popularity and ease of cultivation of the daylily will overcome the widespread dislike of orange.

Most orange flowers are for summer and for sun but I have a little patch in spring shade with *Epimedium* × *warleyense*, an orange form of celandine (*Ranunculus ficaria*), and an orange primrose that turned up among a batch grown from seed of Barnhaven hybrids of *Primula vulgaris*. The celandines are tucked among the roving roots of the epimedium,

where its leaves appear very early in the year. Then come its flowers, with those of the epimedium raised well above them on wiry stems, and finally the epimedium leaves to fill the gap as the celandines go dormant.

More difficult to place than bright orange is a color often called shrimp pink or salmon, as exemplified by that pretty dianthus called 'Helen'. Nearly everyone likes this color but because it rides the borderline between pink and orange it is not easy to combine with either group of colors. Sequester it among blue flowers and gray foliage and the group becomes easier to place.

RED

Even more than orange, red commands attention, yet without the stigma of garishness so often attached to orange. Painters have long recognized its value as a catalyst in an otherwise quiet landscape. The eye roves over the rest of the scene but returns to gaze at the red. Red is at its most riveting in a green setting. In a mixed planting it may stand out less than yellow, bright white, or silver but it still has the ability to hold the eye.

Flowers of pure red are scarce and perhaps that is just as well as a little goes a long way. Most reds veer toward scarlet, a main component of the "hot" color schemes just discussed, others toward crimson, which is red plus a little blue, with each addition of blue moving it toward purple. Roses, tulips, and dahlias provide some of the purest reds. Clear reds are also found among Oriental poppies and peonies, and in *Crassula falcata*, *Crocosmia* 'Lucifer', *Lobelia cardinalis*, *Monarda didyma*, and *Verbena peruviana*. Some "near-misses" include *Lychnis chalcedonica* and *Potentilla* 'Gibson's Scarlet', which lean toward scarlet, and *Schizostylis coccinea* 'Major' which approaches crimson.

It is interesting to note that whilst perennials with orange flowers are predominantly sun lovers, some of the best red flowers are found in plants that perform well in light shade, and prefer this in the South. These include *Lobelia cardinalis*, *Monarda didyma*, the fire pink (*Silene virginica*), *Spigelia marilandica*, and the red-fruited baneberry (*Actaea rubra*).

Lychnis chalcedonica *with mock orange* (Philadelphus). *Red draws the eye but white is the dominant color, even in sunlight, more markedly so on dull days or at dusk.*

*In green surroundings red does dominate. Berries are associated with autumn but the red fruits of baneberry (*Actaea rubra*) ripen in summer, which makes it a useful plant for enlivening shade plantings of ferns and rhododendrons. (Garden of Roy Davidson, Washington; July)*

Observing the rule that reds containing blue should not be mixed with reds containing yellow, clearly crimson cannot be combined with scarlet or orange, yet I have seen this done most beautifully in a spring scheme employing crimson peonies and orange poppies, brought into harmony by pale apricot tulips streaked with crimson. Yellow doronicums were also present, and a sprinkling of blue throughout from forget-me-nots and *Brunnera*. Nature often manages to harmonize in a single flower colors we think to clash, and such flowers are invaluable when trying to integrate two colors otherwise thought incompatible.

There are differences of opinion as to whether the three primary colors, red, yellow, and blue, or any two of them, combine attractively as pure, fully saturated hues. Some enjoy such cheerful combinations, others consider them gaudy. Certainly the three together contrast quite stridently. The contrast between red and yellow is abrupt but if orange is added as intermediary the grouping is less well adapted to beds that also contain pink. Strong contrasts are usually acceptable if used sparingly, and the scarcity of pure blues and reds makes it unlikely that such combinations will be overdone. The contrast of red with pure white is no less strong but seldom found objectionable.

Most shrubs flower in spring so the role of perennials in providing summer color is an important one. One splash of red among the greens of a shrub garden in summer draws the eye and holds it within the picture, a picture composed of the play of dark and light of the many shades of green and the shadow patterns. Red is also accentuated by the gray of walls or paving.

A strong use of color is the red-and-purple border, of which the one shown on page 158 is a fine example. Such borders rely heavily on shrubs, annuals, and the dahlias that supply some of the truest reds. The reddish brown or purplish brown foliage called "purple" in gardening parlance is comparatively rare among perennials, and most of the few available have flowers of unsuitable color for a red-and-purple theme. Among the few are several new bronze-leaved selections of *Cimicifuga*, *Heuchera* 'Palace Purple', purple-leaved hybrids of *Lobelia cardinalis*, black mondo grass (*Ophiopogon planiscapus* 'Nigrescens'), and purple plantain (*Plantago major* 'Rubrifolia'). Purple-leaved ajugas (the blue flowers having gone by before the red-and-purple theme gets under way) could be included, and possibly *Sedum maximum* 'Atropurpureum', though the dusty pink flowers are less than ideal in this setting and, given its tendency to sprawl, a place behind a silvery plant such as *Santolina pinnata* (which has off-white flowers) would display it better.

Perennials with flowers of this rich reddish brown are few. Some can be found among dahlias and daylilies, and there is the chocolate-scented *Cosmos atrosanguineus*, once a collector's item, but now available from a few American mail-order nurseries. Unfortunately this is not very cold hardy.

Red-and-purple borders invariably include such purple-leaved shrubs as *Berberis thunbergii* 'Atropurpurea', purple selections of the smoke bush (*Cotinus coggygria*), purple-leaf hazel (*Corylus maxima* 'Purpurea') and the sand cherry (*Prunus × cistena*). The dahlias in the border shown include 'Doris Day' and the purple-leaved 'Bishop of Llandaff'. Among the annuals and half-hardy plants, all with red flowers or purple leaves, are cannas, tuberous begonias, pelargoniums, a dark red dwarf coleus, beefsteak plant (*Iresine*), and ruby chard. There are also near-red clematis such as 'Mme. Julia Correvon', and red roses. Because its red flowers are accompanied by foliage strongly red-brown tinted, 'Europeana' would be a very suitable rose, and a new celosia with purple leaves and red

Bicolored tulips orchestrate the crimson of the peonies with the orange of the poppies, helped by a sprinkling of blue and enlivened with yellow doronicums, the strongest color in the scene. (Wallington, England (a National Trust property); June)

The red flowers of Crassula falcata accentuate the textural detail of the seat and paving. (Garden of Harland Hand, Bay Area of California; September)

flowers called 'Red Chief' might have been tailor-made for schemes such as this. Purple orach (*Atriplex hortensis* 'Rubra'), the castor bean (*Ricinus communis*) called 'Dwarf Red Spire', and the annual hibiscus called 'Coppertone' are other possibilities, and perhaps purple perilla, though this actually *is* tinted purple rather than red-brown.

Red-and-purple borders are dramatic—perhaps *too* dramatic for gardens of average size. Because they include many annuals and tender plants they are also labor intensive. Most of us will want to try red and purple on a much smaller scale, or perhaps to soften it with gray. *Monarda* 'Cambridge Scarlet' against a purple-leaved barberry or smoke bush would make a good beginning. A combination enjoyed in my own garden is a patch of the red tulip 'Keukenhof' among white *Phlox subulata* against a background of purple barberry (*Berberis thunbergii* 'Atropurpurea'). In the Chicago Botanic Garden *Celosia* 'Red Chief' was stunning with the gray-leaved, rather tender *Helichrysum petiolatum*.

GARDENER'S PURPLE

This seems an appropriate place to explore further the possibilities of purple foliage. It is so often said that white and gray are the great harmonizing colors, and so they are if one excludes the bright pure whites and scintillating silver-grays that are excellent as *contrast* for other bright colors but not for merging one into another. As harmonizers I would rank the brownish colors gardeners know as "purple" equally with soft white and the less light-reflecting grays.

Foliage colors described by gardeners as purple bear little resemblance to that color as nongardeners envisage it. Very few plants have truly purple leaves, nor would most of us think it desirable that they should. One that does is *Setcreasea pallida* 'Purple Heart', a plant related to tradescantia sometimes used in bedding schemes. Although a perennial, it survives only light frost. The purple or bronze foliage of garden writing is reddish or purplish brown, as compatible with other colors

as brown earth. Soil, however, has a matte, light-absorbing surface, while most purple-leaved plants gain a glow from their shiny light-reflecting surface.

The exact color of "purple" foliage is quite variable, sometimes a very dark brown with a hint of true purple (e.g. *Perilla frutescens* 'Atropurpurea', *Cotinus coggygria* 'Velvet Cloak', 'Nottcutt's Variety', or 'Royal Purple') and sometimes with a bronze sheen over green, but more often the reddish brown of mahogany or the brown shoe polish that used to be called oxblood, a color that appears brown in dull weather but strongly red when backlit by the sun. The difference can be important in fine-tuning a combination. Perennials with flowers of purplish pink benefit by association with purplish brown, but orange flowers need the redder browns.

Plant names are not a reliable guide to the color of purple foliage. *Cotinus coggygria* 'Royal Purple' does have leaves of very dark purplish brown, but *C. c.* 'Purpureus' has green leaves—it's the inflorescence (the "smoke") that is purple—and *Heuchera* 'Palace Purple' is reddish brown. It cannot be

assumed that a plant called 'Atropurpurea' (dark purple) has more purple in the color than one called 'Atrorubra' (dark red). (*Berberis thunbergii* 'Atropurpurea' is called purple barberry, but the dwarf version is called 'Crimson Pygmy'.)

These reddish or purplish browns go with just about every other color. Just about! As usual, the controversial color is orange. Some like it, some don't. Much depends on the precise shade of the orange and the purple, and on what other plants grow nearby. It is orange-peel orange that most find unacceptable, but whatever its exact color the red-browns make better companions for it than the browns that contain some true purple. Many professing a general distaste for orange make an exception for *Lychnis × arkwrightii* 'Vesuvius', which marries reddish orange flowers to chocolate-colored leaves. Dahlia selections with purple leaves and dark apricot flowers are also ready sellers.

Low-growing plants with purple leaves are ineffective against brown earth. Shrubs are tall enough, or dense enough, to rise above it and make their own statement, but such

The leaves of orange-flowered Lychnis × arkwrightii 'Vesuvius' are the color of bitter chocolate. Behind are the silvery leaves of the biennial giant thistle, Onopordum acanthium. *(Garden of Susan Ryley, Victoria, British Columbia; late May)*

plants as black mondo grass (*Ophiopogon planiscapus* 'Nigrescens') or purple-leaved ajugas are visually lost against brown earth or bark-mulch paths, where a cream- or yellow-striped mondo grass or liriope, or a gray-leaved ajuga, would be a better choice, and although purple and green are not incompatible, neither are they mutually enhancing: *Heuchera* 'Palace Purple' is much better displayed alongside a gray path or rock than adjacent to green lawn—more important, however, is that it be placed where sun can shine through and redden the leaves.

Combinations of purple foliage and yellow flowers can be as blatant or as subtle as you please. The brighter the yellow and the more solid the form of the plants, the more vibrant—strident some may think—the combination will be. Purple fennel (*Foeniculum vulgare purpureum*) marries yellow buds and flowers to feathery mahogany foliage with buoyant grace and *Lysimachia ciliata* 'Purpurea' is a charismatic mix of small light clear yellow flowers and leaves of a soft grayed pur-

ple. At the other extreme, 'Crimson Pygmy' barberry with orange-yellow *Coreopsis auriculata* 'Nana' is a real showstopper, exciting as a spot planting but I personally wouldn't care to see it massed. Another association of considerable impact I liked was the contrast in color and form from *Liriope muscari* 'Variegata', with narrow leaf blades striped with creamy yellow, next to the purple plantain (*Plantago major* 'Rubrifolia'), which has broad leaves of dark beet red in a large rosette.

A little gem for the rock garden or raised bed is a celandine (*Ranunculus ficaria*) rejoicing in the name 'Brazen Hussy', a well-chosen name on all counts. Brazen it is, in its bold display and in the high, burnished gloss of both its purple leaves and starry buttercup yellow flowers. And a hussy in that this diminutive minx multiplies rapidly. It puts up leaves very early in the year and flowers in early spring, at which time it likes moist soil. Soon afterward it goes quickly and neatly dormant and is then indifferent to summer drought.

Herb gardeners can take their pick among numerous yellow- or purple-leaved annuals and perennials, including purple sage (*Salvia officinalis* 'Purpurascens'), purple fennel, purple perilla, purple orach (*Atriplex hortensis* 'Rubra'), golden oregano (*Origanum vulgare* 'Aureum'), and golden thyme. Golden lemon balm (*Melissa officinalis* 'All Gold') is what its name says; *M. o.* 'Aurea' is only mottled with yellow.

In rich, moist soil the yellow-edged leaves of *Hosta* 'Frances Williams' could combine boldly with the purple-lined leaves of *Ligularia* 'Desdemona' or 'Othello'. Add a golden sedge, *Carex stricta* 'Bowles' Golden', for textural contrast. If you cannot tolerate the orange daisy flowers the ligularias hold above their brownish green, purple-lined leaves, re-

Yellow and purple foliage in the herb garden at Hever Castle, England. (late June)

place them with one of the brown-leaved cimicifugas—theirs is a less intense, bronzed brown and as companion you might prefer a hosta with all-yellow leaves.

Bronze foliage is also found among the rodgersias, with *Rodgersia pinnata* 'Superba' outstanding among those at present available. You have to look closely at the handsome leaves with sharply delineated veining to see that they are indeed pinnate (shaped like a feather) as the name suggests. They appear palmate (shaped like a hand) and held palm up. The color is a soft brown with a metallic sheen, a color unlikely ever to strike a discordant note, but the two pictures, shown on page 162, one pensive, the other provocative, demonstrate the extent to which companion plants influence the mood evoked.

For a very subtle combination, try the pale lemon yellow stars of *Coreopsis* 'Moonbeam' trailing over a patch of bronze-leaved ajuga, or the cream-variegated periwinkle (*Vinca minor* 'Argenteo-variegata') intermingled with dark-leaved *Viola labradorica*. Put

these last two side by side and they'll take care of the intermingling, the violet spreading by seed, the periwinkle with trailing stems that root as they go. The butter yellow ivy called 'Buttercup' is also very pretty with this little violet.

Gray and blue associate extremely well with purple foliage, with or without yellow. I find *Rudbeckia* 'Newmanii' (similar to 'Goldsturm' rudbeckia but spreading less rapidly) very satisfying against a background of purple barberry, and even more pleasing with the addition of gray *Artemisia* 'Powis Castle' (much larger, and more summerproof in humid regions than 'Silver Mound', though not as cold hardy) and blue globe thistle (*Echinops*). In late summer and autumn the same barberry is backdrop for two asters, the blue *Aster patens* and the much deeper violet-blue 'Hella Lacy', with contrast in form provided by a gray-leaved yucca.

Among blue, gray, and purple combinations admired in the gardens of friends, two early summer schemes stand out. First, the blue *Linum perenne* 'Sapphire' in front of a purple cutleaf maple (*Acer palmatum* 'Dissectum Atropurpureum'), with a ribbon of lamb's ears (*Stachys byzantina*) edging the border and allowed to filter through the cascading outer branches of the maple. Second, shown on page 164, purple sumac (*Cotinus coggygria* 'Notcutt's Variety') with one of the taller catmints (*Nepeta gigantea*), lamb's ears, a white peony, and just a sprinkling of rose-pink flowers-of-Jove (*Lychnis flos-jovis*) in the foreground. In that same garden the blue, gray, purple, and white combination was repeated in a completely different way with *Veronica teucrium* 'Crater Lake' lining both sides of a gray paved path, backed by the purple sumac, with the annual white-flowered *Omphalodes linifolia* massed on the other side of the lawn.

One of the nicest foliage shrubs for mix-

ing with perennials is an almost thornless shrub rose with grayish purple leaves. The actual color varies so much with site, climate, and season that it has been given two names at different times. Long known to gardeners as *Rosa rubrifolia* (red-leaved rose), it is now called *R. glauca* (leaves with a gray, grapelike bloom). The gray overlaying the purple gives this rose a delicate, misty effect. Grow it for its foliage, not for its small pink single flowers. It mixes with most colors but particularly well with pink.

White-and-purple is a theme I've been exploring. The abundance of white-flowered perennials gives greater flexibility than is usual in schemes employing limited color. A row of three purple barberries (*Berberis thunbergii* 'Atropurpurea') is backdrop for a succession of white flowers from perennials and small shrubs that include the blackberry rose (*Rubus rosiflorus* 'Coronarius') and the low, spreading *Deutzia gracilis* 'Nikko'. The perennials year begins with little *Arabis sturii* and white *Phlox subulata* on the front edge, a snowy white unnamed form of *Phlox divaricata* and the equally bright white daisies of *Chrysanthemum leucanthemum* 'May Queen', which will continue to bloom through summer if dead stems are removed. Then comes *Phlox* 'Miss Lingard' (repeat blooming

Same plant, same season (early June), but two different moods. Top, *bronze-leaved* Rodgersia pinnata 'Superba' *is combined with* Euphorbia palustris *and* Hosta 'Bucksaw Blue'. *Yellow-variegated* Euonymus 'Emerald n' Gold' *and purple-leaved* Viola labradorica, *not shown in the picture, were also part of this lively composition. (Great Dixter, England)* Bottom, *the same rodgersia is dreamily combined with gray* Helichrysum angustifolium *and a pale pink form of* Clematis montana *on the wall behind. (Muckross Gardens, Ireland)*

if cut back after the first flush), and, overlapping this in bloom, the silvery-leaved, white-flowered *Lychnis coronaria* 'Alba' (a short-lived perennial that self-sows), and one of the white-flowered baptisias (probably *Baptisia pendula*). By then *Astermoea mongolica* will be opening its little white pompom flowers and will keep going well into autumn, joined in summer by *Phlox paniculata* 'Mt. Fuji' and then by *Boltonia* 'Snowbank', succeeded, as the season draws to a close, by a Korean chrysanthemum with large white single flowers.

In late May Rhododendron *'Scintillation', hostas, and ferns (also see the photograph on page 190) are the focus of attention in the garden shown below. Soon interest will shift to the long border of perennials, where a ribbon of gray-leaved* Stachys byzantina *runs past such early flowers as* Linum perenne *'Sapphire', top right, and has been allowed to mingle with the outer branches of the purple cut-leaf maple anchoring the end of the border,* bottom right. *Later in summer there'll be a fresh burst of color from daylilies. (Garden of Sydney and Martin Eddison, Connecticut; May)*

Nepeta gigantea *(also called 'Six Hills Giant') with* Stachys byzantina, Artemisia lactiflora, *a white peony,* Cotinus coggygria *'Notcutt's Variety', and a sprinkling of pink* Lychnis flos-jovis *'Hort's Variety'. (Garden of John Treasure, Burford House, Tenbury Wells, England; June)*

Far left: *Purple barberry (*Berberis thunbergii *'Atropurpurea')* *and purple perilla (*Perilla frutescens *'Crispa') with* Miscanthus sinensis *'Variegata',* Pennisetum *'Hameln', and* Astermoea mongolica *in September.* Left: *the seed plumes of the miscanthus with a late white chrysanthemum in late October. (Virginia)*

There is more purple foliage from *Ajuga* 'Jungle Bronze' and the self-sowing annual purple perilla, and white-striped foliage from *Miscanthus sinensis* 'Variegatus', which adds its own quota of smoky brown when it blooms in early autumn. Black mondo grass (*Ophiopogon planiscapus* 'Nigrescens') is interplanted with white autumn-flowering *Crocus speciosus* 'Albus'.

Elsewhere in my garden *Gaura lindheimeri* leans over 'Crimson Pygmy' barberry and *Viola labradorica* has self-sown among the trailing stems of a white variegated euonymus. An autumn combination spotted in Beth Chatto's English garden was the white-flowered form of *Cyclamen hederifolium* peeking through purple-leaved *Viola labradorica*.

When you see a grouping you admire, don't be discouraged from attempting something similar because some of the plants cannot be grown in your region. There are usually other plants you can grow that could be substituted. The focus of a grouping I saw in Ireland was an arching clump of a cream-striped New Zealand flax (probably a selection or hybrid of *Phormium colensoi*) flanked by small purple barberries amidst the yellow-green foam of *Alchemilla mollis*, the group spiced up by the magenta flowers of an adjacent geranium. New Zealand flax is not hardy at temperatures lower than 20°F but a variegated liriope could take its place, or the much hardier *Yucca* 'Golden Sword'. The taller New Zealand flaxes (*Phormium tenax*) enable us to select more precisely the degree of purple leaf color desired, choosing between dark purplish red, lighter purplish red, brownish red, and a dark green kind just flushed with maroon that makes a flattering background for pale lemon yellow daylilies. These, however, are the prerogative of those in regions where only light frosts occur.

In general, purple foliage plays a supporting role to other plants. One exception is *Aeonium arboreum* 'Zwartkop', so rewarding of close inspection that it is best equipped to serve as a specimen, in the ground or in a container, though only, alas, in such favored climates as coastal California. The yellow flowers on three-foot branched stems are of minor importance; its beauty lies in the play of light on the six-inch succulent rosettes, their color an arresting combination of almost black, velvety purple highlighted with rich ruby red where sunlit from side or back, and shading to pale yellowish green at the heart.

GRAY

Gray, the harmonizer, helps other colors give of their best and never strikes a really jarring note though it can be a tad out of tune with a cream-flowered or chartreuse-leaved neighbor. Silver-gray and scarlet make a brilliant pair, and silver-gray with lemon yellow looks deliciously cool, but with golden yellow or orange, gray is merely inoffensive. A symbol of serenity, gray is an indispensable component of that most enchanting of all color schemes, the "white" garden.

Grays are not, however, all alike, nor all harmonious with each other. They differ considerably in appearance and they also differ much more than is generally realized in their soil, site, and climate requirements. The most carefully considered color scheme will fail if the plants selected are not suitable for the environment. We need to look afresh at the grays in the light of our individual niches within the varied climates of the United States.

Many gray-leaved plants come from the Mediterranean, where they grow in hot, dry sites, but in those parts of the United States where the sun is hotter and more prolonged than it is in Europe, some of these may benefit from shade during the hottest part of the day. They may also do better in a soil enriched with compost or leaf mold, provided it does not get soggy. This makes possible some nontraditional combinations: *Stachys byzantina* might, for instance, grow next to primroses. Even when drainage is faultless, however, gray-leaved plants adapted to dry heat often rot in humid weather. It is disheartening to see that drift of silvery gray lamb's ears become overnight a patch of brown mush. But don't then despair of growing gray-leaved plants.

The only way to be sure how a plant will perform is to try it, but there are some clues to guide us, especially if *Hortus Third* is on hand for checking descriptions. Books and catalogues merely say that a plant has gray or silver leaves. *Hortus Third* describes them as glabrous (smooth and hairless), glaucous (coated with the fine gray dust or "bloom" found on plums, grapes, and cabbage leaves),

The gray of Senecio cineraria *does nothing for orange marigolds. (England; September)*

or pubescent (coated with hairs). Sometimes the hairs on a leaf are so fine that it may appear glaucous, but if it is, the gray farina can be rubbed off to reveal the green beneath. It is plants with pubescent leaves that are most likely to rot in wet or humid weather, seldom those with glabrous or glaucous leaves, though, as usual, there are exceptions: I've found the glaucous-bladed grasses *Helictotrichon sempervirens* and *Agropyron pubiflorum* intolerant of hot and humid summers and *Festuca* 'Sea Urchin' rotted in a wet one.

What purpose is served by the farina on glaucous leaves is hard to fathom, because the group encompasses plants for sun and shade, dry soils or wet ones. What most have in common is tolerance of humidity. Since the dictionary makes "damp" synonymous with "humid," I should say that I make this distinction: England is damp (chilly and moist), Virginia is humid (hot and moist). Many gray-leaved plants don't like damp weather but humid heat is a greater killer. Wrapped in their warm, wet blanket, plants with hairy leaves turn to mush. Humidity makes me perspire, dampness does not, and I conjecture that smooth gray leaves tolerate humidity better than hairy ones because they are better able to transpire (sweat).

In general, plants with glabrous or glaucous leaves are a less silvery color, often bluish gray. If, however, we count bracts as leaves, the most scintillating metallic silver of all comes from a biennial sea holly, *Eryngium giganteum*. The glaucous leaves of the yellow- or orange-flowered horned poppy (*Glaucium flavum*) are also very silvery. Other glabrous- and glaucous-leaved plants include *Euphorbia myrsinites* and the similar *E. rigida*, prickly poppy (*Argemone grandiflora*, a perennial in mild climates, elsewhere an annual), sea kale (*Crambe maritima*), the biennial Scotch thistle (*Onopordum acanthium*), blue rue (*Ruta gra-*

veolens), many pinks (*Dianthus*), and king's spear (*Asphodeline lutea*), which gets its gray sheen from multiple light-reflecting surfaces created by alternating ridges and channels in the smooth, linear leaves. These all want well-drained soil and plenty of sun.

But then there are the glaucous-leaved blue hostas such as *Hosta sieboldiana*, which need moist soil. One of the handsomest foliage perennials, *Rudbeckia maxima*, also prefers moist soil, and although the ethereal *Lysimachia ephemerum* has the sort of narrow, rather leathery gray leaves associated with drought-resistant plants, it does not thrive in dry soil nor insist on sharp drainage. The smooth-leaved yuccas are deservedly eulogized for their drought resistance, but some at least—gray-green *Yucca filamentosa* among them—are far more tolerant of shade and wet soil than is generally supposed. A welcome addition to the gray-leaved plants for shade is *Ajuga reptans* 'Kingwood', which arose as a sport on 'Silver Queen' at Kingwood Center and was named by Henry Ross. 'Gray Lady' is the same or similar.

Pubescent plants differ a lot, but what

The most widely grown of all gray-leaved perennials, lamb's ears (Stachys byzantina), growing with primroses in light shade. (Garden of Mr. and Mrs. A. Van Vlack, Connecticut; May)

Glaucous-leaved perennials for sun and shade respectively: left, Euphorbia myrsinites with Dianthus deltoides 'Brilliant' (Viette garden, Virginia; early June), and right, a Hosta tardiflora × sieboldiana hybrid with Lamium maculatum 'Shell Pink'. (Beth Chatto Gardens, Essex, England; early July)

they have in common is the need for sharp drainage. Mixing in the grit used for surfacing roads gives them the sort of soil they like. The silky hairs that coat the leaves sunproof them by restricting transpiration and reflecting the light. They are apt to look as dejected as wet cats during prolonged wet weather, and their leaves then become less gray. There is one puzzling exception. *Anaphalis triplinervis*, one of the pearly everlastings, does not like dry soil. This was the sole gray-foliaged survivor when a Seattle friend's white garden was flooded during an exceptionally wet spring.

The floss on the most silvery pubescent leaves is very noticeable. Among these are lamb's ears (*Stachys byzantina*) and *Salvia argentea*. Lamb's ears is one of the first plants to rot because the leaves lie on the soil and mound up on each other, restricting air circulation. *Senecio cineraria* is intensely silver but the leaves are well spaced and held well above the soil, enabling it to tolerate muggy weather. Horehounds (*Marrubium*) also come fairly well through summer humidity in spite of the

dense felt on their nettlelike leaves. Silver horehound (*M. incanum*) is a softer gray than the name suggests, a very good blender and equally attractive whether cut back in spring to maintain it as a hummock or allowed to sprawl over the edge of a path. The flowers are white. Mat-forming *M. cylleneum* is also a soft gray-green but each finely scalloped, rounded leaf is rimmed with silver, giving it a frosted look. The flowers are pale lavender.

The hairs on pubescent leaves are often so tiny that a magnifying lens is needed to see them. Artemisias have this kind of leaf. There is no clear pattern of rotting within this group but it does seem that the more finely cut and silvery the leaf, the more it is likely to rot: *Artemisia* 'Silver Mound' often rots, *A*. 'Powis Castle' and *A*. 'Huntington' seldom do.

Gray is considered a soft, melding color, and it usually is, but gray is as variable as other colors and there are exceptions. The intense silver-grays and silver-blues are dominating colors: does any plant have more impact than the glistening silver-blue selections

of Colorado spruce (*Picea pungens*)? One intensely silver perennial (annual in cold regions) is *Senecio cineraria* 'Cirrus', one of the dusty millers, and the similar 'Snow Cloud'. This silver-gray does not clash with any other color but it does dominate the scene and, like the hot colors, seems nearer than it is. Such strong silvers can make cream and off-white look dirty but pure, bright white can hold its own and ease the transition from silver-grays to blue-grays.

Blue-grays, such as rue (*Ruta graveolens*) and blue lyme grass (*Elymus glaucus*), are best kept well away from bright silver-gray, for they are, if not combative, wasted on each other. The yellow-greens found often in foliage (golden oregano, *Origanum vulgare* 'Aureum', for example) and occasionally in flowers are also at odds with silver-gray—they don't fight, they just sulk in each other's company—but greenish yellows can be very attractive with blue-grays and blue-greens and hostas alone provide countless opportunities for exploring the subtleties of such combinations.

The softer grays and gray-greens are quieter plants and these, with white, form part of most popular color themes: with mixtures of pastels; with pink and blue; with yellow and blue; with yellow and purple—true purple, that is; and with the bronze and mahogany foliage usually called purple. All-gray gardens can be very serene and restful if just a few kinds of contrasting form are used in quantity, with contrast between dark gray-greens and paler grays. Numerous different kinds gathered together make for an interesting collection but the effect will be spotty and probably dull.

Colors that seem harsh alone are softened by the presence of gray, but the ability of gray to integrate discordant colors is sometimes overstated—it takes an extensive sweep

of gray (or soft white) to keep them sufficiently apart and it is usually easier to move one of the combatants out.

WHITE AND CREAM

Much said about gray is also true of white. The role of soft whites as harmonizers was discussed under form. Pure, luminous white is a strong, advancing color. Put it between two other brilliant colors and, far from pacifying them, it joins the fight for attention. Pure white may make adjacent cream or off-white look in need of a wash when there is only one of each, but not as a rule in mixed plantings.

It isn't often enough said that there are degrees of white. Take the ground-covering phloxes (*Phlox subulata*, *Phlox nivalis*, *Phlox bifida*, and their hybrids). 'White Delight' is a pure and sparkling white. By contrast the smaller round-petaled flowers of 'Sneewitchen' are a chalky or slightly grayed white, and the notched petals of 'Snowflake' (which

Artemisia lactiflora looks dirty by comparison with the silvery gray of Artemisia *'Silver King'. The pink flowers are* Anemone vitifolia *'Robustissima'. (Pennsylvania; September)*

seems to be the same as 'Ellie B.') are a creamy white. I had thought dogwood flowers to be snowy white but by contrast with *Phlox* 'White Delight' they are slightly creamy; so are those of *Viburnum plicatum tomentosum* in their early stage of bloom, and an underplanting of 'White Delight' exaggerated their creaminess. *Phlox* 'Snowflake' would have been better but it isn't as vigorous, so instead I'm alleviating the whiteness by dotting in some blue: when only two colors are used they have to be just right for each other, but a third can act as referee.

The serene but sparkling association of white, green, and gray appeals to everyone, and whilst we may long for a white garden on the Sissinghurst scale, there is enchantment in a single plant with gray leaves and white flowers: *Lychnis coronaria* 'Alba', perhaps, or *Argemone grandiflora*. Successful "white gardens" on a larger scale usually include touches of pastels, especially pale lavender and pale yellow.

There is certainly no shortage of white flowers, and the addition of green comes about naturally from their foliage. Because white gardens always include gray foliage, and because this is less fleeting than flowers, a white garden or border is effective longer than most color schemes even when limited to annuals and perennials, but to get the most from it we need to draw on a full range of plants: shrubs for height, bulk, and spring flowers, roses for early summer, and, space permitting, a small tree or two—the willow-leaved pear (*Pyrus salicifolia* 'Pendula') would add more gray, or the similar *Elaeagnus angustifolia*. Bulbs should play their part: white tulips for early bloom, white lilies (none better than *Lilium regale*) for fragrance. Ground covers can conceal bare ground and flow out over paths: *Lamium* 'White Nancy' is a good one where there is a little shade, or in a cool climate. The soft form of ornamental grasses is being increasingly appreciated: several have white-striped leaves, with *Miscanthus sinensis* 'Silberpfeil' ('Silver Arrow') one of the best.

Romantic in mood, ethereal at dusk—white shows up in the gloaming when other colors can no longer be seen—the white garden also needs vines, on fences, arbors, poles, or clambering into trees and bushes. My first choice would be the night-blooming annual moonflower, *Ipomoea alba*, easily grown from seed, which opens its great white fragrant platters at dusk. In my Virginia garden hummingbirds work it for an hour or so before retiring for the night, then the whir of wings continues with hawkmoths. To go out with a flashlight and try to follow them in flight is the best reason I can think of for holding a mid-

A white garden with touches of cream, yellow, and lavender. Plants include yellow-banded Miscanthus sinensis *'Zebrinus', fluffy, creamy* Artemisia lactiflora, *gray artemisias, white phlox and garlic chives (* Allium tuberosum*), and lavender perovskia. (Garden of Ron Johnson and George Schoellkopf, northwestern Connecticut; August)*

The shrubs in this white border include mock oranges (Philadelphus 'Virginal' and P. coronarius 'Variegatus'), the shrubby potentilla 'Abbotswood', Deutzia scabra 'Candidissima', and Spiraea 'Snowmound'. Perennials include Anthericum liliago, artemisias (Artemisia ludoviciana, A. 'Powis Castle', A. 'Lambrook Silver'), Centranthus ruber 'Albus', Delphinium 'Icecap', Geranium pratense 'Album', white-striped Iris pallida 'Variegata', Lychnis coronaria 'Alba', Malva moschata 'Alba', Physostegia 'Summer Snow', Pulmonaria 'Sissinghurst White', Romneya coulteri, Viola cornuta 'Alba', white-flowered columbines and penstemons, and shasta daisies. There are white lilies (Lilium regale), a white-striped grass (Arrhenatherum elatius bulbosum 'Variegatum'), and Clematis 'John Huxtable' and 'Marie Boisselot'. (Garden of Mr. and Mrs. David Hodges, Brook Cottage, Alkerton, Oxfordshire, England; June)

night party. In the South the large seeds can go straight into the ground in early April, but it flowers earlier if plants are started indoors and this is probably necessary where the growing season is short. Sweet autumn clematis (*Clematis maximowicziana*, but often sold as *C. paniculata*) looks like a lace tablecloth hung out to dry and is magical at dusk. It is at its best in the Southeast, where it needs cutting back before the seed ripens if seedlings are not to become a nuisance. *Clematis flammula* is equally good, flowers earlier, and does not self-sow to the point of becoming a nuisance. Where winters are not too severe *C. armandii* provides fragrant flowers in spring. This needs substantial support. White potato vine (*Solanum jasminoides* 'Album') is delicate enough to ramble through large shrubs and small trees.

Cream flowers present no problems, mixing well with just about everything, though looking, in my opinion, a trifle drab when combined with pure white flowers or silver foliage. They are equal to gray as peacemakers among such strong colors as magenta, those with their flowers in soft plumes (the majority) serving this purpose particularly well. Many white flowers are cream in bud but remarkably few stay cream when fully open. Those that come to mind are *Artemisia lactiflora*, *Aruncus dioicus*, *Camassia leichtlinii* 'Plena', some peonies, *Rodgersia podophylla*, and, for shade, *Symphytum grandiflorum* and *Smilacina racemosa*. *Achillea* 'Creamy' starts off pale sulfur yellow, slowly fading to cream. *Achillea* × *taygetea* also fades to cream. A combination I enjoy is cream with purple or violet and I have sought, unsuccessfully so far, a cream-flowered companion for the violet-blue berries of the shrubby callicarpas. *Artemisia lactiflora* would be perfect, but it flowers too early in my region. I haven't tried shearing it to see if this would delay the bloom.

MAGENTA, PURPLE, AND PINK

"Malignant magenta" (Gertrude Jekyll) or "maligned magenta" (Louise Beebe Wilder)? If you really cannot tolerate magenta, you'd better beware of catalogue descriptions, where it frequently masquerades as cerise, rosy red, crimson-purple, bright pink, and a host of other euphemisms for what is thought to be an unpopular color. Someone, however, must have loved the name, if not the color, because there's a very beautiful rose called 'Magenta' that isn't magenta at all but a grayed or mauvish pink of great charm. In general, though, magenta gets few compliments, and it seems to have been in disrepute for a very long time, else why "rose mullein" for magenta-flowered *Lychnis coronaria* when magenta mullein would have been more honest, besides providing a nice bit of alliteration? Disapproval notwithstanding, again and again travelers and garden visitors are spellbound by magenta: bougainvillea cascading over a gray stone or white-painted wall with the blue sky beyond,

Chairs of mellowed magenta echo the stronger pink of Geranium sanguineum *growing through a carpet of woolly thyme (*Thymus pseudolanuginosus*). (Design by Michael S. Schultz for Mr. G. Beasley, Oregon; May)*

Pale apricot poppies sprinkled through Lychnis coronaria. *(Beth Chatto Gardens, Essex, England; late June)*

purple loosestrife in a wet meadow, ice plants (*Carpobrotus chilensis*) on Californian beaches, purple pea (*Lathyrus latifolius*) sheeting a roadside bank, or money plant (*Lunaria annua*) naturalized in a woodland clearing. For that matter, foxgloves (*Digitalis purpurea*) come mighty close to magenta, and who dislikes foxgloves? It becomes apparent that when leavened with green, gray, white, blue, or sand, magenta affronts no sensibility.

What puts us off magenta is seeing it joined with yellow and orange in what Louise Beebe Wilder so well described as a "terrible if joyous racket." Magenta with bright yellow strikes too shrill a note for most of us, and fewer still like magenta with orange. But there are always exceptions. Magenta and orange are put together by the color blind and the contrary, but also by those with sufficient flair

to make it work. A few light orange poppies popping up cheekily through a patch of rose mullein struck me as a charmingly impudent touch, and a water garden with rodgersias, ostrich ferns (*Matteuccia struthiopteris*), and massed candelabra primroses in magenta, purples, and pinks was the better for being highlighted with a few bright yellow primroses.

Few of us so delight in magenta that we'll struggle with temperamental plants of that color. Conversely, we may tolerate a plant in spite of its color if it is easy to grow: *Geranium sanguineum* is such a plant, seen in gardens more often than any other hardy geranium despite its color. A carpet of woolly thyme (*Thymus pseudolanuginosus*) interplanted with clumps of this geranium is a combination I'd certainly copy if the climate permitted—alas,

woolly thyme rots in hot and humid summers.

There aren't so many flowers of this villi-
fied color that they can't be avoided if you so
choose—*Geranium sanguineum* also comes in
a soft purplish pink ('Glenluce'), in white (*G.
s.* 'Album'), pale pink (*G. s. striatum*), and
sunrise pink (*G. s.* 'Shepherd's Warning')—
but there are among them some very good
plants, plants that most do enjoy, covet even,
when seen in the right company. If your sensi-
tively composed scheme of soft pinks, grays,
and whites seems somehow lackluster, an in-
jection of shrieking magenta may be just what
is needed to bring it to life. Tempted by one

of those cheap offers that usually turn out to
be a false economy, I bought a quantity of
Spanish bluebells, expecting them to be blue.
They turned out to be a wishy-washy pink and
were discarded in disgust, action regretted the
following spring when, in a friend's garden, I
saw the same pale bluebell interplanted with
Geranium sanguineum.

Do you want bright nonclashing contrast
or the gradual melting of one color into another? Bright white makes magenta more brilliant, off-white tones it down and so do green,
gray, and cream, including the pale creamy
yellows. A combination I particularly enjoyed

was *Geranium sanguineum* with cream-variegated, curly-leaved *Hosta undulata* in front of pink and cream roses. That was in the Northeast; in the Southeast, this geranium flowers with the peonies, which also give us pink and cream. Blue is seldom amiss, the effect varying with the particular blue, sometimes sharpening magenta, sometimes subduing it. Blue-green hostas and some of the blue-gray grasses, such as *Helictotrichon sempervirens* and the fescues (usually found lumped under the name *Festuca glauca*, but numerous and varied in color) set off magenta particularly well.

But if magenta is to be seen at its best, blend it into paler tints and darker shades of itself, the sort of opulent mix found in classic roses: pink, crimson, carmine, ruby red, maroon, velvety violet, and sultry grayed purple, with lesser amounts of soft white and creamy yellow. Then magenta comes into its own— sumptuous, sensuous, and wholly satisfying. A never to be forgotten picture was the glowing crimson-magenta of the rose 'Henri Martin' with the softer cerise plumes of *Filipendula purpurea*.

On a simpler scale, in the Rockies nature painted a picture far from garish with a single

Geranium psilostemon with a pink form of Astrantia major. (Oregon; July)

clump of magenta locoweed (*Oxytropis*) amidst a drift of the same species the color of raspberry mousse. Alert for similar associations in gardens, I found rose mullein (*Lychnis coronaria*), the magenta flowers tempered by its own silvery foliage, underplanted with pale pink *Geranium sanguineum striatum*, and then the exceptionally pretty association of *Geranium psilostemon*'s magenta with the pink-and-white blend of an astrantia, each enhancing the other, neither dominant, a partnership of rare perfection. In the rock garden try *Geranium sanguineum* with a pale pink form of *Armeria maritima*.

What else do we have that might loosely be called magenta? Some bergenias to begin with, but they flower so early, and their own foliage is so bold, that they disturb no one. *Lespedeza thunbergii* flowers at the other end of the season and although the color is brash, the plant is graceful in form and delicate of foliage. At this time of year there are white, blue, pink, and purple asters aplenty to keep it agreeable company. The creeping thyme called 'Coccineus' harmonizes naturally with other thymes in a potpourri of white, pink, or pale purple flowers and green or gray foliage.

Two of rock garden stature are *Geranium subcaulescens* 'Splendens' and wine-cups, *Callirhoe involucrata*. Both are stunning trailing over gray rock, or gray paving for that matter. *Lychnis viscaria* 'Splendens Flore-pleno' is also quite small but its audacious color shouts a cheerful greeting from afar: ". . . the magenta flowers are not admired by all gardeners," says *Wyman's Gardening Encyclopedia*. I've admired it as underplanting for *Weigela florida* 'Variegata', a medium-sized shrub with white-variegated leaves and pale pink flowers that coincide with those of the lychnis.

There are phloxes that verge on magenta, but with so many others to choose from they are usually ignored by nurseries and garden-

ers alike. Not so, however, *Astilbe taquetii* 'Superba'. Few who can grow this well (it needs rich, moist soil) would disdain it, though I must say that rusty brown doesn't enhance magenta and that's what you get for a while when the flowers on half the spike are dead. There's a time to turn a blind eye with most plants—"You don't always look your best either," said a well-known landscape architect, defending such occasions. Paler pink

Rosa 'Henri Martin' with Filipendula purpurea and Mimulus lewisii in the rose garden at Sissinghurst Castle, England. (June)

Magenta Lythrum salicaria *in the background is calmed down by pale pink astilbes and* Geranium endressii. *(Garden of Kathleen Hudson, England; July)*

astilbes would be nice with *A. t.* 'Superba' if they did not disobligingly decline to coincide at this late time of year. It is gorgeous in a drift all on its own in the cool of a lightly shaded water garden, or with its spirelike flowers accentuated by the broad blue-gray leaves to be found in many hostas. In English gardens it is frequently combined with the bright yellow grassy leaves of *Carex stricta* 'Aurea' but that's a bit too strong for me.

Blue-gray hostas are also perfect companions for the cerise of *Filipendula purpurea*.

The paler pinks are seldom a topic for debate. Pink, white, and gray is a romantic combination many enjoy. In this the "pinks" (*Dianthus*) serve us well and none I know has flowers more exquisite nor foliage more silvery than one called 'Inchmery'. It is not, however, long-lived—few of the hybrid border pinks are. Simpler old selections of *Dianthus plumarius* have lower, denser mats of finer foliage and these go on forever. There are more pink flowers available than any of us can find room for, so if a particular plant isn't quite the right color, finding a replacement isn't hard. Be wary of the salmon pinks, and don't handicap yourself by making *Sedum* 'Autumn Joy' the basis of a pink theme. It is such a good plant that this might seem a good idea, but there is salmon and brick red in its late stages and this will limit what you can put with it.

Freed of the pinkish cast that characterizes magenta, strong purple is generally liked, at least if judged by the popularity of such flowers as *Liatris* 'Kobold' and *Allium giganteum*. Its stridency was made purposeful in a Victorian-style conservatory displaying foliage houseplants of the stolid dark green kind. The light was dim, the atmosphere somber, but in one corner purple impatiens was banked with bright yellow chrysanthemums. Shocking, yes, but also enlivening. Eye and mind soon weary of such strong color but here, where visitors came and went it struck a note of cheer in what might have been a gloomy place on a dull and rainy day.

Pale purple is a restful color and can be used to soften the harsher purples. Try *Liatris* 'Kobold' echoed by the paler purple of bergamot (*Monarda fistulosa*). Some prefer to keep all purples away from blues, others delight in just such combinations. Pale purple is at its

most winsome with white, cream, creamy yellow, and silver-gray. A pretty ornamental mint, *Mentha longifolia*, combines pale purple flowers with gray leaves most appealingly—unfortunately it is, like most of the mints, extremely invasive.

COLOR ECHOES

Leafing through a magazine in a doctor's office I came across a personality quiz that asked this question: "Do you see the woods, or the trees?" In gardening, designers see the woods, plant collectors see the trees. The two can be synchronized, but most of us lean one way or the other. I'm among those who see the trees, absorbing gardens as a series of separate pictures and noticing how they fit (or not) into the overall design only with a conscious effort. Among the most satisfying vignettes are groups of plants creatively combined, whether complete in themselves or part of a larger picture. The group doesn't have to be large, two or three plants are sometimes enough.

When I find myself lingering to analyze a composition of exceptional charm, it is likely to be what I've come to think of as an echo. By this I mean some aspect of a plant repeated in another one nearby. It might be two tones of the same color in close proximity, or neighboring flowers or leaves of the same color but different form, or the repeating in an adjacent plant of one of the colors in a bicolored or multicolored flower or leaf. Bicolored or multicolored foliage is the basis for some of the most satisfying themes. Too much sameness is boring, too much diversity bewildering, and what pleases me so much about color echoes is, I think, that although united by similarities, there is also contrast.

The possibilities are greatly increased if

Allium giganteum rises over blue columbines and a blue form of Iris tenax, *toned down by its backing of* Syringa 'Palibin'. *(Jane Platt's garden, Oregon; May)*

a full range of plants is grown: perennials, bulbs, shrubs, grasses, vines, ferns—an echo came about by chance in my own garden when pink primroses picked up the pink in the gray fronds of the Japanese painted fern (*Athyrium niponicum* 'Pictum'). Even vegetables can be put to ornamental use—ruby chard and red dahlias make a striking couple. Annuals are particularly good because they flower longer than most perennials.

Among the most versatile plants I've found for creating color echoes are hostas, daylilies, *Ajuga* 'Burgundy Glow', yellow-striped liriopes and mondo grass (*Ophiopogon*), variegated forms of sage (*Salvia officinalis*) and euonymus, pansies, and tulips.

Echoes between two kinds of flower are the hardest to coordinate and seldom effective for much more than a month. Among gardening's many disappointments are those near-misses where imagined combinations fail when put into effect because flowering times do not quite coincide. This won't happen with *Achillea* 'Salmon Beauty' because it orchestrates its own symphony with tints from cream to deep salmon in the plates of flower. Though complete unto itself it could be accentuated by echoing one of its tints with an appropriate daylily from the great range available.

Bearded irises lend themselves to exquisite echoes. The effect is fleeting but iris collectors are used to that, so for irisarians willing to spare a bit of space for something else here are a couple of ideas to encourage color scheming. A yellow iris (choose your own) could echo the yellow in such scarlet-and-yellow columbines as *Aquilegia canadensis* and *Aquilegia formosa*, and the daintiness of the columbines would counterbalance the stateliness of the iris. At Ladew Topiary Gardens in Maryland, a clump of white and citron yellow irises was placed in front of the yellow-leaved barberry (*Berberis thunbergii* 'Aurea'), over a carpet of yellow creeping Charlie (*Lysimachia nummularia* 'Aurea'). Delectable, and there'd be continuing color when the irises were but a memory until the next year.

Several longer-lasting combinations that have held me spellbound were based on yellow—usually soft yellow. Creamy yellow *Anthemis* 'Wargrave', with its mustard yellow eye, was used in two summer duos of similar color, contrasting form. In one it was paired with a goldenrod, *Solidago* 'Golden Mosa', in the other with yellow loosestrife, *Lysimachia vulgaris* (a pretty though invasive plant). Why not, then, combine all three, and maybe add pale sulfur yellow *Achillea* × *taygetea?* Perhaps, but part of the composer's skill is knowing when to leave well enough alone—a theme too much repeated might become monotonous.

Many torch lilies (*Kniphofia*) have bicolor pokers of yellow and orange. In one artistic grouping the yellow was palely echoed by fluffy *Thalictrum speciosissimum*, both further enhanced by the nearby glaucous foliage of a Scotch thistle (*Onopordum*). An autumn picture was painted with the creamy yellow, darker eyed single flowers of *Chrysanthemum* 'Mary Stoker', the brighter yellow double ones of *Chrysanthemum* 'Target', and the distant echo of *Patrinia scabiosifolia* seen across blue-gray rue. Earlier, in the same bed, touches of green and lemon yellow in the ivory flowers of the little daffodil 'W. P. Milner' were echoed in the brilliant lime green inflorescences of *Euphorbia myrsinites*. Another variation on the yellow theme had a haze of greenish yellow fennel merging into the brighter yellow of a plumed goldenrod, with contrasting form from spikes of gladiolus of pale primrose yellow with a lime green eye. An echo of a different kind came from the yellow starry flowers along the rods of king's spear (*Asphodeline lutea*), repeated in a mat of smaller yellow stars from *Sedum middendorffianum* at its feet.

The flower spikes of lamb's ears (*Stachys byzantina*) are frequently scorned and cut off. Half hidden in gray wool, just a hint of pink from the flowers is revealed, but that little was just the right faint echo for a musk mallow (*Malva moschata*), itself a delicate color. A pink early autumn threesome seen in the Midwest matched the purple eye of a phlox ('Bright Eyes', perhaps) to a purple bergamot (*Monarda*), then picked up the baby pink of the phlox with a haze of *Gypsophila* 'Pink Fairy'. But my favorite combination of pinks was the dusty pink fuzzy globose heads of *Phuopsis stylosa* (synonym *Crucianella stylosa*) next to a flat-faced pansy of blackberry-stain pink, possibly one called 'Blackberry Rose'.

Shrubs extend the scope for spring, especially in the Southeast, which is famed for spring displays of azaleas and criticized for the overuse of too few kinds. Gorgeous as these are, opportunities are missed for using their sheets of color as backdrop for other early flowers. My own favorite azalea is strappetaled, pale purple 'Koromo Shikibu', beautiful enough alone but enhanced when the darker purple spots on the petals are matched in an underplanting of purple *Primula sieboldii*. Not all such schemes work out: *Daphne* 'Carol Mackie' carpeted around with *Arabis procurrens* gives scattered white and green of similar daintiness from both, pleasing enough but calling for more contrast, something I hope to achieve by planting among the arabis a single clump of *Ligularia tussilaginea* 'Argentea', which has bold green leaves edged and margined white. This is evergreen but marginally winter hardy for me. If it doesn't make it, one of the hostas with white-edged leaves will be tried—round-leaved *Hosta decorata* would do nicely.

A simple echo, with the pale blue of catmint picked up in the deeper blue of the viola, left, and a double-echo from Anthemis 'E. C. Buxton' sprawling over a bicolored Viola tricolor seedling, bottom. Most of the plants sold as Anthemis 'E. C. Buxton' in the United States are not true to name, so if the exact color is important to your plans, see before you buy. (England; July)

Iris tectorum
'Album' with
Hosta undulata
'Albo-marginata'.
This hosta does
best in light shade
but is fairly sun
tolerant even in
hot regions. The
iris does well in
full sun or light
shade. (Virginia;
May)

Color echoes are easier to orchestrate, and more certain of success, when one or more of the plants involved is a foliage plant. Among perennials, hostas top the bill, for there are so many with white or yellow variegations that can be matched to white or yellow flowers. Try a white-edged kind (*Hosta undulata* 'Albo-marginata' is inexpensive and can still hold its own with the newcomers) with white peonies, *Lamium* 'White Nancy', the upfacing white flowers of the Japanese roof iris (*Iris tectorum* 'Album'), or fragrant white sweet rocket (*Hesperis matronalis* 'Alba'). Or how about the greenish yellow foam of alchemilla flowers tumbling over such yellow-edged hosta leaves as *Hosta fortunei* 'Obscura-marginata', or the pale chartreuse of *H.* 'August Moon' in front of the taller chartreuse-flowered *Euphorbia* × *martinii* amidst a drift of the chartreuse biennial *Smyrnium perfoliatum*? Still pursuing the greenish yellow theme, this time with herbs, carpet around yellow-flowered rue (*Ruta graveolens*) or fennel (*Foeniculum vulgare*) with golden oregano (*Origanum vulgare* 'Aureum').

The many variegated kinds of euonymus are as versatile as hostas, getting extra marks for being evergreen, losing a few in cold regions for their lesser hardiness. *Euonymus fortunei* 'Emerald Gaiety' is one of the best, a responsive shrub, easily persuaded to do what you want it to do, whether flattening itself against a wall or fence, carpeting the ground, or mounding up to three feet or more. It changes its colors as the year progresses, the edge of the green leaf rich cream in spring, becoming white and finally, with frost, gaining a touch of pink. I grow it along the front of a bed and encourage it to stay low by snipping off upward-heading sprays. Through it, right at the front, grow small clumps of a winter-dormant sedge (*Carex siderosticta* 'Variegata') with wide, cream-striped leaf blades, and the

cream of both is echoed in spring by a dainty columbine of palest primrose yellow (*Aquilegia canadensis* 'Corbett') interspersed with the evergreen fronds, coppery in spring, of Japanese sword fern (*Dryopteris erythrosora*). *Euonymus* 'Emerald n' Gold' is similar but with a bright yellow edge to the leaf. A friend matched this with the varnished yellow bobbles of a double-flowered buttercup (*Ranunculus bulbosus* 'Flore Pleno').

Those who share my penchant for creamy and citrine yellows will want to try the yellow-variegated culinary sage called 'Icterina', while I look on in envy, for it doesn't, alas, take kindly to hot and humid summers. Nor does *Alchemilla mollis*, but where these two do well they make delightful partners. An enchanting summer ensemble in a Seattle garden, as cool and refreshing as lemonade, combined this sage with the vanilla and lemon yellow torch lily 'Little Maid', the pale tint echoed in the rounded flowers of the mounding *Scabiosa ochroleuca*, echoed again in the creamy edge to the large leaves of a comfrey (*Symphytum* × *uplandicum* 'Variegatum'), then both lemon and cream repeated in the sheaves of tiny daisies borne by a perennial sadly in need of a prettier name than *Solidaster*, child of a mixed marriage between goldenrod (*Solidago*) and aster.

If pink is your preference, there's another form of culinary sage called 'Tricolor', with leaves of green, cream, and pink. This, with a purplish pink selection of *Verbena canadensis* trailing over it, stopped me in my tracks. This verbena (which can also be had in blue or white) is much hardier than most and it flowers for a very long time. In another garden I saw it used with the finely incised ornamental kale called Pink Peacock. 'Tricolor' is also the name of a rather temperamental form of the shrubby little *Hypericum moseranum*. This dislikes extremes of heat and

Ajuga 'Burgundy Glow' with purple thyme. 'Burgundy Glow' is not as winter hardy as most ajugas and a proportion of its leaf rosettes revert to purple or green. It is the prettiest of the ajugas and well worth a little effort but not one to use where extensive ground cover is wanted. Where summers are hot it needs shade. (England; June)

cold and is happiest in the Pacific Northwest. The leaf edge is a rosier, less blued pink than that of the sage, and the prettiest association I've come across was with a double dianthus, name unknown, of exactly the same color.

The beet red mixed with cream and green in the leaves of *Ajuga* 'Burgundy Glow' is the basis for many an echo. In England it looked very fetching intermingled with a light purple thyme, but this wouldn't work in most parts of the United States where the thyme needs sun, the ajuga shade. What has worked for me, in light shade, is the ajuga interplanted with bright pink *Oxalis braziliensis* (invasive, I should warn, and not hardy in the Northeast), which flowers in spring, then goes summer dormant. The late summer- or autumn-flowering Japanese anemone (*Anemone × hybrida*) 'Margarete' is a perfect color match for the pink in 'Burgundy Glow' ajuga.

If you've read this far, you know about my passion for purple foliage. I've saved some echoes for now, like the myriad glinting gray-and-purple needles of a little juniper (*Juniperus communis* 'Berkshire') in winter with the large burnished purple leaves of *Ajuga* 'Jungle Bronze', or a pale apricot daylily with its dark crimson eye matched to 'Crimson Pygmy' barberry, or the purplish bracts in the lupinelike spikes of *Acanthus spinosus* backed by a purple-leaved elder (*Sambucus nigra* 'Purpurea'), or a coppery orange pansy with a bitter-chocolate "face" enlivening an adjacent mat of a geranium with little dark brown leaves (*Geranium sessiliflorum* 'Nigricans'). A combination that held me enthralled early in the season was the little viola called 'Jackanapes', with bright yellow lower petals and purple-brown upper ones, in front of purple-leaved *Lobelia fulgens*—I wish I could have had another, later look when the lobelia bore its red flowers.

I've neglected orange, but it produced a spectacular echo in a California garden where leopard-spotted scarlet-and-yellow tigridias were growing through a carpet of scarlet-, orange-, green-, and yellow-tinted *Sedum rubrotinctum*. And in one of this year's catalogues I noticed a new pansy called 'Flame Princess', an unusual combination of yellow upper petals and orange-scarlet lower ones. Now let me see, what would go nicely with that?

Combinations between two foliage plants make the longest-lasting echoes of all. The first such memorable association I recall was at England's Sissinghurst, where the green-and-cream of hosta leaves (*Hosta fortunei* 'Albo-picta', variegated with creamy yellow, not white as the name implies) recurred in the smaller cream-edged leaves of *Euonymus fortunei* 'Silver Queen'. More recently, in the golden garden at Crathes Castle, near Aberdeen, I spotted the same hosta color matched to chartreuse-leaved golden oregano (*Origanum vulgare* 'Aureum'), and in an Ohio garden *Hosta* 'Shade Fanfare'—greenish yellow with a white rim—rose out of a drift of corresponding color from the small leaves of the yellow creeping Charlie, *Lysimachia nummularia* 'Aurea'. Plants with variegated foliage all have echo potential, among them yellow-

Helenium 'Waldtraub' with the faded flowers of Euphorbia characias wulfenii. (Garden of Mr. and Mrs. J. Carnwath, Washington; August)

and-white striped yuccas, irises, liriope, and mondo grass (*Ophiopogon*). I've played matchmaker with a cream-striped mondo grass and the little cream-and-green *Sedum lineare* 'Variegatum', a combination not dependent on a few weeks of flower and pretty nine months of the year.

Echoes can come from things other than flowers—seedheads for example. August in Seattle found a tawny helenium called 'Waldtraub' mistily echoed by the mellow bronze and copper and creamy green seedheads of *Euphorbia characias wulfenii*. October in New York offered the rusty red heads of *Sedum* 'Autumn Joy' palely echoing the rosy tints in the leaves of 'Rose Glow' barberry. In my own garden, *Abelia* × *grandiflora* complements the same sedum, its dark bracts repeating the sedum's color in airier form, a long-lasting combination that endures to the end of the year, enlivened through November by a smattering of small white abelia flowers. In Washington, D.C., a brighter autumn echo came from orange chrysanthemums banked below the sweeping branches of an orange-berried pyracantha.

Echoes can come from structure, too. At the New York Botanical Garden, in October, a large mound of the Nippon daisy (*Chrysanthemum nipponicum*) echoed in color and shape the white dome of the distant conservatory. At the Ladew Topiary Gardens in Maryland, the tawny daylily (*Hemerocallis fulva*) matched the dark apricot paint of a pagoda. Brick paths invite echoes and I found one of great artistry in a friend's Long Island garden. Alongside a path of terra-cotta brick grew a clump of a bearded iris with the palest lilac standards, deepest purple falls, and a dark orange beard to echo the paving. Bronze-tinted rodgersia leaves and brown seedheads against a patch of brown crushed lava rock made another unusual echo. Intentional or happenstance? Who knows—some of the best echoes do come about by chance.

Just as some can carry a tune and some cannot, so can some carry a color in their minds more accurately than others. It is easier to carry out color (and flowering time) combinations on the spot. In my garden one mid-February morning I paused to consider a patch of *Helleborus abchasicus* (*H. orientalis abchasicus* to some taxonomists). I grew this from seed, rushed to me by a friend in England, freshly collected—it is hard to grow from seed stored more than a week or two. The flowers of this hellebore are a color similar to that of *H. atrorubens*, which might be the better choice in cold regions because it is deciduous, whereas *H. abchasicus* is by nature evergreen. My clumps of *H. abchasicus* were happy and healthy where I'd put them but completely ineffective. There was ample light but direct sun was blocked and the flowers appeared a sullen maroon. Rendered translucent by the sun they are ruby red netted with purple. They needed to be sunlit for some part of the day and I wandered round the garden seeking a better place for the six clumps.

The flower color matched exactly the beet pink in the leaves of 'Burgundy Glow' ajuga, so one hellebore went in there (leaving me with five, which is an easier number to arrange attractively than six). *Daphne odora*, an evergreen shrub, was also in bloom, and in front of it were three clumps of an arching sedge (*Carex* 'Evergold') with showy leaves striped yellowish cream, a combination about which I was ambivalent. Had you asked me what color the daphne was, I'd have said deep pink. Period. It isn't: the fully opened flowers are almost white, with a faint blush of bluish pink, but there's a deeper, more brilliant pink from the unopened buds.

To my surprise the hellebore flower I had in my hand was, when sunlit, a very close

Rusty seedheads and a touch of rust in the leaves of Rodgersia pinnata *echo the crushed lava rock of the path. (Washington; August)*

The terra-cotta sculpture by Anne Entis is picked up by touches of terra-cotta in the feather-rock (hand-picked for this color conforma-tion) and in the striping on the leaves of Hakone-chloa macra *'Aureola' which, looking yellow overall, echoes* Hosta *'Frances Williams' in the background. (Gar-den of the late Richard Meyer, Ohio; August)*

match, but with a soupçon more purple that made it just right with the creamy sedge. Tucked among the sedges the hellebores have turned a less than perfect partnership into a satisfying trio. I toyed with the idea of adding some 'Burgundy Glow' ajuga in front of the sedge, but it wouldn't work because the sedges are right on the edge of a path and their skirts sweep the ground, leaving no room for an underplanting. It might, anyway, have over-pursued the theme, but one of my other daphnes may get a carpet of ajuga underneath, perhaps with an interplanting of *Cyclamen coum* in a near-magenta form.

Most of these echoes involve plants growing close to each other, but two of the most memorable I've seen were echoes across space. One was a triple echo. In an Ohio garden a beautiful grass with a windswept look and a tongue-twisting name (*Hakonechloa macra* 'Aureola') echoed the yellow of a distant *Hosta* 'Frances Williams'. The grass looks yellow but when you get close you see the streaks of white and terra-cotta in the narrow blades. Behind the grass was a terra-cotta sculpture, and the front of the bed was edged with lumps of feather-rock handpicked for the touches of terra-cotta mixed with the gray. The second, in an English garden, was simpler, possibly accidental, ephemeral, and magical. Color called to color across a lake, with an iris in two tones of purple echoing wisteria on the opposite bank weeping over its own reflection in the water.

There are no flowers in this picture, yet the scene lacks neither color nor interest. Among the many foliage plants are ferns and hostas in great variety (the largest hosta, center left, is 'Sum and Substance'), Helleborus orientalis and H. foetidus, Asarum canadense, purple-leaved ajuga, and American pachysandra (Pachysandra terminalis), which has marbled leaves. (Little River Farm Perennial Nursery, North Carolina; May)

The flowers of Rhododendron 'Scintillation' are a highlight of the year, but the textural interest from ferns (Osmunda claytoniana) and hostas will still be there when the rhododendron flowers are just a memory. (Garden of Sydney and Martin Eddison, Connecticut; May) Also see the photographs on page 163.

5 | Foliage Plants

Foliage lasts much longer than flowers. Take bloodroot (*Sanguinaria canadensis*), for example, one of our most beautiful native woodland plants. The snowy flowers are enchanting but they last only a few days. As if to make amends for their hasty departure, they then put up handsome, rounded and lobed leaves that last well into summer. These look very beautiful with small ferns or such ferny-leaved shade perennials as Jacob's ladder (*Polemonium reptans*).

Foliage plants vary so much in color, form, and texture that satisfying gardens can be created with foliage alone. Colored foliage is discussed in the chapter on color, so here we look primarily at shape and texture.

Hardy flowering perennials favor the north, but southerners can grow a broader range of foliage plants of lasting structural quality. Many of these need shade. So do we! I'd never heard of a shade tree when I gardened in England—cloudy skies are shade enough. In Virginia the shady parts of my garden get weeded more punctiliously than the sunny ones through the summer months. It is sanctimonious of us to criticize the Amazonians while destruction of America's own jungles goes on apace to make way for yet one more unneeded supermarket. Gardeners in the Deep South could help by voting with their pocketbooks and viewing with disfavor lots denuded of trees, ignoring the fashion for perennials borders, and reveling in the luxuriance of exotic foliage plants that actually enjoy heat and humidity.

Among the many handsome foliage perennials for shady gardens in the warmer zones (Zone 8 and up) are aspidistra (of which there are some attractive variegated forms), and *Ligularia tussilaginea*, which includes not only the fairly well known yellow-spotted leopard plant, but the solid green species, a form edged and dappled with cream usually called 'Argentea', and a fascinating form called 'Crispata' with curled and crinkled leaf edges. *Rohdea japonica* is slightly hardier (Zone 7). This too has at least one form with white-edged leaves. If these aren't available locally, look for them in the catalogues of mail-order nurseries specializing in houseplants.

Among the rather tender foliage plants for sun or light shade are elephant's ears (*Alocasia*), New Zealand flax (*Phormium*), and umbrella plant (*Cyperus alternifolius*).

When, however, we come to the most popular, and most varied, of all foliage perennials, hostas, gardeners in the warmest zones are at a disadvantage. Hostas are very cold hardy, and they need sufficient cold to induce winter dormancy. Nor are they seen at their best where summers are dry or intensely hot—at present, anyway: hosta breeders have sun and heat resistance among their aims. Breeders have made an unsung conservation contribution by so enlarging the summer potential of tree-shaded sites that the trees are less likely to be sacrificed to make way for plants that need sun. Hosta leaves vary not

A clump of hostas becomes a focal point where a path branches to the left and right. There is a splash of bright color from the orange-flowered azalea but most of the color comes from foliage plants. The yellow-leaved shrub in the background is Physocarpus opulifolius *'Luteus'. The golden grass on either side of the path is* Milium effusum *'Aureum'. The white flowers at the front are* Geranium clarkei *'Kashmir White' (G.* rectum *'Album' of nurseries). (Garden of Mrs. Arnold Rakusen, England; June)*

only in size and color but also in shape, from almost round to narrowly straplike, so there is abundant scope for contrast within the genus, but still they are the better for other companions, especially ferns, grasses, and liriope. An edging of liriope would not only contrast in shape with large-leaved hostas but give much needed cohesion to the mishmash of a collector's garden.

In shade, where flowers are few once spring has passed, thoughtful combinations of foliage plants are crucial to continuing interest. Woodland gardens come first to mind, and either side of a woodland path would be a good place for foliage plants if the shade is not too dense and the root competition not too severe. Where tree roots are a problem many gardeners have had success covering the ground with the fabric sold as landscaping cloth and growing their plants in a layer of rich soil on top of this. Water passes down through the cloth but tree roots are restrained. How well this works depends on the depth of soil and its richness, and on the ability or willingness to keep it moist if natural rainfall is not sufficiently abundant. It should be re-

Bold-leaved hostas and ferny-leaved astilbes complement each other. The astilbe is 'Fanal'. (Washington; July)

membered that trees can be killed by raising the soil level over a large proportion of their roots. This is unlikely to happen if fairly narrow beds are made alongside a woodland path, but one often sees circular raised beds around a solitary tree in a lawn and doing this does put the tree at risk. Placing a few large containers under the tree and growing foliage plants in these might be the better way.

The most favorable place for shade-loving foliage plants is not, however, the woodland garden but a bed or border in the shade cast by buildings, walls, and fences. Here they get the shade they want without root competition. This will usually be against a north- or east-facing wall, but many city gardens are shaded throughout for most of the day by tall surrounding buildings. This is not the handicap many seem to think, it is just a matter of fitting the plants to the site.

In the sunny bed or border flowers have precedence, but keeping foliage as well as flowers in mind will make the border much more satisfying than it otherwise would be, especially in spring, before the crescendo of bloom distracts us from other considerations. Combining different shapes and textures is every bit as satisfying, and as challenging, as orchestrating colors. The many shades of green are satisfying in themselves but there are also other colors from such early-to-emerge perennials as *Iris pallida* 'Aurea-variegata', the purple-tinted leaves of *Iris* 'Gerald Darby', golden feverfew (*Chrysanthemum parthenium*), and purple-tinted *Sedum* 'Vera Jameson'. The late summer flowers of *Sedum alboroseum* 'Medio-variegatus' are much less important than the creamy-yellow foliage, which is at its showiest early in the season and particularly effective next to the dusty purple leaves of *Lysimachia ciliata* 'Purpurea'. Green-leaved *L. ciliata* is a pretty but modest plant with dainty pale yellow flowers

in summer, never particularly popular until the advent of this purple-leaved form. It likes moist soil, is somewhat invasive, and is doing very well in a part of my wet ditch where water is sometimes a foot or more deep. Astilbes look so fresh and ferny. They won't flower until late spring or summer but in early spring the color of many is apparent—white ones have green leaves, while those with reddish flowers also have red-tinted leaves.

Some perennials have a quality uniquely their own—the way alchemilla's leaves hold glistening quicksilver droplets of moisture, for example, or the slim-fingered leaves of *Helleborus foetidus*, or the pleated leaves of the veratrums, or the way the arching blades of the hardy orchid (*Bletilla striata*) flutter with the slightest breeze. Few plants in my garden get more attention than *Baptisia perfoliata*, which has round leaves threaded along arching stems. But for purposes of considering contrast, many perennials can be roughly grouped as ferny, bold, grassy, or variegated. Group the sword-shaped leaves of an iris with the large round ones of a hosta and the ferny ones of an astilbe and you have an ideal combination for foliage contrast.

A plant's character is largely influenced by the texture of the leaves, but the size and shape of the plant also has a bearing. Daylily leaves are usually quite broad, but because they arch in a rather formless manner the clumps fall somewhere between grassy and bold. This makes for poor textural contrast with plants in either of these categories. That's exactly what we want when we put daffodils among clumps of daylilies, the better to conceal their leaves, but when foliage is lastingly attractive, do the opposite, emphasizing it by means of contrast. Daylily foliage is set off less well by adjacent clumps of bearded irises with their swordlike leaves, or Japanese irises with narrower, grassy ones, than it is,

for example, by feathery achilleas, fine-cut *Coreopsis verticillata*, the soft mounds of maple-like leaves found in many geraniums, or the large divided leaves of peonies.

Many perennials grown mainly for their flowers have foliage of textural beauty but the plants mentioned here are those whose foliage is of primary, or at least equal, importance.

FERN-TEXTURED FOLIAGE PLANTS

The words "ferny" and "feathery" evoke an image of dainty, insubstantial texture. Such plants include, as well as the ferns (not all of which are ferny!): astilbes, columbines, *Corydalis* (these are long-flowering, too), sweet cicely (*Myrrhis odorata*), nice for the flowers but better for foliage, thalictrums, and *Vancouveria*. The bleeding hearts (*Dicentra* are grown for their flowers but earn a place for their foliage alone, and don't overlook a closely related self-sowing annual or biennial vine of singular delicacy, the Allegheny vine, *Adlumia fungosa*. If only *Selinum tenuifolium* (or the similar *S. carvifolium*), with flowers like Queen Anne's lace, weren't so hard to come by, for this can out-fern the ferns with the filminess of its frondlike leaves. Two plants of similarly delicate texture that have recently become available are *Athamanta* and *Meum athamanticum*. These all need a bit of relief from hot afternoon sun.

For sun there are numerous achilleas and artemisias, feverfew (*Chrysanthemum parthenium*), threadleaf coreopsis (*Coreopsis verticillata*), and such fernleaf peonies as red-flowered *Paeonia tenuifolia* (the most finely cut) and the taller 'Windchimes' with lilac-colored flowers. A favorite of mine is one of the mountain mints, *Pycnanthemum virginianum* (there are other, similar species), with aromatic leaf slivers piled into an airy mound. Tansy (*Tanacetum vulgare*) has graceful fernlike leaves, and the more congested "fronds" of the lower, bushier curly tansy (*T. v. crispum*) are among the most exquisite of all leaves, resembling bright green crinkled feathers. In good soil this might be too much of a spreader, but poor, dryish soil and sun restrain it. The leaves look invitingly crunchy, and tansy has in the past been used to flavor puddings, but in her book *Herbs for Every Garden* Gertrude Foster warns: "Tansy is considered dangerous if taken as an infusion. It is one of the prohibited herbs for dealers in botanical drugs. It cannot be sold as a dried herb in drugstores or by mail. As little as ten drops of the essential oil will produce dizziness and more could be lethal, if taken internally. It is one of the embalming herbs of ancient days, when the leaves were placed about a corpse to preserve it." It probably takes a lot of leaves to produce ten drops of the essential oil, but better safe than sorry. I wonder if it would be fatal to deer!

A beautiful feathery plant getting some enthusiastic press of late is dog fennel (*Eupatorium capillifolium*). The specific name means "like hair." This is a weed of exceptional beauty, bushy and feathery, averaging five feet in height, sometimes more, but always self-supporting. It was on our lot when we bought it and getting rid of it was a long struggle. The tiny white flowers are not ornamental but they do the job they are made for—perpetuating the species—all too well and puppy fennels appeared all over the garden. The flowers come quite late and it might perhaps be less weedy where the season is short but its native range goes as far north as Massachusetts. Think twice before you spend your money on this; it is inexpensive but Roundup isn't.

You'll certainly regret it if you bring the beautiful, feathery, extremely invasive mare's tails (*Equisetum*) into your garden; instead, I recommend asparagus. Asparagus fern (*Asparagus densiflorus* 'Sprengeri') isn't a fern and it can only be grown outside by those in frost-free regions, but take a look at the leaves of ordinary culinary asparagus—this isn't just a delicious vegetable but also an elegant ornamental plant for a sunny border, especially the variety *Asparagus officinalis pseudoscaber*. Sweet fern (*Comptonia peregrina*) isn't a fern either, it is a small suckering shrub, but this too is a fine addition to a sunny border, retaining the bright green freshness of its aromatic foliage all through the growing season despite heat, drought, and low-fertility soil.

Ferny plants such as these add a light and graceful look to borders, as well as being helpful in separating warring colors.

Tulips seen through the newly emerged foliage of Asparagus officinalis *'Pseudoscaber'. (Virginia; early April)*

BOLD-LEAVED FOLIAGE

Bold-leaved plants include bergenias; many hostas; the hand-shaped leaves of the Lenten rose (*Helleborus orientalis*); most rodgersias; the ornamental rhubarbs, *Rheum palmatum* (culinary rhubarb also has boldly handsome leaves); the broad arrows of the hardiest calla lily (*Zantedeschia aethiopeca*); the large hosta-like glaucous leaves of *Rudbeckia maxima*; the angel-wing, red-lined leaves of the hardy begonia (*Begonia grandis*); the large rounded ones of some ligularias; umbrella plant (*Peltiphyllum peltatum* in most books and catalogues but now changed to *Darmera peltata*); the skunk cabbages, and, if you dare, the invasive *Petasites*. Theoretically any of these would make good partners for plants with ferny leaves, but artistry and craftsmanship go hand in hand in garden making and requirements for sun, shade, and moisture must be kept in mind. Large leaves often indicate a need for shade and/or abundant moisture. If this is lacking, rodgersias in particular will shame not only themselves, with their brown and shabby leaves, but also the adjacent plants and you, the gardener. One way of dealing with this is to sink a large tub for the moisture lover. If the plant likes to grow in a bog there may be no need to make holes in the tub. If it merely wants moist soil, drill holes in the tub then line it with a layer of newspaper sufficiently thick that water seeps very slowly away.

Gertrude Jekyll liked to use the bold round leaves of bergenias as a border edging, and for this they are excellent where they fare well. Unless you have observed them through the season where you live, start small, with just a clump or two, for in many parts of the United States they are happy in neither sun nor shade, while their cabbagelike leaves provide safe harbor for slugs. They seem to be at their best located in full sun in regions where 80°F is a heatwave. The beet red or burnished mahogany of the winter leaves is a valued characteristic of *Bergenia purpurascens* and many of the hybrids. One of the loveliest, but the least adaptable, bergenias is *B. ciliata*, which has large round leaves coated with short glistening bristles. The leaves are killed by hard frost, though the roots may survive.

"Bold" is a relative term, of course: the round leaves of the gingers (*Asarum*) are bold by comparison with the ferny little *Aruncus aethusifolius* or the lacy leaves of *Vancouveria planipetala*. Not all gingers have round leaves, some are arrow-shaped, but all are beautiful. This is a widely distributed genus. The very hardy winter-dormant *Asarum canadense* has its West Coast equivalent in *A. caudatum*, and the evergreen southeastern *A.*

The bold leaves of Peltiphyllum peltatum (synonym Darmera peltata) *contrast well with the surrounding ferns. The castlelike ornament is an old chimney pot. (Garden of Roy Davidson, Washington; July)*

The burnished mahogany leaves of bergenia growing in full sun in a large rock garden. (Mr. and Mrs. Clair Stewart, Ontario; October)

virginicum, *A. arifolium*, and *A. shuttleworthii* 'Callaway' have a similarly gray-marbled counterpart in *A. hartwegii* from California and Oregon. Some exquisite Japanese species, among them *A. kumageanum*, recently made their debut. The hardiest and most versatile of the evergreen kinds is the European ginger (*A. europaeum*), with polished bright green rounded leaves. All of these are the prettier for the company of ferns or other plants with lacy leaves.

Large-leaved hostas make good companions for the Japanese bleeding heart (*Dicentra spectabilis*), not only because of contrasting texture, but because the bleeding heart comes early into growth and, in the South, is shabby by midsummer. It does no harm to cut it down once it starts to wither. In the meantime, the hostas, having made a later start, are ready to fill the gap. Where it is hardy, the calla lily (*Zantedeschia aethiopeca*) can also play this gap-filling role. So can *Brunnera macrophylla*, its bright blue forget-me-not flowers lovely with the pink or white of the bleeding heart, while its large coarse leaves do not attain their full size until a bit later in the season.

The bold category subdivides into two groups: the bold and more-or-less rounded already mentioned, and the bold, usually more-or-less upright swordlike or strap-shaped leaves. These include *Agapanthus orientalis* (some species have narrower leaves), agaves, aloes, aspidistra, many irises, New Zealand flax (*Phormium*), *Rohdea*, and yuccas.

Among the bold-leaved groups are some of the best architectural plants, for use as accents or focal points, bringing a sense of structure and permanence to the garden. Where autumn does not bring the gardening year to an end, the evergreen kinds serve best. I have found triangular groups of three V-shaped yuccas (*Yucca filamentosa* 'Variegata' is my favorite) invaluable for interplanting with little bulbs. The bulbs do not get stepped on when dormant, nor dug up by mistake when seeking a home for some new arrival. The strong form of the yuccas draws attention away from the withering leaves of crocuses and holds the space together when the ground between is bare, though this can be kept to a minimum by surrounding them with drifts of annuals.

The rounded, leathery leaves of Asarum virginicum *contrast with the ferny ones of* Vancouveria planipetala. *Both are evergreen to about 20°F. The asarum is clump-forming, the vancouveria a spreader, but at controllable speed. (Virginia)*

Where winter is a time for hugging the wood stove, the large-leaved hostas can be put on display as specimen clumps in prominent positions *if* you are sure you can keep them free of slug damage. Many hostas make such colossal clumps of bold leaves in just a few years that they could reduce adjacent plants to insignificance. Let them be center stage, as focal points, perhaps, rising out of a ground-cover carpet. The leaves of *Hosta* 'Sum and Substance', for example, may measure more than fifteen inches across. They are a pale lime green and a large clump looks magnificent surrounded by a carpet of purple-flowered periwinkle (*Vinca minor* 'Atropurpurea') or a purple-leaved ajuga such as *Ajuga reptans* 'Royalty', with scalloped leaves of a purple so dark it approaches black.

GRASSY LEAVES

Apart from the grasses and sedges, which are discussed on pages 249–258, liriopes and ophiopogons are the best of the grassy-leaved plants for foliage contrast with ferny leaves or boldly rounded ones. The hardiest of them, *Liriope spicata*, is too invasive for the border. *Liriope muscari* is clump forming and there are many selections to choose from. Even in the Southeast, where liriope is so common, garden centers offer little choice, but one mail-order specialist sells more than two dozen different kinds. Most have lilac-to-purple bloom spikes but there are two with white flowers: green-leaved 'Monroe's White', and one with white flowers and variegated leaves.

The leaves of many irises are swordlike and bold—notably the bearded irises and such moisture-loving species as *Iris pseudacorus*. Although the leaves of Siberian irises are narrower, the dense, upright shape of the clumps gives them a bold appearance. Among the irises with grassy leaves my favorite is *I. graminea*, valued more for its foliage than for its flowers. The scent of the purplish flowers is so strongly fruity that it has been called the plum-tart iris, but you have to get down on hands and knees to smell them because they are quite small and nestled among the dense clumps of narrow, shiny leaves. It is an easy iris to grow, in sun or light shade, and maintains its good appearance throughout the growing season. Other irises with grassy foliage include such native kinds as *I. verna* and the West Coast species and hybrids often grouped as "Pacificas."

Tradescantias have grassy leaves but they may or may not have summer-long value, depending on the kind, and where you live. The one I grow, *Tradescantia hirsuticaulis*, goes summer dormant, reemerging with the cooler weather of autumn. Being inclined to sprawl, the grassy leaves of torch lilies (*Kniphofia*) are not much of an adornment, so concealment rather than contrast might better be one's goal. The smaller montbretias (*Crocosmia*) have grassy leaves, while those of such tall ones as 'Lucifer' are bold.

Many bulbs have grassy foliage but it is usually too short-lived to be an important factor in design. Exceptions include several of the ornamental onions, especially garlic chives (*Allium tuberosum*), which would be worth growing even if it never flowered. In one part of my garden several clumps of it are interplanted with scarlet-flowered *Geum* 'Red Wings', which in the coastal Southeast flowers in April or early May on somewhat sprawling stems rising from basal rosettes of lobed paddle-shaped leaves. The firmly shaped, lightly textured clumps of the onion give the flowering stems of the geum just the support they need, without overwhelming the scattered flowers as a plant with coarser foliage might.

One of the daintiest grassy-leaved plants

in my garden is St. Bernard's lily, a species of *Anthericum* usually listed as *A. liliago* but I think it may really be *A. algeriense*. In any event, the one I have is the one you are likely to come across in gardens (rock gardens, usually) and catalogues. It makes exceptionally graceful fifteen-inch high clumps of leaves only a quarter-inch wide and seeming even narrower because they are channeled. If they die down by midsummer, as they may where it is very hot, especially if the soil gets dry, they do so without the mess associated with, for instance, daffodil leaves. Over the leaves, in spring or early summer, rise wiry stems bearing flights of starry snowy white flowers. The leaves and flower stalks are coated with a glaucous bloom, giving the clump a gray-green look. In front of mine is ferny-leaved pasqueflower (*Anemone pulsatilla*), which bears its goblet-shaped flowers a little earlier. Behind the anthericum is a large clump of *Hosta* 'Francee', its great rosette of broad, white-edged leaves contrasting with the grassy leaves of the anthericum and echoing its white flowers. A large shrub to the west (*Chimonanthus praecox*) casts shade over the hosta by early afternoon, leaving the others in sun for an hour or two longer.

VARIEGATED LEAVES

American garden writers have tended to be patronizing about the English passion for variegated leaves (English writers are equally disparaging about the variegated flowers popular in the United States), but hostas have brought about a change of heart.

I'm inclined to turn a blind mind to spotted leaves, with a few exceptions like leopard plant (*Ligularia tussilaginea* 'Aureomaculata') and pulmonarias, and I find quite repulsive . . . well, never mind—as Thumper

The yellow-striped leaves of Iris pseudacorus *'Variegatus' turn green in summer but the white-striped leaves of* Iris laevigata *'Variegata' retain their variegation throughout the growing season. Yellow-striped* Carex *'Evergold' is evergreen where winters are not excessively cold. (Wisley Gardens, England; Spring)*

said to Bambi: "If you can't say anything nice, don't say anything at all." I *can* think of nice things to say about leaves with cleanly defined variegation. They add long-lasting color to the garden, and a white or cream edging to a leaf makes us more aware of its shape. Leaf variegation is also a major ingredient in the color echoes that give me so much pleasure.

Much of the scorn heaped on variegated plants results from collections gathered together in one bed. One variegated plant with another can be mutually enhancing if their sizes or shapes are different: the narrow blades of a variegated liriope or the grassy *Hakonechloa* 'Aureola' with a large-leaved hosta, for example. Gather a lot of different ones together and the eye is befuddled. Taller variegated plants show well against a plain dark green or bronze-purple background. *Astrantia major* 'Sunningdale Variegated' benefits from such a showcase: the leaves are hand-shaped, the lobes striped in white, cream, and yellow, elegant but intricate and in need of plain accessories.

Lamium maculatum with Geranium 'Johnson's Blue', growing in light shade. (England; late June)

There's a great range of variegated plants. They can be found in every textural category but there are few ferny ones, which is perhaps as well. When the pattern is fancy it is better that the shape be plain. Ferny-leaved rue (*Ruta graveolens*) is a beautiful plant but the variegated form looks messy.

There is a host of hostas and ivies, several lamiums, and don't overlook the white-edged pachysandra, a plant so often massed as a workhorse but much more distinguished as a single clump or small drift echoed by white flowers—*Geranium sanguineum* 'Album', perhaps (in the South this benefits from a bit of shade), or white columbines. The variegated Solomon's seal (*Polygonatum odoratum* 'Variegatum') would be a good plant even if it had plain green leaves: the variegation puts it up in my top ten. It takes a while to settle down but once it does it increases quite rapidly and needs robust companions. Little blue-flowered *Iris cristata* used to dwell at the feet of mine but when I wasn't looking it got crowded out. Such vigorous plants as periwinkle (*Vinca minor*) or sweet woodruff (*Galium odoratum*) could hold their own.

Pulmonarias get a high mark. They'd be on my "best plant" list if they weren't quite so demanding of a cool site. In England they'll grow in dry shade, in coastal Virginia absolutely not. I can grow them well only with careful choice of site, and soil not so much improved as replaced with rich compost and manure. They hate hot sun; even morning sun can cause them to wilt. Pulmonarias decline, as plants so often do, to be slotted neatly into categories. Some are grown for their foliage, others for their flowers, which are among the first of the year. Coral pink *Pulmonaria rubra* comes first for me, with the others hard on its heels. *Pulmonaria angustifolia* is among the brightest and purest of blues. The plain green leaves of these two are, to put it kindly, undistinguished. Not so those of *P. saccharata*, invariably sold as 'Mrs. Moon', whether it is or not, which is among the best of the bold foliaged plants, the small stem leaves at flowering time followed by great ground-hugging rosettes of broad leaves dappled with aluminum gray. An edging of these can hold a shady border together throughout the growing season. The flowers are pretty too, pink-and-blue bells in glistening silky-haired calyces. Gardeners are a contrary lot; if a flower is white, we want it blue, if it is blue we want it white, or pink, or something else. In my opinion pulmonarias don't do white well, but there are some around if that's what you want. Pulmonaria seed produces a multitude of variations on a theme, most of them salesworthy, so it is hard to be sure just what you are getting, but the best of those called 'Argentea' are indeed argent (silver) all over. *Pulmonaria longifolia* has long, narrow, spotted leaves and brilliant blue flowers. Those of *P.* 'Roy Davidson' are a bit wider—don't miss this one, the leaves are prettily marked with silver and the flowers are a soft sky blue unlike any other.

The plant sold as *Disporum sessile* 'Variegatum' (incorrectly, I'm told, by one expert on the genus) is an elegant variegated plant. The nodding greenish white narrow bells are cute but the spear-shaped white-edged leaves are the main attraction. I paid $15 for my first plant, a good many years ago, then soon had plenty to give away for it is quite invasive. No one who has it seems to mind. Rambling over the woodland floor is the best place for it; it spreads thinly and could highlight a mat of creeping phlox in white, pink, or blue. *Iris foetidissima* 'Variegata' has similar cleanly defined white stripes but this one doesn't roam, rather it makes broad architectural clumps where it does well. In cool regions it isn't demanding but in hot ones the soil must be moisture retentive and it needs

afternoon shade. *Iris japonica* 'Variegata' has broader, slightly arching white-striped leaves. It runs all over the place but the stringlike stolons are barely under the surface of the leafy soil it likes and are easily pulled out. For several years I let it roam around a white-flowered peony, then a bad winter killed it and I had to start again. Zone 8 is its hardiness limit. Mine have never flowered.

In a garden that leaves a lot to be desired, one of the plants I can boast about, growing alongside a path shaded by pines, is a selected form of *Arum italicum* 'Pictum' with slightly frilled arrow-shaped leaves handsomely marbled with silver. Buying plants so named has been a bit of a pig-in-a-poke because it varies quite a lot and good forms are scarce, but at least one nursery is building up stocks. It comes into growth with the cooler days of autumn and is seldom seriously winter damaged where the temperature stays above 15°F. On frosty days the leaves huddle down on the ground, perking up when the temperature rises, much as the leaves of daffodils do. If, at its hardiness limit (probably Zone 6), the leaves are winter-killed, it makes new ones and is then at its showiest in early spring. It copes with summer heat by going dormant but after the leaves have gone there are chunky spikes of brilliant red berries, so use only low carpeters to cover the ground it occupies. Periwinkle would do: one with white flowers would be especially nice with the white-patterned leaf of the arum. I use the irridescent *Selaginella uncinata*, which plasters itself flat on the ground. This isn't very hardy and even in Zone 8 takes a beating in unusually cold winters, nor does it like dry summers.

If only the beautiful variegated brunneras (*Brunnera macrophylla* 'Variegata' and 'Hadspen Cream') would learn some such trick as dormancy for getting through the dog days of summer. Seldom do they have more than a brief burst of beauty in spring, when the cream edge of the large leaves exquisitely combined with sky blue flowers makes these among the most covetable of plants. Dry soil, wind, hot sun, or high temperatures (even in shade) all cause the leaf edges to shrivel. Pick off the disfigured leaves and it makes new ones, only to repeat the process. Only those who can offer rich, moist soil in a protected site are likely to rise to the challenge. If you are one of the lucky ones you could combine one of these brunneras with the similarly demanding creamy globeflower (*Trollius*) called 'Alabaster' for the stuff of which garden dreams are made.

The three-foot variegated comfrey (*Symphytum* × *uplandicum* 'Variegatum') with pendulous clusters of light blue flowers at azalea time is a bit more accommodating but still quite hard to please, and it has another shortcoming of its own—infant plants have cream-edged leaves but after a couple of years they often revert to green. The shorter *Symphytum grandiflorum* is one of the most vigorous and accommodating plants I know, and very tolerant of dry shade, so the fairly new *S. g.* 'Variegatum' offered greater promise—and still does: in my garden the leaf edge has scorched but not so badly as to make me give up hope of finding just the right spot for it. It looks good next to the arching cream-striped sedge (*Carex*) called 'Evergold'. If you have the soil and site to suit these brunneras and comfreys you'll probably also do well with *Scrophularia aquatica* 'Variegata', a form of the water figwort found alongside England's rivers and ponds. Shade is advisable for this where summers are hot, but where they are cool it can take sun if the soil is moist and could go on the edge of a bog garden, where I can imagine it combined with blue or pale primrose Japanese or Louisiana irises.

Those who can't provide for plants that demand cool conditions and moist soil can comfort themselves with *Chrysanthemum pacificum*, which revels in the heat. It isn't exactly variegated but the leaves, diamond-shaped with notched edges held in upfacing rosettes, are margined with the silver that lines the undersides. This newish plant was an instant winner, making its way through the horticultural hierarchy—collector, momma-and-poppa mail-order nursery, wholesaler, and garden center—with extraordinary speed because it is easy to grow and easy to propagate. It is a plant to grow in drifts, in the foreground, along with just about anything. It is primarily a foliage plant but in the Southeast it is valuable too for its somewhat frost-resistant flowers. The flower buds, as hard, round, and glistening as ball bearings, are a good match for the greeny yellow flowers of *Patrinia scabiosifolia*. They open into little petalless bright yellow balls with a foetid but not pervasive smell attractive to flies. Its hardiness limit is not yet established.

Iris pallida 'Aurea-variegata' can be grown in sun or a little shade but an opportunity has been lost if it can't be seen with the sun shining through from behind at some time of day, for only when backlit is it at its most exciting. The white-striped form I've found less robust and the better for protection from hot afternoon sun. Their leaf fans have an architectural value similar, on a smaller scale, to that of yuccas. If, for you, the leaves hold their good looks through summer, try spacing three or more fans well apart and letting them rise up over an interplanting of low annuals. For me they are at their best from April through June and their summer shabbiness is disguised by dainty white-flowered *Euphorbia corollata* and the trailing stems of a prickly poppy (*Argemone grandiflora*) with gray leaves and white flowers. Iris rhizomes, you've probably read, are supposed to be fully exposed to

Iris foetidissima 'Variegata' seldom flowers but it earns its place in the garden with handsome evergreen foliage. It is not very cold hardy (Zone 7) but where it thrives it retains its good looks the year around. In England, and in the Pacific Northwest, it tolerates dry soil, but where summers are hot the soil should be well drained but moisture retentive. The gray, ground-covering foliage is a more or less evergreen New Zealand bur (Acaena). (Jane Platt's garden, Oregon; early August)

Fans of Iris pallida *'Variegata' are interplanted with clumps of* Arctotis *'Flame'. Where summers are hot this iris needs some shade from afternoon sun, otherwise the leaves are likely to become scorched and shabby. (England; August)*

the sun and not overgrown by other plants, but that rule can be bent in hot regions.

With foliage combinations, as with flowers, one can have too much of a good thing. I had put together a combination of Japanese painted fern, lance-leaved, white-edged *Hosta* 'Louisa', gray grassy *Allium senescens glaucum* (which I find the better for shade in my hot garden), gray carpeting *Ajuga* 'Kingwood', gray-spotted *Pulmonaria longifolia*, and the form of hardy orchid (*Bletilla striata*) with white flowers and white-edged leaves. Feeling rather pleased with this, I added a clump of *Asarum virginicum* with its round, gray-patterned leaves. Suddenly it was too much and I longed for a patch of strong bright red. Voles have since gobbled up the hosta so perhaps I'll fill the gap with red impatiens.

Don't overlook fall color. In regions where frost comes early, foliage may get blackened before it has time to change color. Most flowers fade quickly in hot southern summers but fall brings recompense. The year winds slowly and gently down, making autumn the favorite time of year for many southern gardeners. The amber autumn foliage of amsonias, especially *Amsonia hubrectii*, is far showier than the flowers were earlier, and platycodons turn a warm banana yellow one can enjoy without the daily chore of removing dead flowers. The leaves of these will fall as the year draws to a close, but the red, orange, and yellow leaves of some geraniums remain to cheer the winter days, a reminder that the garden isn't dead, just resting for a while.

6 | Covering Ground:

Ground Cover, Massing, Invasive Plants, Lawns and Paving, and the Modified Meadow

It may not be immediately apparent but there is in these headings a common denominator: the ability to cover the ground. Lawns and paving are, after all, "ground covers."

INVASIVE OR GROUND COVER?

Whether the plant vigor needed for ground cover is an asset or a nuisance depends on a number of things, especially climate and soil. One of my worst "weeds" has been a little plant esteemed in rock garden circles, *Nierembergia rivularis*. It is very beautiful, with flowers like dimunitive white morning glories held just above a mat of little leaves. I wanted a small patch but it proved to be an all-or-nothing plant. It spreads by threadlike running roots and each year I'd weed out a barrowful but leave just a little, only to repeat this chore the following spring. Much of the spreading goes on when it seems to be dormant. In the end it had to go. Nowhere else have I seen it mentioned as an invasive plant. *Oenothera speciosa* has been, for me, a larger pink-flowered version of the same problem,

and this too had to be cast out of the garden, but I found a place for it on the roadside verge.

Plants spread fastest with a combination of sandy soil, warm climate, and high rainfall fairly evenly distributed throughout the year. A plant that runs rampant under such conditions might be quite restrained in clay and a cold climate: mistflower or hardy ageratum (*Eupatorium coelestinum*) is one example—it beautifies roadside ditches all around me but is too invasive for the garden. Friends further north find it quite controllable. Any meadow plant growing wild in abundance where you live should, as a garden candidate, be viewed with suspicion.

Occasionally the reverse may apply and a naturally vigorous plant be handicapped by a hot climate. One of the first invasive plants I had to contend with when I started gardening in England was *Campanula poscharskyana*, desirable but not for mixing with less robust things. Soon after coming to live in the United States I was given it by a friend on Cape Cod. This and sweet violet (*Viola odorata*) were the main carpeting plants under tall pines in his garden. Still "thinking English," I lost it several times before realizing that in Virginia's heat it cannot take dry sandy soil and full sun. In light shade, watered in times of drought, it is steadily but controllably extending its territory year by year. It makes a pretty carpet between gold-leaved hostas. This again makes the point that nothing one reads, hears, or even observes should be considered gospel. In this varied country a plant's performance may differ greatly from one place to another and its function change accordingly.

Vigorous plants can't be stereotyped; they play many roles. Carpeting kinds can unify a plant collection, display an ornament or specimen plant, be partner in a color echo, or flow over and soften paving. Tough, dense kinds can cover the ground where grass will not grow or is difficult to mow. Not all vigorous plants are spreaders, though, nor are all ground covers carpeters: the ornamental grasses combined with sturdy perennials so much in vogue are upscaled ground-cover plants.

Useful mat-forming perennials through which bigger plants could grow include acaenas, periwinkle (*Vinca minor*), thymes, creeping raspberry (*Rubus calycinoides*), oregano (*Origanum vulgare*), *Arabis procurrens*, *Campanula portenschlagiana*, *Lamium maculatum*, ('Beacon Silver' and 'White Nancy' being the most desirable cultivars), *Linaria aequitriloba*, *Laurentia fluviatilis*, *Lysimachia nummularia*, several of the low-growing sedums, sweet woodruff (*Galium odoratum*), and the unique beige-gray *Orostachys furusei*.

Such popular ground covers as ivy and pachysandra are required to be dense and vigorous; they couldn't otherwise do their job, which often is a tough one. These are generally used alone but a few perennials can compete, including the tough old tawny daylily (*Hemerocallis fulva* 'Europa') and some of the older hostas, such as *Hosta undulata* 'Erromena', the toughest of the lot. These can also compete, for a few years at least, with bugleweed (*Ajuga*). Periwinkle is vigorous, but vining and less dense, so many perennials can grow through this. A combination that gives me a lot of pleasure in April is the purple-flowered periwinkle interplanted with clumps of *Ranunculus ficaria* 'Flore Pleno' and 'Colarette', compact forms of the tuberous English wild celandine, the first with bright yellow fully double burnished flowers, the second an orange-yellow anemone form. These make flattened clumps of rounded leaves very early in the year, going quickly and neatly dormant soon after flowering finishes. An unnamed hosta seedling with narrow lime green leaves is a recent addition that seems to be thriving.

Ground-cover perennials for shade are plentiful but there are few that can stand the combination of extreme heat and full sun. Moss pink (*Phlox subulata*) is one of the best and there are dozens of selections, varying in vigor and quality of foliage as well as in flower size and color. For large scale ground cover, the best I've tried is 'White Delight'. One of the best new plants of a decade, *Chrysanthemum pacificum* (described in detail on page 202) is a valuable addition to the limited range of ground covers for hot sun.

Problems often arise when aggressive plants are mixed with, and overrun, less assertive kinds of similar or smaller size. They are not bad plants, just good plants in the wrong place. "Pick on someone your own size," my mother used to say when bullying went on. With plant bullies, go a step further and give them something bigger to contend with. However pugnacious a perennial may be, trees and shrubs can rise above it. My own garden is a mixed one and many a good perennial that couldn't be let loose among its fellows has found a place among shrubs, some in the shade of the woodsy areas, others in sun.

Where it is marginally hardy (about Zone 5) blue plumbago (*Ceratostigma plumbaginoides*) is kept under control by winter cold. For me, with winter temperatures occasionally sinking to 0°F but freezes seldom prolonged, it is far too invasive for a perennial border, but it barely survived on the hot west-facing side of surface-rooting trees. Compromise was reached in a bay between a group of three abelias (*Abelia* × *grandiflora* 'Prostrata Alba', a shrub that keeps its roots to itself).

It came as a surprise to me that many "mum" chrysanthemums are by their nature invasive. In England and New England the climate keeps them in check but in Virginia some have shown an amazing burst of speed, notably a little one called 'Mei Kyo', which began its sojourn in my garden as a tiny sprig and within a year had spread to fill a square yard—clearly not a plant to mix with less competitive things. It now makes a low-maintenance carpet alongside the drive, hemmed in to the left by a dogwood, to the right by a magnolia, and behind by a group of *Spiraea japonica* 'Shibori' ('Shirobana'). It is reliably perennial and does not require annual division, or indeed any division at all, just occasional thinning, accomplished here in casual fashion by pulling out bunches of spent flowering stems, roots and all, as I pass back and forth to the mailbox during the winter months. In March I cut off the remaining stems, a two-hour job with clippers, ten minutes with an electric hedge trimmer. 'Mei Kyo' is sold by several southeastern nurseries. It does not have time to flower where winter starts in October. *Chrysanthemum* 'Bronze Elegance' is a pale brick-red counterpart.

Another overeager plant I've let loose among trees and shrubs is the anemone sold as *Anemone vitifolia* 'Robustissima', a name

that is probably wrong but at least the last part is descriptive. Other perennials of rapid spread that could be used this way include *Alstroemeria pulchella* (in the Deep South—in the Northeast it isn't hardy and in the Northwest it doesn't spread fast enough to need much restraining), sweet woodruff (*Galium odoratum*), bee balm (*Monarda*), *Anemone canadensis*, *Oenothera pilosella*, and *Disporum sessile* 'Variegatum', which in my garden adds a dainty touch to a shaded area as it wanders widely but harmlessly among the suckering stems of *Rhododendron atlanticum* hybrids. *Physostegia virginiana* likes its namesake state all too well and the popular name "obedient plant" (from the way the flowers can be pushed around on the stem) struck me as ironic as I struggled to remove a barrowful or two of its invasive roots, but the white form (a trifle less invasive) gives me a lot of pleasure wandering among bushes of a three-foot ruby-red crepe myrtle (*Lagerstroemia indica* 'Victor').

Indigofera incarnata (or *I. decora*) tolerates dry shade, which makes it just the sort of plant a lot of gardeners need. It has running roots and I'd hesitate to let it loose among choice perennials, but it hugs the skirts of such evergreen shrubs as azaleas and *Osmanthus americanus* very pleasantly and gives me no trouble at all. Botanically *incarnata* means flesh-colored. If the flower color of this indigo resembles flesh at all, it is very sunburned flesh—the color is, in fact, mighty close to magenta, but if you don't like the sound of that, there's one with white flowers as well. Usually no more than one foot high, this could be fitted in nicely between foundation plantings and a path. So could lily-of-the-valley (*Convallaria majalis*).

Symphytum grandiflorum could also get out of hand in rich, moist soil but is the answer to a gardener's prayer for dry shade. This has creamy tubular flowers. *S. g.* 'Hidcote Blue' is about the same size with a hint of blue in the flowers, but by no means the bright blue one expects from the borage family. *S. g.* 'Hidcote Pink' has a touch of pink in its creamy flowers and grows taller than the others at about eighteen inches.

Where the soil is moderately fertile and not dust dry, one of the best ground-covering perennials for light shade is *Geranium macrorrhizum*, which never looks more beautiful than when used in quantity in bays between shrubs. It self-sows abundantly but is easily pulled up—so easily that it won't work in places where fallen leaves are raked up. It tends to grow itself out of the ground and benefits from a topdressing of soil or mulch every year or two. Pale pink 'Ingwersen's Variety' is the daintiest selection but if you'd pre-

fer a brighter color, look for 'Bevan's Variety'.

For a few perennials the only safe place is solitary confinement. Among the worst are those that spread stealthily by underground rhizomes (lily-of-the-valley, for example). Fred McGourty talks about "thugs," Bob Hebb calls them "plants with taking ways," while others have called them things less printable. In innocent enthusiasm I've grown a lot of them and am still, from time to time, beguiled by a catalogue description or the plant's observed beauty into adding another. *Houttuynia cordata* 'Chameleon' was one of them. I've seen it described as a good ground cover but it isn't dense enough for that. Hither-and-yon is its habit, one shoot here, another a foot away—even, on light soil, on the other side of a concrete path. It *can* be tamed, but only if grown in a container stand-

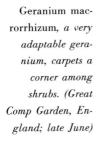

Geranium macrorrhizum, *a very adaptable geranium, carpets a corner among shrubs. (Great Comp Garden, England; late June)*

ing on crack-free concrete paving. *Eomecon chionantha* was my latest indiscretion, and I knew it within one season but kept it for another year in hope (realized) of flowers to photograph. By then the ropelike roots had spread for yards, in and out of other plants in the nursery bed. I've encountered nothing as invasive as this since coltsfoot (*Tussilago farfara*) in my English garden, and if anyone tries to sell you *that*, have they got a deal for you.

No plant has—yet—defeated me once battle was drawn but Chinese lanterns (*Physalis alkekengi*) nearly managed it, adding insult to injury by failing to produce the lantern-like seedpods which are, as far as I'm concerned, its only reason for being. It is often said that invasive plants shouldn't be grown in small gardens, but in fact it is in large ones that they are most likely to become a nuisance. The plants in a very small garden are always under the eye, therefore more likely to be checked, or eradicated, before this becomes a major operation. At the other extreme, such invasive plants as *Campanula rapunculoides* and the good old tawny daylily may be just what is wanted for a meadow. Here follow a few more invasive plants I've encountered, with uses (if any) to which I've put them or seen them put.

Variegated goutweed (*Aegopodium podagraria* 'Variegatum') is a very beautiful foliage plant. At the shady end of a courtyard garden in North Carolina, against a boundary wall, drifts of it alongside a white-painted swinging seat were surrounded by paving on all sides—cool, refreshing, and under control. The paving must be solid, though, or goutweed will run along the cracks, and it mustn't be allowed to go to seed. At White Flower Farm in Connecticut it surrounded an urn at the corner of a lawn, with gravel driveway on the other two sides. Below-ground barricades may have

prevented its spread into the lawn or gravel but, if not, mowing would control it on one side, weedkillers on the other.

Variegated lamiastrum (*Lamiastrum galeobdolen* 'Variegatum') is equally beautiful, and equally invasive, but it spreads by surface runners and if these are kept cut off (feasible only in fairly small spaces), it is not hard to control. If the runners aren't removed, they romp on, rooting as they go, until they run out of horizontal space—unlike ivy, it cannot climb trees. The best use of it I've seen was as a carpeter on a large bank with a path along the top to halt its passage and a paved driveway below. Cypress spurge (*Euphorbia cyparissias*), a European immigrant that has become a native weed so rapidly does it spread, could be similarly used, and so could *Hypericum calycinum*.

If one species of plant is invasive, it doesn't necessarily follow that others in the genus will be cast in the same mold. *Physostegia virginiana* is invasive, but the form with variegated leaves is difficult to establish.

Lamiastrum galeobdolen 'Variegatum' covers a bank in an English garden. This makes an excellent container plant, or it could cascade down a terrace wall. In hot summer regions it needs shade. If you need a less vigorous kind, consider Lamiastrum 'Herman's Pride', which has white-checkered leaves. Both have yellow dead-nettle flowers. (Garden of Mrs. N. A. Laurie, England; June)

Ajugas spread fast, by runners and seed, but *Ajuga pyramidalis* is a clump former. *Liriope muscari* is also a clump former as a rule (I've had a couple of exceptions, possibly allocated to the wrong species in this very confused genus), but beware of the rampant *Liriope spicata*, which is, nonetheless, a valued evergreen weed-suppressing, erosion-controlling carpeter in my garden, spreading through gravel and sand between the drive and the bank of a creek, checked by wheel compression from crossing the drive but tough enough to be parked on occasionally. No epimedium is going to be a nuisance, but some make clumps (*Epimedium grandiflorum*, *E.* × *rubrum*, *E.* × *youngianum*), some spread densely (*E.* × *versicolor*), and some spread too thinly to make good ground cover (*E.* × *warleyense*). If you want a foamflower (*Tiarella*) for ground cover, choose the stoloniferous *T. cordifolia*, but if you want it to stay in its clump, choose *T. wherryi*.

All of the mints are invasive, the saving grace being that their roots, though by no means shallow, don't descend to unexcavatable depths. One friend made an ornamental feature by housing several invasive herbs, including mints, in tall flue tiles sunk close together but with their tops at different levels. Large plastic pots could be used, or buckets with holes drilled in the bottom, if they are lined with a thick layer of newspaper. This lets water through but restrains the roots. Confined this way I commend as a fine ornamental *Mentha longifolia*, with its gray leaves and pale purple flowers.

Lily-of-the-valley could be treated the same way, but the best place for this where it is invasive (in some regions it is choice and difficult) is an otherwise unplanted area where it can romp to its heart's content. I have such a place behind our house, where an apron of land is surrounded by water. There are pine trees and the natural mulch they provide, but I wanted no bright flowers to conflict with the view. There are daffodils, of the simpler kinds, but nothing else except a big expanse of lily-of-the-valley, started under a bedroom window so that the fragrance might waft in, and encouraged to spread even more rapidly than is its way by slicing out a few circular clumps each year and moving them further out. It grows dense and weed suppressing, green and cool-looking through summer, gold in autumn, with a shabby period of only a couple of weeks before going winter dormant.

Another aggressive plant that can be tamed by growing it in a container is blue lyme grass (*Elymus arenarius*). Because it thrives in the summer humidity that rots so many gray-leaved plants, I do grow a single large clump of it in one of my beds, but several hours have to be spent each year removing roving roots, so when I get around to it, it will go in a large plastic tub sunk not quite to its rim. Its arching habit is nowhere better displayed than in a large free-standing container. It is not evergreen but the dead leaves remain attractive through much of winter.

Glaucous-leaved Elymus arenarius, *safely contained in a whiskey barrel, remains attractive in winter. (Garden of Norman Beal, Virginia; February)*

Three ways of using the very invasive Vinca major: *Top left, the green-leaved species is allowed to go its way among trees, interplanted with odds and ends of bulbs left over from other plantings—tulips, daffodils, wood hyacinths, anemones (Colonial Williamsburg, Virginia; April); top right, the variegated form, in containers, cascades down from a balcony (Garden of J. Liddon Pennock, Meadowbrook Farm, Pennsylvania; September); and right, in a barrel standing on paving, combined with a purple-leaved barberry (Garden of Gladys and Alain Huyghe, Virginia; June).*

Containers aren't always the complete answer, though; it depends where you put them. The large-leaved variegated periwinkle, *Vinca major* 'Variegata', is a very attractive plant, with or without the flowers that are sparingly borne, but it is extremely invasive so I put it in a whiskey barrel standing at the junction of two bark-mulch paths. I soon learned that the trailing stems must be sheared off repeatedly to prevent them from reaching and rooting into the ground, a task that would be less urgent if the container stood on paving. The length to which these vining stems grow in a single year is quite remarkable. I saw this trait put to imaginative use with containers of this periwinkle (wintered in a greenhouse) spaced along a railed second floor balcony, from where the vining stems cascaded down to form a living curtain in front of a doorway below. Elevating plants this way displays them well and keeps them under control (at the cost, of course, of the need for regular watering). Things like the periwinkle, lamiastrum, and creeping Charlie (*Lysimachia nummularia*) are a good choice for hanging baskets.

There's a fine and wavering line between usefully vigorous and overly aggressive. *Ajuga*, moss pink (*Phlox subulata*), *Mazus reptans*, and the little, not very hardy (Zone 7/8), blue star creeper (variously called *Laurentia*, *Isotoma*, or *Pratia*) are popular plants, but all are capable of making a takeover bid. Often there is a choice: there are moss pinks of every persuasion—rampant, restrained, and little rock garden gems. With others, why not make virtue out of necessity? *Mazus reptans* will infiltrate a lawn. It stays lower than the mower blades and doesn't get in the way, so why not let it have its head? Most lawns would be prettier for its presence. I didn't, though, want it to spread from a shaded bark mulch path (it can stand occasional foot traffic) into the beds

alongside and after a bit of experiment found that an edging of dense dwarf ophiopogon halts it in its tracks. Blue star creeper is scarcely more than a film over the ground and would be a nuisance only, perhaps, in a rock garden. Little creepers like this, and some bigger ones such as *Cerastium tomentosum* and creeping Charlie don't usually get out of hand when used to stitch together joins in steps or paving. A friend paved part of his town garden with the small square concrete pavers sold by garden centers, but here and there he used a round one instead, which left little open corners into which such plants were tucked and from where they soon spread along the cracks between the pavers.

Invasive plants aren't limited to those with spreading roots. Some take seriously the injunction to go forth and multiply, and their seed will germinate on stony ground or any other kind. A friend gave me the double form of the greater celandine (*Chelidonium majus* 'Flore Pleno'), saying "It's invasive but you'll love it." It is, and I did, but not enough to give

*Confined to the cracks between steps, mouse-eared chickweed (*Cerastium tomentosum*) cannot get out of hand. (Hestercombe, England; August)*

up to it my whole two acres. The leaves are beautiful and the small yellow poppy flowers delightful, but these open in succession from late spring through fall, and all this time the seedpods are ripening and scattering seed—compound interest less welcome in the garden than in the bank account. Double flowers are often sterile, but not these. Still, it has a place. In a garden in coastal Maine it was naturalized among a shelter belt of trees near the water. On the other side was extensive lawn, and then a walled flower garden. I daresay a few seeds make even this long journey, but not enough to be a nuisance.

Other self-sowers to beware of are brunnera, ornamental onions, feverfew (*Chrysanthemum parthenium*), money plant (*Lunaria*), lemon balm (*Melissa*), oxeye daisies (*Chrysanthemum leucanthemum*, including most of those sold as 'May Queen'), and most violets. Sometimes the vigor of its reproduction depends on where you live. I was asked for a picture of *Salvia lyrata* by someone assembling a program on endangered plants. Endangered! Only by me with Roundup spray! It grows wild where I live and self-sows by the million.

Removing spent flowers prevents most such plants from taking over your garden, but will you remember, and will you be there? It doesn't always do the trick with violets anyway because many of them manage their reproduction differently from most plants, forming not only the seedpods you see but a bigger batch, unfertilized but fertile, just below the surface of the ground.

Perennials can't climb trees, and most can't swim. Outside the moat of your castle might be the place for some of the more vigorous kinds. My own "moat" is the roadside ditch outside the front boundary, with a mown free-for-all beyond. Mown, that is, by everyone but me—mowing is a chore I decline to

take on and our verges disgraced the neighborhood while I was deciding how best to deal with them. This was my lesson in meadow gardening! I knew better than to rototill and bring up buried dormant weed seeds, so the grass was bumped off with Roundup. It gave up fairly quickly but for two years thereafter monthly applications of Roundup were needed to keep pace with annual weeds. What then to do with it? Inspiration came during a winter drive between Interstate banks planted with weeping love grass (*Eragrostis curvula*). This forms fine-bladed arching clumps of a foot or so, broader than they are high. It goes winter dormant but the clumps hold their shape and resemble some of the brown-leaved sedges. This I am now using on the roadside verge, interplanted with the very vigorous old double 'Kwanso' daylily, which can't cross the deep ditch on one side, nor the blacktop road on the other. This would be the place for such other overly vigorous plants as wild yarrow (*Achillea millefolium*), *Artemisia* 'Silver King', most of the lysimachias, bouncing Bet (*Saponaria officinalis*), including the double form, the tawny daylily, and probably anything given to you by a neighbor. Because they are tough, and because they spread, these are all good meadow plants.

With some only moderately invasive plants the "set a thief to catch a thief" approach works well. The crux of the style so much in the limelight as the "new American garden," which I prefer to call the modified meadow, is the combining of sturdy plants that can fight it out on equal terms. Because maintenance is reduced, it makes large plantings manageable, but it also lends itself to quite small groupings. It is a pity that exaggerated statements implying a labor-free Eden of year-round unflawed beauty are leading to skeptical rebuttals because it is a timely style in an era when skilled garden labor is a scarce

*The tawny daylily (*Hemerocallis fulva *'Europa') is often thought to be a native plant, so widely has it naturalized by spreading roots. It is sterile, so there'll be no un-wanted seedlings, and it remains a fine plant for roadside verges, meadows, or any-where other peren-nials don't have to compete with it. The flowers look much less slovenly when dead than those of most large-flowered hy-brids. (Virginia; June)*

commodity. Certainly it is more practical for most than the sort of wildflower meadow garden so much talked and written about but so seldom achieved.

MEADOWS AND THE MODIFIED MEADOW

It seems to me that the idea of a meadow garden attracts two kinds of people, those who want a work-free garden, and those who are willing to work but want something more natural than lawn and foundation plantings. Misleading advertising must be causing a lot of disappointment, because meadow gardens will not fulfill the dream of bliss without blisters: put on a pretty dress and smart shoes (or none)

and dance over your lawn or weed patch shaking a can, and what you'll have next year is exactly what you had to begin with, except that your bank balance will be lower. A natural garden is assumed to be carefree, but only in prairie regions, devoid of trees, is a meadow natural; elsewhere, nature will strive to return cleared land to woods and will soon succeed if the meadow is left to take care of itself.

If a meadow garden is to be attempted, the flowers most likely to succeed are those already growing wild (though not necessarily native) in the region, among which, very likely, will be found some of these: asters, bouncing Bet (*Saponaria officinalis*), butterfly weed (*Asclepias tuberosa*), goldenrods, yarrow (*Achillea millefolium*), black-eyed Susan (*Rudbeckia hirta*), hawkweeds (*Hieracium*), *Liatris*, *Verbascum thapsus*, and the ubiquitous

oxeye daisy (*Chrysanthemum leucanthemum*) and tawny daylily (*Hemerocallis fulva* 'Europa'). *Hemerocallis* 'Nashville' is another rapidly spreading daylily recommended for meadows and banks, growing fourteen inches high and bearing green-throated dark burgundy flowers. Foxgloves (*Digitalis purpurea*) will naturalize in full sun where summers are cool but are usually the better for light shade.

Even for such tough plants as these it is advisable to first remove the existing vegetation. Neil Diboll, plant ecologist with Prairie Nursery which specializes in wildflowers and grasses, puts it succinctly: "Possession is nine-tenths of the law in this game." If the area is not extensive and you have the patience to wait a year, the existing vegetation can be smothered out by covering it with a layer of newspaper topped with mulch. For quicker results, burn it off, or use a herbicide. Seed can then be sown into slits, or clumps set out, disturbing the soil as little as possible to avoid bringing dormant weed seeds to the surface where they can germinate.

A meadow garden may not match the maker's dream even when successful. It may prove to be too unstructured, or untidy for urban and suburban settings, and sometimes a cause of neighborhood strife. Plants don't recognize property boundaries and your self-sowing "meadow flowers" may be "weeds" to those next door. It is not unknown for injunctions to be granted requiring that suburban "meadows" be mown before they can go to seed.

"Natural garden" is a contradiction in terms, but the modified meadow is a better compromise than we have seen before except in woodland wildflower gardens. Experiments with this more relaxed, less labor-intensive method of gardening have been going on in Germany for many years. Stylized in America by landscape architects Oehme, van Sweden and Associates, it requires that the soil be cleaned of weeds, including grass, just as it would be for a flower border. It is then planted with drifts of comparatively few kinds of sturdy perennials and ornamental grasses, choosing those adapted to the region and that don't require staking, deadheading, frequent watering, or regular division. When these perennials meet and mingle, there is no space for weeds. This kind of planting is more ordered than a meadow and needs less maintenance than a mixed border, but it is not maintenance-free. At the beginning of each growing season, dead top growth must be cut away and most perennials will still require occasional division; *Sedum* 'Autumn Joy', for example, splays out and becomes less attractive when clumps get overcrowded, and the spread of other plants will have to be curtailed if their proportions in the garden are to be maintained. Many grasses get bare in the middle after several years, and dividing such big ones as *Miscanthus* is extremely arduous work. Many grasses are very drought resistant but occasional fertilizing may be needed, especially in areas of heavy rainfall where nutrients are rapidly leached from the soil, particularly if it is sandy.

Massed perennials are dramatic. Some of the most impressive displays come from great sweeps of a single kind—a scene found in the wild more often than in gardens, for the very good reason that the display, though breathtaking, is not very prolonged. With informed choice of plants, the modified meadow spreads the display through much of the year: *how much*, once again, depends on where you live. Many ornamental grasses are even more at-

tractive in their autumn and winter buffs and browns than they are in their summer greens, but where there is heavy snow or constant rain they do not retain their structure through winter, and when this comes early some won't have time to form the flowering plumes that are a major part of their appeal.

Massed plants being easier to arrange, install, and manage than more intricate combinations, the modified meadow has much to commend it if approached in an exploratory frame of mind, but one risks boredom from overuse of the same few plants if the approach is merely imitatory. The leading perennial actors in this play must by now be known to everyone: *Sedum* 'Autumn Joy' and *Rudbeckia* 'Goldsturm'. They are splendid plants, but the range needs to be widened and the style adapted to different regions. Other suitable plants include *Achillea* 'Coronation Gold' and 'Moonshine', astilbes, bergenias, *Caryopteris*, *Chrysanthemum* 'May Queen', *C.* × *rubellum* 'Mary Stoker' (also Korean chrysanthemums in the South), coreopsis (especially *Coreopsis verticillata*), daylilies, epimediums, *Iris sibirica* (the flowering time is short but the

Miscanthus, or eulalia grass, was common in the Southeast long before it became fashionable. The photograph, showing it with asters in October, was taken at Gloucester Daffodil Mart, Virginia, in 1975.

The sculptural winter habit of Lespedeza thunbergii *'Albiflora', a plant that stays attractive most of the year. (Virginia; January)*

foliage stays neat and adds textural variety), joe-pye weed (*Eupatorium*), leadplant (*Amorpha canescens*), liriope, and Russian sage (*Perovskia*). And grasses, of course, which I'll get to presently.

Perennials that remain attractive in winter are to be preferred for this style of gardening. *Lespedeza thunbergii* is a favorite of mine. During the growing season its habit is wide and arching, but after the leaves have fallen it becomes quite architectural, the slender branches becoming upright and turning in to meet each other at the tips. During a freak eighteen-inch snowfall that bent and snapped evergreens and flattened most grasses, the lespedeza shed the snow and looked untouched. Until growth begins again from the base in spring it occupies little ground space and can be surrounded with bulbs, later cascading out and concealing their dying foliage. Even where frosts come before it flowers, it might earn a place for its attractive foliage and sculptural winter form.

The modified meadow is an innovative style with much greater potential than has yet been developed. The concept can be applied to any kind of garden: border, rock garden, woodland garden, small city garden, foundation plantings, or just a small patch in the corner of a lawn. Just choose sturdy, fairly self-sufficient plants of long-lasting good appearance adapted to, and of a size in scale with the site, then group them in numbers appropriate to the area being planted. Caring for ten plants of the same kind takes only a fraction of the time needed for ten different ones.

When massing hostas, daylilies, or bearded irises it is safer to stay with those older cultivars that have been tried and not found wanting; modern hybrids are often selected for qualities other than sturdy self-sufficiency. Hardy geraniums are still more or less as nature made them and, where they do well, lend themselves nicely to a mix-and-match massing of white, pink, blue, lavender, and violet flowers united by their common form.

So give consideration to the modified meadow approach, which may be just what you want, or the best compromise, but don't just jump on the bandwagon; it is not a style for everyone. It may not satisfy those wanting a very structured garden, though massed plantings can be very effective in a formal setting. At the other extreme, it certainly will not suit the plantsman or collector and, at least in stereotyped form, it won't meet the needs of the artist because it limits opportunities for creative and original combinations. Part of the charm of a garden is the day-to-day changes, the ephemeral nature of a flower often adding to its appeal. The modified meadow does change, but not to the same extent as a mixed garden. But artists and plantsmen are in a minority, as are those wanting to devote most of their spare time to a garden, and the modified meadow is certainly an attractive alternative to the sterility of lawn and foundation plantings.

LAWN ALTERNATIVES

An extensively planted paved courtyard, with hostas, alchemilla, ferns, Campanula portenschlagiana, *and a touch of scarlet from monkey flower (*Mimulus*). The courtyard is primarily an ornamental feature. (Garden of Mr. and Mrs. David Hodges, Brook Cottage, Alkerton, Oxfordshire, England; July)*

Lawns are being swept away, I read, and replaced by paving. Not where I live or travel they aren't, though I do agree that some of them should be, for reasons of aesthetics or water shortage. Paving has the advantage in very small gardens but lawn would be hard to replace in large ones. A paved area or wood deck near the house has, of course, long been customary. Paving requires less maintenance (it does have to be swept, and the bird droppings washed away) and it doesn't have to be watered, but it doesn't look or feel as cool and fresh, children who fall on it may skin their knees or noses, and it is far more expensive to install than lawn (prohibitively so for most, except on a small scale). It is also permanent, which can be a serious disadvantage for do-it-yourself gardeners (most of us), who seldom get the layout quite right the first time around.

If you opt for paving, consider leaving spaces for plants. Planted paving is picturesque but not very practical for surfaces in constant use, nor where litter from trees necessitates frequent sweeping up. Where summers are very hot many plants cannot contend with the heat reflected from the paving. If the paving is near the house, winter-dormant plants that leave large bare gaps might make the paving unsightly but creeping plants could be planted in the cracks. Sometimes a minor path, away from the house, is a better place for playing with plants in paving. Keep in mind, though, that weeds also like to grow in paving cracks. Life can be made more difficult for them by laying such a path on plastic, slitting it where you want to sow seed or insert a small plant between the paving stones.

Gravel or sand is another possibility, eliminating the need to mow and water at lower cost and with greater flexibility than paving, but requiring more work to keep the surface clean of weeds. Gray crushed rock is

*Plants in the concrete paving in one of the "rooms" of Harland Hand's terraced California garden. The plants include dwarf yarrow (*Achillea*), ophiopogon,* Iberis sempervirens, *and thrift (*Armeria maritima*). (May)*

A sand garden with clumps of alchemilla at the corners. The cushion-shaped plants to the left are heathers. Among the plants in the narrow border behind are sages (Salvia officinalis 'Purpurascens' and S. o. 'Tricolor'), dianthus, Ceanothus 'Marie Simon', and Hypericum moseranum 'Tricolor'. Alchemilla needs shade where summers are hot, and even then it gets too shabby in summer to merit such prominent placement. (Garden of Patricia Fountain, England; late July)

the most common surfacing for drives in my area, but I found this too harsh and light reflecting on sunny summer days. Golden brown gravel sets off flowers almost as well as grass and permits less structured beds, with plants allowed to spread or seed out into the gravel. Seeds germinate freely in gravel and that, of course, includes weed seeds, so those totally averse to the use of chemicals (one or two applications a year is usually sufficient) will need to lay the gravel over plastic.

What of the other lawn alternatives one reads about? I've seen more kinds of alternative lawn in America than I did in England, among them dichondra, ophiopogon, and *Laurentia fluviatilis*, but their application is regional. Moss makes a beautiful grass substitute in moist shade but it isn't easy to establish where it doesn't naturally exist. Moss grows naturally around a few of the trees in my own garden and I've found it to be impervious to Roundup, which makes it very easy to keep free of weeds, including grass. I don't know if this is true of all mosses, so conduct your experiments on a small scale first. Moss is

easily damaged and one owner of such a lawn requires that visitors not wear high-heeled shoes.

In the rather few regions where they do well, herb lawns (thyme, chamomile, oregano) can be very attractive but they are best regarded as garden features, not as substitutes for grass, except in very small spaces.

The main complaint about grass is its need for frequent mowing, but the mowing is a renewal, like replacing old worn clothes with new ones. If the same grass blades remained all season, they would get flattened, damaged, and brown when the lawn is walked or played on. It is the ability of grass to renew itself so quickly that enables it to grow over spilt earth or other deposits that would remain unsightly on such flatter ground covers as thyme or, for that matter, paving. With demands for water continuing to grow it may not, for much longer, be feasible to have lawns in regions where summer drought is normal. Where rainfall is ample, grass remains the most versatile, uniform, hard-wearing, and resilient ground cover, unequaled as green open space for setting off beds and borders of flowers.

An attractive alternative to lawn in a plantswoman's small front garden, with gaps in the paving filled mainly with woolly thyme (Thymus pseudolanuginosus). A clump of Kniphofia 'Little Maid' can be seen in the corner near the road. (Garden of Pam Snow, Seattle, Washington; August)

Two scenes from a mixed garden in Virginia. The same garden is shown in the photograph on page 2. Every kind of plant is grown, including a great many in containers. The photograph below shows the privacy attained for a corner patio by screening it with mixed plantings of shrubs and perennials. (Garden of Gladys and Alain Huyghe, Virginia; early July)

7 | Perennials in the Mixed Garden

American garden designers tell me that what their clients most want is "an English border." This is a bit of a misconception: few English gardeners now maintain the kind of border that prompts the request. The English herbaceous border came about in an age of considerable affluence for a few. As England entered an era of plantsmanship, with a wealth of plants of every kind available, borders were only one component of grand gardens, which might also have included a shrubbery, rose garden, walled fruit and vegetable garden, fernery, woodland walk or wilderness, and water of some kind, whether formal pool, pond, stream, or bog.

That era ended, few grand estates remain in private hands, and with less help available or affordable most of those few have had to be simplified. Many remain much as they were under the management of The National Trust—England's "national treasures," a source of pleasure and inspiration to visitors from home and abroad. It is in these gardens that visiting Americans see most of the fine borders they find so enviable—enviable but not realistically imitable for most of us, nor for most English gardeners.

England today has more gardens than ever before, and more enthusiastic gardeners, interested in plants of every kind, but most gardens aren't big enough to segregate a perennials border so the mixed bed or border is usually preferred. In it is grown something of everything: small ornamental trees, conifers, shrubs, roses, vines, perennials, ferns, grasses, ground covers, bulbs, and annuals.

Mixed beds, being so varied, can provide something of interest and beauty every month of the year. Southerners, obviously, have the advantage in winter, but even in the coldest zones there can be winter structure from the firm outlines of conifers, the white bark of birches, and the colorful red, orange, or yellow twigs of red osier dogwoods and willows. The mixed border, or mixed garden, like every other style, cannot be formularized for American gardens, it must be tailored to individual sites, soils, climates, and life-styles, but a once-over-lightly of the components of mixed borders might help in fitting a few bits into the puzzle.

TREES AND SHRUBS

First, a recommendation. Read *Shrubs and Trees for the Small Place* by P. J. Van Melle, published in 1943 and out of print but available in many libraries. It is based on northern experience but has descriptions and assessments of value for everyone and covers the subject far more comprehensively than is possible here. Each plant is rated for floral effect, fragrance, foliage value, seasonal color, decorative fruit, summer blending value, winter value, relative freedom from insects and diseases, tolerance of shade, adaptability to various soils, suitability as hedging or specimen and—an important consideration for those of us who like to play with color and combinations—transplantability.

In touching briefly on trees I am not concerned with woodland gardens and forest-sized trees but with small ornamental trees suitable for a flower border. They can be a mixed blessing. Nothing in my garden gives me more pleasure for less work than some of the ornamental trees, particularly those chosen for their attractive bark: crepe myrtles (in sun, underplanted with *Juniperus conferta*); coralbark maple (*Acer palmatum* 'Senkaki', also called 'Sango Kaku') underplanted on the east side with snowdrops and *Campanula garganica*; paperbark maple (*Acer griseum*) underplanted on the east side with bloodroot (*Sanguinaria canadensis*) and *Campanula poscharskyana*; lacebark pine (*Pinus bungeana*) partly underplanted with hellebores; and Cornelian cherry (*Cornus officinalis* or *C. mas*) with its shaggy bark and very early yellow flowers underplanted with ajuga.

But there's no denying that tree roots can handicap perennials. The thing to bear in mind when deciding where to plant an ornamental tree is that plants adapted to shade usually have a shallow root system enabling them to grow in the surface duff that accumulates under trees. Most of them flower in spring, and many go summer dormant. Plants that grow in sun usually need a deeper root run. One of my crepe myrtles (*Lagerstroemia fauriei*) was originally surrounded by butterfly weed (*Asclepias tuberosa*) and gaillardia but its roots eventually crowded them out. Crepe myrtles grow large and their roots spread wide and dense.

There are trees, though, that can be combined with perennials in a sunny bed. *Xanthoceras sorbifolium* is my best. Only six feet high after fifteen years, it has flowered faithfully from its foot-high beginnings as a small sucker from a friend's tree. The shiny leaves are finely pinnate and the flowers, borne in

The most popular of all cherries, Prunus 'Kwanzan', *puts on a glorious though brief display of flower each spring and its bark is also ornamental. Under it, in a garden planned for year-round interest and low maintenance, grow white and yellow-variegated selections of* Euonymus fortunei *and perennials that do not have a long shabby period. Bergenias, primroses, columbines, and geraniums flowered earlier.* Sedum 'Autumn Joy' *is yet to come. To the left is* Weigela florida 'Variegata'. *(Garden of Mrs. L. D. Willmott, England; September)*

spring, are white stars with dark red eyes loosely clustered in pendent bunches. The branches slope upward and don't smother out plants growing beneath it and the roots are not dense—the perfect little border tree, reportedly perfectly hardy in Poughkeepsie, New York. It does not transplant well and should be put out as a young container-grown plant. Books differ about its soil and site preferences but mine is happy in full sun and sandy, acid soil.

Planting right up to the trunk of small ornamental trees with branches well clear of the soil isn't usually a problem on the shady (north- or east-facing) side. Tree roots absorb a lot of moisture so the soil will tend to be dry. Perennials and ground covers likely to succeed in such places include pachysandra and periwinkle (*Vinca minor*), epimediums, vancouveria, Solomon's seal (*Polygonatum*), *Symphytum grandiflorum*, and *Indigofera decora*. For those willing and able to water when necessary, there is an abundance of suitable plants, including hostas and ferns.

Finding plants to grow on the sunny (south- or west-facing) side is much more difficult, especially where summers are hot or dry. Few perennials that remain in growth through summer flourish when they have to contend with both heat and root competition. *Phlox subulata* is one possibility, and perhaps *Potentilla tridentata* if the tree roots aren't too dense and watering can be done in periods of drought. The least suitable plants for such a hot, dry place are those described as "drought resistant." Most of these are deep-rooting meadow plants that haven't evolved to compete with the roots of trees. I have found one exception, the sundrops passed from gardener to gardener as *Oenothera fruticosa* (correctly, I am told, *O. pilosella*). This is a toughie, as plants passed from neighbor to neighbor usually are. It spreads rapidly but shallowly, is easily pulled out, delights in heat, doesn't mind poor, dry soil, and although it flowers for no more than a month (less in hot climates), the glossy foliage rosettes cover the ground for much of the year.

If there's a tree in the border with branches that sweep the ground, this is the perfect spot for a massed planting of early bulbs. They get the sun they need in late winter and spring, then take their summer rest without the risk of being walked on or disturbed. One of the prettiest scenes in my garden in April is a mass of bright blue *Anemone coronaria* under a large dogwood at one end of a border. The two flower together, for about the same length of time. By the time the anemone is ready to go dormant for the summer, the dogwood has leafed out to hide the bare earth. This anemone (which comes in many different colors) isn't very hardy, and even where it is, it diminishes year by year and needs to be supplemented from time to time. My first choice was *A. blanda*, which, once established, self-sows and increases, but when they flowered they proved to be not the deep blue I had ordered but a wishy-washy color far too pale to be effective under the white flowers of the dogwood. This kind of problem is one I've encountered often with the bulb industry and I recommend placing small trial orders before buying anything in substantial quantity. The hardiest anemone, and the one that increases most rapidly in my garden, is *A. nemorosa*. There are several beautiful white forms, single or double-flowered, and several blues but none as deep a blue as the brightest forms of *A. coronaria* and *A. blanda*.

Earlier, in February, *Narcissus* 'February Gold' flowers under the gnarled, spreading branches of a tree wisteria (*Wisteria sinensis* 'Alba') which, in April, will be hung with chains of white, fragrant flowers. By late spring the wisteria has leafed out and hides the withering leaves of the daffodils, which in the course of five years have increased from fifty to several hundred.

Other suitable early flowering bulbs include aconites (*Eranthis*), snowdrops (*Galanthus nivalis*), chionodoxas, starflower (*Ipheion uniflorum*), and such little early crocuses as *Crocus chrysanthus*. Where it is hardy you could have winter flowers from *Cyclamen coum*.

Autumn-flowering bulbs are a bit more difficult to place. You need to know the habits of both the bulb and the tree. I grow *Crocus medius* under *Prunus mume*, which sheds its leaves at about the time the crocus comes into bloom without burying it. The leaves of the crocus come with or soon after the flowers and are gone by the time the tree leafs out in spring. Most colchicums flower in autumn but produce their leaves in spring. I can grow these under the American fringe tree (*Chionanthus virginicus*), which drops its leaves early in autumn and leafs out late in spring, but not under the oriental *C. retusus*, which holds its leaves (which are also a lot messier when they fall) a month or more longer.

If I'm not sure that the place I have in mind for bulbs will work out in practice, I plant the bulbs in pots and plunge these to the rim in a nursery bed or odd corner of the garden. They can then be put in place at flowering time.

SHRUBS

Shrubs are the main component of the mixed garden and they have many functions. Among them can be found not only flower for almost any time of year but variegated or colored foliage, fragrance, colorful fruits, autumn leaf color, and colorful winter bark and twigs. In shape and size shrubs range from treelike (*Viburnum plicatum tomentosum* could substitute for dogwood) and columnar accent points (*Juniperus* 'Skyrocket', for example) to low mounds and prostrate carpeters. Small evergreen shrubs, such as Kingsville boxwood (*Buxus microphylla* 'Compacta'), Helleri holly (*Ilex crenata* 'Helleri'), or dwarf mugo pines (*Pinus mugo*) can anchor the ends of borders or provide formal punctuation along the front. Taller evergreens could be brought forward to divide long borders into separate color schemes: Southerners have plenty of choice; in cold regions a compact form of the inkberry (*Ilex glabra* 'Compacta') might be used.

The lasting structure of shrubs holds a border together when perennials are dormant. Vines can ramble through some of them and others can prop up perennials. Purple-leaved shrubs are the mainstay of red-and-purple color schemes, and yellow-leaved ones the main component of golden gardens. Shrubs can be used for screens and hedges, evergreen or deciduous, high or low, formal (clipped) or informal (allowed to assume their natural shape). A row of shrubs on a front boundary, perhaps on a berm for added height, could screen a front garden where fences aren't permitted and provide a background for border flowers. As hedges, or individually, shrubs create microclimates of shade and shelter for smaller plants.

Shrubs can frame a garden, or divide up space within it. Beds of perennials much more than eight feet wide make it hard to spray, deadhead, or weed around those at the back without stepping on those in front. Suppose, though, there exists a bed too wide for easy management. It may be of pleasing proportions or there may be other practical reasons for not making it narrower—perhaps there are paths or walls in place. Shrubs could be used at the back, or to divide an island bed

The shrubs, perennials, and bulbs included in this small island bed are all of long-lasting good appearance. They include Cotinus coggygria *'Notcutt's Variety',* Weigela florida *'Variegata',* Astrantia major, Sedum *'Autumn Joy',* irises, *and* Allium christophii. *In hot summer regions of the United States, the astrantia needs shade. (Garden of Mark Rumary, England; late June)*

down the center. They need little routine management and any major pruning can be done in wintertime when perennials are dormant. A fourteen-foot bed split down the middle has some advantages over two separate beds. The amount of sun will be different on the two sides, broadening the range of plants that can be grown, and a center row of shrubs can provide a visual barrier between two different color schemes. Evergreens could be used for strongly defined partition, or deciduous shrubs of loose, rounded habit to blend in less noticeably.

The proportions of shrubs to perennials can be whatever you wish but at the extremes we have shrubs combined with perennials in two very different kinds of garden: the predominantly sunny, and the predominantly shady. Site and climate may determine which it will be but there are infinite variations: a

Shrubs predominate in my garden. Left: *The tip of a large island bed encircled by the drive. The center of the bed is filled with azaleas and camellias, over in early July when the picture was taken.* Hydrangea macrophylla *'Ayesha' and* Hemerocallis *'Hyperion' are in bloom on the east-facing side. Hellebores in front of the hydrangea flowered earlier,* Tricyrtis hirta *(center bottom), which has seeded itself into the drive, will flower later. To its left is the Japanese painted fern underplanted with snowdrops.* Right: *This photograph, taken in April, shows a favorite azalea, split-petaled 'Koromo Shikibu', underplanted with* Hosta undulata. *The hosta is still among the best in spring but becomes less attractive as the season progresses.*

woodland garden is shady, so is a city lot surrounded by tall buildings, or a border against a north wall. Densely wooded sites are not hospitable to shrubs; there is insufficient light and too much root competition from surrounding trees. Unless the trees are thinned, underplantings will be limited to woodland plants—not necessarily only native kinds—that flower before the trees leaf out and then go summer dormant.

What is often called a shrub garden (nearly always a mixed garden) differs from the wildflower or woodland garden in having few, if any, forest-sized trees but it still has a good deal of shade, cast by large shrubs and such small ornamental trees as crab apples,

cherries, and magnolias. In the light shade under scattered trees, or where the shade comes from buildings or a tall hedge, many more plants can be grown than in a woods, including (climate permitting) such evergreen shrubs as mountain laurels (*Kalmia latifolia*), rhododendrons and azaleas, aucubas, camellias, hollies (*Ilex*), mahonias, and pieris. Here can be grown the full range of perennials preferring, or tolerating, shade: anemones, columbines (*Aquilegia*), brunnera, bleeding hearts (*Dicentra*), hellebores, liriope, woodland phloxes, (*Phlox divaricata, P. stolonifera*), primroses (*Primula*), pulmonaria, toad lilies (*Tricyrtis*), and all the native wildflowers adapted to the particular region. Most flower will come in spring, with summer interest provided by such foliage plants as bergenia, variegated Solomon's seal (*Polygonatum odoratum thunbergii* 'Variegatum'), hostas, and ferns.

Adding shrubs to sunny beds and borders of summer-flowering perennials lengthens the season of interest at both ends, and reduces the amount of work required. Space for space, most shrubs require less attention than perennials. Shrubs bring early bloom to borders but those grown for foliage and form make a longer-lasting contribution, especially evergreens with gray, purple, gold, or variegated foliage to match or contrast with nearby perennials. Conifers of pyramidal, spirelike, or mounded shape are invaluable for their strong, permanent form, but be careful when choosing their close companions—lush foliage sprawling over evergreen shrubs can kill or disfigure them; conifers are particularly vulnerable. Because they are very vigorous and quickly replace damaged stems, *Euonymus* 'Emerald n' Gold' (gold variegated) and 'Emerald Gaiety' (cream variegation turning to white) make excellent evergreen shrubs for the front of a border. Left unchecked they make long vinelike branches, and if there's a solid surface nearby they will adhere to it, but occasional clipping of wayward branches will

Hosta 'Buckshaw Blue' with Euonymus *'Emerald n' Gold', a combination that will remain attractive all the growing season (if slugs aren't permitted to chew the hosta leaves!). The euonymus is evergreen. (England; early July)*

Philadelphus 'Belle Etoile' is one of the nicest small mock oranges. Here, in my garden in June, it flowers with yellow achilleas and blue veronicas. Under it is lamb's ears, interspersed with tulips in those years when vole depredations haven't wiped them out. (Virginia)

maintain them in a mounded shape. These are trouble-free shrubs for the most part but scale can be a serious problem so an annual spraying with dormant oil is advisable. Where they can stand the climate (the milder parts of the West Coast), hebes (*Hebe*) are excellent front-line evergreens.

Shrubs can be added to existing flower borders but ideally the bigger ones for the back of a border or middle of an island bed should be positioned before the perennials. They will be permanent, with adjustments made to the perennials as the shrubs increase in size. Very large shrubs are out of scale in most beds and borders, and would cast too much shade for sun-loving perennials, but there is no shortage of small and medium-sized shrubs to choose from: not large lilacs but such smaller ones as 'Palibin' or the

dainty cutleaf *Syringa persica* 'Laciniata'; not *Viburnum carlesii* but *V. c.* 'Compacta'; not the large weigelas and deutzias but such smaller kinds as *Weigela florida* 'Variegata' (recommended for its long-lasting variegated foliage), and *W. f.* 'Foliis Purpureis', with its pink flowers and purple-flushed foliage. Small deutzias include *Deutzia gracilis* and the low mounding *D. g.* 'Nikko'. The popular *Spiraea* × *vanhouttei*, foaming with white flowers in spring, could be kept in scale by pruning, but why endure this chore when there are similar smaller kinds such as *S. trilobata* and *S. nipponica* 'Snowmound'? Most flowering cherries and almonds are trees but *Prunus glandulosa*, with pompoms of white or baby pink double flowers along the stems, and the bright pink, single-flowered *P. tenella* are small bushy shrubs. These are all deciduous and bear their pink or white flowers in spring.

Suitable yellow-flowered shrubs include *Kerria japonica*. This can take full sun but in hot regions light shade prevents the flowers from bleaching out. It is a spreading, suckering shrub, but easily controlled, graceful and arching to about four feet, with willowy stems that remain green in winter. Double-flowered *K. j.* 'Pleniflora' continues to produce a smattering of flowers after the main spring flush but is on the large side at six feet or so. The smallest, and the loveliest, is *K. j.* 'Variegata', with single yellow flowers at azalea time and prettily shaped small leaves patterned in white.

Sundry shrubby potentillas and hypericums mix well with perennials, but they vary a lot in regional adaptability. Where neither summer heat nor winter cold are severe the best hypericum might be the large-leaved, large-flowered 'Hidcote' which, when happy, blooms from midsummer through autumn. Where summers are very hot *Hypericum frondosum* would be a better choice, evergreen with small blue-green leaves, fast growing to three feet or so but, like many fast-growing shrubs, not very long-lived. Though smaller than those of 'Hidcote', the flowers are showy and abundant. *H. f.* 'Sunburst' is a low-growing cultivar, not much more than two feet. Where winters are very cold, go for *H. kalmianum*, with inch-wide flowers and very small blue-green leaves. This survives temperatures down to −30°F. The shrubby potentillas are extremely cold hardy and capable of flowering for months at a time, but disappointing where summers are hot. Some are of doubtful parentage but they are usually listed as *Potentilla davurica* or *P. fruticosa*. There are many yellow-flowered kinds, from bright yellow to pale primrose, and also some good whites, the best white I've grown being 'Abbotswood'. Potentillas also come in pink, or-ange, or red but cultivars in these colors (I'm told there are better ones in the offing) are frequently inconstant in color.

SHRUBS WITH COLORED FOLIAGE

For foliage color all the Japanese barberries (*Berberis thunbergii*) excel. They are very hardy (to Zone 4), and tolerant of most soils, in sun or slight shade. The purple foliage of *B. t.* 'Atropurpurea' makes a fine background for flowers of almost any color, whether as a hedge or as a single specimen, and it bears a good crop of bright red berries in winter, for which you later pay a labor toll as you weed out unwanted seedlings: this, and occasional light pruning are the only maintenance required. *B. t.* 'Rose Glow' is similar but with pink streaks in the leaves. As a low hedge or a frontal mound there is the popular 'Crimson Pygmy', the newer 'Bagatelle' (said to be more

In the barrel is Berberis thunbergii 'Aurea', matched to the bright yellow of Aurinia saxatilis growing at the base of blue bearded irises. (Garden of Gladys and Alain Huyghe, Virginia; April)

compact), and the green-leaved 'Kobold'. *B. t.* 'Aurea' is brilliant yellow in spring. A friend used this in a half barrel, color matched to *Aurinia saxatilis* below and contrasting with deep blue irises alongside.

There are many other yellow-leaved shrubs. Among the best for borders are several cultivars of *Spiraea japonica*, which we'll come to later; *Abelia* 'Francis Mason'; and the golden privets (*Ligustrum*), which would like to become small trees but can be pruned as hard as you wish. For fine texture, the best yellow-leaved shrub is *Lonicera nitida* 'Baggesen's Gold' but it isn't very hardy. By contrast the yellow ninebark (*Physocarpus opulifolius* 'Luteus') is coarse-leaved but ultra hardy (Zone 2). Then there are the numerous evergreen conifers of varying hardiness, all of them superb backgrounds for blue, white, or orange flowers. (See photo on page 236.)

Abelia × grandiflora is one of the very best border shrubs. Van Melle (*Shrubs and Trees for the Small Place*) accords it a higher total score than any other shrub except *Berberis thunbergii* 'Minor', with perfect marks for summer blending value, which is what we are after in the flower border. Root hardy to about −20°F, in the warmer zones it is evergreen and can reach ten feet high. It can be cut back hard but you won't have to do that often if you plant the compact 'Sherwood', 'Prostrata', or yellow-leaved 'Francis Mason'. *Abelia* 'Edward Goucher' is quite small, and the flowers are a deeper pink but it isn't as hardy. At temperatures below 15°F, abelias lose their leaves, and at their hardiness limit they are winterkilled to ground level, regrowing and flowering within a year. The late season flowers are small, white, tubular, and plentiful but it is for its overall color that it excels, made softly purple by a combination of dark leaves and the reddish calyces that remain long after the flowers fall.

DIEBACKS, CUTBACKS, AND SHRUBLETS

This brings me to a very useful group, the diebacks, or cutbacks, (abelia is one of these at its hardiness limit), and those I call shrublets (also called sub-shrubs or woody-based perennials)—plants of indeterminate character, straddling the fence between shrubs and perennials, most not much more than three feet high. Shrublets mix extremely well with perennials. Among those in widespread use are lavender, rosemary, sage (*Salvia officinalis*), santolina, rue (*Ruta graveolens*), germander (*Teucrium chamaedrys*), helianthemums, and such artemisias as *Artemisia abrotanum* and 'Powis Castle'. Pruned hard in early spring, santolina and rue form sculptured domes excellent for anchoring bed ends and corners. In the warmer zones, gray-leaved *Phlomis fruticosa* gives year-round gray foliage, and rondels of yellow flowers at peony time, Cape figworts, or Cape fuchsias (*Phygelius*), dangle their tubular flowers for weeks on end, and *Erysimum* 'Bowles' Variety', or 'Bowles' Mauve', a bushy wallflower with narrow gray-green leaves and purplish flowers, not long-lived but easily raised from cuttings, blooms for most of the growing season.

The merits of such tender (Zone 8), more or less evergreen southern native shrublets as Texas sage (*Salvia greggii*), gray-leaved *Conradina canescens*, and the clinopodiums are slowly becoming recognized now that they are available from nurseries. Texas sage blooms with the autumn asters and boltonias and typically the flowers are the same bright reddish pink as *Aster* 'Alma Potschke' but other color selections have been made, including white. The little leaves are very aromatic and it is evergreen. In sandy soil it is fairly long-lived but gets gaunt and brittle unless cut back hard every year or two. In my garden the two-foot

Clinopodium coccineum bears its scarlet tubular flowers in abundance from July on, a great attraction for butterflies. Its lengthy bloom period is overlapped toward the end by lavender-flowered *C. georgianum*, which keeps the color going through autumn. Both are content with poor, dry soil. They are not long-lived but easily rooted from cuttings.

Diebacks are shrubs that are killed to the ground by winter cold but, where they are root hardy, throw up new stems the following spring. They include such fine "perennials" as *Lespedeza thunbergii*, the indigoferas, the rather tender (Zone 8) *Ceratostigma willmottianum* (a two-foot bushy version of the well known creeping blue plumbago), willow-leaf jessamine (*Cestrum parqui*), with greenish yellow flowers that scent the evening air, and the captivating *Lavatera thuringiaca* 'Barnsley', with rounded gray-green leaves and mallow-like flowers of soft rosy pink with a darker eye. In an English garden *Clematis viticella* 'Purpurea Plena Elegans', with little maroon pompom flowers, wended its way through this winsome mallow, a combination I'm eager to try. Most autumn-blooming plants are the prerogative of the South, which makes northerners the more appreciative of mint shrub (*Elsholtzia stauntonii*), a hardy dieback shrub that bears purplish flowers in September in the north, sometimes as early as June in the South.

Cutbacks are shrubs that may or may not be topkilled but are amenable to cutting back if the gardener chooses, and often the better for it. *Caryopteris*, *Perovskia*, and *Hypericum* 'Hidcote' fall into this category. Heading my list of cut-and-come-again shrubs is *Spiraea japonica*, which nowadays includes those usually listed as *S. × bumalda*, an old-time favorite but with many fine new cultivars of fairly recent introduction. They are all easy to grow, at their best in full sun but tolerant of light shade. They vary in height but none grows too large for our purpose and all can be pruned as hard as you wish, including right down to the ground. All have fuzzy-looking plates of multistamened flowers, varying in color from white to bright pink. *S. j.* 'Alpina' makes a mound perfect for a frontal position. *S. j.* 'Little Princess' stays low for a number of years but will reach three feet in time if left unpruned. The latest additions to the range are yellow-leaved kinds of similar size such as 'Lime Mound' and 'Golden Princess'.

Next as we move up the scale comes the old 'Anthony Waterer', two to three feet high with bright pink flowers and a few gold splashes on the leaves. 'Gold Flame' is usually about the same size though I've seen it much taller, an extremely popular shrub and nearly faultless, the only snag being the quite horrid combination of bright pink flowers with copper-tinted yellow leaves. What we still lack in this group is cultivars with yellow leaves and white flowers. 'Shibori' (also sold as 'Shirobana') is about the same height, with the curious habit of bearing white, pale pink, and bright rosy pink flower heads on the same plant—sometimes. Of five plants I bought, one is white, the others white-and-pink, so perhaps the part of the plant from which cuttings are taken is important. In any event it is a good plant, and excellent for massing. My own favorite of the group is *S. j.* 'Fortunei' (synonym 'Crispa'), long sold as *S. dolchica*. This has bright pink flowers and beautiful incised leaves. It can reach six feet but mine are kept about half this height. The rankest beginner can hardly go wrong with these spiraeas. Shear them, or hack them back as you will, they'll regrow, bush out, and flower. The correct way to do it is called renewal pruning, periodically removing some of the older branches at the base, then cutting the others back to the desired height. They flower

Spiraea 'Gold Flame' is one of the most popular foliage shrubs, despite the unloved combination of bright pink flowers with yellow foliage. With it here are Alchemilla mollis and a double-flowered form of Geranium pratense. (Garden of Mrs. J. R. McCutchan, Bates Green Farm, Arlington, Sussex, England; July)

for many weeks and if then sheared back give an equally long repeat performance. Where the growing season is long, a third repeat is possible.

Stephanandra incisa is a close relative of the spiraeas and equally amenable to pruning. The flowers are not showy but *S. i.* 'Crispa' has very pretty leaves and its low, mounding form makes it well suited to the front of a border. The dwarf flowering almond, *Prunus glandulosa*, with double pink or, less common, double white flowers, seldom exceeds four feet in height but can be cut back if you'd prefer it shorter. Do this immediately flowering ends in spring.

Many large shrubs flower on branches made that year and can be cut back hard to maintain them at a size suited to the border. Candidates for this treatment include the chaste tree, *Vitex agnus-castus*, which in the South does indeed make a tree and one well suited to the large flower border. *Hibiscus syriacus* is also capable of becoming a small tree, but it flowers much more profusely if kept to bush size. *Hydrangea arborescens* can be cut back to the ground and so can lead-plant, *Amorpha canescens*, an excellent small shrub for hot, dry places, with ferny gray-green leaves and arched plumes of light violet flowers. Its height is usually given as three feet but I've seen it reach six. *Tamarix pentandra* (Zone 2) can take the worst of wind, cold, and poor soil, but if left unpruned is likely to be shapeless and sprawling. Cut back to a foot at the end of winter, it makes a feathery silver-gray spire about six feet high, bearing plumes of pink flowers somewhere between late May and October, varying with region. Purple-

A daylily and pale yellow An-themis *'Wargrave' are played off against yellow-variegated* Cornus alba *'Spaethii', treated as a cut-back shrub to limit its size. (England; July)*

leaved sumacs (*Cotinus coggygria*) are often treated as cutbacks in English gardens to maintain them as mounds of purple foliage. In southeastern gardens they are capable of making six feet of growth by summer and may have to be cut back twice, while in zones colder than 5 it may fail to survive winter or become a dieback shrub. The much hardier purple-leaved sand cherry (*Prunus × cistena*) could be used instead.

Cold winters kill top-growth of butterfly bush, *Buddleia davidii*, but where this doesn't happen it will be a more gainly and manageable bush if pruned to the ground in spring. The hardier *B. alternifolia* 'Argentea' has willowy gray leaves, and pale lavender flowers wreath the slender arching branches in spring or early summer. It is often grown as a small weeping tree. In my Virginia garden it is stolo-niferous, giving me an abundance of young plants with which to experiment. A group of three cut back to six inches in March made a large, loose corner patch of willowy stems about two feet high. Behind them went an August-blooming lavender-flowered liatris (*Liatris microcephala*) that tends to fall over when heavy with flowers but got enough support from the buddleia to keep it upright. In front went the beautiful late flowering chrysanthemum called 'Mary Stoker' (*Chrysanthemum × rubellum*), which wends its way by means of stoloniferous roots in and out of the buddleia, gaining support for its lax flowering stems and mingling its soft yellow flowers touched with apricot with the gray leaves of the buddleia.

Callicarpa dichotoma is a cutback shrub highly regarded for its growability in sun or

In sandy soil and a warm, wet climate, root suckers must be regularly removed if Buddleia alternifolia *'Argentea' is to be grown as a small weeping tree or large shrub, as it usually is. This patch, in my garden, cut back hard in late winter, has made a thicket of slender gray-leaved stems which are interwoven with the spreading* Chrysanthemum × rubellum *'Mary Stoker'.*
(Virginia; early October)

light shade and almost any soil, including dry ones, its blendability, moveability, controllability, and for the brilliant violet-purple berries strung along the small-leaved arching branches in autumn. It flowers and fruits on branches of the current year's growth and, if winter cold doesn't do this for you, I find it the better for being cut back nearly to the ground every other year. *Salvia leucantha* (Zone 8) flowers when the callicarpa berries are at their showiest and the two make a good color match.

Then there are cutback or dieback shrubs grown not for fruit, flower, or foliage color but for texture. Sweet fern (*Comptonia peregrina*), described elsewhere, is best in poor, dry soil because in rich ones it spreads too fast. *Salix purpurea* 'Nana' (also sold as

'Gracilis'), like most willows, doesn't like to be dry but otherwise isn't fussy. This makes a cloud of slender purplish stems and narrow gray-green leaves. It is usually seen about three feet high but it can be clipped as hard as you like and makes a good low hedge. These are blenders, supporting cast for the perennials, but, for the favored few who can grow it, *Melianthus major* should have the specimen status befitting one of the world's most beautiful foliage plants. The large leaves are a gleaming gray-green and deeply incised. Frost kills it to the ground but the roots are a little hardier. In England I was familiar with it only as a winter dieback, in summer a ferny mound under two feet high. When, in southern California, I saw it for the first time as a sprawling eight-foot shrub I thought it much less appealing. As a cutback it would make a beautiful container specimen for those who could winter it in a frost-free greenhouse.

Northerners have an advantage when shrubs grown for their winter bark color can be staged against a carpet of snow. There are ultra hardy (Zone 2) cutbacks for this purpose among the dogwoods (*Cornus*) and willows (*Salix*). Color is brightest on one-year wood, so it is customary to cut them back hard at the end of winter, either cutting back all the branches or, if more height is wanted, cutting out half the branches each year. The red-stemmed dogwood, *Cornus alba* 'Sibirica', has bark of the brightest red, but you might prefer to settle for a bit less winter color for the sake of the white-variegated leaves of *C. a.* 'Elegantissima'. Next in order of brightness comes the red osier or scarlet willow, *Salix alba* 'Chermesina' (also sold as 'Britzensis'), and the yellow-barked golden willow, *S. a.* 'Vitellina'. If a large thicket is wanted, then look to the red-stemmed *Cornus stolonifera* and yellow-stemmed *C. s.* 'Flaviramea'. Any of these is guaranteed to strike a cheery winter note, but only if placed where you see them frontlit by the sun. Their dense, competitive roots can be kept in check by root pruning, slicing a circle around them with a sharp spade once a year.

The next suggestion, only for hot and humid regions where woody plants grow with junglelike speed, seems almost sacriligous, but we need to keep open minds and learn new ways of doing things suited to local conditions. An eight-year-old coralbark maple (*Acer palmatum* 'Senkaki', also known as 'Sango Kaku') in my garden, lightly pruned when branches grow out of balance, is now over ten feet high. A cutting rooted from it grew to six feet in four years. The best color is on new wood so I decided to test its potential as a cutback shrub. Cut back by half in late winter, it made new four-foot branches that season. Cut back to eighteen inches the following year, new growth was even more vigorous. This is an expensive shrub compared to *Cornus alba* 'Sibirica', and the twig color is much the same, but the maple leaves are beautiful, those of the dogwood nondescript.

EVERGREENS AND DWARF CONIFERS

In warm regions, where winter isn't a closed garden season, beds devoted to perennials alone leave inappropriate bare patches, which may not matter if they are out of sight of the house and main walkways, but that is seldom the case. Consider including some broadleaf evergreens along the front of the border or the most visible side of an island bed. They should be low-growing kinds, so that the perennials, in their season, are not concealed. If spaced along the front, with low perennials allowed to flow between them, they blend informally into the summer scene but hold the

space together when perennials are dormant. Possibilities include *Abelia* 'Prostrata' or 'Sherwood', *Berberis candidula, Berberis × gladwynensis* 'William Penn' and the one called 'Lucky Sport' which I'm told is more weather resistant in Ohio than 'William Penn', dwarf nandinas (*Nandina domestica* 'Nana Purpurea' or 'Harbor Dwarf'), small kinds of euonymus such as 'Emerald Gaiety', and such Indian hawthorns (*Raphiolepis*) as 'Enchantress'. All can be controlled by pruning if they get too tall for your purpose.

Dwarf conifers have year-round appeal. The real midgets need a rock garden or raised bed to show to advantage but there are many of medium size that can contribute year-round form to the mixed border. Among the most popular are the feathery, loosely pyramidal blue-gray *Chamaecyparis* 'Boulevard', bright green dwarf Hinoki cypress (*C. obtusa* 'Nana Gracilis'), coppery gold *Thuja* 'Rheingold', and such slender junipers as 'Skyrocket'. The bright green, tightly conical dwarf Alberta spruce (*Picea glauca* 'Conica') is a good choice where summers are cool. It is widely planted in the Southeast but it shouldn't be because it is always, sooner or later, defoliated by spider mites.

ROSES

The rose is a much-loved and extremely varied plant. Name any other flower and there's a chance nongardeners won't know what you mean, but everyone recognizes a rose. There are climbing roses to train on posts, walls, trellises, fences, or arbors, bushes of greatly varying shape and height, ground-cover roses, and miniature roses. The common image, though, is of what might be called the "bedding rose."

In public gardens, and in the gardens of

The orange torch lily, an unnamed Luther Burbank hybrid, glows even more brightly against a golden conifer. (Western Hills Nursery, northern California; July)

many rosarians, beds are devoted to roses alone, with no underplantings. There are good reasons for this. Large collections of hybrid teas, floribundas, and grandifloras need frequent feeding, watering, spraying, fertilizing, deadheading, and pruning, and it is easier to give these attentions if the roses are grouped together with nothing else to get in the way. Without regular spraying, such collections of roses are much more likely to be damaged by pests and diseases than are individual bushes surrounded by other kinds of plant.

Another reason for growing modern roses on their own is that many were bred for the show bench more than for the garden and the grandeur of the flowers and gawkiness of the bush make them poor blenders with perennials. This never was true of all: the hybrid tea rose 'Dainty Bess' and the floribundas 'Betty Prior' and 'Nearly Wild', all singles, are just three examples of roses well suited to the flower border.

Collectors of old-fashioned and species roses usually do combine them with perennials, and need to, to keep the interest going when the roses have had their rather brief fling. Such gardens are the very essence of romance. The drawback is summed up in that old verse about the seasons: "June brings tulips, lilies, roses." Yes, June, or thereabouts (often May in the South), and June only for most of the old kinds. But how sweet a time it is, heady with the fragrance of such ladylike and aristocratic old charmers as 'Maiden's Blush', 'Königin von Dänemark' ('Queen of Denmark'), 'Mme. Hardy, 'Mme. Isaac Pereire', and 'Reine des Violettes' (Queen of Violets). Because pink is the most common color in roses, the color scheme employing old roses is usually pink, blue, white, and gray. Popular perennials and shrublets to associate with them include artemisias, lavender, sage (*Salvia*), lamb's ears (*Stachys byzantina*),

Rosarians often keep their roses separate from other plants for ease of maintenance. Artists prefer the romance of mixed plantings. Here we see a compromise with the rose 'Mary Rose' separate and accessible yet in close association with Geranium sanguineum 'Striatum' (G. s. 'Lancastriense') and G. 'Russell Prichard' on the other side of the narrow path. All geraniums associate well with pink roses. (Garden of Mr. and Mrs. David Hodges, Brook Cottage, Alkerton, England; June)

hardy geraniums, irises, and pinks (*Dianthus*). Lupines and delphiniums are frequently included for the contrast of their spikelike form with the rounded shape of the rosebushes.

Increasingly we can have the best of both worlds, and no longer can the line between "old-fashioned" roses and modern hybrids be clearly drawn. The shrub rose 'Bonica' is one example of what breeders have done for us; it is like a larger edition of the polyantha rose 'The Fairy' and nearly as trouble-free. 'Carefree Beauty' is another, well deserving of its name, and the Meidiland range are getting good marks. Those in very cold zones haven't been neglected either; the Explorer roses de-

veloped at the Government Research Center in Ottawa were bred for hardiness. Many of the new shrub roses do have the softer form of the old ones, and they keep on blooming through summer, but fragrance is still largely lacking, so David Austin's new "English roses" offer great promise. They were bred to combine the charm, fragrance, blending form, and relative freedom from pests and diseases of the old roses with the long blooming period and wider color range of the hybrid teas and floribundas, but we have yet to find out how well they will perform under the very un-English weather conditions of many parts of the United States.

I'm sure they exist, but I've never seen a blue-gray-and-yellow scheme based on roses. Perhaps, in the past, there weren't enough good yellow kinds. There are now—from the species *Rosa hugonis*, with ferny foliage that has no equal (this blooms only once, in spring) and the early rugosa hybrid 'Agnes', to such summer- and autumn-flowering beauties as the single-flowered shrub rose 'Golden Wings', introduced in 1956, and the new warmer yellow 'Graham Thomas'. From Californian breeder Ralph Moore comes *R. rugosa* 'Topaz Jewel', heralded as the first reblooming yellow rugosa. In front of mine I've planted a group of dark violet-blue *Salvia* × *superba* 'May Night'. Some of the apricot blends could be added, the best of the old and the new with, for instance, the subtle old 'Buff Beauty' and the striking new 'Brandy'. With these could go the same blue and gray perennials as those customarily mixed with pink roses, along with yellows like *Coreopsis* 'Moonbeam', *Kniphofia* 'Little Maid', oenotheras, and daylilies.

Bliss seldom comes unalloyed and there is the risk of getting scratched when perennials are mixed with roses. I've suffered less from those with obvious thorns than from the almost hairlike prickles that coat the stems of *Rosa rugosa* and defy extraction from the fingers. Avoid very stoloniferous roses. The two most rapid spreaders I've grown are *R. rugosa* (the species, not the hybrids) and *R. gallica* 'Versicolor'. I have them still, but not among perennials. Hybrids of *R. rugosa* are more manageable: 'Frau Dagmar Hartopp' consistently draws a high mark in tests and my own favorite of the group, carnation-flowered 'Pink Grootendorst', runs a close second. The very hardy *R. virginiana*, with good autumn color and red twigs in winter, is hard to beat for year-round interest, but its thicket-forming nature disqualifies it from the border.

Miniature roses are becoming increas-

ingly popular—make your own choice for the front of the border, rock garden, or raised bed from the hundreds available. As one-of-each collections many are too toylike for border use but three or more of a kind (how many depends on the size and habit of the rose and the size of the border) planted close enough to intermingle look more natural. Better for the purpose, though, are those of a flowing habit. 'Nozomi' is sometimes classified as a minia-

Shrub rose 'Kathleen Ferrier' matched to pink penstemons at Wisley Garden, England. (July) ture, and the tiny flowers certainly qualify, but unless trained to climb, this is a vigorous ground-cover rose that roots where its tips touch the ground. After several years I have discarded it, not because it flowers only once but because cleaning out the fallen leaves that collected among its viciously thorny stems left me scratched and bleeding once too often. In its place is 'Petite Pink Scotch', a very old rose recently rediscovered. This smothers itself with little pink pompoms in early summer. Unfussy about soil, pest- and disease-resistant, dense, shearable, almost evergreen in the South, flowing in habit (rooting where its tips touch the ground), and with tiny, almost ferny, leaves, it is a near-perfect front-of-the-border rose, lacking only extended bloom. I've obviated this shortcoming by planting a not overly vigorous clematis, 'Mme. Julia Correron', to ramble through it.

If climbing roses are to be trained on walls or fences behind borders, it is advisable to have a path, or at least stepping stones, at the back to make them accessible for pruning,

Rosa 'Petite Pink Scotch' at North Carolina State University in late May. It will make a mound two feet or more high but can be pruned to keep it very low. In Zone 8 it is evergreen.

training, or spraying, but spraying can be kept to a minimum, sometimes eliminated, by choosing those least prone to disease. Climbing roses are not self-supporting; they have to be fastened to their supports. There are many ways of supporting them other than walls and fences. One of the prettiest uses is the arch over a garden path and several manufacturers now sell ready-made arches if you don't feel up to constructing your own. Roses trained as climbers make excellent support for clematis and this is a time-honored combination. *Clematis* 'Huldine' would be a good choice for an arch because it is at its loveliest at or above head level, where backlighting renders the white sepals translucent and reveals the purple veining on their backs. The easiest support to construct for climbing roses grown among perennials is a tripod of three sturdy poles fastened together at the top in wigwam fashion. In windy areas, hammer the poles well into the ground. Keep the need for restraint to a minimum by avoiding roses overvigorous for the available space. Many miniature roses can be trained as climbers—'Red Cascade', for instance. Any ground-covering or trailing rose also has potential as a climber.

The American Rose Society publishes each year an inexpensive ($1.00 for 1990) *Handbook for Selecting Roses*, assessing nationwide garden merit of a wide range of roses on a scale of 1 to 10. This is a great help, especially if you can't make up your mind which of several shall be the chosen one, but there's so much regional variance in vigor, health, and hardiness that local Rose Society recommendations are better still. When you've decided what you want, the "Combined Rose List" published each year by Beverly R. Dobson (215 Harriman Road, Irvington, NY 10533) will tell you who sells it.

Rosa 'Sea Foam' was bought based on the description "a white counterpart to 'The Fairy.' " It turned out to be of a much more vining habit and has been encouraged to ramble among the multiple trunks of a crepe myrtle, flanked by Hydrangea quercifolia *'Snowflake'. In front are* Hosta rhodeifolia *(in the United States erroneously distributed as* H. helonioides *'Albo-picta', which is a different plant),* Carex siderosticta *'Variegata', and* Liriope *'John Burch'. (Virginia; late May)*

VINES

If you think your garden is already crammed to capacity, recall what crowded cities do— build skyscrapers. The roots of most perennials occupy less space than their tops do when in full growth, so there's root room between

for vines that can rise above them, as well as for bulbs that flower at a different time. Because vines occupy mostly vertical space, they add another dimension and increase the range of color and interest that can be fitted into a bed or border. You can even combine the edible with the ornamental by growing the scarlet runner bean on a tripod in the border.

In my own garden a selected form of trumpet honeysuckle (*Lonicera sempervirens* 'Superba' or 'Magnifica') on a post-and-rail fence covered with chicken wire makes a scarlet backdrop in June for a hot-color border. When vines are grown on a fence, the most profuse bloom (and sometimes *all* of it, especially with roses) will be on the sunny side and this is the case with this honeysuckle, but it also produces quite a lot of flowers on the outer north-facing side of the fence. Further along, Carolina jessamine (*Gelsemium sempervirens*) flowers in spring but provides a green backdrop all year. It calls for several hours of pruning once a year to remove long trails of growth rooting into the ground. For another fence, behind a border of pinks, whites, and blues, I try to remember to raise the annual moonflower (*Ipomoea alba*, formerly *Calonyction aculeatum*) from seed early each year. The great white flowers open at dusk and their fragrance attracts hawk moths. It self-sows and the seeds are winter hardy in my garden, although the vine is not, but they get off to a later start than plants raised under lights indoors. I had native wisteria (*Wisteria floribunda*), both white and blue, on this fence, but in my sandy soil the roots are too invasive— mistakes are inevitable in an experimental garden, and what is true in one soil and climate may not be so in another. Maypops (*Passiflora incarnata*), herbaceous and much hardier than other passionflowers, grows wild along my road. With plants native or naturalized in an area, there's always the possibility

(indeed the likelihood) that they'll be invasive in the garden, but the only way to be sure is to try them and I'm about to plant the lovely white form of this native passionflower on my fence. Heavier soils restrict root spread and it would then be an excellent choice for a cane tripod or wire tomato cylinder in the border. You can get it from Woodlanders Nursery.

To assess the suitability of a vine for the purpose you have in mind, you need to know how it climbs. Some, sometimes called scandent, or climbing shrubs, have no obvious means of support; they climb by insinuating their long stems in and out of the branches of a host shrub or tree. Climbing roses do this, also hooking themselves into place with their curved thorns. Potato vines (*Solanum*) and Cape plumbago (*Plumbago capensis*) are other examples. These can fend for themselves once up among the branches of a tree or shrub but need help getting started and have to be tied in to such supports as poles and trellises.

A few shrubs, sometimes called wall shrubs, might be found listed with vines in catalogues because they are so suitable for training against a wall. Pyracantha is such a shrub, needing relatively little support to hold it against a wall. Grown this way and allowed to branch out, it makes the perfect host for clematis and is also a safe haven for nesting birds. Pyracantha can be grown as a kind of vertical carpet against a wall and it still provides excellent support for clematis or other not-too-vigorous tendril vines. It does, however, take a good deal of clipping to keep it flat and it does not then bear berries. In the United States *Cotoneaster horizontalis* always seems to be grown as a ground cover. In England it is commonly grown against a wall. It tends naturally to flatten itself against its support, with few outgrowing branches, and very little support is needed, none usually to a height of two or three feet. In England I grew this under a window with the scarlet climbing nasturtium *Tropaeolum speciosum* growing through it, but the nasturtium comes from Chile and, like most Chilean plants, is not very adaptable, liking to be cool and moist but insufficiently hardy for those parts of the United States where such conditions prevail. I have found one possible alternative for the South in the firecracker vine (*Manettia cordifolia*) from South America, which rambles through Gumpo azaleas in my Virginia garden and has survived all the heat and cold to which it has been subjected through ten Zone 8 years.

Some vines climb by means of adhesive roots or discs. Ivy (*Hedera*), climbing fig (*Ficus pumila*), some kinds of euonymus (*Euonymus fortunei radicans*), and climbing hydrangeas (*Hydrangea anomala petiolaris*, *Schizophragma*, and *Decumaria*) are examples. They need something solid to which they can adhere. In the wild it would be a tree trunk, in the garden usually a wall. What a blessing these vines are for those of us handicapped by brick walls of a harsh red unsympathetic as a background for most flowers. Ivy is the ideal disguise where it is fully evergreen. There are hundreds of kinds, varying a great deal in hardiness, vigor, and density. Use the vining kinds that tend to grow as single strands when you want just a tracery against a pretty wall, the dense self-branching ones for total concealment. The American Ivy Society offers a lot of information to help in the selection. My own choice for dense wall cover is the sweetheart, or shield, ivy (*Hedera helix* 'Deltoidea'), often sold in pots at nurseries for Valentine's day. When young, the leaves are perfect hearts, becoming larger and shield-shaped at maturity. *Hedera colchica* has much larger heart-shaped leaves. Once well established on a wall, ivy can provide support for a secondary vine such as clematis. So can the climbing hydrangeas, but these attach themselves less firmly, so don't add a secondary vine of great weight. The annual clock vine or black-eyed Susan vine (*Thunbergia alata*) would be suitable, or one of the clematis (*Clematis × jackmanii* for example) that flowers on new growth and can be cut to the ground each year.

Perhaps you have an ugly fence you'd like to conceal. Chain-link fences provide perfect support for most vines (sections of chain link affixed to a wall make excellent trellis), so make virtue of necessity by turning them into "fedges," a term coined in England to describe a combination of fence and hedge. Ivy is excellent for this purpose; it climbs solid surfaces by adhesive holdfast roots but will

The annual clock vine, Thunbergia alata, *is supported on strings attached to the post and anchored to the ground. (Garden of Gladys and Alain Huyghe, Virginia; September)*

to fairly slender supports.

Then there are the twiners, in which the whole stem lassoes its support, sometimes wrapping itself round and round so tightly that it throttles the host tree—wisteria, for example, and some honeysuckles. Annuals don't live long enough to do that sort of damage but many do make an amazing amount of leafy growth in a single season. Twining annual climbers include hyacinth bean (*Dolichos lablab*), clock vine (*Thunbergia alata*), and morning glories (*Ipomoea*). The prettily shaped, greeny yellow leaves of the golden hop (*Humulus lupulus* 'Aureus') make a strong color accent against a wall or fence. Although perennial, it can be cut back to the ground each year.

Clematis climb by curling their leaf stalks (petioles) around some slender support. Climbing nasturtiums (*Tropaeolum*) do this too. Gloriosa lily (*Gloriosa rothschildiana*) has an original way of climbing a little, hitching a lift by tendrillike leaf tips. This tuberous plant is not frost hardy but it is easily grown in a large pot and the flower is so showy that it is worth the effort to plunge it into a border during summer, putting it on the shady side of a larger perennial or small shrub. Grown this way it seldom exceeds two or three feet in height, often needing no support at all. If it does, the stems of a perennial, a small shrub, or a short bamboo cane or two will suffice. When frosts come, take the pot indoors, cease watering, and let it go dormant for the winter.

Tendril and twining climbers vary a lot in the diameter of the support they can encircle: wisteria isn't safe anywhere but on a forest tree or large wall, while at the other extreme spurred butterfly pea (*Centrosema virginianum*) is so delicate and lightweight that it can climb grass stalks or the stems of tall perennials. All climbers, except those clinging by holdfasts, can be accommodated with some

also weave itself in and out of chain-link fencing with a little direction at first to make it go up instead of out along the ground. Many other vigorous vines can also be used to weave through or drape over ugly fences.

Many vines climb by means of fine tendrils that curl themselves around some slender support. In the wild it would be branches and twigs. Examples are coralvine (*Antigonon leptopus*), the annual cup-and-saucer vine (*Cobaea scandens*), *Eccremocarpus scaber* (a tender perennial vine with small tubular scarlet flowers that can be grown as an annual if started early), the climbing peas (*Lathyrus*), and passionflowers (*Passiflora*). Species of *Parthenocissus*, which includes Boston ivy and Virginia creeper, have two means of climbing—tendrils and adhesive discs, so these can attach themselves to walls and fences or cling

The post of a rustic arbor wrapped with chicken wire provides support for the climbing pea, Lathyrus latifolius *'Albus'. Other plants in the picture include verbascums, poppies, sea hollies (*Eryngium*), and, in the background, alchemilla and* Helenium *'Moerheim Beauty'. (Garden of Mrs. J. R. McCutchan, Bates Green Farm, Arlington, Sussex, England; July)*

combination of posts, rails, wigwams of bamboo canes or poles, trellises, chicken wire, plastic netting, wires, string, or the longer-lasting fishing line. One friend attached strings to the arms of the post holding a lantern at the entrance to her garden, anchored them in the ground (you can do this by wrapping the string round a brick or rock and burying it) as support for clock vine (*Thunbergia alata*).

Chicken wire stapled to fences, molded over garden walls, or wrapped around tripod poles is not conspicuous. If local ordinances restrict the height of fences, a strip of trellis on top might be permissible. When clothed with vines this would raise the screening height of the fence. The cylinders and cones sold for supporting tomatoes (for which purpose they are frequently too weak) make excellent supports for small vines grown among perennials. The easiest way of supporting many of the less vigorous vines is, however, to let them ramble through a small tree or shrub. This works particularly well with clematis, which all too often climb themselves while one's back is turned, forming a tangled skein of brittle stems impossible to unravel. Grown through a shrub, the strands distribute themselves more evenly and pruning becomes simple—just cut off whatever sticks out too far or too untidily. No training is needed, provided you remember that most vines grow toward the sun. Clematis like their roots in shade, their flowers in sun, so plant on the shady side of a shrub and let the stems make their way over or through it to the sun.

Clematis are the very best climbers for mixing with perennials. The large-flowered hybrids come in a great range of whites, pinks, and blues to mix and match with perennials. I've enjoyed the color echo of the popular violet-blue clematis called 'Ramona' with the blue columbines and Siberian irises that

flower at the same time. Such vigorous clematis as *Clematis montana*, the sweet autumn clematis (*C. maximowicziana* but usually sold as *C. paniculata*), and the similar earlier-flowering *C. flammula* need a wall, fence, or tree for support. Behind one of my borders, *C. maximowicziana* looks like a lace tablecloth tossed over the fence in late summer and early autumn, sweetly fragrant and ethereal at dusk. The seedheads too are beautiful, but I've had to limit my enjoyment of these and cut the plants to the ground before the seed ripens, otherwise self-sown seedlings become a nuisance. This isn't a problem with the similar *C. flammula*, which flowers for me in midsummer. The easiest clematis to use in the flower border are those that flower on growth of the current year, so that top growth can be tidied away with that of other perennials at the

Clematis × jackmanii *trails down over lamb's ears. (England; July)*

end of the season. I particularly like the small-flowered *C. texensis* hybrids such as 'Duchess of Albany' and 'Gravetye Beauty' and I find these more drought resistant than most—clematis need well-drained soil but they don't like it poor or dry. *Clematis* × *durandii* isn't a climber but makes each year long trailing stems that bear large flowers of a very lovely dark blue. This flowers at the same time as the late Satsuki azaleas and the pinks (*Dianthus*) and mine trails over these. My special favorite for mixing with perennials is the summer-flowering small-flowered hybrid 'Betty Corning'. Stems reach out to secure themselves lightly yet firmly to whatever is within reach (in my case the stems of a lily and twigs of a dwarf Japanese holly), starting about July to bear the succession of nodding blue pagoda-shaped flowers that go on for a couple of months, with potential for longer, given summer pruning I'm not always around to do.

Some clematis flower on growth of the current year and on older stems too, and some flower only on growth arising from older wood. At least that's what the books say. Get one of them (Christopher Lloyd's has long been my standby) for general guidance but realize that in those parts of the United States where summers are hot and the growing season long, many clematis listed as flowering only from stems of a previous year have time to make, ripen, and bear flowers on growth of the current year. American gardeners must experiment and find out what works in their region.

Vines don't always have to climb. Ivy, euonymus, and climbing hydrangeas (*Hydrangea anomala petiolaris*, *Schizophragma*, and *Decumaria*) cleave to walls by adhesive discs but will also root into the ground and can be trained over tree stumps, rocks, or wellheads. Many honeysuckles can also be used this way or kept cut back as bushes. *Lonicera* × *heckrottii* is a good one for the border because it continues to produce flowers all summer but it does need need frequent cutting back, otherwise the twining stems will twine around each other in an unattractive tangle. Star jasmine (*Trachelospermum jasminoides*) can be grown as a free-standing bush and the variegated star jasmine (*T. asiaticum* 'Variegatum') makes a pretty flowerless white-and-green foliage hummock if wandering strands are removed. Ivy can be trained across steps between riser and tread. So, if there is shade, can Kenilworth ivy (*Cymbalaria muralis*), with trailing stems that root at the nodes.

Clematis can trail over the ground and intertwine with perennials or low shrubs, including the ubiquitous ground-covering junipers, through which they lift their flowers to the sun while benefiting from shade for their roots. I've enjoyed a combination that arranged itself in my garden when *Parthenocissus henryana*, very like Virginia creeper but with a silvery stripe in the center of each leaflet, spread some of its stems out along the

Clematis *'Betty Corning' with* Chrysanthemum leucanthemum *'May Queen' and* Miscanthus sinensis *'Variegatus'. (Virginia; June)*

Clematis
'Comtesse de
Bouchaud' peeps
through a fence to
delight passersby.
The border inside
includes purple
coneflower
*(*Echinacea
purpurea),
Veronica *'Icicle',*
and Salvia
farinacea. *(Garden*
of Mr. and Mrs.
A. Van Vlack,
Connecticut; July)

ground over a carpet of purple-leaved ajuga. In another garden I visited, the golden-leaved hop (*Humulus lupulus* 'Aureus') trailed over a carpet of variegated greater periwinkle (*Vinca major* 'Variegata'), an attractive combination, but one to be eschewed where the periwinkle is invasive.

The climbing perennial pea (*Lathyrus latifolius*) is on the "top ten" list of one of my flower arranger friends. Accustomed to seeing it rampant on roadside banks, some West Coasters tend to despise it and that's a pity, for it is a fine plant, and very adaptable. The flowers look just like garden sweet peas but lack the fragrance. It climbs by tendrils to six feet or more and can be grown on a fence, trellis, or other kind of support, but it also makes an excellent trailer. It is vigorous enough to cover a bank, but if old stems are cut out it keeps up a succession of fresh young vining shoots from the base and it goes on flowering all season. Doing this also prevents self-sowing. Magenta is the most common color but it can also be had in pale lavender, pink, and a snowy white.

The climbing pea is a vine that can be treated as a perennial. Conversely, some perennials can be treated as vines. One imaginative friend with a small town garden attached pig wire a couple of inches clear of his solid wood fence and planted tight against it perennials that would normally be too tall for a small garden, among them *Boltonia asteroides, Salvia guaranitica*, and *Salvia azurea* (the last a noted sprawler and always a challenge to gardeners). As growth began in spring, stems, kept limited in number, were tucked behind the pig wire. By midsummer the fence was papered with perennials in bloom. Treated this way, they grow taller than they otherwise would.

GRASSES

Grasses are conspicuous by their absence from most gardens. Taught for several decades that neatness is next to godliness in gardens, many homeowners see grasses as untidy and remain to be convinced that dead is beautiful. A yearning for more romantic gardens is evident in the reawakened interest in perennials but the leap from mown lawns and sheared evergreens to undisciplined grasses is a big one. Praise, then, to landscape architects Oehme, van Sweden and Associates who, by their use of grasses within a firm structure, bridged the gulf between nature's unruliness and man's desire for order. No more than any other is this a style pleasing, or practicable, for everyone, but by adding a new dimension to professional garden design and bringing grasses into prominence, Wolfgang Oehme and Jim van Sweden tossed into the pool of garden artistry a stone that is creating ever-widening ripples. As other designers and innovative home gardeners pick up the ball we shall see more imitable examples of creative use of grasses. "Familiarity breeds contempt" says the old maxim. Not so—most cleave to the familiar, and in matters of fashion familiarity breeds compliance. How many women, refusing to raise or lower their hemlines at fashion's whim, find one day that the old length looks wrong? They haven't changed and the skirt hasn't changed, but it just doesn't look right. In part it is a matter of retraining the eye.

As grasses become more popular they'll sometimes be put where they aren't suited or aren't suitable but they have so much to contribute that there'll still be a net gain. Designers say that their clients ask for color. Red-leaved Japanese blood grass (*Imperata cylindrica* 'Red Baron') and the several grasses with yellow leaves give a longer dis-

play of color than most flowers, but most grasses have a quieter beauty and the use of these as single clumps, surrounded by colorful flowers, will probably win more converts than grasses used in rustic wildness or semitamed mass.

Lauded on the one hand, ignored on the other, what are the facts about grasses, what the hyperbole? Ornamental grasses are not new to gardens but interest in them has been peripheral and, in the United States, largely confined to the shrub-sized pampas grass, *Cortaderia* (not a good mixer but impressive as a specimen), and eulalia, *Miscanthus*, in the South, and the wandering white-striped ribbon grass, or gardener's garters (*Phalaris arundinacea* 'Picta'), further north. English gardeners have preferred grasses grown for their gray, yellow, or variegated summer foliage. Many of these prefer cool climates: *Molinia caerulea* 'Variegata', for example, and *Holcus mollis* 'Variegata'. *Miscanthus sinensis* is one of the most adaptable grasses and Miss Jekyll used *M. s.* 'Zebrinus', with its yellow-

The "New American Garden" designed by landscape architects Oehme, van Sweden and Associates, at the National Arboretum, Washington, D.C., photographed in October when newly planted, top left, *and again in October two years later,* top right. *The massed planting under the tree in the foreground is* liriope. *The photograph at the* bottom *is a shot of the hedge of* Calamagrostis acutiflora 'Stricta' *along the front of the garden.*

banded leaves, in her famous border. She also used blue-gray *Elymus glaucus* but is not on record as having constrained it within a sunken container, a wise precaution with this stoloniferous species. An excellent assessment of grasses for English gardens (appropriate, too, to the Pacific Northwest), with suggestions for their use, is contained in Graham Stuart Thomas's book *Perennial Garden Plants*.

What *is* new is the use of grasses that look their best in autumn. It is these that have brought—in political parlance—a kinder, gentler look to the landscaping of the nation's capital. In this modified meadow style rugged grasses are used in quantity, mixed with drifts of sturdy perennials. In America this style was launched around the Mason-Dixon line, where the moderate winters, early springs, hot summers, and especially the long, sunny autumns, suit well such flowering grasses as miscanthus, reed grass (*Calamagrostis*), and fountain grass (*Pennisetum*). They need sun to give their best, can look very bedraggled in rain-sodden summers, and some do not flower where summers are cool and winter comes early. English books have little knowledge to impart about the use of these types, so we must work out the where's and how's for ourselves.

Because the sun never lights them from behind, flowering grasses are poorly served by south-facing borders, or any orientation where the sun's rays are blocked from behind by a tall wall or hedge. Island beds display them best, for then they are backlit in turn from east, south, and west as the day progresses. This applies also to the red leaf blades of Japanese blood grass (*Imperata cylindrica* 'Red Baron') which, glowing like stained glass when lit from behind, competes with such contenders as yellow foxtail grass (*Alopecurus pratensis* 'Aureus') for the "most colorful grass" award.

The range of available grasses is now much greater than our knowledge of how to use them. Foliage colors include not only every shade of green, but yellow, variegated, silver-gray, brown (not only in death—sedges such as *Carex buchanani* are brown the year around), and occasionally red. Flower colors are variable but never garish. There are grasses for wet sites and dry ones, for sun and for shade. Some are upright, some are arching, some make dense tuffets and some are stoloniferous. They range in height from a few inches to three times the height of a man. There are grasses for use as ground cover, for edgings, as specimens and focal points, for screening, and even for hedges.

The roles grasses play as companions for perennials will vary with soil, site, climate, species, and individual choice, but there is something for nearly everyone. Those in Zones 6 to 9 are spoilt for choice. Few survive in the coldest zones but some are proving hardier than expected where insulation by snow cover can be relied upon. One of the evergreen sedges, the two-foot tall *Carex grayi*, is exceptionally hardy, so you could use this as your "canary down the mineshaft." Nor are most grasses well suited to humid Zone 10 regions but sweet flag (*Acorus calamus*) might succeed, also the giant reed (*Arundo donax*), cattails (*Typha latifolia*), and pampas grass (*Cortaderia selloana*). "Grasses," you will note, is being interpreted to include such other grass-like plants as the reeds and sedges. Not, however, bamboos, a group I shy away from as generally invasive and frequently shabby. White variegated *Arundinaria variegata* and yellow-variegated *A. viridistriata* would be attractive additions to the flower border were they less aggressive. Sinking them in tubs might work but I wouldn't bet on it.

With a few exceptions, grasses remain attractive throughout the growing season, and, if not ruined by snow or heavy rain, often long thereafter. If they have an off-time, it is usually in early spring, just after they've been cut back, but at that season there's so much else to occupy our attention that the grasses are not missed. Soft in texture and graceful yet decided in shape, grasses of neutral color (the majority) make perfect companions for perennials, never creating conflict, ornamental in their own right, and also functioning as keystones round which more colorful plants come and go. Because they are seldom disfigured by pests and diseases, extending the use of grasses is a practical approach to reducing the use of chemicals in the garden.

If repetitive tasks are to be kept to a minimum, leaving more time for the creative aspects of gardening, it is necessary, from time to time, to take a hard look at the plants being grown and assess their pleasure/work ratio. Are grasses labor-saving? Yes, with a few exceptions, though minimal maintenance depends on choosing the right plant for your purpose. Case histories of a few I grow might help put things in perspective.

Throughout the year I pause as I enter our driveway to enjoy the weeping Japanese love grass (*Eragrostis curvula*) on the front verge, where, interplanted with 'Kwanso' daylilies, it has eliminated the need to mow and keeps weeding to a minimum. Kept under control by a ditch on one side and a tarmac road on the other, it serves my purpose admirably, but it is too fecund for the border.

The apron of land behind our house is lapped by the tidal water of a creek. Former owners had mown the marsh grasses round the edge and resown each year the struggling lawn under the pines. Having ample space at the front for garden making I decided from the start to let the back apron return to nature, only removing seedling shrubs and trees that would block our view of the water. Now it is

carpeted with pine needles and rimmed by wind-tossed sussurant marsh grasses, sprinkled with salt-tolerant wildflowers that appeared of their own accord: sea lavender, goldenrod, sea oxeye (*Borrichia frutescens*), and such salt-marsh mallows as *Hibiscus moscheutos* and *Kosteletzyka virginica*, punctuated by occasional mounds of saltbush (*Baccharis halimifolia*). In autumn the saltbushes become white clouds of silky seed parachutes which do cause me quite a lot of work by coming to rest and germinating in the nursery beds at the side of the house. This part of the garden is otherwise self-sustaining, self-perpetuating, and largely labor-free, but the natural beauty I enjoy there strikes many as unkempt. Among the grasses is *Panicum virgatum*, a shimmering cloud in November, backlit by the eastern sun and the glinting wind-rippled water. Across the creek is our neighbor's bulkheaded neat green lawn. This, too, is beautiful in its way, and certainly a better setting than mine for the crab apple and cherry trees that flower there, briefly, in spring, but maintaining the lawn involves considerable labor and expense.

Few are blessed with sites of natural beauty. The untamed panicum in the marsh brings me delight of a different order but no greater degree than a single clump in association with dead astilbe heads in a border at the New York Botanical Garden, a more imitable object lesson for most of us than grasses used on the grand scale. The grasses in our front garden are grown in single clumps or small ground-covering drifts, some in sun, others in shade. The soil is an acid sand, enriched in varying degree by compost and manure. Because it has pretty white-striped leaves *and* autumn flowers *Miscanthus sinensis* 'Variegatus' is one of the most popular grasses and one of my own favorites. Growing in full sun, it is the hub around which white-flowered perennials revolve in a white-and-purple-foliage color scheme. Of its companions, only *Astermoea mongolica* flowers from late spring well into fall. Other perennials come in sequence as the year progresses: *Chrysanthemum leucanthemum* 'May Queen', *Baptisia pendula*, *Lychnis coronaria* 'Alba', *Phlox* 'Miss Lingard' followed by 'Mt. Fuji', *Boltonia* 'Snowbank', and finally, in November, white chrysanthemums. The miscanthus remains a beautiful constant factor as the others come and go, the vase-shaped clump of white-striped leaves no less showy than the flowers and never yet marred by pest or disease. In late summer a haze of purplish flowers echoes the purple barberries behind, drying and curling into golden crosiers so long-lasting that they must be sacrificed when the clump is cut back in early March. Delaying the cutting back risks disfiguring emerging new leaves. Cutting back miscanthus or other large grasses stem by stem isn't hard work but it is time-consuming. A hedge trimmer does the job faster. Most years this haircut is the only maintenance needed but I water if a summer month passes without rain. In a wet year a sparring match went on between the grass and the downpours—down, up, down, up, as the canes splayed out under the weight of the water then stood up again when they dried. Finally, as one deluge followed another, they stayed out for the count, dense skirts of foliage smothering their companions. Designer Edith Eddleman paid a timely visit. "Cut them off," she said. I did, sacrificing some flower, and the center bushed out into renewed beauty.

To keep it in proportion, this clump is divided every third year, not a quick or easy job but manageable. Dividing a long-established clump of *Miscanthus sinensis* 'Zebrinus', however, took an axe, a saw (feasible only if the soil is free of stones), broke a fork and nearly broke my back, really a task beyond the strength of the average gardener. Dividing such large grasses before the clumps assume formidable proportions seems to be advisable.

The combination of large size with gracefully arching narrow leaves makes miscanthus a background against which the cartwheel flowers of hybrid mallows seem less vulgarly large, and yellow-banded 'Zebrinus' goes nicely with the velvety violet flowers of the autumn-flowering Mexican bush sage, *Salvia leucantha*. 'Zebrinus' is cut back in February to clear the field for early daffodils snuggled up at the base, their dying foliage later concealed by the new leaves of the miscanthus.

In spring the broad stripes in the corn-like leaves of *Arundo donax* 'Variegata' are a gleaming white. They first make a match with the snowy flowers of *Phlox* 'Miss Lingard', then later with those of *Phlox* 'Mt. Fuji'. Then they take on a creamy tinge. It is this sort of seasonal change that makes color scheming such a challenge. By late summer most of the leaves are green, with just the odd thin stripe

Dead is beautiful. Panicum virgatum *with astilbe plumes at the New York Botanical Garden in October.*

of cream, but now attention focuses on the glistening squirrel-tail flower plumes atop the twelve-foot stems. This grass rejoices in wet summers—drought might find its Achilles heel if the soil is thin. The canes, thicker and fewer than miscanthus, are sturdy enough to remain upright in the face of a downpour. A single clump of this imposing plant needs scarcely an hour's annual maintenance, and it is more effective as a single clump than grown in mass. It is not an asset in winter and if not cut down, the large leaves scatter messily by Christmastime.

If you haven't grown grasses before, *Pennisetum alopecuroides* would be a good one to begin with. For me this has thrived through drought and deluge, needing only an annual cutting back and an hour now and then removing unwanted seedlings. It benefits from division about every fourth year but could be left longer. A single large, arching clump looks good for at least nine months of the year, the constant yet changing element among a progression of flowers: white *Begonia grandis* and blue and white *Iris tectorum*; purplish pink *Allium senescens; Sedum* 'Autumn Joy' in its progression from sea green through pale pink, rosy pink, terra-cotta, and rust; blue asters; white chrysanthemums; and, finally, in winter, the red berries of nandinas. This is a role many grasses play supremely well, complementing all colors and giving stability to an otherwise changing scene. *Pennisetum alopecuroides* 'Hameln' is a compact version for smaller gardens, or for grouping in large ones. *P. a.* 'Viridescens' has showier inflorescences, nearly black when young, enchanting when dew-spangled, as are so many grasses. This one does self-sow in overabundance but mostly in the vicinity of the parent clump, not all over the garden. Because the seedheads shatter early, it doesn't have great winter appeal. I hear complaints that grasses shipped

out from mail-order nurseries don't look much for the money, but most grow fast and many transplant best while small. My *P. a.* 'Viridescens', bought in October in a gallon can, made a clump three feet across by the following autumn.

A single clump of blue fescue (*Festuca* 'Sea Urchin') was divided into three after one year, and into nine the next. Blue fescues do particularly well in light, acid soils in full sun. They look especially lovely with pink flowers. Grouped at one end of a pink/white/blue border, mine thrived for three years, staying good-looking twelve months of the year. In their fourth summer, a wet one, they rotted out, in part, perhaps, because overdue for division. Dividing them isn't a big chore; they can be sliced into sections with a sharp spade, but the need to leave space for expansion between reset clumps gives them a gappy bedding plant look. For one year in three they fill their space and assume an appearance of permanence, then they need dividing again. This need for frequent division detracts from their value. There's a big range of blue fescues to choose from, some a soft blue-gray, others such as 'Blausilber', an intense, dominating silvery blue. The flowers are usually a creamy tan, never offensive, if not an ideal combination with the blue-gray foliage. If you'd prefer that they didn't flower, look for one called 'Solling'. If you want an outstanding flowering form, choose pinkish-flowered 'Superba'.

Carex glauca, a blue-gray sedge requiring richer soil and light shade, is stoloniferous but it gets shabby when congested, so once again fairly frequent division is the order of the day. Looser and less congested than the fescues, if reset with the tips of one arching clump just touching the next, they retain their individual form without the bunlike look of newly divided blue fescues. It makes a good path edging, sometimes a bit bedraggled in winter but smartening up when given a spring haircut. Much better for this purpose, though, at least where the growing season is long, is the evergreen silver sedge, a plant of uncertain nomenclature at present most often listed as *Carex conica* 'Variegata' and frequently described as a dwarf, which in my experience it is not except when stunted by climate or growing conditions. The pencil-line edge of white to the one-eighth-inch wide leaves gives the clumps their overall silvery look. A drift of eight-year-old clumps, never divided and showing no sign of needing it, mingle at the edges but remain individual flattened mounds barely six inches high but over two feet across. *Ajuga* 'Burgundy Glow' trickled between the clumps when they were young but eventually got crowded out. Sedges prefer moist soil but most of them are fairly drought tolerant when grown in light shade and deep soil. Clumps of silver sedge put in full sun soon perished but probably could stand it where summers are cool. For me it would be maintenance-free were it not for the pines overhead, which necessitate occasional combing out of fallen needles. As companions it has hostas, hellebores, blue phlox (*Phlox divaricata*), the hardy orchid (*Bletilla striata*), and glossy-leaved, white-flowered *Penstemon digitalis*, which likes moister soil than most penstemons and doesn't object to light shade. There used to be another grass, the white-flowered woodrush, *Luzula nivea*, enchanting for two years with a pink-flowered form of foamflower (*Tiarella*), but then the voles that are the scourge of sandy pineland gardens did it in.

Obfuscation, not artistry, was the intent with another grouping—an identification challenge for visiting friends. *Carex siderosticta* 'Variegata', is grouped with *Liriope muscari* 'Variegata' and a hosta acquired as *Hosta helonioides* 'Albo-picta' but correctly, it seems, *H. rhodeifolia*. All have similar cream-striped leaves, narrowest in the liriope, widest in the hosta, too much alike for contrast, too different to meld into a single unit, definitely not an example of good design. The carex would be far better displayed at the base of a large-leaved yellow-variegated hosta such as 'Frances Williams'. Our opinions of plants are often based on comparisons—if nothing but crabgrass would live we'd value that—and this pretty and vigorous sedge is highly regarded further north, but because it goes winter dormant, the leaves show tip-burn where summers are very hot or the soil gets dry, and it looks quite similar to cream-striped liriopes and ophiopogons; it is outranked by them where they are reliably hardy and evergreen.

But by no means is advantage always to the south. My failures include *Molinia caerulea* 'Variegata' and *Hakonechloa macra* 'Aureola', which prefer cooler summers. Bulbous oat grass (*Arrhenatherum elatius* 'Variegatum') also makes this clear—pretty in spring, disgracing the garden in summer, taking on a new lease of life in autumn. Blue oat grass (*Helictotrichon sempervirens*) can take dry heat (in Denver, for example) or cool damp (England), but it rots when heat and humidity are combined. So does that lovely new blue-gray grass from England, *Agropyron pubiflorum*, which is quickly and easily raised from seed.

Here are some creative combinations culled from other gardens. Bowles' golden grass, *Milium effusum* 'Aureum' (not to be confused with Bowles' golden sedge mentioned later on), brings welcome patches of simulated sunshine to lightly shaded beds (in deep shade the leaves turn green). In Oregon it was combined with yellow-leaved *Hosta* 'Golden Scepter' for matching color, contrasting texture. Flank this with the brilliant blue of *Omphalodes cappadocica* for a striking spring display. In another Oregon garden the

Deschampsia
flexuosa *'Aurea'*
in Jane Platt's
rock garden in
May, top, *and*
August, bottom.
(Oregon)

taller, more substantial clumps of cream-striped *Molinia caerulea* 'Variegata' punctuated a carpet of golden oregano (*Origanum vulgare* 'Aureum'. I haven't done well by these two grasses so far—they can't stand extreme heat unless in shade and moist soil—but I haven't yet admitted defeat and am trying to persuade the milium to make a match with the yellow coin-dotting in the glossy green leaf platters of the leopard plant (*Ligularia tussilaginea* 'Aureo-maculata'), which also bears, very late in the year, flowers of matching yellow.

Asters and chrysanthemums held sway in Nancy Goodwin's North Carolina garden early in November but the composition that had me enthralled was a water figwort (*Scrophularia aquatica* 'Variegata') with leaves of green and creamy yellow combined with a cream-striped sedge (*Carex* 'Evergold')—rich yellowish cream, as it comes from a cow, not the bleached concoction of the supermarket—both rising cheerfully through a carpet of fallen magnolia leaves with silvered undersides. The arching habit of this evergreen sedge is best displayed in a slightly raised bed.

The wee flowering perennials we call rock garden plants are colorful in spring, but rock gardens seldom have much to say for themselves in summer if they depend on these alone. Some of the little grasses would keep the interest going: mosquito grass (*Bouteloua gracilis*), for instance, with little pinkish combs of flower rewarding close inspection. In an Oregon garden the eighteen-inch *Deschampsia flexuosa* 'Aurea' contributed a clump of hair-fine golden leaves and a haze of golden flowers to the spring and early summer scene, continuing to shimmer in its dried golden brown late summer garb.

In the moist border, bog garden, or at the margin of a pond, Bowles' golden sedge (*Carex stricta* 'Aurea') makes a fine companion for blue and white Japanese irises, or such natives as *Iris versicolor* or *I. virginica*, keeping the color going long after the iris flowers are gone. At Sissinghurst in England this golden sedge was combined in eye-catching brilliance with orange-flowered *Geum* 'Borisii'. In the Botanic Garden of the University of British Columbia in Vancouver *Hakonechloa macra* 'Aureola' made a cheerful spring partnership with orange-flowered *Trollius* 'Fireglobe'.

Many tall flowering grasses make excellent see-through plants, none better than the airy *Stipa gigantea*, which in England and in Oregon I saw used as a kind of exterior lace curtain to give privacy to windows. Certainly the shapely clumps of *Helictotrichon sempervirens*'s silver-blue leaves belong at the front of the border. It featured in two fine combinations by Connecticut designers Fred and Mary Ann McGourty—in their own garden with pink-flowered *Chrysanthemum* 'Clara Curtis', and in a client's garden rising out of a carpet of purple-leaved ajuga.

In Ohio a billowing mass of *Miscanthus sinensis* 'Variegatus' lightened a border of mixed daylilies in a collector's garden, while Longwood Gardens in Pennsylvania two combinations employing this miscanthus demonstrated how much a plant's character is influenced by its companions—dramatic with *Rudbeckia* 'Goldsturm', ethereal with the creamy plumes of *Artemisia lactiflora*.

Grasses and perennials can do so much for each other. At Great Dixter in England *Lychnis coronaria* added piquancy to the arching blades and lax, feathery plumes of the *Stipa calamagrostis* with which it was intermingled, the grass in its turn softening the stridency of the mullein's magenta flowers. Buoyancy and stolidity were mutually enhancing at Brookside Gardens, Maryland, in October, where the airy pinkish purple plumes of

*Stipa gigantea im-
mediately outside
a front sitting
room window gives
privacy without
making the room
dark. (Garden of
Kathleen Hudson,
England; August)*

maiden grass (*Miscanthus sinensis* 'Gracil-limus') were color-echoed and firmly anchored by an underplanting of pale and deep pink chrysanthemums (see page 260).

FERNS

Many American houses are built on wooded lots. Even when the developer put a chain saw to most of the trees, a site that was sunny to begin with gets shadier as the survivors fatten out and the innocent little newcomers bought in gallon cans assume mature proportions. So "What can I grow in the shade?" is a fre-

quent, often plaintive, question. If the trees are deciduous, quite a lot, though some thinning or limbing up of trees may first be necessary. Woodland wildflowers of the region are the obvious starting point, though some from other lands with similar soil and climate may do as well or better. Woodland flowers nearly all flower in spring, before the trees come into leaf, but there need be no dearth of interest thereafter—that's when foliage plants come into their own. Once ferns are recognized as the foliage perennials they are, their place becomes apparent.

With ferns, as with wildflowers, those locally native are the most likely to succeed.

Some may be *too* successful, but whether a particular kind stays in its clump or roams all over the forest floor (hay-scented fern, *Dennstaedtia punctilobula*, for example) can be ascertained from local observation or field guides. Many from far-off places will do equally well, sometimes better. Ferns from Japan adapt well to the East Coast, those from Europe to the Pacific Northwest. Species moved from one coast of the United States to the other may not settle down so readily.

Most deciduous ferns are extremely cold hardy, evergreen kinds much less so. For northeasterners the evergreen fern of choice is the Christmas fern (*Polystichum acrostich-*

oides). Where the average winter low is no colder than 15°F and the ground seldom freezes there are many beautiful evergreen kinds. Holly fern (*Cyrtomium falcatum*) makes substantial arching clumps of firm, glossy fronds. In a Virginia garden a row of these formed the foundation planting under the windows against a shady wall of white-painted brick, a pleasant change from the usual clipped evergreen shrubs. The planting was sprinkled with the bright pink flowers of red campion (*Silene dioica*) planted behind the ferns—rambuctious magenta money plant (*Lunaria annua*—annual but self-sowing) would be another possibility for mixing with

Stipa calamagrostis with Lychnis coronaria at Great Dixter, England, in July.

Miscanthus sinensis 'Gracillimus' with chrysanthemums 'Grandchild' and 'Daisy Royal'. In the background is a purple-leaved form of Hibiscus acetosella. (Brookside Gardens, Wheaton, Maryland; October)

A brick path curves informally through plantings of ferns, wildflowers, forget-me-nots, Spanish bluebells (Scilla hispanica), and other shade-loving plants. To the left is ostrich fern. Perennials include Smilacina racemosa, Geranium maculatum, pulmonarias, and columbines. (Design by Michael S. Schultz for Mr. G. Beasley, Oregon; May)

the ferns against a white wall, or the white form against a red one.

In ferns, spores (rusty scalelike dots arranged in fascinating patterns on the backs of the leaves) take the place of seeds as a means of propagation. It is a slower process than seed, and not always successful, but neither difficult nor time-demanding to attempt. Most ferns can be divided in due course but I wanted quicker increase of a favorite glossy-leaved evergreen fern—tassel fern (*Polystichum polyblepharum*, bought as *P. setosum*). It was three years before the baby ferns, having first passed through their intermediate liverwortlike stage, were ready to pot-on but in the meantime they needed almost no attention. If just a few are wanted, spores can be sown on an inverted peat pellet standing in a saucer of water and covered with a transparent plastic picnic glass. All that's then needed is occasional replenishing of the water. I sowed on peat moss in a large pot, covered it with a transparent plastic dome, and put it in a shaded frame. Some forms of soft shield fern (*Polystichum setiferum*) are evergreen and quite similar to tassel fern, "soft," as the name suggests, in appearance, with very finely cut grayish green fronds. Many forms (one of them often distinguished as *P. setiferum* 'Proliferum') have the unusual characteristic of forming infant ferns along the midrib of the frond. Detach these and pot them up until they are big enough to brave the garden and you'll soon have enough to edge a shady path.

Ferns are to shade what grasses are to sun: graceful plants, fine-textured in the main, restful in color, of long-lasting good appearance, and requiring minimal maintenance. They are not as varied in color as grasses— Japanese painted fern (*Athyrium niponicum* 'Pictum') is unique, its gray fronds veined with ruby red. It is a good companion for just about any shade-loving plant but especially

*A foundation planting of the evergreen holly fern (*Cyrtomium falcatum*). (Garden of Julia Bristow, Virginia; May)*

with flowers that pick up the red veining in the fronds, deep pink primroses for example, or the purple flowers of *Bletilla striata*, the so-called hardy orchid—hardy, that means, relative to other orchids. And even if you have it for only one year (I don't know how hardy it is), you won't regret risking your money on *Oxalis regnellii* 'Atropurpurea' once you've seen its dark purple leaves and pale lavender flowers against the painted fern. You can get it from Glasshouse Works or Montrose Nursery.

Most full-grown ferns are green, but new fronds are sometimes a different color. Those of the fern called "English painted fern" (*Athyrium otophorum*) in some catalogues (goodness knows why, when it comes from

Japan and China), are an unusual bleached butter yellow or palest lime green, reminiscent of *Hosta fortunei* 'Aurea' and one of these days I'd like to put these two together and see how they get on. The new fronds of autumn fern (*Dryopteris erythrosora*) are coppery—exquisite with the pale yellow of *Aquilegia canadensis* 'Corbett' or the wild English primrose (*Primula vulgaris*). In San Francisco I viewed with envy the exquisite young pink fronds of frost-tender *Blechnum occidentale* emerging through a carpet of vancouveria.

A few ferns grow in dry, rocky places, in light shade or full sun. These—the lip ferns (*Cheilanthes*), for example—are usually fairly small, suiting them to the rock garden. Most ferns are woodland plants, though, giving of their best in light shade, moist, humusy soil, a natural mulch of leaves and their own dead fronds, and freedom from root disturbance. Where summers are cool, they can stand more sun, giving scope for adding the grace of ferns to the bright color of summer-flowering perennials—the lady fern (*Athyrium filix-femina*) with brightly colored phlox (*Phlox paniculata*), for example. Although most want shade, under trees is not the only place for them, or even the best. Trees compete for moisture (and win), so where rain is not abundant, ferns and other woodland plants may do better, and need less watering, in the shade of a wall or building. The shady side of a large shrub is another possibility—preferably those with compact roots, such as rhododendrons and camellias. When ferns are mixed with flowering plants, morning sun from the east may be an advantage, but sun on frosted flowers and foliage may do damage that wouldn't occur if they thawed out more gradually, so a north-facing location might be better where late spring frosts are common. Many ferns will grow in deep shade but they gain in beauty where the sun's slanting rays from

back or side render the fronds translucent. Few ferns like dry soil but where others have failed the male fern, *Dryopteris filix-mas* would be worth trying, as it is more drought tolerant than most.

None grow in deep water but many ferns inhabit the boggy banks of ponds and lakes, wet ditches, or low-lying places. Under these conditions the royal fern (*Osmunda regalis*) often becomes a massive clump up to six feet high, so it needs companions of a size that won't look dwarfed or get crowded out. *Gunnera*, umbrella plant (now *Darmera* but better known as *Peltiphyllum peltatum*), skunk cabbage (*Symplocarpus foetidus* and species of *Lysichiton*), false hellebores (*Veratrum*), and that most robust of irises, *Iris pseudacorus*, can hold their own, and all have foliage of contrasting rounded or swordlike shape. Cinnamon fern (*Osmunda cinnamomea*) and interrupted fern (*O. claytoniana*) also do well in boggy ground but the most popular midsized fern for combining with such plants as rodgersias and candelabra primroses in muddy places is the shuttlecock-shaped ostrich fern (*Matteuccia struthiopteris*), a very adaptable fern but not at its best in winterless regions. Sensitive fern (*Onoclea sensibilis*) is much shorter in stature, seldom more than eighteen inches, spreads rapidly and thus needs companions that can rise above it. Netted chain fern (*Woodwardia areolata*) is similar but the leaves are a brighter, glossier green. As its common name suggests, marsh fern (*Thelypteris palustris*) also enjoys wet soil, where its fresh, cool green could set off the bright orange of some of the globeflowers (*Trollius*). Add a sprinkling of blue forget-me-nots (*Myosotis*) if you want to further soften the orange; they too do well in wet soil. Despite their penchant for muddy feet, all these ferns can be grown in soil only moderately moist.

Ferns vary a lot in height, from the tree

Pink double-flowered primroses (Barnhaven hybrids of Primula vulgaris) *pick up the pink in the fronds of Japanese painted fern (*Athyrium niponicum 'Pictum'). *(Virginia; April)*

ferns of the tropics to such charming little carpeters as *Blechnum penna-marina*. Each gains distinction from the association when clumps of the taller ferns are set among such flowering carpeters as sweet woodruff (*Galium odoratum*) or creeping phlox (*Phlox stolonifera*), but contrast in height isn't essential when there is contrast in texture or color. In my garden a little oak fern (*Gymnocarpium dryopteris*) runs around among a patch of 'Burgundy Glow' ajuga. It got there by accident but the partnership seems to be to their mutual satisfaction, as well as mine. White and green is always a refreshing combination and I like to see the English woodland geranium (*Geranium sylvaticum* 'Album') or white forms of the American one (*G. maculatum* 'Album') combined with feathery ferns. Adding a clump of a foliage plant with white-striped grassy,

swordlike, or rounded leaves contributes both textural contrast and a color echo—possibilities include silver sedge (a plant that has suffered repeated name changes but is usually listed as *Carex conica* 'Variegata' or *C.c.* 'Marginata'), *Iris foetidissima* 'Variegata', *Aspidistra elatior* 'Variegata', *Rohdea japonica* 'Variegata', various variegated pulmonarias, and numerous hostas.

Ferns don't have flowers but the "cinnamon stick" fertile fronds of *Osmunda cinnamomea* are striking, and those of interrupted fern (*O. claytoniana*), black to bitter-chocolate brown and sandwiched on the stem between the "normal" feathery leaflets, quaint and curious. These are ferns of firm and upright structure, good among carpeters or with the large, rounded leaves of bergenias or *Ligularia dentata*. Ferns are always elegant but they aren't all similarly "ferny." The maidenhairs (*Adiantum*) are exceptionally dainty. Southern maidenhair (*A. capillus-veneris*) trails its lacy fronds of little bright green fan-shaped leaves over the ground, seldom much more than six inches high, so put it in the foreground. Weather permitting, it is almost evergreen, and this can be a trap because old leaves look battered and spoil the fresh spring look of the new ones if not cut off, and this always needs to be done earlier than you think. This applies equally to epimediums, so deal with both at the same time. Northern maidenhair (*A. pedatum*) carries its one- to two-foot fronds in distinctive fingered whorls that look the more lacy and airy, without being overwhelmed, when displayed over a carpet of European ginger (*Asarum europaeum*), with glossy bright green leaves of strong round outline. Maidenhairs aren't plants for stagnant bogs but they do have a great need for moisture and won't succeed without it in hot regions. Perennials with dainty foliage such as epimediums, columbines, and corydalis aren't the best thing to put with maidenhair ferns—they look too much alike—but these

Fringecups (Tellima grandiflora) with sensitive fern (Onoclea sensibilis). (Garden of Elda and Ray Behm, Washington; May)

would contrast well with the bold, once-cut leaves and firmly upright stance of sword ferns such as *Polystichum munitum* and *Nephrolepis cordifolia*, or the broad, undivided wavy straps of the harts-tongue fern (*Asplenium scolopendrium*).

Some associations for the South involve my favorite fern, which actually isn't a fern at all but looks like one and needs similar conditions of moisture and shade. *Selaginella braunii*, which is evergreen to about 15°F, makes clumps of flattened horizontal fronds resembling bright green lace doilies. Not much more than one foot high, it soon gets twice as broad and continues to spread slowly out. I have it with the large arrow-shaped leaves of *Arum italicum* 'Pictum' and the even larger ones of calla lilies (*Zantedeschia*), also with the sword-shaped leaves and white flowers of *Bletilla striata* 'Alba'.

Green is a perfect foil for white, red, or orange, and just about any combination embodying flowers of those colors along with the green of ferns is a certain winner, but the subtlety of green on green can be enchanting when textures contrast. One of the West Coast's native plants, fringecups (*Tellima grandiflora*) is sometimes considered a weed. It isn't a showy plant but in a Seattle garden the most was made of its quiet charm when its rounded leaves and two- to three-foot stems strung with little green fringed urns were given a background of ferns—sensitive fern (*Onoclea sensibilis*), in this instance, but many others would do as well.

BULBS

Bulbs of similar heights, flowering time, and dormancy are easier to fit into flower beds than those that are out of kilter, but the latter are invaluable for extending the season at both ends. Tall late spring and summer flowerers easy to mix with perennials include *Camassia leichtlinii* 'Plena', with upright three-foot stalks of creamy, starlike double flowers, charming against the blue of *Baptisia australis*, crocosmias and the similar *Curtonus*, galtonias (some object to this carrying dead flowers along with the live ones but anyone who grows daylilies can surely cope with that), and the rather tender, heat-loving tuberoses (*Polianthes tuberosa*) with single or double white flowers of intoxicating fragrance. But the most useful and varied summer-flowering bulbs are lilies and ornamental onions. Lilies are indispensable if only for their rich perfume. *Lilium regale*, *L. auratum*, and the later *L. speciosum* are three of the most fragrant. Some hybrids have very little scent.

With so many lilies to choose from, it's hard to go wrong aesthetically (culturally is another matter) unless, as not infrequently happens, what you paid for is not what you get: you may then suffer the annoyance of having a bright orange lily clash with your bright pink phlox. The tallest ones need something bushy in front to hide their legginess, and perhaps to prop them up a bit in the hope that you won't have to stake them, but they come in so many heights and colors that finding one for any spot shouldn't be a problem. Memorable combinations include a few burnt orange lilies rising out of the chartreuse foam of alchemilla flowers; a lily graded in tones of pink from blush to purplish, bought as 'Mabel Violet' but suspiciously similar to 'Pink Perfection', against the large glaucous leaves of *Rudbeckia maxima* (which has yellow flowers but not until a bit later and in any case raised so high that comparison is only with the blue of the sky); white Madonna lilies (*Lilium candidum*) against the hazy pale purple of biennial clary sage (*Salvia sclarea*), with tall dark purple phlox in the background. The Ma-

donna lily is temperamental, so unless you welcome a challenge, substitute the similar, inexpensive, easy, and so very fragrant regal lily (*Lilium regale*). In the white garden at Sissinghurst this was meltingly combined with a cloud of white bowman's root (*Gillenia trifoliata*, also known as *Porteranthus trifoliatus*), and white annual love-in-a-mist (*Nigella damascena*), and in my own garden with *Gaura lindheimeri*, *Lychnis coronaria* 'Alba', and

Madonna lilies with clary sage (Salvia sclarea) backed by purple phlox. (Waterperry Gardens, England; July)

Regal lilies with Festuca 'Sea Urchin', Lychnis coronaria 'Alba', and Gaura lindheimeri. (Virginia; early June)

blue fescue (*Festuca* 'Sea Urchin'), but it is no less lovely and by no means eclipsed among brightly colored flowers.

Some alliums are bulbs, others grow from rhizomes that hold together in tight but readily dividable clumps. From a practical point of view the latter—garlic chives (*Allium tuberosum*) and *A. senescens* among them—are treated like any other perennial, and very good ones they are, so long as you remember to remove ripening heads before they can self-sow, a wise precaution with nearly all the ornamental onions. If you find that the onion smell won't wash off your hands after you've done that job, try rubbing them with baking soda.

Of those with bulbs, the three- to four-foot Yorktown onion (*A. scorodoprasum*) is tall enough to rise above the competition. Very fecund, it is a first-rate meadow plant but also a stunner in the garden with such yellow flowers as *Coreopsis lanceolata*. There are showier ones, however, with bigger knobs of (usually) purple bloom on tall sturdy stalks, in spring or early summer. The blooms, soon gone, are followed by highly ornamental, long-lasting spherical seedheads. Of those I've grown, the first to bloom (usually in April in my southern garden) is purple-flowered *Allium aflatunense*. *Allium rosenbachianum* and *A. nigrum* (usually listed as *A. multibulbosum*) follow, more or less together. *Allium rosen-*

The deadheads of Allium christophii (formerly A. albopilosum) mingle with lavender, crocosmias, and a single flower of Anthemis 'Wargrave'. (Jane Platt's garden, Oregon; August)

bachianum is rosy purple. There's a greenish white form but if this color is wanted, my choice would be *A. nigrum*. This is one of the tallest and most substantial-looking, the lax strap-shaped leaves as much as four inches wide, and the dome-shaped umbels of white flowers with dark green eyes as much as six inches across held on three-foot stalks. The most advertised, the most expensive, but the least reliable of the ornamental onions is *A. giganteum*, which has very large purple flowers. I have never had it return a second year. *Allium christophii* (formerly called *A. albopilosum*) is much more reliable, and many think it the best of the ornamental onions. It is a bit shorter than the others, usually under two feet, but the spherical inflorescence is exceptionally large, sometimes almost a foot in diameter. The leaves of all of these come very early, which makes them vulnerable to frost. Even if they escape that hazard, they are withering by flowering time, so relieve the stately flowers of this embarrassment by letting them rise behind hummocks of perennials or low shrubs. They follow the tulips and could be interplanted with them.

The drumstick onion, *A. sphaerocephalum*, flowers in summer. It has long-lasting leaves, tubular and string fine but lax, so, again, they are better hidden. It is a good mixer, with egg-sized, egg-shaped beet-red heads of flower at daylily and lavender time. It looks good behind the pink daisies of *Chrysanthemum* × *rubellum* 'Clara Curtis' when their bloom times coincide—no guarantees because Clara's flowering time is influenced more than most by climate and shearing.

Allium cernuum and *A. pulchellum* (also known as *A. carinatum pulchellum*) are daintier plants, about eighteen inches tall. *Allium cernuum* has nodding flowers of a rosy pink that matches or blends with many old-fashioned roses, so it makes a good companion for

these, mixed with hardy geraniums and such gray-leaved plants as lamb's ears (*Stachys byzantina*). *Allium pulchellum* has sparkler-like flowers of dusty purple (white in *A. p.* 'Album') light enough to contrast, in my garden, with the dark purple leaves of annual perilla, with gray *Artemisia* 'Powis Castle' behind that.

Purples predominate among onions but there are other colors. *Allium flavum* is similar to *A. pulchellum*, but shorter and with yellow flowers. *Allium caeruleum*, about fifteen inches high, has round heads of clear blue flowers, nice in front of the yellow-striped leaves of *Iris pallida* 'Aurea-variegata'.

Before we leave the onions, let's not forget chives (*Allium schoenoprasum*), accessible for picking and a worthy ornamental in the front ranks of the flower bed.

Of all the spring-flowering bulbs tulips are easiest to mix with perennials. With tulips we bid good-bye to winter and satisfy our color-starved senses with splashes of brilliant color. An assortment of clear reds and yellows among or behind yellow alyssum (*Aurinia saxatilis*) makes a brave show that might be thought gaudy in summer. Tulips make nonsense of our color pretensions, pulling off with aplomb the combination that is anathema to so many gardeners, pink or purple with orange. 'Princess Irene', for example, has flowers of glowing orange flamed with crimson. A patch of this can pull together, say, a crimson peony and an orange geum or poppy, toned down a bit, if you wish, with a sprinkling of blue forget-me-nots.

Bloom time for tulips varies quite a lot. Catalogues are helpful about this, listing them, for example as "single early" or "single late." It still takes experience and observation to find just the right color to coincide with such early perennials as white candytuft (*Iberis sempervirens*), brilliant chartreuse *Eu-*

out the border, at the back where the gaps they leave will soon be hidden, or at the front to be followed by annuals. Most hybrid tulips diminish from year to year but if you've found persistent kinds (which kind these are varies with climate), don't set them close to perennials needing frequent division.

You can grow tulips right through some perennials—threadleaf coreopsis (*Coreopsis verticillata*), for instance—but use early flowering kinds; late ones might be engulfed before they have time to bloom. Red tulips through Russell lupines was one memorable combination. By accident I achieved a showy but one-time effect (no tulips emerged the following spring) with clumps of *Tulipa praestans* 'Unicum' coming up through *Sedum reflexum* 'Oxbow'. This stocky tulip has bright red flowers and white-edged leaves as handsome as those of hostas, while the sedum, which is evergreen in the South, turns purple in cold weather.

Several species, or near species, do persist for me, and some increase. Scarlet *Tulipa tubergeniana* 'Keukenhof', with several flowers to a stem, is stunning growing through white moss pink (*Phlox subulata*) against a background of purple barberries (*Berberis*), and the pink-flushed pale primrose flowers of *Tulipa marjolettii*, with a delicate look belied by its sturdy constitution and rapid multiplication of bulbs, emerge prettily from a carpet of golden oregano (*Origanum vulgare* 'Aureum'), which also provides good color contrast for scarlet *Tulipa sprengeri*, a graceful late spring bloomer (May or early June) for sun or shade but not very hardy, nor easy to find.

The most reliably permanent tulip for the Southeast is the dainty red-and-white candystick tulip, *T. clusiana*, and its sunny scarlet-and-yellow counterpart, *T. clusiana chrysantha*. The first of these I planted under *Sedum* 'Ruby Glow'. By the time this comes

Scarlet Tulipa tubergeniana *'Keukenhof' growing through white phlox, backed by purple-leaved barberries. (Virginia; April)*

phorbia myrsinites (red tulips are stunning with these), yellow doronicums, or dainty purple-flowered *Pulsatilla vulgaris*. It helps if there's a local public garden where big displays of tulips can be observed.

When a border has been planned for peak summer bloom, the tulips will have had their day before the perennials come into flower, so artistry isn't a consideration in deciding where to put them; dispersed through-

Iris pallida
'Aurea-variegata'
interplanted with
Tulipa clusiana
'Tubergen's Gem'.
The leaves of this
tulip are insub-
stantial and die
away early.
(Virginia; April)

into flower, the insubstantial tulip foliage has long since withered away. *Tulipa clusiana chrysantha* 'Tubergen's Gem' brings added zest among the yellow-striped leaves of *Iris pallida* 'Aurea-variegata'. Dainty, starry little *Tulipa tarda*, with several flowers to each stem, is one of my failures but this is one of the most reliable species in colder regions.

Two plants will often share a bed harmoniously, especially when they work different shifts. Lilies and tulips are ideal bedmates. So many of mine made meals for voles that I took to planting them in sunken plastic laundry baskets with holes drilled in the bottom. One basket will hold a dozen tulips inter-

planted with five lilies. It takes a whopping hole to sink a laundry basket, so this is harder work and reverses the usual planting sequence (perennials first, bulbs later) but it forces the close planting that is usually more effective than dibbling the bulbs in thinly here and there. If the basket mesh has holes wider than a quarter-inch, line it with one of the tough but water-permeable mulching or shading cloths available at garden centers.

Two very successful combinations came about using this method. In a hot-color bed, lily-flowered tulip 'Queen of Sheba', a flamenco-dancer swirl of burnished petals, accentuates by repetition the yellow-and-copper new growth of *Spiraea* 'Gold Flame'. Scarlet-and-yellow columbines (*Aquilegia canadensis*), sprinkled in as seed, join this gay spring chorus. Meantime the interplanted 'Enchantment' lilies are just starting into growth, their neon-bright orange flowers coinciding in early summer with the bright yellow bowls of a stoloniferous sundrops (*Oenothera pilosella*), a shallow-rooted, easily controlled wanderer that has wended its way over and around the sunken basket. Dutch irises can also be interplanted with lilies. They put up new leaves in autumn (unharmed by moderate frost), flower in spring, then make way for the lilies.

In a border of cooler colors, small early tulips in the sunken basket turned out to be misnamed and a color nearer scarlet than pink, which didn't much matter because they

have the scene pretty much to themselves at that time of year. Pink 'Corsica' lilies follow, with daylilies in sultry colors (dark wine red 'Cape Cod' and plum purple 'Shadyside') behind them, against a background of pink and white *Spiraea* 'Shibori' (also sold as 'Shirobana'). While this was being put together, the low, creeping *Coreopsis rosea* was spreading apace in the nursery beds and needing a permanent home. If ever a plant was a

Right: *The lady or peppermint-stick tulip (*Tulipa clusiana*) growing through* Sedum *'Ruby Glow' in front of* Yucca filamentosa. *Behind the yucca,* far right, *is* Allium tuberosum. *The tulips flower in April, the sedum and allium in late August or September. (Virginia)*

Part of my hot color border in April with 'Queen of Sheba' tulips in front of Spiraea *'Gold Flame'. Columbines* (Aquilegia canadensis), *sprinkled in as seeds, are just beginning to bloom. The tulips are interplanted with orange 'Enchantment' lilies which, in June, will combine with the bright yellow flowers of* Oenothera pilosella, *the foliage of which can be seen to the right of the tulips.*

nurseryman's delight, this is it, for a lifted clump falls into a hundred separate little rooted plants. In October a dozen of these little plantlets were dibbled in over and around the basket. By lily time they'd meshed into a carpet smothered with flowers of a pink that matched the lilies and spiraea. The soil is light and drains rapidly but this was a summer of almost constant rain, which kept the coreopsis happy. It does like to be wet—sodden, even—and whether it will tolerate a dry summer remains to be seen.

When it comes time to divide (lilies) or supplement (tulips) bulbs in laundry baskets,

it can be managed without lifting the basket. Tulips last longer if planted deeply but most of the showy hybrids do diminish from year to year.

How about hyacinths—a best-seller among bulbs, colorful, fragrant, and so welcome indoors when winter seems to be dragging on too long, but in the garden dumpy bedding plants. Their progenitors, the wood hyacinths or Roman hyacinths, are easier to fit into the garden—tucked in handfuls just behind evergreen candytuft (*Iberis sempervirens*), for instance. Slender, graceful, and with a scent less cloying than the hybrids, they can be bought in white, or pink, or blue, but if the fat ones grown in bowls indoors are planted out they will after a year or two revert to simpler form. To flower well they need sun for at least half the day in spring.

Gladiolus, too, have had grace bred out of them, but there are still some dainty species we can grow, and one at least, *Gladiolus byzantinus*, is hardy where the corms are below frost line (Zone 5, one authority indicates), a goal toward which it cooperates by pulling itself deeper year by year—old clumps I dug up were a good fifteen inches down but I don't know whether they can be planted this deep at the start. It likes light soil, in sun, bears rosy purple flowers flashed with white in spring or early summer on two- to three-foot stems that never topple, comporting itself with such elegance that it makes converts of magenta-haters. There's a white form too, though less easy to find. The leaves are slender but still a bit messy when they die down, so it needs to be behind or among something that will grow up to hide them. I have clumps among *Chrysanthemum* 'Mei Kyo', which is little more than a green haze over the ground when the gladiolus blooms but grows to fifteen inches soon afterward.

That daffodils aren't attractive to rodents is certainly a plus, but their very virtues—long-livedness and fairly rapid increase—makes them hard to fit in with perennials. Early daffodils are best—*Narcissus obvallaris*, for instance, or 'February Gold'. At the front of a bed, use such sturdy ones of moderate size as 'Tete-a-Tete' and 'W. P. Milner'. 'W. P. Milner' makes a captivating combination with the brilliant chartreuse bracts of *Euphorbia myrsinites*. 'Little Gem' is my favorite front edge daffodil: early (February for me), small but robust, and a rapid multiplier. Unlike most daffodils, the bulbs stay quite near the surface and can be lifted in chunks with such

little disturbance that I do this when they are in bud, putting half the clump straight back where it came from and using the other half to extend the patch at the edges or start another planting

When placing the larger daffodils, keep them away from perennials needing frequent division (bee balm and asters, for example). Put them between those that can go undisturbed for years, preferably kinds with foliage sufficiently abundant and widespreading to conceal the withering daffodil leaves. Very early starters aren't suitable—*Chrysanthemum leucanthemum* 'May Queen' (invariably in flower in April in my garden) would engulf most daffodils while they were still in bloom. Late risers are best: hostas, for instance, or *Lespedeza thunbergii*, also such dieback or cutback shrubs as buddleia, caryopteris, *Lavatera* 'Barnsley', and perovskia. *Amsonia tabernaemontana* will serve but its Oriental counterpart, *Rhazya orientalis*, is better because it breaks ground two weeks later. *Hibiscus coccineus* is about the latest riser in my garden, late enough, in fact, to go in front of Oriental poppies, which flower early and then go dormant, leaving bare earth that needs to be concealed. Butterfly weed (*Asclepias tuberosa*) is a late riser, but its foliage is a bit skimpy for hiding daffodil leaves.

Keep daffodils at least a foot away from peonies and gas plant (*Dictamnus albus*). These can stay in place for a lifetime, steadily increasing in size, and they might resent the disturbance when daffodil bulbs that have sunk to nearly unexcavable depths, as old clumps are apt to do, have to be disentangled from among their roots. This would be a better place for early, short-lived tulips.

Daylilies are ideal companions for daffodils. They emerge early in spring, but the foliage clumps, so fresh and neat and even, stay low sufficiently long for the daffodils first to have their day. The leaves of the two are so similar that they merge visually in the brief interim before the daylilies completely hide the shabby leaves of the daffodils. Between daylilies is also a good place for the early-flowering blue camassias, *Camassia leichtlinii*, in such good blue forms (some are wishy-washy blue) as 'Caerulea'. Note, though, that creamy-flowered *C. leichtlinii* 'Plena' flowers quite a bit later than the others and can take its place as a perennial rather than an early bulb.

Daffodils are easier to mix with perennials in the more casual setting of the shrub or wildflower garden. I have white *Narcissus* 'Thalia' behind white primroses (*Primula vulgaris*) on the east-facing (summer-shaded) side of a dogwood, in a part of the garden much visited in spring, largely ignored in summer. Elsewhere I mentioned the invasiveness of the Japanese anemone sold as *Anemone vitifolia* 'Robustissima' (in all probability a hybrid like most of the others) in the sandy soil of my southern garden. It has been allowed to go its way between tall shrubs, interplanted with daffodils. When the time comes to divide the daffodils (as signaled by diminished bloom), the inevitable digging out of some anemone roots will be less a disturbance than a useful thinning of this rambunctious plant. This would also be a good place for Spanish bluebells (*Scilla hispanica* of catalogues but now changed to *Hyacinthoides hispanicus*). Such combinations wouldn't do were I attempting to keep the anemone within a prescribed space in a border.

Bulbs that put up their leaves out of season (our point of view, of course, not theirs) can be a problem. I'd have evicted bergenia from my garden, where it just doesn't do well enough to earn its place, except that it is interplanted with spider lilies (*Lycoris*) and these take so long to settle down that I don't want to upset them. The bergenia's fat leaves make a solid base from which rise in turn the spider lily flowers on their stiff stalks and their quite good-looking strap-shaped leaves.

Colchicums have a well-chosen popular name, naked ladies. The flowers *do* look naked, and they tend to sprawl on the ground in a rather abandoned way, so it seems kind to give them a carpet to lie on. The yellow leaves of creeping Charlie (*Lysimachia nummularia* 'Aurea') would do nicely. I saw a bewitching combination at the Chicago Botanic Garden in October, where *Colchicum* 'Water Lily' rose through a deeper purple form of sweet alyssum (*Lobularia maritima*). There are two challenges with colchicums—where to place them effectively and how to get hold of them at the proper planting time. They are nearly always shipped out in autumn along with the other bulbs. That's much too late and it sometimes takes them years to recover, if they live at all. The most robust and free-flowering kinds are such large-flowered hybrids as 'Lilac Wonder', 'The Giant', and the double 'Water Lily'. All are pale purple. The common name autumn crocus is often applied to them, as well as to the yellow-flowered *Sternbergia lutea*, which leads to confusion with the true autumn-flowering crocuses. I don't have much to say about sternbergia. Where I thought it would look good it failed to grow, and where it has settled down (among *Allium senescens*) it isn't very effective. The yellow flowers need a color of better contrast than the green leaves of the onion. At Longwood Gardens in Pennsylvania it edges long twin borders of blue-flowered *Caryopteris* × *clandonensis*, and I mean to try it through blue plumbago (*Ceratostigma plumbaginoides*).

Unlike those of crocuses, the leaves of colchicums are broad and they appear in spring, which can be a bit of a shock if you aren't expecting them. My most successful bit

*Clumps of star-flower (*Ipheion uniflorum *'Wisley Blue') and a sprinkling of* Anemone blanda *flower among Barnhaven hybrid primroses in an east-facing bay between evergreen azaleas. The leaves of snowdrops, which flowered earlier, can also be seen. (Virginia; April)*

of color-scheming has the pale purple chalices emerging through a patch of the creamy-leaved ivy 'Lemon Swirl'. I can't say which colchicum it is because that's another problem—a large percentage of those sold are not true to name. Behind is *Hosta undulata*, with wavy cream-and-green leaves, and behind that a pale purple azalea. The appearance of this popular old hosta deteriorates in summer but in spring it is peerless and, with the azalea, puts on such a show that the colchicum leaves go unnoticed. Grape hyacinths (*Muscari*) and starflower (*Ipheion uniflorum*) flower in spring but their leaves appear in autumn and go dormant in summer. Take advantage of this by making them co-occupant with winter-dormant perennials and such taller bulbs as tulips and lilies. Their leaves clothe the ground in winter, and when bloom times coincide, the blue of their flowers is always harmonious.

There are countless permutations and I've been wondering if I can pull off a triple with tulips, lilies, and grape hyacinths in the same sunken baskets. Mixed with yellow daffodils they bring spring beauty to beds where peonies are just pushing through the ground, and those which will later be filled with the hostas still out of sight. Starflower is one of the best bulbs for the South and increases rapidly, so I've had ample opportunity to try it in different places. Mine are the one called 'Wisley Blue', a deeper blue and preferred by most, though the rather ghostly milky blue of the species has its own charm. I have two favorite combinations: around and among the cream-edged leaves of variegated Solomon's seal (*Polygonatum odoratum* 'Variegatum'), which is up and about its business by the time starflower blooms, and as part of a medley of blue- and white-flowered bulbs—snowdrops, chionodoxas, and *Anemone blanda*—mixed with primroses (Barnhaven hybrids of *Primula vulgaris*) in assorted shades of pink.

The money I've expended on crocuses that then made meals for mice and voles must rival that spent on sunflower seed for birds. Our two cats helped for a while but took early retirement, so I now plant a good many crocuses in sunken quart or gallon plastic pots. Grown this way they need dividing at least every second year but if this is done just after they flower, when the leaves are there, it doesn't take many minutes to knock out the clump of tangled roots, divide it into two or three, and replant. Spring and autumn kinds can be mixed in the same pot for a double show—*Crocus tomasinianus* (spring blooming) with *Crocus medius* (autumn blooming), for instance.

Along the front edge of a border is a good place for early crocuses, in or out of pots, to be followed by annuals (planted between the sunken pots the annuals spread to cover them), or growing through such front-line plants as *Campanula portenschlagiana*, and blue plumbago (*Ceratostigma plumbaginoides*). In summer my patches of *Crocus chrysanthus* are tucked under the spreading skirts of *Nepeta* 'Six Hills Giant' but this wouldn't work in frost-free climates, where this catmint is evergreen. Mice and voles chomp away underground and once they find a patch of bulbs will clear it out with remarkable efficiency, but if surface digging squirrels and chipmunks are all you have to contend with, a fairly dense ground cover over the bulbs might afford enough protection. The two best I've found are moss pink (*Phlox subulata*) and creeping raspberry (*Rubus calycinoides*).

The host of little bulbs that can grace our gardens are sometimes listed as "minor bulbs," a bit disparaging but better at least than the "botanicals" or "specie" seen in some catalogues. Some are seen at their best in sizable drifts under deciduous trees and shrubs. Others (especially the large-flowered crocuses) do well in lawns, and the tiniest ones are best displayed in rock gardens or raised beds. But many can, with a bit of ingenuity, be fitted into borders. A triangle of three yuccas will hold a patch of ground together structurally and leave space in between where little bulbs can go with less risk of being dug up by mistake.

Fitting little bulbs, or big ones for that matter, into the more relaxed surroundings of the shrub or woodland woodland garden is much easier, especially when there are ferns. I have snowdrops under Japanese painted fern (*Athyrium niponicum* 'Pictum'), snowflakes (*Leucojum*) between other deciduous ferns, and evergreen ferns as a backdrop for the

*Rain lily (*Zephyranthes candida*) with* Yucca filamentosa *'Variegata'. Many bulbs like to be dry in summer but this one thrives on the alternating drought and deluge of the Southeast. It is not hardy where the ground freezes deeply. (Virginia; September)*

ghostly gray-green flowers of *Ornithogalum nutans*. When lungworts (*Pulmonaria saccharata*) open their pink and bright blue flowers toward the end of winter, the leaves on their flowering stems are small and sparse. There's ample space between the clumps for *Scilla tubergeniana* to display its stocky spikes of very pale blue flowers with darker stripes. By the time they've gone, the big basal leaves of the lungworts are expanding to fill the gap. In another garden I noticed clumps of bright blue *Scilla sibirica* tucked among pachysandra. In autumn the little white-and-pale pink flowers of *Cyclamen hederifolium* will pop up through the darker pink-white-and-green leaves of 'Burgundy Glow' ajuga, which retains insufficient of its leaves through winter to get in the way of the cyclamen leaves that follow the flowers.

Most bulbs for shade bloom in spring. One with dainty leaves that blooms from spring through fall is *Oxalis regnellii*. A nursery threw in a dozen tubers as a "bonus" with an order, so I potted them up and put them under lights, where they bloomed all winter. In spring they were planted out, between a hosta and a fern, where they went on flowering without pause. By autumn the clump had doubled in size. I wiggled off enough for one pot and left the rest to the mercy of the weather. In spring, to my surprise, back they came, to flower all summer. This is usually sold as a houseplant and I don't know how much cold it can stand but it isn't much trouble to maintain it in the dual role of houseplant/bedding plant. The species has green leaves and white flowers but *Oxalis regnellii* 'Atropurpurea' has dark purple leaves and pink flowers.

ANNUALS, BIENNIALS, HERBS, AND VEGETABLES

In the past I've likened growing annuals to raising a baby past the diaper stage then tossing it out and starting again but I've come to see that impermanence has its advantages; one can try a few different plants each year, and get quick results when trying out new ideas—little is lost, after all, if it doesn't work out. One very successful creative touch seen in a local garden was impatiens flowing from a barrel tipped on its side and trickling down an ivy-covered bank. Could I copy it with blue lobelia to look more like water or even with a low-growing, blue-flowered perennial—some of the veronicas, for instance? Adding annuals broadens the palette—there are, for instance, few perennials with red or orange flowers but a great many annuals. And because they reach maturity so fast, annuals are marvelous for plugging the inevitable gaps in borders.

Now that I garden where intense heat curtails the display of many perennials, I've also come to value the ability of some annuals to flower profusely and continuously through summer, asking very little in return, except for the few (pansies in particular) that need daily deadheading if they are to go on flowering. Some of the "annuals" that flower the longest are actually perennials that are killed by hard frost. Three I've found outstanding are mealycup sage, *Salvia farinacea* (hardy to about 20°F), especially the compact, darker blue form 'Victoria', about eighteen inches high and wide with branched spires of deep blue flowers; the slightly hardier prickly poppy (*Argemone grandiflora*), with lax stems of glaucous leaves and large satiny white flowers; and annual periwinkle (*Catharanthus roseus*). All start to flower in late spring and keep it up until the temperature drops well

Snapdragons color-keyed to daylilies in a border at Innis-wood Botanical Garden and Nature Preserve, Ohio. (July)

*Supplementing perennials with an-nuals keeps borders colorful longer. Perennials in these beds include butter-fly weed (*Asclepias tuberosa*), Achillea 'Moonshine',* Coreopsis verticillata, C. lanceolata, *and* Echinops ritro. *Annuals include zinnias, dahlias, nasturtiums, and marigolds. (Design by Plimpton Associates, Rhode Island; August)*

below the freezing point.

"Annuals" can even be shrubs—the one called blue daze (*Evolvulus glomerata*), for instance, low and spreading, layering itself as it goes, with little grayish leaves and circular sky blue flowers. This rejoices in the hot, wet summers that do in so many flowers (it is seen a lot in Florida) but also does well through periods of drought. Frost kills it but it is easy to take cuttings, or sever little rooted pieces before frost, and winter these indoors. The same is true of *Cuphea hyssopifolia*, a fine-textured but dense little bushlet that stays pristine and goes on flowering all through summer and autumn. It self-sows during the season and the little plantlets could be potted up before frost and wintered indoors. It is also easy to root cuttings. Typically the small flowers, profusely borne, are medium purple, but there are other color forms, including white.

Annuals do need to be chosen to suit the climate. Many aren't fussy but some rejoice in the heat and dislike constant rain, among them gaillardia, gloriosa daisies (*Rudbeckia* hybrids), marigolds (*Tagetes*), zinnias, and *Portulaca grandiflora*. (*Portulaca oleracea* is drought resistant but also thrives in warm, wet

Salvia farinacea 'Victoria' (a perennial where winters are not severe, elsewhere an annual) with zinnia 'Peter Pan Scarlet' at Denver Botanic Gardens. (September)

weather.) Others need a moderate temperature, or tolerate daytime heat only if the nights are cool—clarkia, godetia, nasturtiums (*Tropaeolum majus*), pot marigold (*Calendula*), Shirley poppies (*Papavar rhoeas*), China asters (*Callistephus chinesis*), mignonette (*Reseda odorata*), and wallflowers (*Cheiranthus cheiri*), for example. Drought tolerance may be a requirement, a quality displayed by wax begonias, lantana, verbena, and the recently introduced *Melampodium paludosum* that has been such an instant hit. Bedding geraniums (*Pelargonium*) are extremely drought resistant but flower poorly in extreme heat. The catalogue of Park Seed Company includes a helpful culture guide, in which annuals are coded *wa* (prefers warm weather) or *ca* (prefers cool weather).

All-America Selections evaluates new introductions in all parts of the country and selects winners from among the most adaptable, but the heat-tolerant kinds favored may not be the best choice where summers are cool or wet. Visit a local trial garden (the AAS publishes a list) and make your own evaluation. The following have been winners in recent years:

Coreopsis 'Early Sunrise' (yellow)
Dianthus 'Telstar Picotee' (crimson and white)
Impatiens 'Tango' (orange)
Marigold (*Tagetes*) 'Golden Gate' (red-and-yellow bicolor)
Torenia 'Clown Mixture' (many colors; best in semishade)
Verbena 'Sandy White' (white) and 'Trinidad' (hot pink)
Celosia 'New Look' (bronze foliage, scarlet plumes) and 'Century Mixed' (plume-type, mixed colors)
Shasta daisy 'Snow Lady' (white, dwarf, and stocky)
Basil 'Purple Ruffles' (glossy purple, aromatic leaves)
Petunia 'Purple Pirouette' (purple-and-white picotee)
Sanvitalia 'Mandarin Orange'
Snapdragon (*Antirrhinum majus*) 'Princess White with Purple Eye' (white-and-purple bicolor)
Cosmos 'Sunny Red' (scarlet-red)
Gazania 'Mini-Star Tangerine'

The bedding plant industry supplies a plenitude of such staples as ageratum, wax begonias, geraniums, impatiens, marigolds, petunias, scarlet sage (*Salvia splendens*), and zinnias—and maybe tobacco plant (*Nicotiana*), but only *N. alata*, not the intensely fragrant white-flowered *N. sylvestris*, or the graceful green-flowered *N. langsdorffii*. Mass production keeps plants affordable but ill serves artistry. Chunky plants predominate: the dainty, ferny-leaved *Tagetes tenuifolia* and the graceful narrow-leaved, small-flowered *Zinnia angustifolia* are seldom to be found among the large-flowered marigolds and zinnias on garden center benches, let alone at the local supermarket. Scarlet sage is certain to be there, perhaps in drab purple or dingy white as well as red, but when did you ever see *Salvia horminum* (synonym *S. viridis*) in its range of pastel pinks and blues?

Less common kinds must be grown from seed. Indoor plant lights are a great asset. Seed catalogues are so enticing, it is all too easy to overorder. When a dab of mustard was the customary accompaniment to roast beef it used to be said that mustard fortunes were made not from what was eaten but from what was left on the plate. If I'm anything to go by, the same is true of the seed trade—in the hurry-scurry of spring a lot of the packets get shoved to the back of the fridge to await another year.

The annual Viguiera porteri, *native to the Southeast, self-sows each year among* Yucca *'Golden Sword'. There were tulips here in early spring. (Virginia; October)*

Raising annuals by sprinkling purchased seed where you want it to grow isn't as successful as if often implied—to be sure it is what nature does, but nature doles out seed with a far more liberal hand than the one that counts seed into packets, and does it, furthermore, at the optimum time. One April I planted out sturdy little plants of love-in-a-mist (*Nigella damascena*). They flowered in early June, but not for long; it was too hot by then. In autumn self-sown seedlings appeared by the hundred, went undamaged through winter, and having got off to an early start flowered before it got hot. I've had nigella ever since, for no more effort than weeding out the surplus. Self-sowers usually set an overabundance of seed, so some about-to-be-parent plants can be pulled out when they get shabby; just be sure to leave enough plants for regeneration.

All self-sowers don't germinate in autumn—nature, no doubt, has her reasons. *Viguiera porteri*, an annual with bright yellow daisy flowers, native to the Southeast, flowers in October. It was a bit too productive for the border, but because the new crop of plants don't appear until late spring it is just what I need for covering the ground between yuccas where early bulbs have bloomed.

Borders shouldn't show bare soil in summer, nor look too rigorously controlled. Art has been said to require a combination of discipline and abandon, and nothing better brings the abandoned look than self-sowing annuals, nudging their way into gaps that were not apparent with the skill of a seasoned rail-car traveler. A tall, loosely branched, red-flowered sage, *Salvia coccinea*—another frost-tender perennial—is one of my best, strewing the all-too-rare red in a scattered way that

Mixed annuals and perennials in a small border at the Mordecai Garden, Raleigh, North Carolina. Vegetables and herbs occupy the center of this garden, with flower borders round the edges. The border includes orange butterfly weed, gray artemisia, yellow achillea, and the yellow spires of Thermopsis villosa. *The blue-and-white flowers are larkspur (*Consolida ambigua, *also called* Delphinium ajacis). *Once established this usually self-sows. (May)*

both brightens and softens the border. Other good self-sowers include cleome, larkspur (*Consolida ambigua*), poppies (including the California poppies (*Eschscholzia*), sweet alyssum (*Lobularia maritima*), and sweet Williams (*Dianthus barbatus*), but fancy kinds and selected colors soon revert to what nature intended. Forget-me-nots (*Myosotis*) are prime self-sowers, of a color that is all things to all plants (there are pink and white ones but blue is the universal favorite), bringing to mind so many lovely combinations: softening orange geums; echoing the deeper blue of 'Hensol Harebell' columbine; lending quiet support to the pristine purity of white trilliums; wistful with gray lamb's ears (*Stachys byzantina*); and, being one of the few annuals that don't mind soggy soil, cheerfully cohabiting with brightly colored candelabra primroses in a bog.

It is probably as border edgings that we think of annuals first, and there's something for everyone—formal edgings of chunky wax begonias, soft drapings of lobelia, sanvitalia, or the dainty Dahlberg daisy (*Dyssodia tenuiloba*), even a mock hedge of kochia. *Portulaca oleracea* is my present pet, the perfect carpeter over resting bulbs. The dense mats make it hard for weeds to get a toehold, yet they come from a single slender root that doesn't interfere at all with the dormant bulbs below. It can be had in nearly any color except blue, as subtle or as gaudy as you choose: pinks neon bright or pale pastel; soft apricot, bright orange, or pinkish orange sunrise hues; cool lemon or warm yellow; white; and many bicolors. Break off a trailing stem, poke it into the ground (even, in my case, into the gravel of the drive), water it in and give it another occasional watering if there is no rain, and after a couple of weeks you have a sizable flowering mat. Stems clad in small fleshy leaf pads radiate out from the center, lying flat on

Forget-me-nots are very adaptable. Because they flower early, before trees have fully leafed out and before the weather has got hot, they can be grown in sun or shade, as well as being one of the few annuals tolerant of wet soil. Top, they carpet a pair of sunny borders, between dormant perennials. (Garden of Edward C. Childs, Connecticut; May) Bottom, they partner trilliums in shade. (Garden of Catherine and Harry Hull, Massachusetts; May)

A hedge of kochia
at the Longwood
Inn, Pennsyl-
vania. (September)

A hedge of kochia at the Longwood Inn, Pennsylvania. (September)

the ground and obliterated each morning by the wealth of the bloom. But let me not gloss over its shortcoming: "in the morning," there's the. rub—the flowers work part time, clocking out soon after lunch, but they do it very neatly, no deadheading called for, and the next day there'll be more.

The term "biennial" means that seed is sown one year to flower the next. Popular biennials include foxgloves, hollyhocks, and sweet Williams. Some of them (or some selections) may, in some regions, behave as annuals or perennials. The Foxy strain of foxgloves, for instance, flower the first year if started early.

It is customary to sow the seed of biennials in late summer and set out the young plants in autumn to flower the following year. Once established in the garden those that

flower early usually provide a self-perpetuating sequence and there'll be flowers every year, provided the young plants survive winter. They are amazingly winter hardy but protecting them with a lightweight mulch (salt hay or evergreen branches, for instance) is helpful in cold regions.

Foxgloves are one of the most valued biennials. They provide the spirelike form that is none too common among perennials and can take their place at the back of the border. Nowadays they come in a luscious array of colors but many of the hybrids lack the elegance of the wild *Digitalis purpurea*, the exquisite white-flowered *D. p.* 'Alba', and the pale pink forms that tend to crop up when these two are grown together. The self-descriptive 'Sutton's Apricot' is very beautiful but seed sold under that name is a bit of a grab

Because red is a fairly scarce color among perennials, ruby chard, shown here with dahlias, is a useful addition to the border. (England; August)

bag. Mine didn't yield a single plant to fit the name but did produce a few of an equally lovely pale primrose color. Once you have a patch established, pull out those of a color you don't like before they can self-sow.

The most exciting combination I've seen utilizing foxgloves also included that problem shrub *Spiraea* 'Gold Flame'—a placement challenge because it bears pink flowers with its yellow leaves. This, just coming into flower in May, was underplanted with a golden carpet of creeping Charlie (*Lysimachia nummularia* 'Aurea'). Foxgloves in purple and pink rose up behind the spiraea, picking up the color of its flowers. Alongside it a roaming patch of *Oenothera speciosa* bore its pale pink bowl-shaped flowers, and in front of these were violas in pale pinks and purples. Many who don't like pink and yellow together would, I think, have been won over by this combination.

Biennials that flower later in the year may not self-sow soon enough for the young plants to reach maturity the following year. If the leaves are ornamental in their own right, as many verbascums are, that's good enough, they earn their place with or without flowers. In my garden the seedlings of clary sage (*Salvia sclarea*) take two years to reach flowering stage, so there's an off-year without flowers, during which the foliage doesn't fully occupy its ultimate space, so the gaps have to be plugged with annuals. I've been given seed of a clary sage said to be perennial and am waiting eagerly to find out if it does behave this way in my garden. Standing cypress (*Ipomopsis rubra*) also has an off-year but this bears its scarlet flowers (occasionally yellow) on such slender, upright feathery spires, occupying mainly skyroom, that parents and babies can be fitted in together and I've got an alternating sequence going by collecting seed

Herbs within a structured framework, and close to the house for easy picking. Included are thyme, sage, chamomile, oregano, garlic chives, and sweet cicely. (Design by Dan Borroff, Seattle, for Mr. and Mrs. J. P. Smith; August)

and saving this for a year before sowing it. Meantime the plants also self-sowed, so half the patch flowers one year, half the next.

Don't overlook vegetables and herbs. I personally can do without the inelegant multicolored cabbages that have become a staple of the nursery trade, but the ornamental "Peacock" kales have a fernlike quality, parsley makes a fine bright green edging, ruby chard has handsome leaves and stalks of an unrivaled bright red, and I've already mentioned asparagus as a graceful foliage plant.

It is customary to grow herbs within an ordered framework and many nondescript kinds do need this firm structure. Others are sufficiently ornamental to claim a place in the border. Golden oregano (*Origanum vulgare* 'Aureum'—also called golden marjoram) is a fine weed-suppressing edging plant. It could be combined with feathery purple fennel, blue-gray rue, purple sage (*Salvia officinalis* 'Purpurascens'), or the annual purple-leaved basil. Mints are too invasive for flower beds, and for picking one wants them close to the house. I found a place for mine between a north-facing house wall and the gravel drive, where it thrusts its way through a carpet of evergreen ajuga. If I don't pick enough and it produces the tough flowering stems useless for the kitchen, shearing it to the ground prompts a burst of neater, more pickable short shoots. And tough though it is, it has not managed to cross the car tracks in the drive.

Garden privies are usually tucked away out of sight and hard to find. At Well Sweep Herb Farm, New Jersey, the privy is an ornamental focal point. Its prominence is accentuated by perspective—the borders of lamb's ears seem to form an arrow pointing the way. (July)

8 | Garden Features and Ornaments

"Every garden should have vistas and features," announced a well-known landscape architect. In most gardens they may amount to the same thing. "Vista" smacks of gardening on a grand scale and a view worthy of framing, but in most residential areas the "view" is more likely to need blotting out. Suburban gardens of average size have to be more inward-looking than large ones in rural surroundings, so "vistas" become focal points, drawing the eye toward a feature but halting it within the garden. The Y where a path forks is a natural focal point, and a good place for a feature.

Focal points aren't new, of course. At many a grand estate I've walked a grassy yew-lined cross axis toward a distant hedge-backed statue, examined it, then turned around wondering if the journey had been worthwhile. Not all grand design is good design, and charm, which seldom goes hand-in-hand with magnificence, is oftener found in gardens of modest size.

Garden ornaments need serve no purpose other than embellishment—a statue or urn tucked among border flowers, for instance. They can also be intrinsic to design, or

the solution to a design flaw. If, for example, a path dead-ends at a wall or hedge there's a feeling of pointlessness. I know it well. Being plantsman more than designer, I all too often paint myself into corners. One of my paths ran alongside a flower bed and terminated at our post-and-rail front fence, with a view beyond of blacktop road and cars in the driveway on the other side. There were two problems: to block the view (cars don't make pleasing focal points!) and to stop the path from dead-ending. A solution struck me while taking a stroll down two local streets. One that ends abruptly has a parade ground feeling—I half expected someone to bawl "Halt. . . . About face." The other street encircles a small island before turning back on itself, so one strolls on without pause. My path could encircle a feature to distract the gaze from what lay beyond and provide a turning point. I toyed with this idea, to the point of having a visiting friend play "statue" or "tree," standing with arms outstretched so that I could gauge the needed height and position of such a view-blocking feature. In the end I expanded the border and adopted another solution—evergreen shrubs inside the fence as background for the exten-

sion, with the path continuing along the front.

If, for better or worse, the view is already blocked by a wall or hedge, putting a seat against the wall is a common ploy. A millstone, or a larger simulated millstone cast in concrete, would make a more interesting, multipurpose roundabout. A circular structure of this kind could be used as a seat, a sundial, the plinth for an ornament, even a water feature with the water piped through a hole in the middle to flow over the surface and down through a cobbled surround to provide change of texture. A half barrel or other circular container filled with flowers would make a simpler, inexpensive turnaround. This would also be a good place for a fountain. One of the best amalgamations of the practical with the ornamental I've seen was in the display garden of an English herb nursery, where a bowl and pedestal fountain stood in a little pool at the end of a grass path between two borders, the

Flowers and ornaments are mutually enhancing: Top: *A terra-cotta caldron of geraniums and petunias stands alongside rose mullein (*Lychnis coronaria*) in the garden of artist Gladys Huyghe. (Virginia; June)* Bottom: *A "bubble pot" by Claud Conover with daylily 'Lilting Lavender' in the Ohio garden of the late Richard Meyer. (July)*

fountain spray adjusted to splash over a surrounding cobbled circle planted with perennials that like moist soil.

If there *is* something worth looking at on the other side of a wall, a wall window or "*claires-voies*" is an attractive feature.

Features do give a garden added charm and interest. When I send a selection of pictures to a publisher, those combining plants with attractive structural or ornamental elements are invariably snapped up fastest. Demand exceeds supply and I began to wonder why I so seldom find pleasing features to photograph. The reason became apparent when I looked through my file of garden ornament pictures; 90 percent fell into two categories— the ornate urns and mythological figures of another place and a bygone age, or the graceless mass-produced products of our own. We could do better. Garden centers aren't, as a rule, the place to look for tasteful garden accessories. Look instead in antique shops, art galleries, potteries, flea markets and garage sales, builder's merchants, and junk yards.

When you see a sculpture you like in another garden, ask who made it: hundreds of talented artists and sculptors are waiting to be discovered.

Pondering on the whys and wherefores of garden ornament led to a group discussion about what works and what does not. Personal opinion is, of course, a factor. So is fashion to a minor degree—"Victoriana," long considered the epitome of bad taste, staged a bit of a comeback. When one garden's piece of junk becomes another's tasteful ornament, the difference lies in artistry, that special seeing eye with which few are blessed. Just why *what* it is and *where* it is seems exactly right in an artist's garden cannot be explained—artists don't follow rules, rules follow artists.

Still, a pattern did begin to form, and it was encouraging to realize that although mass-produced (therefore relatively inexpensive) objects quickly become banal, pleasing garden features have more to do with imagination than money: a simple stone or terra-cotta pot is seldom out of place, and such "found" ob-

A simple fence sets off the daylily flowers in a small garden at Colonial Williamsburg. (Virginia; July)

A "by-product" of the logging industry, old tree stumps are common in the Pacific Northwest. This old relic has been given a second lease on life as garden sculpture. (Garden of Elda and Ray Behm, Washington; May)

jects as driftwood, tree stumps, and glass carboys can become engaging garden features. One of the most appealing wall plaques I've seen was made by molding a mixture of cement and vermiculite (1 part cement, 3 parts vermiculite, plus water to what, in cooking lessons, used to be called "firm dropping consistency") over an attractively patterned street drain cover.

Appropriateness to setting is the main criterion. A bikini on the beach is (or can be) attractive; a bikini worn at a ball is tasteless. Similarly in the garden: urns of a size and ornateness befitting Versailles are out of place in less grand settings, while the axe-carved owl so appealingly placed in the crotch of a woodland tree would look silly perched on a topiary in a formal garden. The sculpted seal that looked just right on a boulder alongside

a pond would look all wrong on a plinth among the flowers; the Lutyens bench so elegant in the sort of setting for which it was intended looks merely pretentious in less gracious surroundings.

Ideally, the structural elements of a garden should themselves be ornamental: the total is greater than the sum of its parts when flowers are associated with such structural ornaments as a stone wall, a picket fence, a brick path, wrought-iron gate, gazebo, or vine-clad arch. At Colonial Williamsburg cannonballs are used with chains as self-closing mechanisms for gates. A Rhode Island gardener used old flatirons instead, adding interest to a small garden without in any way detracting from the flowers.

Chain-link fences are excellent for keeping dogs out, or in, but they are not a thing of

The concrete doves by Marie Gill at Denmans, West Sussex, England, left, would look equally at home in many American gardens, but the sculpted raccoons by John Seymour displayed among hostas and ferns in the Ohio garden of the late Richard Meyer, right, convey "American garden."

beauty—their appearance can be vastly improved by interweaving them with the strapping sold for that purpose. A solid concrete path is serviceable but when inlaid with bricks, pebbles, or strips of wood it, becomes ornamental as well. It is said that necessity is the mother of invention: when I admired the unusual texture of a crazy-paving path I learned that its maker had broken up the concrete path cast in place by a former owner, liked the texture of the underside and used the pieces upside-down. Walls of such ugly materials as cement blocks can be painted, of course, but that makes for high maintenance. A gray cement slurry gives a longer lasting surface or, if the wall isn't too extensive, the sort of hypertufa coating (mixtures of cement, peat moss, and perlite or vermiculite) often used for coating old sinks or making garden troughs could be applied.

Steps can be ornamental of themselves but become more so when creeping plants are inserted between riser and tread. Two of the best perennials for this purpose are *Cerastium tomentosum* and *Campanula portenschlagiana*.

Next to structure, the most appropriate garden features are those that have, or appear to have, a purpose beyond the ornamental: seats, birdbaths, bee skeps, pumps, sundials, lamps, containers, horse troughs, and hitching posts have seeming relevance even though the lamps are never lit, the containers are empty, and a horse never set hoof in the garden. Imagination can be brought into play with, for example, a dry stream to give purpose to a bridge where there is no water.

Age brings the feeling of timelessness that contributes to the tranquility of a garden, and the old—even dilapidated—is more romantic than the new: ruins (real or mock),

These two photographs demonstrate two very different approaches to garden structure.

The white painted gateway makes a focal point at the end of the crazy-paving path in this English cottage garden. This is a plantsman's paradise, with many unusual rock garden and border plants to be seen. This romantic approach is attainable only when the owners devote much of their lives to the making and care of the garden. The plants include Lavatera 'Barnsley', artemisias, white fireweed (Epilobium angustifolium 'Album'), delphiniums, poppies, and violets. The bright pink flowers in and alongside the paving are the annual Salvia viridis (S. horminum). (Garden of Mr. and Mrs. M. Metianu, Kent, England; July)

*In this garden a carpet of white-flowered thyme is interplanted with clumps of evergreen coralbells (*Heuchera *'Bressingham Hybrids') within the flowing semiformal structure of the paving. The narrow outer borders are more varied, with shrub roses,* Coreopsis verticillata *'Zagreb',* Coreopsis *'Moonbeam',* Sedum spectabile, *and* Acanthus mollis. *Because the planting is kept simple, and subordinate to structure, this garden can be professionally maintained. (Design by Dan Borroff, Seattle, Washington, for Mr. and Mrs. J. P. Weyerhaeuser, III; August)*

lichened rock or wood, old gravestones used as paving, copper or bronze containers coated with verdigris, an old wooden wheelbarrow planted with flowers, even a mass-produced concrete statuette of no artistic merit transcends its mundane origin when weatherworn. Stone and concrete can be artificially aged by watering or brushing on concoctions of cow manure, buttermilk, and ground-up moss (the proportions don't much matter). It helps if the surface is first roughened with a wire brush. Nostalgia comes into play with old chimney pots and other bits of memorabilia often to be had for a song. England's old stone sinks and staddlestones are envied, but America has its own artifacts—iron sugar kettles, wagon wheels, and fancy fishing floats, for instance.

Whimsy, humor, and conscious sentiment have a place but overuse makes anything

A dry stream and simple plank bridge at Denmans, West Sussex, England. The flowers are blue ajuga and chartreuse euphorbia. (June)

trite and there's a fine line between the poignant and the mawkish. Whimsy is done well at two of my favorite gardens: Ladew Topiary Gardens in Maryland, and Brookgreen Gardens in South Carolina. At the first I got a chuckle from Hilaire Belloc's words engraved on a sundial: "I am a sundial, I make a botch of something that is done far better by a watch." In a private garden I smiled back when I turned a bend and came across a jolly bewhiskered sculpted sea lion stretched out belly-up among foliage plants in a wet spot.

Restraint is desirable, in color, form, and quantity. Are two really better than one? Simple lines and natural materials are easiest to use: ornaments should complement the flowers, not dominate them. The more elaborate an object is, the better its quality must be. The clumsy design and excessive ornamentation of Victorian stone seats is mitigated by quality of workmanship, also by scarcity. Reproduced in molded plastic such seats would become the ultimate ugliness. Natural materials—stone, wood, terra-cotta—blend best into a garden, but don't be afraid of concrete, which nowadays is being shaped and textured in numerous garden worthy ways, especially as paving. With few exceptions, plastic remains unsympathetic, though some plastic rocks and containers purporting to be stone or terra-cotta are scarcely distinguishable from the real thing.

There is no more welcoming feature, and none more versatile, than a garden seat. Seats can be all things to all settings, from the fallen tree, stone slab, or plank across two rocks, to the elegance of white-painted iron wire. The most common, the park-style bench with slatted seat and back, gains appeal (though losing usefulness) when plants are encouraged to ramble through from a raised bed behind. In matching simplicity or elegance to the setting, beware the "rustic" bench made of gnarled

branches; it is too contrived for such natural settings as a woodland or meadow garden, though quite at home in the flower border which is, after all, itself contrived. Neutral colors (natural wood or rock, white or black paint) are the accepted colors for garden seats, and these are seldom out of place, but it doesn't follow that bright color is always undesirable. Few would want to outshout the flowers with a bright yellow seat, but might not a red one add welcome color to a shady corner of foliage plants?

Musing on this, I realized that our sanctions often spring less from merit than from familiarity; it is to the unfamiliar that we bring our critical faculties. Antiques and artifacts steer a course between the familiar and the commonplace. The innovative will be criticized as often as acclaimed, while the natural (in keeping, that is, with natural surroundings) and the familiar (as things have long been done) are more readily accepted. Hence, presumably, the ubiquity of some hideous "classical" garden seats with bulbous or otherwise malformed supports: the squat legs which on a bulldog have a certain grotesque charm lose their appeal for me when (mis)applied to a stone or concrete bench.

The charm of age in a lichened old wall alongside the drive of a cottage garden, with Primula auricula along the base. (Garden of Mr. and Mrs. A. Van Vlack, Connecticut; June)

Stone or concrete? It is often difficult to tell. The photograph to the left *shows a millstone path with hostas and daylilies. (Ohio; July) The steps in the photograph to the* right *are concrete, interplanted with* Sedum rubrotinctum *and dark green* Muehlenbeckia axillaris. *(Garden of Harland Hand, Bay Area of California; September)*

The yellow autumn foliage of platycodons can be seen behind the stone seat in the herb garden at the Garden Center of Greater Cleveland. In the foreground are two rather tender sages (Zone 8), blue Salvia guaranitica *and the drought-tolerant* S. leucantha *which is a shrub in frost-free regions, top-killed in winter at its hardiness limit. (Ohio; October)*

*This seat, modeled on granite boulders in the Sierras, is made of concrete. Lamb's ears (*Stachys byzantina*) flow from the crevices at the base of the seat. The orange flowers are* Aloe striata, *a fine perennial in frost-free regions. (Garden of Harland Hand, Bay Area of California; April)*

Plants often do poorly in the root-filled soil under a large tree. The cobbled apron provides a change of texture, dry footing for the seat, and a place to stage a sculpture. Underground seepage keeps the soil moist enough for clumps of hosta and astilbe. In drier gardens a flower-filled container could be used instead. (Garden of the late Richard Meyer, Ohio; July)

A blue gate is matched to blue-and-white borders. Forget-me-nots are prominent, with tulips, peonies, and such early geraniums as 'Johnson's Blue' also in bloom. (Design by Michael S. Schultz for Mr. G. Beasley, Oregon; May)

Water, that most captivating of garden features, remains natural in some degree even when used in wholly artificial ways; it need only suit the ambience of the garden. A large oblong water lily pool centered in a spacious lawn of similar shape is in scale and character with its surroundings. In smaller gardens a pool might better be fitted into a corner to avoid breaking up the limited open space. Rock is a natural corollary for water and a small pool fits nicely into a rock garden. It is harder to fit into a bed or border of perennials but, as the pictures show, it can be done.

The sound of splashing water is very appealing on a hot summer day. The need to install some kind of pump deters many from installing fountains but small moving water features can sometimes be devised without the need for this, using plastic water pipe buried just under the ground leading to a hose or tap. No such limitation affects reflecting bowls. In either case such water features look best with some space around them. Fountains make good focal points toward the end of a path, or where two paths cross, but could also be recessed into a border on a paved or cobbled surround to display the feature and protect a pump or piping from disturbance. In the Japa-

A small raised pool in the corner of a front garden. The overall shot was taken from the drive in August, the close-up, bottom, *from the lawn in May. Plants surrounding the pool include epimediums, hostas, ferns, columbines, a bright pink azalea, yellow Welsh poppies (*Meconopsis cambrica)*, and,* front left, *the pink-belled shrublet* Andromeda polifolia. *(Garden of Elda and Ray Behm, Washington)*

A calla lily
(Zantedeschia
aethiopeca), hardy
Zones 7/8, grows
in the shallow
water of a formal
courtyard pool
edged with
Mimulus 'Inshriac
Crimson'. The
junipers at the
corners are
Juniperus sabina
'Tamariscifolia'.
(Garden of John
Treasure, Burford
House, Tenbury
Wells, England;
June)

Right: *Water trickling into this hollowed log ripples the surface and creates movement. (Garden of Mary Ley, Connecticut; May)*

Left: *Because they did not expect it to be their permanent home, the owners of this small garden did not want to spend a lot of money on permanent structure. This small pool was made in a weekend, using a plastic liner laid directly over the lawn. The wood coping anchors the liner and provides a place to sit and watch the goldfish. Behind the uncontained back edge of the pool are the orange flowers of Ligularia dentata. The pool liner was visible but could have been concealed with a layer of pebbles. (Designer Doug Bayley, Seattle, Washington; July)*

Water trickles into a small pool from the pipe through a rock encrusted with sedums, moss, and small ferns. (Garden of the late Yul Brynner, France; June)

nese-influenced garden of friends the roof downspout was led into a water bowl surrounded by cobblestones. Birds are attracted to reflecting bowls, especially shallow ones, and keeping them clear of vegetation makes the birds less vulnerable to lurking cats. Larger bowls could hold a miniature water lily. The half whiskey barrels available for a few dollars when there's a brewery in the vicinity are leakproof if kept filled with water,

but whiskey will have permeated the wood and this turns the water sour, so a plastic liner is advisable. Reflecting bowls have a magic similar to flickering flames, with images constantly changing as the sun or clouds move across the sky or you change your own position. The tiniest puddle will do it. At Folly Farm in England, a famous Lutyens-Jekyll design collaboration, house and surroundings are mirrored in a small water-filled hexagon

carved in the center of a raised stone slab, a touch of genius that could be adapted to the tiniest garden.

Statue . . . sundial . . . birdbath . . . pool? Such features enhance the flowers, much as an expensive gown might be dramatized by its accessories in a boutique window, but don't overdo it. Cramming too many features into a garden makes it look cluttered and restless and a garden should, above all, be restful. Which is not at all the same thing as labor-saving. Perennials will never be that but they reward abundantly every hour devoted to planting and caring for them.

Above: *A raised concrete pool reflects the tree fern overhead.* Right: *Sedum rubrotinctum clings to the rim of the pool. Lamb's ears flow along crevices and agapanthus has self-sown. (Garden of designer Harland Hand, California; September)*

Recommended Reading

Some of these books are out of print. With diligent search, they can usually be obtained from firms specializing in used horticultural books. For the novice, to whom even this short list might be bewildering, *Perennials: How to Select, Grow and Enjoy* by myself and Frederick McGourty is an inexpensive illustrated guide to the most popular perennials. *Perennials for American Gardens* by Ruth Rogers Clausen and Nicolas H. Ekstrom is a more comprehensive, well-illustrated guide. *Perennial Garden Plants* by Graham Stuart Thomas remains, to my mind, the best book on perennials ever written. Sunset's *New Western Garden Book* is an indispensable guide for West Coast gardeners, and also applicable to the Southeast. The general guides to identification I consult most often are *The Complete Handbook of Garden Plants* by Michael Wright, *The Concise Encyclopedia of Garden Plants* by Kenneth A. Beckett, and the *Taylor's Guides*. Those books marked with an asterisk (*) were first published in Great Britain.

Armitage, Allan M. *Herbaceous Perennials Plants.* Athens, GA: Varsity Press, Inc., 1989.

Beckett, Kenneth A. *The Concise Encyclopedia of Garden Plants.* London: Orbis Publishing, Ltd., 1983.*

Beckett, Kenneth A. *Growing Hardy Perennials.* Portland, OR: Timber Press, 1982.*

Bloom, Alan. *Perennials for Your Garden.* Floraprint* (and any other book by this author).

Brookes, John. *The Small Garden.* New York: Crown Publishers, Inc., 1989.*

Brown, Emily. *Landscaping with Perennials.* Portland, OR: Timber Press, 1986 (particularly helpful for California gardeners).

Buckley, Arthur R. *Garden Perennials.* Blaine, WA: Hancock House Publishers, Ltd., 1977.

Chatto, Beth. *The Green Tapestry.* New York: Simon & Schuster, 1989* (and any other book by this author).

Clausen, Ruth Rogers and Nicolas H. Ekstrom. *Perennials for American Gardens.* New York: Random House, Inc., 1989.

Cumming, Roderick W. and Robert E. Lee. *Contemporary Perennials.* New York: Macmillan Publishing Company, 1960.

Druse, Ken. *The Natural Garden.* New York: Clarkson N. Potter, Inc., 1989.

Eddison, Sydney. *A Patchwork Garden.* New York: Harper & Row, 1990.

Everett, Thomas H. *The New York Botanical Garden Illustrated Encyclopedia of Horticulture.* New York: Garland Publishing, 1981.

Ferguson, Nicola. *Ferguson's Garden Plant Directory* (North American editor: Frederick McGourty). London: Pan Books, Ltd., 1984.*

Fish, Margery. *Cottage Garden Flowers.* London: Faber & Faber, 1980* (and any other book by this author).

Foster, H. Lincoln. *Rock Gardening.* Portland, OR: Timber Press, 1982.

Grimm, William Carey. *Recognizing Flowering Wild Plants.* Harrisburg, PA: Stackpole Books, 1968.

Harper, Pamela and Frederick McGourty. *Perennials: How to Select, Grow and Enjoy.* Los Angeles: Price Stern Sloan, Inc., 1985.

Hay, Roy and Patrick M. Synge. *The Color Dictionary of Flowers and Plants for Home and Garden.* New York; Crown Publishers, Inc., 1982.*

Hebb, Robert S. *Low Maintenance Perennials.* Cambridge, MA: Arnold Arboretum.

Hobhouse, Penelope. *Color in Your Garden.* Boston: Little, Brown, 1985.*

Lacey, Stephen. *The Romantic Jungle.* Boston: David R. Godine Publishers, Inc.*

Lawrence, Elizabeth. *A Southern Garden: A Handbook for the Middle South.* Chapel Hill, NC: University of North Carolina Press, 1984.

Lima, Patrick. *The Harrowsmith Perennial Garden.* Charlotte, VT: Camden House Publishing, Inc., 1987.

Lloyd, Christopher. Anything by this author but especially *The Well-Tempered Garden.* New York: Penguin Books, 1985.*

Lovejoy, Ann. *The Border in Bloom.* Seattle, WA: Sasquatch Books, 1990.

McGourty, Frederick. *The Perennial Gardener.* Boston: Houghton Mifflin Co., 1989.

Miles, Bebe. *Wildflower Perennials for Your Garden.* New York: Hawthorn Books Inc., 1976.

Morse, Harriet K. *Gardening in the Shade.* Portland, OR: Timber Press, 1982.

Niehaus, Theodore F. and Charles L. Ripper. *A Field Guide to Pacific States Wildflowers.* Boston: Houghton Mifflin Co., 1976.

Perry, Frances. *Collins Guide to Border Plants.* London: Collins, 1957.*

Peterson, Roger Tory and Margaret McKenny. *A Field Guide to Wildflowers of Northeastern and North-central North America.* Boston: Houghton Mifflin Co., 1975.

Sheldon, Elisabeth. *A Proper Garden.* Harrisburg, PA: Stackpole Books, 1989.

Still, Steven. *Manual of Herbaceous Ornamental Plants,* Third Edition. Champaign, IL: Stipes Publishing Co., 1988.

Stresau, Frederick B. *Florida, My Eden.* Port Salerno, FL: Florida Classics Library, 1986.

Sunset, editors. *New Western Garden Book.* Menlo Park, CA: Sunset Lane Publishing Co., 1988.

Taylor's Guides. An inexpensive series of illustrated guides to garden plants, including: *Annuals; Perennials; Ground Covers, Vines and Grasses; Shrubs; Roses; Bulbs.* Boston: Houghton Mifflin Co.

Thomas, Graham Stuart, *Perennial Garden Plants,* Second Edition. London: J.M. Dent & Sons Ltd., 1982.*

Van Melle, P. J. *Shrubs and Trees for the Small Place.* New York: Charles Scribner's Sons, 1943.

Wilder, Louise Beebe. *Color in My Garden.* New York: Atlantic Monthly Press, 1990.

Wright, Michael. *The Complete Handbook of Garden Plants* (American consultant, John Elsley). New York: Facts on File Publications, 1984.*

Wyman, Donald. *Wyman's Gardening Encyclopedia.* New York: Macmillan Publishing Company, Inc., 1986.

Yeo, Peter. *Hardy Geraniums.* Portland, OR: Timber Press, 1985.*

Societies and Sources

The Association of Specialty Cut Flower Growers. Executive director, Judy Laushman, P.O. Box 2796, Friday Harbor, WA 98250.

The Hardy Plant Society (Great Britain). Membership secretary, Simon Wills, The Manor House, Walton-in-Gordano, Clevedon, Avon BS21 7AN England.

The following societies are affiliates:

The Hardy Plant Society of Oregon, Connie Hanni, 3530 S.E. Bluff Road, Boring, OR 97009.

Mid-Atlantic Hardy Plant Society, Mrs. Joanne Walkovic, 529 Woodland Avenue, Media, PA 19063.

The Northwest Perennial Alliance, P.O. Box 45574, University Station, Seattle, WA 98145.

The Perennial Plant Association. Executive secretary, Steven M. Still, 3383 Schirtzinger Road, Hilliard, OH 43026.

Providing useful source lists always presents a dilemma. The addresses of many societies change each year and when membership secretaries have completed their terms of office, it is a nuisance to them to be deluged with enquiries from out-of-date source lists. As for nurseries, hundreds now sell perennials, and what they offer changes from year to year. Here and there throughout the text I have named a nursery from which an uncommon plant can be obtained. The addresses of these nurseries and hundreds of others, along with those of specialist plant societies (daylily, hosta, peony, fern, etc.) can be found in the following source guides:

Barton, Barbara. *Gardening by Mail.* Boston: Houghton Mifflin Company, 1990. This invaluable source book, frequently updated, lists hundreds of nurseries, trade associations, and specialist plant societies.

Brooklyn Botanic Garden (1000 Washington Avenue, Brooklyn, NY 11225). *Perennials: A Nursery Source Manual.* No. 118, 1988/89. Sources are named for several thousand perennials and rock garden plants.

Dobson, Beverly R. (215 Harriman Road, Irvington, NY 10533). *Combined Rose List.* Sources are named for thousands of roses. Updated annually.

Index

Page numbers in *italics* indicate illustrations.